Another Classic Cookbook from
The Junior League of Denver, Incorporated
Creators of **Colorado Cache Cookbook**

Crème de

C O O K B O O K

Colorado

Crème de Colorado…
Offering you more than recipes,
Offering you Colorado!

Table of Contents

Additional copies of *Crème de Colorado* may be obtained by writing:
Crème de Colorado
The Junior League of Denver, Inc.
6300 East Yale Avenue, Suite 110
Denver, Colorado 80222
(303) 782-9244

Please enclose your return address with a check payable to *Crème de Colorado* in the amount of $16.95 per book plus $2.00 postage and handling. Colorado residents add $.70 sales tax per book.

First Edition, First Printing: 60,000 copies
September 1987
Second Printing: 60,000 copies
September 1987
Third Printing: 120,000 copies
December 1987
Fourth Printing: 60,000 copies
May 1988

Library of Congress Catalogue Number
87-410429
ISBN 0-9603946-2-1

The Junior League of Denver, Incorporated, is an organization of women commited to promoting voluntarism and to improving the community through the effective action and leadership of trained volunteers. Its purpose is exclusively educational and charitable.

The proceeds realized from the sale of *Crème de Colorado* will be returned to the community through projects of The Junior League of Denver, Incorporated.

The Committee

Chairman and Editor
Constance Fox Graham

Marketing Chairman
Sally Hewitt Daniel

Marketing Co-Chairman
Hindi Bergmann Roseman

Testing Coordinator
Kimberly Watkins Schroeder

Appetizers
Merlaine Meyers Peede
Kathleen Edwards Schmidt

Soups
Linda Green Hanson

Salads
Elaine Sack Woodworth

Breads
Barbara Young Hart

Brunch
Lorinda Stewart Swenson

Pasta
Nancy Ervin Panasci

Fish & Seafood
Billee Leonard Madsen

Poultry
Judy Sewald Fitzgerald

Meats
Sherry Sieck Lohmeier

Colorado Wild
Randall H. Lortscher

Vegetables
Melissa Pickering Miller

Desserts & Chocolate
Lee Yanus Doyle
Loyce Helgerson Sorrell

Mexican
Marcia Langton Wood

HealthMark
Susan A. Stevens

Feasts
Karlene Alt Elder
Anne Kuzell Hackstock

Index
Lorinda Stewart Swenson

Graphic Design Liaison
Patricia Schweiger Harmon

Production Coordinators
Merlaine Meyers Peede
Kathleen Edwards Schmidt

Copy Editor
Elizabeth Alexander Holtze

Computer Production
Susan White Siegesmund

Advisors
Kay Durey Johnson
Karen Keck Albin

Design
Matrix International Inc.

Photography
Gregory D. Gorfkle
(Cover: Inset photo)

Michael Bush
(Cover: Landscape photo)

John Fielder
(Inside: Colorado landscape photography)

Copy Writer
Heidi Dake Keogh

Typography
Bradford/Will Graphics

Crème de Colorado...
our name says it best!

Crème de Colorado is a selection of exciting, fresh recipes that reflect Colorado's lifestyle and rich heritage. We have encouraged using only the freshest ingredients in recipes that are designed to accommodate our on-the-go society; upscale, yet uncomplicated; inspiring, yet reliable; and in the tradition of our best-selling *Colorado Cache*. We have responded to contemporary trends toward "lighter" eating, without compromising our desire to bring you American food...with the Colorado flair!

Crème de Colorado represents the best of Colorado cooking. Through a discriminating selection process, nearly 700 recipes were chosen from the over 4,000 that were submitted. Each recipe was tested, retested, and tested again, before it earned our enthusiastic recommendation. Our clean format, clear instructions, and cross-referenced index insure cooking gratification — whether at sea level or in our high altitude kitchens.

We have enhanced our book with color images by the renowned Colorado naturalist photographer, John Fielder. His work so perfectly captures the arresting beauty of a grove of aspen igniting the mountainside with shimmering gold; the effect of fresh snowfall exposing the character and glacier-carved profile of each mountain peak; the delicacy of a wildflower tucked into a rocky slope; and the tranquility and sensitivity of our treasured wilderness. Mr. Fielder grasps the essence of Colorado with his lens and the results invite you to feel a part of our region. For, it is this mystique of Colorado that lends itself to our lifestyle, prompts our food preferences, and flavors our cooking.

Colorado has been a "melting pot" of America's mobile society since it was first colonized by Mexico in the 1840's. That rich Hispanic influence survives and has blended with the rush of gold and silver miners, trappers, and other homesteaders who ventured West at the prospect of a better life. What they discovered was incredible natural beauty. The parades of pioneers who passed through our gentle, fertile plains were greeted by majestic, rugged peaks framed in deep blue sky, and knew their journeys were over. Colorado's beauty, temperate climate, and its immigrants from every part of America have together molded a relaxed and casual style of living that is fresh, healthy, and hearty. It follows that Coloradans have a penchant for outdoor cooking and entertaining, and that our foods reflect our natural bounty: from wild game to Rocky Mountain trout to our rich harvests of wheat, melons, peaches, sugar beets, and vegetables from our valleys and plains.

Crème de Colorado, likewise, has its own interpretation of favorite recipes (as well as new creations from our test kitchens) that makes them a little fresher…a little more Colorado! We have attempted to capture this essence so that a brook trout tastes almost as good in your kitchen as it did over the campfire when you fished our mountain streams last summer.

Crème de Colorado has reached beyond the realm of the ordinary cookbook. Our style, format, and selections are as appealing to men, as they are to women. We believe, too, that traditional American cooking can be as imaginative as it is delicious, so we have assisted the host and hostess with presentation ideas, menu planning, and serving suggestions.

Furthermore, we have offered tips and techniques to easily modify any recipe to a lighter, healthier form.

Crème de Colorado features "Colorado Wild," a game section…because game and game birds are a popular and not uncommon by-product of Colorado; a Mexican section…because we owe a debt of gratitude to their seasonings, style, and influence in Colorado cooking; and a chocolate section…because we can not ignore the persistence of the American sweet tooth!

Crème de Colorado…
offering you more
than recipes,
offering you Colorado!

Landscape photographer John Fielder has been recording Colorado's remote areas on film for thirteen years. During that time he has traveled hundreds of miles by foot, and thousands by four wheel drive.

His first large format book, *Colorado's Hidden Valleys,* was published in 1982, and quickly proved a commercial and artistic success. In 1985 he released two additional books: *California, Images of the Landscape* and *Colorado, Images of the Alpine Landscape.*

Wherever he works, his vision of nature seeks out understated, often bypassed beauty. His images bring new meaning to the natural world.

Pages 2 and 3: October aspens enjoy their last week of foliage below Sierra Blanca Peak in the Sangre de Cristo Range.

Pages 4 and 5: The color of immature aspen leaves is spectacular, yet transitory in duration; even more so than their better known fall state.

Pages 6 and 7: Scarlet gilia and penstemon proliferate, near Crested Butte.

Page 8: Aspen protect a cold ridge, near Telluride on Wilson Mesa.

Page 9: Pinecones old and new color the landscape.

Page 10: Aspen boles and their autumn leaves, along Deep Creek near Telluride.

Page 11: A puddle of October rainwater collects falling aspen leaves just above the Huerfano River and just below the Sierra Blanca massif.

Page 12: Barren aspen play games on a fresh December snow.

Page 13: Forget-Me-Not and Clover compose at 13,000 feet, Mosquito Range.

Page 14: A trio of columbine bask in the sun along Marisposa Creek in the White River National Forest.

Page 15: In a state of transition, September's aspen greet a late summer storm.

Page 16: Orange Sneezeweed wilts in the wet, Maroon Bells-Snowmass Wilderness.

Appetizers

Appetizers

Surrey Ridge Shrimp

16	jumbo shrimp in shells
2	tablespoons oil
32	large fresh spinach leaves, rinsed and stemmed

Sauce:

2	medium shallots, minced
3	tablespoons sherry wine vinegar
2	tablespoons bottled clam juice
1	cup unsalted butter, chilled
1-2	tablespoons caviar, rinsed

Garnish:

pimiento strips

8 servings

Fry shrimp in hot oil until barely opaque. Cool, peel and devein. Immerse spinach leaves in boiling water and remove immediately. Transfer to a bowl of ice water to cool. Drain and pat dry. Wrap each shrimp in 2 spinach leaves and arrange in buttered 9x13-inch baking dish or individual ramekins. Cover with plastic wrap and refrigerate for up to 8 hours.

In medium saucepan, combine shallots, wine vinegar and clam juice. Boil until liquid is reduced by half. Strain liquid and boil until reduced to 1 tablespoon. Add cold butter, 1 tablespoon at a time, stirring constantly. Add caviar and blend.

Bake shrimp at 400 degrees for 10-15 minutes. Arrange 2 shrimp on each plate and top with sauce. Garnish with pimiento. Serve immediately.

This fabulous appetizer, perfect for a very special evening, can also be served at a cocktail buffet.

Mushroom Croustades

48	very thin slices bread
4	tablespoons soft margarine, room temperature
4	tablespoons butter
3	tablespoons finely chopped green onions
½	pound mushrooms, very finely chopped
2	tablespoons all-purpose flour
1	cup heavy cream
1	tablespoon minced fresh parsley
1½	teaspoons minced chives
½	teaspoon fresh lemon juice
½	teaspoon salt
⅛	teaspoon cayenne pepper

48 servings

Cut a 2½-inch circle from each of 48 slices of bread. Lightly spread softened margarine on both sides and press into 1¾-inch mini muffin tins. Bake 10 minutes at 350 degrees or until bread is lightly toasted. Cool. *Store in airtight container overnight or freeze until ready to use.*

In a 10-inch skillet, melt butter. Add green onions and cook over moderate heat for 4 minutes, stirring constantly. Add mushrooms and cook for 10-15 minutes. Remove from heat and sprinkle flour over mixture, stirring to blend. Return to heat. Pour in heavy cream; stir and heat to boiling. When thickened, simmer and cook 1 minute. Remove from heat and add parsley, chives, lemon juice, salt and cayenne pepper. Cool. *May be refrigerated or frozen until ready to use.*

Fill shells just before baking. Bake at 350 degrees for 10 minutes. Let cool 5 minutes before serving.

Perfect for the hostess, because this recipe can be made partially or completely ahead, and filled shells can be frozen. Bake frozen shells for 20 minutes.

Appetizers

Shell Creek Lemon Scallops

3	large lemons
¼	cup dry white wine
1	pound sea scallops, quartered
1	cup butter or margarine
1	small clove garlic, crushed
1	tablespoon minced fresh parsley

6 servings

Halve the lemons. Squeeze juice from pulp to measure ½ cup. Remove all pulp. Remove a thin slice from bottom of each lemon shell to make shell stand level. Set shells aside.

In heavy enamel or stainless saucepan, blend ¼ cup lemon juice and wine. Add scallops and simmer covered for 5 minutes or until tender. Drain scallops well. Discard liquid.

In same saucepan, melt butter. Add remaining ¼ cup lemon juice and garlic. Heat gently to blend flavors. Remove from heat, add scallops and toss carefully. Fill lemon shells with scallops and lemon butter sauce. Place under broiler for 2 minutes to brown edges of scallops. Remove from broiler and sprinkle with minced parsley. Serve immediately.

Scallops served in lemon shells make an impressive first course. Serve on lettuce cups and accompany with French bread for soaking up the delicious butter.

Apricot Brandied Brie

1	1-pound round imported Brie cheese, rind removed
	lemon leaves
1	cup apricot preserves
¾	cup Mandarin Napoleon brandy
2	French bread baguette loaves, sliced in ½-inch slices

Garnish:
  strawberries
  red or green seedless grapes

6-8 servings

Let Brie come to room temperature for about 1 hour. Pierce with fork in several places. Arrange lemon leaves on serving platter and place Brie on top. In medium saucepan, mix preserves and brandy. Heat until hot but not boiling. Pour hot mixture over Brie. Garnish with strawberries and/or grapes. Serve with baguette slices.

A sophisticated appetizer that can be made in minutes.

Appetizers

Glacier Cheese Tart

1½ cups all-purpose flour
5 tablespoons unsalted butter, cut into pieces
¼ teaspoon salt
1 large egg yolk
3 tablespoons ice water
½ pound imported Brie, rind removed
2 cups coarsely shredded Gruyère cheese
½ teaspoon salt
½ teaspoon ground white pepper
4 large egg yolks
½ cup cream cheese, softened and cut into small pieces
¼ cup heavy cream
4 large egg whites

8-10 servings

In food processor, blend flour, butter and ¼ teaspoon salt until mixture resembles coarse meal. With motor running, add 1 egg yolk and 3 tablespoons ice water, or enough to form a ball of dough. Dust dough with flour and chill, wrapped in waxed paper, for 1 hour. Roll dough ⅛-inch thick on floured surface and fit into a 9-inch pie plate, crimping around the edge.

In large bowl, mash Brie with a fork. Stir in Gruyère, ½ teaspoon salt, pepper and 4 egg yolks and combine mixture well. Stir in cream cheese and cream; mix well. In separate bowl, beat egg whites until soft peaks form and fold them into cheese mixture gently but thoroughly. Turn filling into pastry shell and bake in lower ⅓ of oven at 400 degrees for 25 minutes, or until golden. Let tart cool for 10 minutes before serving.

First course fare, and a tempting addition to a brunch buffet or luncheon.

Mushrooms Escargot

12 medium escargot
12 medium mushroom caps
½ cup butter, melted
1 tablespoon minced fresh parsley
1 teaspoon minced garlic
 salt and freshly ground black pepper to taste
2 tablespoons fine dry bread crumbs

12 pieces

In medium bowl, combine escargot, mushrooms, melted butter, parsley, garlic, salt and pepper. Set aside for 5 minutes. Remove mushroom caps. Put ½ teaspoon bread crumbs in bottom of each mushroom cap. Spoon 1 escargot and garlic butter into each cap. Bake at 350 degrees for 10-15 minutes.

Mushrooms stuffed with a savory mixture of escargot and garlic butter. Rich and delicious.

Appetizers

Coconut Beer Batter Shrimp (Gallery Louisiane)

Seasoning Mix:
- 1 tablespoon cayenne pepper
- 1½ teaspoons paprika
- 1½ teaspoons freshly ground black pepper
- 1¼ teaspoons garlic powder
- 2 teaspoons salt
- ½ teaspoon onion powder
- ½ teaspoon dried thyme
- ½ teaspoon dried oregano

Flour Mixture:
- ½ cup all-purpose flour
- 1½ teaspoons *Seasoning Mix*

Batter:
- 2 eggs
- 2 teaspoons *Seasoning Mix*
- 1½ cups all-purpose flour
- 1 cup beer
- 1 tablespoon baking powder
- 4 dozen medium or 2 dozen jumbo shrimp (2 pounds)
- 3 cups grated coconut (6 ounces)

Sweet and Sour Sauce:
- 1 18-ounce jar orange marmalade
- 3-4 tablespoons Creole or brown mustard
- 2-3 tablespoons prepared horseradish

4 dozen

Combine all seasoning mix ingredients and mix well; set aside.

In medium bowl, combine ½ cup flour and 1½ teaspoons seasoning mix; set aside.

In another medium bowl, combine all batter ingredients. Mix well; set aside.

Peel and devein shrimp. Sprinkle both sides with remaining seasoning mix. Dredge each shrimp in flour mixture. Then dip into batter mixture, except for tail. Allow excess batter to drip off. Coat generously with coconut; set aside.

In deep fryer, heat oil to 350 degrees. Drop shrimp one at a time into oil and fry to golden brown, about 1 minute per side. Drain on paper towels. Serve warm with **Sweet and Sour Sauce.**

Combine all ingredients in small bowl.

When it's time to dazzle, serve this spectacular appetizer with its intriguing sauce.

Appetizers

Mandarin Chicken Bites

2	whole chicken breasts (about 2 pounds)
1¾	cups chicken broth
¼	cup soy sauce
1	tablespoon Worcestershire sauce
1	pound fresh spinach leaves, rinsed and stemmed
8	cups boiling water
2	16-ounce cans mandarin oranges, drained

5 dozen

In 10-inch skillet, combine chicken breasts, broth, soy sauce and Worcestershire. Heat to boiling over medium heat; cover, reduce heat, and simmer until chicken is fork-tender (about 15-20 minutes). With a slotted spoon, remove chicken from broth and let cool slightly. Remove and discard skin and bones. Cut meat into 1-inch cubes.

Place spinach leaves in a colander. Pour boiling water over leaves. Drain and set aside to cool.

Place a cube of chicken at stem end of a spinach leaf and wrap leaf around chicken so that chicken still shows on sides. Secure end of leaf with a wooden pick. Refrigerate at least 1 hour. *Recipe can be prepared up to this point one day ahead.*

To serve, place one mandarin orange at the end of each wooden pick. Serve with **Curry Mayonnaise Dip.**

Curry Mayonnaise Dip:

¼	cup mayonnaise
¼	cup sour cream
2	teaspoons curry powder
2	tablespoons chopped Major Grey's Chutney
1	teaspoon freshly grated orange peel

Blend all dip ingredients in a jar and refrigerate.

A most impressive cold delectable with outstanding color.

Appetizers

Sterling Salmon Torte

Torte Layers:

4	tablespoons butter
½	cup all-purpose flour
2	cups milk
4	egg yolks
1	teaspoon sugar
⅛	teaspoon salt
4	egg whites
⅛	teaspoon cream of tartar

Smoked Salmon Layer:

8	ounces cream cheese
½	cup sour cream
2	tablespoons fresh lemon juice
¼	cup chopped green onions
⅓	pound smoked salmon, shredded (reserve 1 whole slice)
¼	cup peeled and chopped cucumber
¼	teaspoon dried dill weed or 1 tablespoon fresh dill weed

Sour Cream Frosting:

½	pint sour cream
1	teaspoon onion powder
1	tablespoon fresh lemon juice

Garnish:

1	slice smoked salmon (reserved above)
	pitted black olives, sliced
	chives or green onion tops, cut into thin strips for stems and leaves
	chives or green onion tops, cut for leaves
	sprigs of fresh dill or parsley

12 servings

To prepare torte layers, melt butter in small saucepan. Stir in flour and cook over low heat until well blended, about 2 minutes; do not brown. Stir in milk and continue cooking until sauce comes to a boil and thickens. In small bowl, lightly whisk egg yolks, sugar and salt. Stir small amount of hot mixture into yolks; stir yolks into saucepan. Cook for 1 minute, stirring constantly. Remove from heat. Beat egg whites until frothy, add cream of tartar, and beat until stiff peaks form. Fold sauce into whites.

Line bottoms of 2 9-inch layer cake pans with rounds of waxed paper; grease paper and sides of pans. Divide torte mixture between 2 pans, spreading evenly. Bake at 350 degrees for 15 minutes; rotate cakes and bake for an additional 20-25 minutes or until lightly browned and top springs back when pressed. Cool in pans for 10 minutes. Invert onto cake racks and pull off paper. Cool completely.

To prepare salmon filling, beat cream cheese, sour cream and lemon juice with electric mixer until smooth. Add green onions, salmon, cucumber and dill weed. Mix until blended.

Place one torte on serving platter and spread with filling. Place second torte on filling. Several hours before serving, mix all frosting ingredients together until smooth. Frost torte and decorate top with flowers cut from smoked salmon and olives. Make stems and leaves from chives and green onions. Garnish with sprigs of fresh dill or parsley. Cut like a cake to serve.

Gorgeous and irresistibly delicious!

Appetizers

Shrimp and Artichoke Vinaigrette

2   15-ounce cans artichoke hearts
      packed in water, drained and
      quartered
1½ pounds medium shrimp, cooked,
      peeled and deveined
1   egg, beaten
½   cup vegetable oil
½   cup olive oil
½   cup wine vinegar
2   tablespoons Dijon mustard
2   tablespoons minced chives
2   tablespoons minced green onions
½   teaspoon salt
½   teaspoon sugar
      dash of freshly ground black
      pepper

12 first course servings
20 servings for buffet

In large bowl, combine all ingredients. Marinate, refrigerated, for at least 6 hours or up to 2 days. Drain before serving.

Beautiful served as a first course in a shell or lettuce cup. For a buffet, serve in a large glass bowl lined with blanched snow peas.

Chicken Liver and Mushroom Pâté

1   pound chicken livers
¾   cup butter
1   cup chopped onion
1   clove garlic, minced
2   cups chopped mushrooms
      (about ¼ pound)
1   teaspoon salt
¼   teaspoon freshly ground black
      pepper
      pinch of ground nutmeg
1   tablespoon cream, brandy or
      bourbon
      sprigs of parsley (optional)
      crackers

Pâté Frosting (optional):
3   ounces cream cheese, room
      temperature
1   tablespoon Dijon mustard

2-3 cups

In large skillet, sauté chicken livers in butter until just pink, about 5 minutes. Remove livers and set aside. Add onion, garlic, mushrooms, salt, pepper and nutmeg to pan and cook until onion is transparent, about 10 minutes. In food processor, combine livers, onion-mushroom mixture and cream or liquor; blend until smooth. Pour pâté into a small, greased mold. Cover and refrigerate until firm. To serve, dip mold in hot water to release, and turn over onto plate. Frost. Garnish with sprigs of parsley, if desired, and serve with plain crackers.

A rich, smooth pâté. Flavor improves if prepared a day or two in advance and refrigerated.

In small bowl, combine ingredients.

Appetizers

Pâté Poulet

2	pounds chicken livers
½	cup chopped onion
2	tablespoons butter
½	cup sherry
½	teaspoon salt
½	teaspoon dried thyme, crumbled
1	tablespoon anchovy paste
3	ounces cream cheese, softened
½	cup butter, softened
½	cup minced fresh parsley
5-6	Granny Smith apples, cored and sliced ¼-inch thick

3 cups

In skillet, sauté chicken livers and onion in 2 tablespoons butter until livers are just done. In food processor or blender, blend mixture until smooth. In small saucepan, heat sherry until reduced to ¼ cup. Add to chicken liver mixture. Blend in salt, thyme, anchovy paste, cream cheese and butter. Continue blending until smooth. Press into oiled mold and chill until firm. Garnish with parsley. Serve with apple slices.

*Frost with **Pâté Frosting** for a more festive presentation.*

Pawnee Ham Pâté

8	ounces cream cheese, softened
¼	cup mayonnaise
1	tablespoon minced onion
1	teaspoon dry mustard
1	tablespoon minced fresh parsley
⅛	teaspoon Tabasco sauce
2	cups finely chopped ham
	crackers

2 cups

In food processor, blend cream cheese, mayonnaise, onion, mustard, parsley and Tabasco. Add finely chopped ham and mix well. Refrigerate until firm enough to shape into a mound. Serve with crackers. *This may be made several days in advance.*

*Ice with **Pâté Frosting** or form into a ball and roll in slivered almonds.*

Appetizers

Caviar Torte

1 tablespoon unflavored gelatin
¼ cup cold water

12-16 servings

In glass measuring cup, soften gelatin in cold water. Dissolve gelatin in microwave oven for 20 seconds at low setting. Use dissolved gelatin in making three molded layers.

Homemade Mayonnaise:
1 egg
1 teaspoon fresh lemon juice
1 teaspoon red wine vinegar
1 teaspoon Dijon mustard
1 teaspoon salt
freshly ground black pepper to taste
1½ cups vegetable oil

In food processor, combine egg, lemon juice, vinegar, mustard, salt, pepper and 3 tablespoons of oil. Blend for 5 seconds. With machine running, pour remaining oil in steady stream through top opening, blending until smooth. Use mayonnaise in *Caviar Torte* and refrigerate remainder for future use.

Egg Layer:
4 hard cooked eggs, chopped
½ cup *Homemade Mayonnaise*
¼ cup minced fresh parsley
1 green onion, minced
dash of Tabasco sauce
freshly ground black pepper to taste

Line bottom and sides of 9-inch springform pan with plastic wrap. Oil lightly. Combine all egg layer ingredients with 1 tablespoon dissolved gelatin. Neatly spread egg mixture into pan, smoothing top. Wipe any egg mixture from pan sides with paper towel.

Avocado Layer:
1 medium avocado, peeled, pitted and puréed
1 medium avocado, peeled, pitted and diced
1 large shallot, minced
2 tablespoons fresh lemon juice
2 tablespoons *Homemade Mayonnaise*
½ teaspoon salt
dash of Tabasco sauce
freshly ground black pepper to taste

Combine all avocado layer ingredients with 1 tablespoon dissolved gelatin. Spread evenly over egg layer.

Sour Cream Onion Layer:
1 cup sour cream
¼ cup minced onion

Combine sour cream, onion and remaining 2 tablespoons dissolved gelatin. Spread carefully over avocado layer. Cover mold tightly. Refrigerate overnight.

Caviar Layer:
3½-4 ounces black or red caviar
fresh lemon juice

thinly sliced pumpernickel bread

Place caviar in fine sieve and rinse gently with cold water. Sprinkle with lemon juice. Drain well. Remove sides from springform pan. Transfer molded layers to serving platter with sour cream layer on top. Spread caviar on top. Serve with pumpernickel bread.

*Serve this spectacular appetizer with champagne and **Homemade Melba Toast.***

Appetizers

Carrots Florentine (Gallery Louisiane)

20 large carrots, peeled and cut into 1-inch pieces
¼ pound bacon, cut into small pieces
1 clove garlic, minced
2 teaspoons minced fresh chives
½ cup chopped onion
2 ounces Pernod
4 pounds fresh spinach, rinsed, stemmed and cooked
1 tablespoon cornstarch
2 cups heavy cream
1 teaspoon celery salt
¼ teaspoon cayenne pepper or to taste

80-100 pieces

Steam carrots until tender; cool. Using a very small melon-ball scoop, remove centers, leaving sides and bottom intact.

In large skillet, sauté bacon until almost crisp. Add garlic, chives, onion and Pernod. Sauté for a few more minutes. Add spinach and cook until onions are transparent. In small bowl, whisk cornstarch into heavy cream. Add to spinach mixture along with celery salt and cayenne pepper. Stir and simmer until thickened. Stuff each carrot with ½-1 teaspoon of spinach mixture. Place stuffed carrots on lightly greased baking sheet. Heat at 350 degrees for 10 minutes or until stuffing is hot. *Carrots can be prepared 4 hours in advance and refrigerated. Heat chilled carrots for 20 minutes or until stuffing is hot.*

3 10-ounce packages frozen chopped spinach, cooked and thoroughly drained, can be substituted for the fresh spinach.

Smoked Oyster Log

1 medium clove garlic, crushed
1 tablespoon finely chopped onion
16 ounces cream cheese, softened
1 tablespoon mayonnaise
1 tablespoon milk
2 teaspoons Worcestershire sauce
¼ teaspoon salt
⅛ teaspoon ground white pepper
dash of Tabasco sauce
2 3¾-ounce cans smoked oysters, drained
½ cup finely chopped pistachio nuts, pecans or walnuts
crackers

Garnish:
sprigs of parsley
pimiento strips

8-10 servings

In food processor with metal blade or in mixing bowl, mix garlic, onion, cream cheese, mayonnaise, milk, Worcestershire, salt, pepper and Tabasco until well blended. Spread into 8x10-inch rectangle on foil-lined baking sheet.

In same bowl, purée or mash oysters. Spread over cream cheese mixture. Cover loosely with plastic wrap. Refrigerate for several hours or until firm. *Mixture can be refrigerated overnight.*

Using a long, narrow spatula to help release cream cheese from foil, roll up like a jelly roll. Do not be concerned if it breaks and cracks. Shape into a long log; roll in nuts, covering log completely. *May be refrigerated, wrapped in plastic wrap for 3 days.* Garnish with parsley and pimiento, if desired. Serve with crackers.

This is especially festive with pistachio nuts and pimientos during the Christmas holiday season.

Appetizers

Pine Mountain Pesto

8	ounces cream cheese, softened
½	pound unsalted butter, softened
1¼	cups lightly packed fresh basil leaves (2½ ounces)
½	cup freshly grated Parmesan cheese
3	tablespoons olive oil
3	tablespoons chopped pine nuts
	salt and freshly ground black pepper to taste
	cheesecloth
1	French baguette loaf, thinly sliced
	sprigs of basil

7-8 servings

In food processor, beat cream cheese and butter until smooth. Set aside.

In clean food processor bowl, blend to a paste the basil leaves, Parmesan and olive oil. Add pine nuts and season to taste with salt and pepper.

Moisten two 12-inch squares of cheesecloth with water and wring dry. Lay flat, one on top of the other. Use cheesecloth to smoothly line a 2½-cup straight-sided plain mold or plastic container. With spatula or fingers, spread ⅙ of cheese mixture in prepared mold. Cover with ⅕ pesto filling, extending it evenly to sides of mold. Repeat until mold is filled, finishing with cheese mixture.

Fold end of cloth over top of cheese-pesto loaf and press down lightly to compact. Chill until firm, 1-1½ hours. If allowed to stand longer, cloth will dry and cause filling color to bleed into cheese. Invert onto a serving dish and gently pull off cloth.

May be made up to 5 days ahead if unmolded, covered with plastic wrap and kept refrigerated. Garnish with additional sprigs of basil. Serve on French baguette slices.

Carr's Wheatmeal Biscuits, slightly sweet, complement the flavor of pesto.

Maroon Bells Cheese Spread

2½	cups shredded New York white Cheddar cheese (10-12 ounces)
⅓	cup grated onion
2	tablespoons mayonnaise
½	cup raspberry preserves
	Triscuit wafers

2 cups

In mixing bowl, combine cheese and onion and mix well. Blend in mayonnaise. Form into a flat mound on serving dish and top with preserves. Serve with Triscuit wafers.

With its brilliant red color, this recipe is a show stopper to serve near Christmas or on Valentine's Day, garnished with raspberries.

Appetizers

Chile Cheese Ball

16	ounces cream cheese, softened
2¼	cups shredded sharp Cheddar cheese
1	7-ounce can diced green chiles, drained
2	tablespoons chopped onion
2	teaspoons Worcestershire sauce
¾	cup chopped walnuts or pecans
	tortilla chips or crackers

2 1-pound balls

In food processor or large mixing bowl, thoroughly blend cream cheese and Cheddar cheese. Add chiles, onion and Worcestershire and blend carefully so chiles are not mashed. Chill several hours. Divide in half and shape into 2 balls. Roll each ball in nuts. Chill overnight. Serve with tortilla chips or crackers.

Can be prepared 1-2 days in advance and can easily be doubled.

Chutney Cheese Ball

8	ounces cream cheese, softened
2	tablespoons sour cream
2	teaspoons curry powder
½	cup chopped green onions
½	cup raisins
½	cup coarsely chopped dry roasted peanuts
1	cup chutney
	crackers

3 cups

In medium bowl, combine cream cheese and sour cream. Blend in curry powder. Add onions, raisins and peanuts and mix thoroughly. Form into a ball. *Can be made 4 days ahead, but flavors will intensify.* To serve, pour chutney over the cheese ball and serve with crackers.

As a variation, roll cheese ball in coconut before pouring on chutney. Garnish with kumquats and green onion brushes.

Coors Legacy Cheese

8	ounces cold pack sharp Cheddar cheese, softened
½	cup butter, softened
¼	teaspoon garlic powder
¼	cup *Coors* beer, room temperature
	crackers or pretzels

1½ cups

In mixing bowl, blend together cheese and butter. Add garlic to taste. Blend in beer. (Do not worry if mixture looks curdled.) Chill. Let stand at room temperature for 1 hour before serving.

Delicious with crackers, pretzels or raw vegetables. When choosing vegetables, use the freshest possible and keep both color and texture in mind.

Appetizers

Dynasty Cocktail Rolls

Marinade:

1½	teaspoons salt
1	tablespoon light soy sauce
1½	teaspoons rice wine or dry Sherry
1½	teaspoons cornstarch
1½	pounds pork loin, chicken breast or raw shrimp, shredded, or any combination of the meats
1	green onion, shredded
¼	cup vegetable oil
4	black Chinese mushrooms, soaked in water until soft, then shredded
6	ounces bamboo shoots, shredded
1	pound Chinese cabbage, shredded
2	stalks celery, shredded
1	pound bean sprouts
½	teaspoon freshly ground black pepper
2	tablespoons light soy sauce

Sauce:

2	teaspoons light soy sauce
½	cup water
3	tablespoons cornstarch
1	tablespoon oyster sauce
90	wonton skins
1	egg, beaten

Condiments:

Chinese Mustard or *Champagne Mustard*
Sweet and Sour Sauce

90 cocktail rolls

In large bowl, combine all marinade ingredients. Stir in shredded meat. Marinate for 15 minutes.

In wok or large electric skillet, stir fry green onion in 2 tablespoons oil for a few seconds. Add mushrooms, bamboo shoots, cabbage, celery and bean sprouts and cook for 5 minutes. Mix in pepper and soy sauce; set aside.

In small bowl, combine all sauce ingredients and stir well; set aside. In clean wok, stir fry meat in 2 tablespoons oil until color changes. Add cooked vegetables and continue cooking for 5 more minutes. Mix well and stir in sauce. Stir until thickened. Cool filling in refrigerator for several hours.

To assemble, place 1 heaping teaspoon filling on wonton skin. Bring bottom corner up and around filling; bring side corners to center over filling. Roll lengthwise. Brush remaining corner with beaten egg and press to close. Deep fry until golden brown. *Fried eggrolls may be frozen and reheated, still frozen, at 450 degrees for 30 minutes, turning once.* Serve with **Chinese Mustard** or **Champagne Mustard** and **Sweet and Sour Sauce** for dipping.

Always a favorite. Prepare these when you have extra time and freeze them to have on hand for unexpected company.

Chinese Mustard

1	cup cider vinegar
4	ounces Coleman's dry mustard
4	eggs, beaten
1	cup sugar

3 cups

In medium bowl, combine vinegar and mustard and refrigerate overnight. In double boiler, cook all ingredients until thickened, about 10 minutes. Cool and refrigerate in an airtight container.

Homemade mustards will keep about a month and make excellent holiday gifts.

Appetizers

Champagne Mustard

2 ounces Coleman's dry mustard
1 cup sugar
⅔ cup Regina champagne vinegar
3 eggs

2 cups

In double boiler, whisk together mustard and sugar. Add vinegar and eggs. Cook over boiling water 7 minutes or until thick. Stir with whisk the entire time. Remove from pan immediately. Cool and refrigerate in an airtight container.

Nana's Italian Meatballs

Basic Italian Sauce:
1 18-ounce can tomato paste
8 cups water
4-6 tablespoons sugar
½-1 teaspoon salt
1 teaspoon freshly ground black pepper
1 tablespoon dried sweet basil
½ cup finely chopped onion
1 clove garlic, minced

8 cups sauce

In large saucepan, mix tomato paste with water. Add sugar, salt, pepper, basil, onion and garlic. Heat to boiling, reduce heat and simmer for at least 1 hour. Stir frequently. If sauce becomes too thick, add a small amount of water. Add meatballs or Italian sausage to sauce. Simmer 20 minutes and serve in a chafing dish.

Meatballs:
1½ pounds ground beef
2 eggs
½ teaspoon salt
¼ teaspoon freshly ground black pepper
1 tablespoon water
½ cup cracker crumbs
3 tablespoons freshly grated Parmesan cheese
¼ cup finely chopped onion

60-65 meatballs

In large bowl, mix together all ingredients. Form into meatballs 1 inch in diameter. Place on rack on cookie sheet. Bake at 350 degrees for 15-20 minutes. Add to ***Basic Italian Sauce.***

Italian Sausage Variation:
2 pounds hot Italian sausage links
1 tablespoon sausage drippings

Place sausage in 9x13-inch baking dish. Cover and bake at 350 degrees for 30 minutes. Cool. Slice into ¼-inch slices. Add sausage and 1 tablespoon drippings to ***Basic Italian Sauce.***

Watch these disappear at your next cocktail party!

Appetizers

Teriyaki Beef Nuggets

⅓	cup soy sauce
2	tablespoons honey
¼	teaspoon ground ginger
1	clove garlic, crushed
1	teaspoon grated onion
¼	cup dry white wine
¾	pound boneless top sirloin, cut into ½-inch diagonal slices
1	6-ounce can water chestnuts, halved

24 pieces

In shallow bowl, combine soy sauce, honey, ginger, garlic, onion and wine. Wrap 1 slice of meat around each water chestnut half and secure with a wooden pick. Marinate beef nuggets in soy sauce mixture for 1 hour. Place nuggets in broiler pan and broil for 3-4 minutes on rack 5-8 inches from heat, turning once or twice. Serve immediately.

These tasty nuggets are a snap to fix.

Piggyback Shrimp

1	cup finely chopped onion
2	tablespoons unsalted butter
¾	cup chili sauce
¼	cup water
3	tablespoons Worcestershire sauce
3	tablespoons packed light brown sugar
1	tablespoon distilled white vinegar
1	tablespoon tomato paste
¼	teaspoon dry mustard
⅛	teaspoon Tabasco sauce
20	medium or large shrimp, peeled and deveined
20	2½-inch strips of bacon

20 pieces

In saucepan, sauté onion in butter until transparent, about 5-6 minutes. Add chili sauce, water, Worcestershire, brown sugar, vinegar, tomato paste, mustard and Tabasco. Heat until boiling; reduce heat and simmer for 20 minutes or until thickened. Remove from heat. Dip each shrimp into sauce and set aside for 20 minutes. Wrap each shrimp in 1 piece of bacon and place on broiler tray. Broil 4-inches from source of heat until bacon is crisp, 3-4 minutes on each side. Warm reserved sauce. Serve shrimp accompanied by sauce.

Here's a succulent combination of shrimp and bacon broiled to perfection and accompanied by a zesty sauce.

Appetizers

Queen City Mushrooms

15	slices white bread
8	ounces cream cheese, softened
2	egg yolks
1	clove garlic, minced
⅛	teaspoon salt
1	pound mushroom caps
¼	cup butter
	paprika (optional)

60 rounds

Cut four 1-inch bread rounds from each slice of bread. On cookie sheet, toast lightly on 1 side under broiler; set aside. In food processor or medium bowl, combine cream cheese and egg yolks. Add garlic and salt and blend well. Thinly coat untoasted side of bread rounds with cheese mixture.

Sauté mushroom caps in butter. Drain on paper towels. Place 1 mushroom cap on top of each prepared bread round and fill with remaining cheese mixture. Sprinkle with paprika for color, if desired. *Up to this point, mushroom rounds can be prepared in advance and refrigerated for up to 8 hours.* To serve, broil until lightly browned.

The savory combination of mushrooms and cream cheese makes this a cocktail favorite.

Durango Drummettes

2	cups water
1	cup soy sauce
1	cup Reese cooking sherry
½	cup packed light brown sugar
⅓	cup chopped green onions
24	chicken drummettes with skin removed

24 drummettes

In large skillet, combine water, soy sauce, sherry, brown sugar and green onions. Add drummettes and stir to coat. Heat to boiling and lower heat. Simmer covered for 30 minutes. Uncover and simmer for 10-15 minutes more, stirring and basting frequently. Serve warm.

These chicken wings will get nibbled up very quickly. Remember to provide a bowl for disposal of bones.

Silverton Drummettes

⅔	cup soy sauce
2	cups packed light brown sugar
24	chicken drummettes with skin removed

24 drummettes

In medium mixing bowl, mix soy sauce and brown sugar. Arrange drummettes in greased, 9x13-inch baking dish. Pour sauce over drummettes and bake at 300 degrees for 3 hours. Serve warm.

Drummettes would be a wonderful addition to a picnic basket.

Appetizers

Wagon Wheel Gap
Filled Biscuits

Biscuits:

2	1-ounce packages yeast
1	cup warm water (105-115 degrees)
3	cups all-purpose flour
1	teaspoon salt
⅓	cup sugar
⅓	cup vegetable shortening
2	eggs, beaten
4-5	tablespoons margarine, melted
¾	cup shredded Cheddar cheese

5 dozen biscuits

Add yeast to warm water. Stir and set aside. In large bowl, combine flour, salt and sugar. Work in shortening by hand until mixture resembles coarse meal.

Add beaten eggs to yeast and water; stir well. Pour yeast mixture into dry ingredients. Mix for 100 strokes. Dough will be very sticky. Shape dough into ball and place in bowl with melted margarine. Turn to coat all sides. Cover and allow to proof for 30 minutes.

Turn dough out onto lightly-floured board. Pat or roll to ½-inch thickness. Cut into biscuits with 1½-inch cutter. Place on cookie sheet brushed with melted margarine. Let stand for 15 minutes.

Bake at 450 degrees for 5-7 minutes or until golden brown. Watch carefully, as these biscuits brown quickly. Remove from oven and brush tops with melted margarine. Cool. *Biscuits may be made 1 day ahead and stored in an airtight container.*

Using a melon-ball scoop, cut a marble-size ball from the top center of each biscuit. Be careful not to pierce the bottom. Fill with **Chili** or **Crab.** Top with shredded cheese. *May be frozen at this point. Defrost 3-4 hours before baking.* Bake at 350 degrees for 5 minutes or until chili is piping hot. Serve immediately.

Chili Filling:

1¼	pounds ground beef
½	cup finely chopped onion
1½	cups boiling water
2	tablespoons chili powder
1	tablespoon ground cumin
1	teaspoon salt
1	teaspoon freshly ground black pepper
1½	teaspoons garlic powder
1½	teaspoons paprika

2½ cups

In large kettle with tight-fitting lid, steam beef and onion. Stir often and cook until meat is tender, about 40 minutes. Be sure to keep kettle covered to retain juices. Stir in boiling water, chili powder, cumin, salt, pepper, garlic powder and paprika. Cover and simmer for 15 minutes, stirring occasionally. Cool and refrigerate. Use 1 tablespoon chili to fill each biscuit.

Appetizers

Crab Filling:
- ½ pound American cheese, shredded
- ⅔ cup chopped green bell pepper
- ½ cup butter, melted
- ½ cup medium-hot salsa
- 4-6 ounces crabmeat

2½ cups

In medium mixing bowl, combine all ingredients. *May be prepared 1 day ahead. Cover and refrigerate.* Use 1 tablespoon crab mixture to fill each biscuit. Place filled biscuits on cookie sheet and bake at 350 degrees for 30 minutes or until filling is piping hot.

For best results, do not double the biscuit recipe. Larger quantities should be made in separate batches.

Centennial Shrimp

- 1 cup shredded Cheddar cheese
- 1 cup mayonnaise
- 6 ounces tiny shrimp
- 1 teaspoon curry powder
- 3 green onions, chopped
- 6 English muffins, split

48 pieces

In medium bowl, mix Cheddar cheese, mayonnaise, shrimp, curry powder and onions. Toast muffins. Spread shrimp mixture on muffin halves and broil until bubbly. *Can be made in advance and frozen before broiling.* Cut each muffin into 4 pie-shaped wedges and serve warm.

Garnish with chopped peanuts and shredded coconut. Serve whole muffins as a lunch entrée with soup or salad.

Legendary Crab Rounds

- 1 cup mayonnaise
- ½ cup grated onion
- 1 cup shredded Cheddar cheese
- 6 drops Tabasco sauce
- ¼ teaspoon curry powder
- 1 6½-ounce can crabmeat, drained
- 2 French bread baguettes, sliced ½-inch thick

50-55 rounds

In medium bowl, combine mayonnaise, grated onion, Cheddar cheese, Tabasco, curry powder and crab meat. *This may be made 1 day in advance.* To serve, place mixture on bread rounds and broil until golden brown. Serve immediately.

Simple to prepare and absolutely fantastic.

Appetizers

Chile Verde Cheese Puffs

Puffs:
- ½ cup butter
- 1 cup water
- 1 cup all-purpose flour
- 1 teaspoon salt
- 4 eggs

Filling:
- 8 ounces cream cheese, softened
- 1 4-ounce can of chopped mild green chiles, drained

48 puffs

In saucepan, melt butter in water. Bring to full boil. Add flour and salt all at once. Reduce heat to low and continue cooking for 3 minutes, stirring constantly. Place mixture in bowl of food processor with steel blade. With motor running, add eggs one at a time. Blend until dough is satiny in appearance. Drop batter from teaspoon onto ungreased cookie sheet. Bake at 375 degrees for 15 minutes.

In food processor with steel blade, blend cream cheese until smooth. Add chiles, and blend briefly. Slice puffs and fill with cream cheese mixture. Place puffs on cookie sheet and heat at 350 degrees until hot, about 10-15 minutes. Serve immediately.

Filled with a delicious chile cream cheese mixture, these wonderful puffs are best served piping hot.

Sheepherder's Brie

- 1 1-pound round loaf Sheepherder's bread, one day old
- 1 ½-pound loaf French bread, cubed
- ½ cup olive oil
- 2 cloves garlic, minced
- 1 pound imported Brie cheese, rind removed, cubed

Garnish:
- green and red seedless grapes

8 servings

Cut through top of Sheepherder's bread with serrated knife and remove the center, leaving a shell ½-inch thick on sides and bottom. Cut center of Sheepherder's bread into 1-inch cubes. Around rim of bread shell, make cuts 1½-inches deep and 1½-inches apart. *Can be made one day ahead up to this point; wrap breads in plastic wrap and refrigerate.*

In small mixing bowl, combine oil and garlic. Brush inside of shell with 3 tablespoons of oil mixture. Brush all bread cubes with remaining oil. Put Brie cubes in bread shell. Place shell and oiled bread cubes on baking sheet. Bake at 350 degrees for 10 minutes. Remove bread cubes and continue baking cheese filled shell about 10 more minutes or until shell is golden brown and cheese melts. Remove from oven and serve shell surrounded by bread cubes. Garnish with green and red seedless grapes.

Spectacular flavor, yet easy to make.

Appetizers

Stroganoff Sausage Dip

1	pound hot bulk pork sausage
½	cup finely chopped onion
½	pound mushrooms, thinly sliced
2	tablespoons all-purpose flour
1	cup sour cream
1	cup milk
1	tablespoon Worcestershire sauce
1	teaspoon soy sauce
1	teaspoon paprika
	large corn chips

4 cups

In large skillet, cook sausage, crumbling with a fork, until well browned. Remove sausage with a slotted spoon and set aside. Add onion and mushrooms to fat in skillet and cook rapidly so mushrooms do not give off liquid. Stir often, until onion is golden. Drain fat and return sausage to skillet.

In small bowl, gradually whisk flour into sour cream. Add milk, Worcestershire, soy sauce and paprika. Whisk to blend well. Add this mixture to meat mixture in skillet. Cook over moderate heat until thickened. Serve immediately with large corn chips.

An interesting interpretation of a classic.

Hot Mushroom and Clam Dip

1	pound mushrooms, sliced
2	tablespoons butter
8	ounces cream cheese
16	ounces sour cream
2	6½-ounce cans minced clams, drained
1	tablespooon soy sauce
¼	teaspoon freshly ground black pepper
½	teaspoon seasoned salt

4 cups

Sauté mushrooms in butter until tender. In double boiler, melt cream cheese and sour cream, blending well. Add mushrooms, clams, soy sauce, pepper and seasoned salt. Place in chafing dish and serve with **Homemade Melba Toast.**

Homemade Melba Toast:
butter
very thin slices white bread, crusts trimmed

Butter bread slices and cut into quarters. Bake at 250 degrees until crisp. *These store well in airtight tins and may be done well in advance.*

Adorn this hot dip with fluted mushrooms dipped in lemon juice to prevent discoloration.

Appetizers

Silver Plume Sausage Puffs

1	pound pork sausage
½	cup chopped green onions
½	pound mushrooms, chopped
3-4	cloves garlic, minced
2	eggs, lightly beaten
½	cup fresh bread crumbs
1	tablespoon whole mustard seed
½	teaspoon cayenne pepper
1	pound puff pastry
4	tablespoons butter, melted

2 sausage puffs, 15 pieces each

In medium skillet, cook sausage until browned. Drain and transfer to a bowl. Add green onions, mushrooms, garlic, eggs, bread crumbs, mustard seed and cayenne pepper; mix well. Roll puff pastry into 2 rectangles. Spread each with ½ of sausage filling and roll up like a jelly roll. Seal seam with cold water. Place on broiler pan, seam side down. Bake at 425 degrees for 45 minutes. Brush with butter. Remove from oven and let stand for 5 minutes. Slice and serve immediately.

Frozen puff pastry is a versatile, convenient aid to the hostess.

Chili Dip

1	16-ounce box processed cheese
2	tablespoons chopped, pickled jalapeño peppers
1	tablespoon chili powder
1	teaspoon ground cumin
1	pound ground beef, cooked and drained
½	cup shredded Cheddar cheese
1	6-ounce can spicy tomato juice (optional)
	tortilla chips

4 cups

In large double boiler, melt cheese over low heat. Add peppers, chili powder, cumin, beef and Cheddar cheese. Stir over low heat until well blended. If mixture is too thick, add tomato juice, one tablespoon at a time, until desired consistency is reached. Serve hot with tortilla chips.

Here's an old favorite for those who enjoy the hot, spicy seasonings of Mexico.

Appetizers

Colorado Calzone

1   **loaf frozen Rhodes bread dough,**
      thawed
      Italian Sausage Filling **or** *Spinach*
      Filling
1   **egg white**

10-12 servings

Roll out bread dough on floured counter to thickness of ¼-½ inch. Prepare filling and spread over dough. Roll up carefully so loaf looks like long loaf of French bread. Seal long edge and tuck under ends. Place rolled loaf on greased cookie sheet, seam side down. Glaze with egg white before baking. Bake at 350 degrees for 30-40 minutes, or until golden brown. Slice into ¾-inch slices and halve each slice.

Italian Sausage Filling:
1   **pound mild Italian sausage**
1   **cup shredded Provolone cheese**
1   **cup shredded Mozzarella cheese**
¼   **cup freshly grated Parmesan**
      cheese
      dash of dried basil
      dash of salt
      dash of freshly ground black
      pepper
      dash of dried rosemary

In medium skillet, cook sausage and drain. Combine sausage, cheeses, basil, salt, pepper and rosemary and mix well. Spread over prepared dough.

Spinach Filling:
6   **ounces center cut bacon, chopped**
½   **cup chopped onion**
1   **10-ounce package frozen chopped**
      spinach, thawed and squeezed
      dry
¼   **teaspoon garlic salt**
1   **cup shredded Monterey Jack**
      cheese

In medium skillet, cook bacon until almost crisp; drain grease. Add spinach and garlic salt and cook several minutes. Stir in cheese and mix well. Spread over prepared dough.

A hearty appetizer for after skiing or a football game. Kids love it! Could easily double as a main dish if accompanied by a mixed green salad.

Appetizers

Spinach Dip with Pita

1 tablespoon chopped jalapeños
¾ cup chopped onions
2 tomatoes, chopped (about 2 cups)
1 10-ounce package frozen spinach, thawed and squeezed dry
8 ounces cream cheese, softened
2 cups shredded Monterey Jack cheese (8-ounces)
⅓ cup half and half

8-10 servings

In medium bowl, mix all ingredients together and pour into buttered oven-proof dish. Bake at 400 degrees for 20-25 minutes. Serve warm with **Pita Toasts.**

Pita Toasts:

2 teaspoons lemon pepper
2 teaspoons ground cumin
½ cup butter, melted
6 pita bread loaves

In sauce pan, stir pepper and cumin into melted butter. Halve pita breads; with tip of knife, open up each half into 2 pieces. Cut pieces into triangle shapes. Dip into butter mixture and place on broiler pan. Broil until crisp.

This new toast idea will instantly become an "old" favorite.

Broccoli Prairie Basket

1 1½-pound round loaf Sheepherder's or sourdough bread
1 ½-pound loaf French bread, cubed
½ cup olive oil
2 cloves garlic, minced
⅔ cup chopped red bell pepper
⅔ cup chopped yellow bell pepper
⅔ cup chopped celery
⅔ cup chopped onion
2 tablespoons margarine
2 pounds processed cheese, cubed
20 ounces frozen chopped broccoli, cooked and drained
½ teaspoon dried rosemary, crushed

2⅔ cups filling

Cut through top of Sheepherder's bread with serrated knife and remove the center, leaving a shell ½-inch thick on sides and bottom. Cut center of Sheepherder's bread into 1-inch cubes. Around rim of bread shell, make cuts 1½-inches deep and 1½-inches apart. *Can be made one day ahead up to this point; wrap breads in plastic wrap and refrigerate.*

In small mixing bowl, combine oil and garlic. Brush inside of shell with 3 tablespoons of oil mixture. Brush all bread cubes with remaining oil. Place shell on cookie sheet with top slice and oiled bread cubes. Bake at 350 degrees for 15-20 minutes.

In large saucepan, sauté peppers, celery and onions in margarine until tender. Add cheese, stirring constantly over low heat until melted. Stir in broccoli and rosemary and heat thoroughly. Pour into bread shell; serve with prepared bread cubes. Can also serve with an assortment of vegetables.

Another time, try this recipe with chopped spinach, thawed and squeezed dry, in place of the broccoli.

Appetizers

Garden Pizza

1　8-ounce can refrigerated crescent rolls
8　ounces cream cheese, softened
⅓　cup mayonnaise
1　teaspoon dried dill weed
1　teaspoon minced onion
2　cups finely chopped raw vegetables (cauliflower, green bell pepper, celery and broccoli)
½　cup chopped green onions
½　cup shredded carrot

10-12 servings

Spread crescent rolls out on 12-inch round, ungreased pizza pan, pressing all seams together. Bake at 400 degrees for 10 minutes. Cool.

Blend cream cheese, mayonnaise, dill and minced onion until smooth. Spread on baked, cooled crust.

Mix together raw vegetables and sprinkle over cream cheese mixture. Top with green onions and shredded carrots. Lightly press into top. Chill until served. Cut into squares.

Use any fresh vegetable combination you like. A fun change of pace from vegetable dips.

Spinach Dip in Rye Loaf

1　10-ounce package frozen chopped spinach, thawed and squeezed dry
1　cup mayonnaise
½　cup chopped green onions
½　cup minced fresh parsley
¼　cup plain yogurt or sour cream
½　teaspoon fresh lemon juice
¼　teaspoon seasoned salt
¼　teaspoon dried dill weed
⅛　teaspoon freshly ground black pepper
2　1-pound loaves rye or pumpernickel bread, round or oval
　radish slices (optional)

8 servings

In medium bowl, mix together spinach, mayonnaise, onions, parsley, yogurt, lemon juice, salt, dill and pepper. *Dip can be prepared 24 hours before serving. Cover and refrigerate.*

Cut ¾-inch slice from top of 1 bread loaf. Cut and scoop out inside and tear into ½-inch chunks. Tear second loaf into chunks. *Store in plastic bag if done ahead.* To serve, fill loaf with spinach mixture, garnish with radish slices, and use bread chunks for dipping.

Surround the dark loaf with crudites of glorious color and various shapes, such as steamed crisp-tender asparagus spears, sliced cooked beets, red, green and yellow bell pepper strips, snow peas and jícama sticks.

Appetizers

Cumberland Cucumber Dip

8 ounces cream cheese, softened
¼ teaspoon garlic powder
¼ teaspoon salt
¼ teaspoon freshly ground black pepper
1 tablespoon Worcestershire sauce
¼ cup mayonnaise
¾ cup chopped onion
2 cups chopped cucumber
large corn chips

4 cups

In medium mixing bowl, combine cream cheese, garlic powder, salt, pepper, Worcestershire and mayonnaise. Add onions and mix well. Mix in cucumbers 4 hours before serving. Refrigerate. Serve cold with large corn chips.

A perfect summertime dip. Serve in a hollowed-out purple cabbage, garnished with sprigs of fresh dill.

Evergreen Avocado Dip

1 6-ounce package frozen avocado dip, defrosted
8 ounces cream cheese, softened
4 medium avocados, peeled, pitted and cubed
½ cup finely chopped onion
1 tablespoon fresh lemon juice
1 teaspoon garlic salt
¼ teaspoon Tabasco sauce
½ teaspoon Worcestershire sauce
½ teaspoon seasoned salt
2 medium tomatoes, chopped
freshly ground black pepper to taste
tortilla chips

6½ cups

In a food processor with metal blade, process avocado dip, cream cheese and half the cubed avocados until smooth. Add onion, lemon juice, garlic salt, Tabasco, Worcestershire and seasoned salt and process a few seconds. Add remaining avocado cubes and tomatoes and pulse a few times, leaving avocados and tomatoes chunky. Add pepper to taste. Serve with tortilla chips.

Best when made the night before, this dip will stay "evergreen" for your crowd. Add salsa for a spicier dip.

Chutney Fruit Dip

16 ounces cream cheese, softened
1 teaspoon salt
½ teaspoon curry powder
⅓ cup chutney
¾ cup sour cream
¼ cup sherry
fruit for dipping

4 cups

In medium mixing bowl, beat cream cheese until fluffy. Add remaining ingredients and blend. Chill until ready to use.

Accompany with an attractive assortment of fruits such as sliced apples, strawberries, pineapple spears and banana chunks.

Toasted Pecan Fruit Spread

3	tablespoons honey
1	tablespoon apple-flavored brandy
2	tablespoons milk
8	ounces cream cheese, softened
½	cup dried apple chunks, chopped
¼	cup chopped pecans, toasted

1¾ cups

In medium bowl, gradually add honey, brandy and milk to cream cheese, mixing until well blended. Stir in apples and pecans. Cover and chill.

For a variation, use ½ cup dried fruit medley (apricots, apples, peaches, pears and raisins) in place of the apples. Delicious spread on crackers or as a dip for fruits.

LaSalle French Nuts

1	egg white
1	teaspoon water
1	12-ounce can salted mixed nuts (2 cups)
1	cup sugar
2	teaspoons ground cinnamon

2 cups

In medium bowl, beat egg white until frothy; add water and beat again. Fold in nuts, stirring to coat. In small bowl, stir sugar and cinnamon together. Add to nut mixture and stir to coat well. Cut a brown paper bag to line a 14x17-inch cookie sheet. Spread nuts on lined cookie sheet. Bake at 350 degrees for 20-25 minutes, stirring occasionally. Mixture will foam. Remove from sheet and cool. Store in covered, airtight container.

A sweet departure from usual cocktail nuts.

Soups

Soups

Chilled Colorado Fruit Soup

6 medium-size ripe peaches, peeled, pitted and sliced
¼ cup dry white wine
6 tablespoons fresh lemon juice
2 tablespoons honey
¼ teaspoon ground cinnamon
dash of nutmeg
1 cup fresh orange juice
1 medium-size ripe cantalope, peeled, seeded and cut into ½-inch pieces

Garnish:
sprigs of fresh mint
fresh blueberries

4 servings

In heavy saucepan, combine peaches, wine, lemon juice, honey, cinnamon and nutmeg. Heat to boiling. Lower heat, cover and simmer for 10 minutes. Remove from heat, cool to room temperature, and purée in blender or food processor.

In blender or food processor, purée orange juice and ¾ of cantalope until smooth. In large bowl, combine peach and cantalope mixtures. Chop remaining cantalope and stir into soup. Cover and chill. Serve soup in chilled bowls, garnished with mint and/or fresh blueberries.

This soup is perfect when Rocky Ford cantalopes and western slope peaches are in abundance.

Fresh Blueberry Soup

1 cup fresh blueberries, washed and stems removed
juice of ½ lemon
1 cinnamon stick
2 cups water
pinch of salt
¼ cup sugar
1 tablespoon cornstarch
2 tablespoons water
¼ cup heavy cream

Garnish:
sugar to rim glasses
¼ cup heavy cream, whipped
blueberries

4-6 servings

In large saucepan, simmer blueberries, lemon juice and cinnamon stick in 2 cups water for 15 minutes or until berries are soft. Stir in salt and sugar. Mix cornstarch with 2 tablespoons water and add to blueberry mixture. Heat to boiling, reduce heat and simmer for 2 minutes. Remove from heat and discard cinnamon stick. When cool, purée soup in blender. Stir in ¼ cup cream. Refrigerate until cold. Serve in champagne glasses rimmed with sugar crystals. Garnish with whipped cream and blueberries.

This elegant summer soup must be made ahead and chilled thoroughly.

Soups

Minted Kiwi Soup

6 kiwis
10 fresh mint leaves
2 cups plain yogurt
¾ cup heavy cream
3 tablespoons cider vinegar
1 cup sugar
¾ cup apricot nectar
1 cup heavy cream
¼ cup sugar

Garnish:
sprigs of fresh mint

8-10 servings

Cut each kiwi in half and scoop out fruit with spoon. Discard skins. Put kiwi fruit and mint leaves into blender or food processor and purée. Add yogurt, ¾ cup heavy cream, cider vinegar, 1 cup sugar and apricot nectar. Blend until smooth. Pour into large bowl. In small mixing bowl, whip 1 cup heavy cream to soft peaks, beating in ¼ cup sugar. Fold into kiwi mixture and chill. When ready to serve, pour into champagne glasses and garnish with sprigs of mint.

A particularly cool and refreshing soup.

Iced Chicken Curry Soup

2 tablespoons butter
1 onion, finely chopped
1 Granny Smith apple, peeled, cored and sliced
¼ cup all-purpose flour
2 teaspoons curry powder
dash of chili powder
dash of cayenne pepper
3 cups chicken broth
½ cup cooked, puréed peas
1½ cups heavy cream
½ cup finely diced, cooked chicken breast

Condiments:
chutney
flaked coconut
toasted sliced almonds
fresh mint leaves

6-8 servings

Melt butter in medium saucepan. Stir in onion and apple slices and cook slowly until soft but not browned. Add flour and curry powder and simmer for 5 minutes. Mix in chili powder, cayenne pepper and chicken broth. Stir until smooth. Add puréed peas, stirring over high heat until soup boils. Remove from heat, cool slightly, and purée in blender or food processor. Chill thoroughly. Before serving, stir in cream and diced chicken breast. Serve in chilled bowls accompanied by chutney, flaked coconut, almonds and mint leaves.

Use a hollowed-out squash lined with a bowl as an unusual soup tureen, and serve condiments in small bowls surrounding the squash.

Soups

Jellied Herbed Consommé

2   10½-ounce cans beef consommé, undiluted
½   cup chopped celery
¼   cup chopped green bell pepper
¼   cup chopped green onions
2   teaspoons Spice Islands Fine Herbs
4-6   tablespoons sour cream
1½   teaspoons curry powder
4-6   tablespoons sliced almonds

4-6 servings

In medium bowl, mix together consommé, celery, green pepper, green onions and Fine Herbs. Refrigerate until jelled. In small bowl, mix together sour cream and curry powder. When ready to serve, put 1 tablespoon sliced almonds in each chilled individual glass bowl. Spoon consommé over almonds and garnish with a dollop of curried sour cream.

This subtle soup makes an elegant first course for a dinner party.

Vichyssoise de Pomme

5   Granny Smith apples, peeled, cored and quartered
    juice of 1 lemon
1   cup dry white wine
2   cinnamon sticks
3   thin slices fresh ginger
5   tablespoons sugar
1   tablespoon Applejack
¼   cup sour cream
1   cup beef bouillon
1   cup heavy cream
½   teaspoon salt

Garnish:
    fresh blueberries

6-8 servings

Cut 2 apple quarters into julienne strips, sprinkle with lemon juice and set aside. In heavy saucepan, combine remaining apples, wine, cinnamon sticks, ginger and sugar. Heat to boiling. Lower heat, cover and simmer for 10 minutes or until apples are thoroughly cooked. Cool and remove cinnamon sticks and ginger slices. Purée cooled apple mixture, Applejack and sour cream in blender or food processor until smooth. With machine running, pour in beef bouillon, then heavy cream in a slow, steady stream. Drain lemon juice from reserved apple strips and add juice to soup. Stir in salt and chill completely. Serve in chilled bowls garnished with reserved apple strips and blueberries.

This refreshing soup combines a creamy apple taste with a hint of ginger.

50

Soups

Fire and Ice Soup

Hot Tomato Ice:
- 1   14-ounce can Italian plum tomatoes
- ½   cup chicken broth
- 1   tablespoon fresh lemon juice
- 1   teaspoon sugar
- ½   teaspoon Tabasco sauce

Avocado Soup:
- 4   ripe avocados, peeled and pitted
- 6   tablespoons fresh lemon juice
- 1½   teaspoons ground cumin
- 4½   cups chicken broth
- ½   cup minced green onions
- 2   tablespoons diced canned jalapeños
- ¼   cup sour cream
      salt and freshly ground black pepper
      to taste

12 servings

In blender or food processor, purée tomatoes with liquid. Strain purée through fine sieve into bowl, pressing hard on solids. Mix in chicken broth, lemon juice, sugar and Tabasco sauce. Freeze in ice cube tray or similar container for 3 hours until firm but not frozen solid. Chop into pieces and blend in food processor until smooth. Return to container and freeze for 2 hours longer or until firm.

In medium bowl, mash avocados with lemon juice and cumin. Heat chicken broth to simmering and whisk into avocado mixture. Stir in green onions and jalapeños. In food processor or blender, purée mixture in two batches to avoid spilling. Pour into large bowl. Whisk in sour cream, salt and pepper to taste. Cover and chill soup for 2 hours or until very cold. Ladle soup into chilled sherbet glasses and put 1 spoonful of tomato ice in the center of each serving.

The spicy ice enhances the cool smoothness of this special avocado soup.

Elegant Pimiento Soup

- 1   16-ounce jar pimientos, drained and chopped
- 2   cups chicken broth
- 5   tablespoons butter
- ¼   cup all-purpose flour
- 3   cups half and half
- 3   cups chicken broth
      salt and freshly ground black pepper
      to taste

Garnish:
- sour cream
- sprigs of watercress or
- fresh dill or
- minced fresh parsley or
- minced fresh chives

6-8 servings

In medium saucepan, heat pimiento and 2 cups chicken broth until simmering. Purée in blender or food processor and set aside. In medium saucepan, melt butter. Stir in flour and cook until bubbling. Gradually add half and half, stirring constantly. Simmer for 3 minutes or until thickened. Stir in puréed pimiento mixture and 3 cups chicken broth. Simmer for 3 minutes or until heated thoroughly. Season with salt and pepper to taste. Chill if desired. Serve with a dollop of sour cream topped with herbs of choice.

This unique soup may be served hot or cold, and is an excellent first course for a special dinner party.

Soups

Tomato Basil Soup

3   tablespoons butter
1   large onion, sliced
1   large carrot, peeled and grated
4   large ripe tomatoes, peeled, seeded
    and chopped
½   cup lightly packed chopped fresh
    basil
¾   teaspoon sugar
⅛   teaspoon ground white pepper
1¾ cups chicken broth
    salt to taste

Garnish:
    thin slices of lemon
    fresh basil leaves

6-8 servings

In 3-quart saucepan, melt butter over medium heat. Add onion and carrot and cook until onion is transparent, stirring frequently. Stir in tomatoes, basil, sugar and white pepper. Heat to boiling, stirring constantly. Reduce heat and simmer covered for 10 minutes. Cool slightly. Pour into food processor or blender and purée until smooth. Return to pan and stir in broth and salt. Heat until steaming. Ladle into individual bowls and float 1 thin lemon slice topped with a basil leaf in each bowl.

For a luncheon, this flavorful soup is also excellent served cold with a pasta salad.

Not Just Another Spinach Soup

2   10-ounce packages frozen chopped
    spinach
2   tablespoons butter
1   small onion, minced
3   tablespoons all-purpose flour
1¾ cups chicken broth
2   cups milk
1   cup half and half
½   teaspoon salt
½   teaspoon ground nutmeg

Garnish:
    crumbled blue cheese or
    freshly grated Parmesan cheese

6-8 servings

In medium saucepan, cook spinach until tender. Drain, put in food processor or blender, and blend until finely chopped. In large heavy saucepan, melt butter and sauté onion for 3 minutes. Blend in flour. Add chicken broth and spinach and cook for 2 minutes. Stir in milk, half and half, salt and nutmeg. Heat to simmering and serve garnished with blue or Parmesan cheese.

Parmesan Bread Sticks *add a finishing touch to this soup. Try serving it chilled in the summer.*

Soups

Oriental Hot and Sour Soup

4	dried Shiitake (Chinese) mushrooms
¼	cup dried cloud ear mushrooms
10	tiger lily buds (golden needles), pulled apart
2	tablespoons cornstarch
3	tablespoons rice wine or dry sherry
¼	pound lean pork loin
4½	cups chicken broth
¼	cup sliced bamboo shoots
1	tablespoon soy sauce
2	tablespoons red wine vinegar
1	teaspoon salt
¾	teaspoon freshly ground black pepper
1	egg, lightly beaten
8	ounces fresh tofu (bean curd), diced
2	teaspoons hot sesame oil
1	green onion, chopped

4-6 servings

In medium bowl, soak Shiitake mushrooms, cloud ear mushrooms and tiger lily buds in warm water for 20 minutes. Drain, squeeze out excess moisture and cut into ¼x¼x1-inch pieces. In small dish, combine cornstarch with rice wine or sherry; set aside. Simmer pork in water to cover until tender. Cool and shred.

Heat chicken broth to boiling. Stir in shredded pork, Shiitake mushrooms, cloud ears, tiger lily buds and bamboo shoots. Simmer for 10 minutes. Add soy sauce, vinegar, salt, pepper and cornstarch mixture. Stir until thickened. Remove from heat and add beaten egg, stirring constantly. Add tofu. Just before serving, stir in hot sesame oil. Ladle into bowls and sprinkle each serving with chopped green onion.

*Serve this soup with **Maifun Salad** for a memorable luncheon.*

Chinese Wonton Soup

Wontons:

1	egg, beaten
¼	cup finely chopped onion
¼	cup finely chopped water chestnuts
1	tablespoon soy sauce
2	teaspoons grated fresh ginger
½	teaspoon sugar
¼	teaspoon salt
⅛	teaspoon freshly ground black pepper
½	pound ground pork
4-5	ounces tiny shrimp, chopped
20	wonton skins
8	cups water

Soup:

6	cups chicken broth
1	cup thinly sliced Chinese cabbage
1	cup thinly sliced mushrooms
⅓	pound snow peas
½	cup thinly sliced bamboo shoots
4	green onions, diagonally sliced into 1½-inch pieces

6-8 servings

In medium bowl, combine egg, onion, water chestnuts, soy sauce, ginger, sugar, salt, pepper, pork and shrimp; mix well. One at a time, position wonton skins with point towards you. Place 1 rounded teaspoon of filling in center of each skin. Fold bottom point up over filling, tucking point under filling. Roll once to enclose filling. Wonton should now look like a triangle with 1 inch at top and to sides of filling. Press down on both sides of filling. Moisten right corner of wonton with water. Grasp both the right and left corners of the skin and bring them together below the filling, overlapping the left corner over the right and pressing to seal. In large saucepan, heat water to boiling. Drop wontons into boiling water one at a time, keeping water boiling. Simmer uncovered for about 5 minutes. Remove and rinse with cold water. Drain thoroughly.

In large saucepan, heat chicken broth to boiling. Three minutes before serving, stir in Chinese cabbage, mushrooms, snow peas, bamboo shoots and wontons. Immediately before serving, stir in green onions. It is important not to cook the vegetables longer than 3 minutes so they will remain crisp.

Soups

Sherried Wild Rice Soup

  1   cup wild rice
  4   cups water
  1   tablespoon salt
  4   tablespoons butter
  1   medium onion, finely chopped
  2   cups sliced mushrooms
  ½   cup thinly sliced celery
  ¼   cup all-purpose flour
  5¼ cups chicken broth
  ½   teaspoon salt
  ½   teaspoon curry powder
  ½   teaspoon dry mustard
  ½   teaspoon dry chervil
  ¼   teaspoon ground white pepper
  2   cups half and half
  ⅔   cups dry sherry

Garnish:
  minced fresh parsley or
  minced chives or
  thinly sliced mushrooms

6-8 servings

Rinse wild rice until water runs clear. Heat water and 1 tablespoon salt to boiling. Add rice and simmer covered for 45 minutes or until rice is tender. Drain off excess water. In heavy saucepan, melt butter, stir in onion and cook 5 minutes or until golden. Stir in mushrooms and celery and cook 4 minutes. Mix in flour and gradually blend in chicken broth, stirring constantly until slightly thickened. Stir in wild rice, ½ teaspoon salt, curry powder, dry mustard, chervil and white pepper. Lower heat and stir in half and half and sherry. Heat to simmering, stirring occasionally. Do not boil. Garnish with parsley, chives or mushroom slices.

This delicious soup can be prepared the day before serving.

7th Avenue Artichoke and Mushroom Soup

  2   tablespoons finely chopped onion
  ½   pound mushrooms, thinly sliced
  3   tablespoons butter
  3   tablespoons all-purpose flour
  2   cups chicken broth
  1½ cups half and half
  1   9-ounce package frozen artichoke
      hearts, thawed
  1   teaspoon onion salt
      dash of cayenne pepper
  2   teaspoons Beau Monde seasoning
  ¼   cup dry vermouth

Garnish:
  chopped green onions or
  minced chives

6 servings

Sauté onion and mushrooms in butter for 5 minutes. Stir in flour and cook slowly for 2 minutes. Slowly add chicken broth and half and half, stirring over low heat until thickened. Cut each artichoke heart into 8 thin wedges. Add artichokes, onion salt, cayenne pepper, Beau Monde seasoning and vermouth and heat thoroughly. Ladle into bowls and garnish with chopped green onions or chives.

An inspired combination of flavors.

Soups

Sensational Senegalese Soup

1 cup butter
7 shallots, minced
3 celery stalks, finely chopped
½ cup all-purpose flour
¾ cup dry sherry
¾ cup apple cider
¾ cup chicken broth
4 cups milk
1 pound raw chicken breast, chopped
1½ teaspoons curry powder
½ teaspoon finely chopped fresh dill
1 teaspoon freshly ground black pepper
   salt to taste
1 large tart green apple, peeled, cored and chopped

Garnish:
   minced fresh chives
   apple slices

10-12 servings

In heavy saucepan, melt butter and sauté shallots and celery for 10 minutes. Whisk in flour and cook 3 minutes. Slowly stir in sherry, apple cider and chicken broth; simmer, stirring constantly, until liquid thickens, about 2 minutes. Gradually whisk in milk. Stir in chicken and bring to a simmer. Cook chicken for 5 minutes or until tender. Blend in curry powder, dill weed, pepper and salt. Right before serving, stir in chopped apple. Heat thoroughly. Ladle soup into bowls and garnish with minced chives and apple slices.

*Pair this with **Tandoori Lamb Kabobs** for an exceptional meal.*

Reuben Soup au Gratin

1 cup beef broth
1 cup chicken broth
¼ cup chopped celery
¼ cup chopped onion
¼ cup chopped green bell pepper
1 tablespoon cornstarch
2 tablespoons water
¼ pound corned beef, shredded
1¼ cups shredded Swiss cheese
¾ cup sauerkraut, drained, rinsed and squeezed dry
4 tablespoons butter
2 cups half and half
   salt and freshly ground black pepper to taste
4 rye bread rounds, toasted
¾ cup shredded Swiss cheese

4 servings

In heavy saucepan, heat beef broth, chicken broth, celery, onion and green pepper to boiling. Reduce heat and simmer covered until vegetables are crisp-tender, about 5 minutes. Dissolve cornstarch in water and blend into soup. Cook until soup thickens, stirring constantly. Remove from heat and stir in corned beef, 1¼ cups Swiss cheese and sauerkraut.

In top of double boiler over simmering water, melt butter and stir in half and half. Add soup and stir until smooth and thoroughly heated. Do not boil. Season with salt and pepper. Ladle soup into 4 oven-proof bowls. Cover bread rounds with equal parts of the ¾ cup Swiss cheese. Float 1 bread round in each bowl of soup and place under broiler until cheese is bubbly and golden.

Do not make ahead. This soup must be served immediately.

Soups

Garden Cheddar Soup

- 2 carrots, peeled and sliced
- 2 small zucchini, halved and sliced
- 2 tomatoes, peeled and cut into wedges
- 1 celery stalk, sliced
- 1 cup sliced mushrooms
- 1 onion, halved and sliced
- 2 cloves garlic, minced
- 4½ cups beef broth
- 1½ cups V-8 juice
- 1 tablespoon minced fresh basil
- ½ cup dry red wine
- ½ teaspoon salt
- ½ teaspoon freshly ground black pepper
- 2 tablespoons minced fresh parsley
- 1 cup shredded Cheddar cheese

6-8 servings

In stockpot, combine carrots, zucchini, tomatoes, celery, mushrooms, onion, garlic, beef broth and V-8 juice. Heat to boiling, reduce heat and simmer covered for 30 minutes or until vegetables are just tender. Stir in basil, red wine, salt, pepper and parsley. Add shredded Cheddar just before serving.

*Serve with **Herb Bread** for a light dinner.*

Curried Seafood Soup

- 8 cups chicken broth
- 1 teaspoon curry powder
- 3 cups diced Red Delicious apples
- 3 cups diced pears
- ½ fresh pineapple, peeled and diced
- ½ cup raisins
- ½ cup flaked coconut
- ½ teaspoon anise seeds
- ½ cup sugar
- ½ teaspoon ground nutmeg
- 1 teaspoon ground allspice
- ½ teaspoon ground cinnamon
- 3 tablespoons butter
- 3 tablespoons all-purpose flour
- 2 cups heavy cream
- ¼ cup dry sherry
- ½ pound shrimp, peeled and deveined
- ½ pound bay scallops, rinsed
- ½ pound crabmeat
- 2 tablespoons butter

Garnish:
- toasted coconut
- toasted sliced almonds
- paprika

8 servings

In large pot, combine chicken broth, curry powder, apples, pears, pineapple, raisins, coconut, anise seeds, sugar, nutmeg, allspice and cinnamon. Heat to boiling, lower heat and simmer covered for 2 hours. Strain broth, discarding fruit and spices. Pour broth back into stockpot and boil until volume is reduced by half, leaving about 1 quart. In small saucepan, melt 3 tablespoons butter. Stir in flour until well blended. Stir in broth in a steady stream, whisking until smooth and thickened. Stir in cream and sherry and heat to simmering. Do not boil.

Sauté shrimp, scallops and crab in 2 tablespoons butter for 2 minutes or until opaque. When ready to serve, stir sautéed seafood into soup. Serve immediately garnished with coconut, almonds and paprika.

A deliciously different Indian seafood soup.

Soups

Salmon Bisque

½ pound fresh salmon
4 tablespoons butter
¼ cup minced green onions
1 clove garlic, minced
¼ cup all-purpose flour
2 cups milk
3 cups half and half
½ cup tomato purée
2 tablespoons dry sherry
1 teaspoon salt
1 tablespoon minced fresh dill
¼ teaspoon ground white pepper

Garnish:
sprigs of watercress
fresh dill

6-8 servings

Poach salmon. Cool, flake and set aside. In large saucepan, melt butter, stir in green onions and garlic, and sauté until onions are transparent. Blend in flour. Cook, stirring constantly, for 5 minutes. Slowly whisk in milk and half and half, stirring until thickened. Add flaked salmon, tomato purée, sherry, salt, dill weed and white pepper. Simmer covered for 15 minutes. To serve, garnish with sprigs of watercress or fresh dill.

*Accompany this smooth soup with **Silverglade Spinach Salad** for a satisfying supper.*

Jazzy Jambalaya

1 pound Andouille sausage (New Orleans-style sausage), sliced
⅔ cup chopped green bell pepper
2 cloves garlic, minced
¾ cup minced fresh parsley
1 cup chopped celery
1 tablespoon olive oil
2 16-ounce cans chopped tomatoes
5¼ cups chicken broth
1 cup sliced green onions
1 teaspoon dried thyme
1 bay leaf
1 teaspoon dried oregano
¼ teaspoon cayenne pepper
¼ teaspoon freshly ground black pepper
1 teaspoon chili powder
6 cups cooked long-grain white rice
1½ pounds shrimp, shelled and deveined
1¾ cups chicken broth

10 servings

In heavy, 5-quart kettle, brown sausage. Remove with slotted spoon and set aside. In skillet, sauté green pepper, garlic, parsley and celery in olive oil for 5 minutes. When soft, put sautéed vegetables into kettle along with the undrained tomatoes, 5¼ cups chicken broth, green onions, thyme, bay leaf, oregano, cayenne pepper, black pepper and chili powder. Add cooked rice. Cover and simmer for 30 minutes. Stir occasionally so rice does not stick. Just before serving, add the shrimp and 1¾ cups chicken broth and simmer gently until shrimp turn pink.

Soup can be frozen. When reheating, add more broth as needed. Served with a green salad, this makes a complete meal.

Soups

Rich and Famous Seafood Gumbo

Roux Mixture:
- ½ cup vegetable oil
- ½ cup all-purpose flour
- 4 celery stalks, chopped
- 2 medium onions, chopped
- 1 small green bell pepper, seeded and chopped
- 1 clove garlic, minced
- ¼ cup minced fresh parsley
- ½ pound fresh okra, sliced, or 1 10-ounce package frozen sliced okra
- 2 tablespoons butter

Gumbo:
- 1 quart chicken broth
- 1 quart water
- ¼ cup Worcestershire sauce
- 18 dashes of Tabasco sauce
- ¼ cup ketchup
- 1 medium tomato, peeled and chopped
- ½ teaspoon salt
- ½ pound Andouille sausage (New Orleans-style sausage), sliced
- 1 bay leaf
- ⅛ teaspoon dried thyme
- ⅛ teaspoon dried rosemary
- ¼ teaspoon crushed red pepper flakes
- 1 cup diced cooked chicken
- 1 pound crabmeat
- 2 pounds shrimp, peeled and deveined
- 1 teaspoon molasses

¾-1 cup cooked white rice per serving

4 quarts

In stockpot, combine oil and flour and cook over low heat, stirring constantly, until roux is the color of a copper penny. This could take 1-1½ hours. Do not let roux burn. Stir in celery, onion, green pepper, garlic and parsley. Cook for 45 minutes, stirring occasionally. In skillet, cook okra in butter until browned. Add to roux mixture and stir over low heat for 5 minutes. *At this point mixture may be cooled, packed and refrigerated or frozen for later use.*

Add chicken broth, water, Worcestershire, Tabasco, ketchup, tomato, salt, sausage, bay leaf, thyme, rosemary and red pepper to roux mixture. Simmer covered for 2½-3 hours, stirring occasionally. Thirty minutes before serving, stir in chicken, crabmeat, shrimp and molasses. Pack cooked rice into a measuring cup and turn cup over in individual soup plates to form an island of rice. Ladle soup around rice mound.

Since preparation time is long, consider making roux mixture one day and completing gumbo the following day. It is well worth the effort and gumbo freezes beautifully.

Soups

Sopa de Maiz
(Mexican Corn Soup)

3½ cups fresh or frozen corn kernels
1 cup chicken broth
4 tablespoons butter
2 cups milk
1 teaspoon ground cumin
1 clove garlic, minced
1 4-ounce can diced green chiles
3 dashes Tabasco sauce
1 teaspoon ground white pepper
8 corn tortillas
  oil for frying
  salt to taste
1 cup diced tomatoes
2 cups diced cooked chicken breast
1 cup shredded Monterey Jack cheese
    with jalapeño peppers

Condiments:
    chunky salsa
    sliced black olives
    sour cream
    sliced green onions
    diced avocados

6-8 servings

In blender or food processor, purée corn and chicken broth. Melt butter in stockpot. Add corn purée and simmer over low heat for 5 minutes, stirring constantly. Stir in milk, cumin and garlic. Heat to boiling, reduce heat, and stir in green chiles, Tabasco and white pepper. *Soup may be cooled and frozen at this point.*

Stack tortillas and cut into 1-inch squares. Heat ½ inch oil in heavy skillet and fry tortilla squares until golden. Drain on paper towels and sprinkle with salt. Put equal amounts of diced tomatoes and chicken in individual soup bowls. Add shredded cheese to simmering soup and stir until cheese melts. Spoon soup into bowls and garnish with tortilla squares. Serve with condiments to be added as desired.

A great version of a traditional Mexican soup.

Soups

San Luis Green Chile Soup

6   medium fresh Anaheim chiles
1   large red bell pepper
1   fresh jalapeño pepper
2   ounces salt pork, diced
½   pound boned chicken breast, thinly sliced
½   pound pork butt steak, thinly sliced
6   tablespoons butter
1   medium onion, diced
½   cup all-purpose flour
1½ teaspoons chili powder
1   teaspoon ground cumin
1   small clove garlic, minced
¾   cup tomato sauce
2   quarts chicken broth, warmed
½   cup peeled, seeded and diced tomatoes
1   tablespoon minced fresh cilantro

Garnish:
avocado slices
sour cream

8 servings

Roast Anaheim chiles, red pepper and jalapeño under hot broiler close to heat until skins blister, turning to char on all sides. Place in plastic bag for 10 minutes. Peel, dice and set aside.

In large skillet, cook salt pork until fat is rendered. Remove salt pork with slotted spoon; drain on paper towel. Increase heat and sauté chicken and pork quickly until browned. Drain and set aside. Melt butter in large saucepan. Add onion and cook until transparent. Add flour and cook stirring until roux is golden brown. Remove roux from heat and stir in chili powder, cumin, garlic and tomato sauce. Whisk in warm chicken broth and heat to simmering. Add chiles, red pepper, jalapeño, salt pork, chicken and pork to soup. Heat thoroughly and stir in tomatoes and cilantro. *Can be made to this point 1 day ahead.* Heat to simmering. Serve garnished with avocado slices and a dollop of sour cream.

Served with warmed flour tortillas, this is sure to become a family favorite.

Spicy Red Bean Soup

1   teaspoon cayenne pepper
1   teaspoon freshly ground black pepper
2   bay leaves, crumbled
1   teaspoon ground cumin
1   pound dry red kidney beans
3   quarts water
1¼ pounds lean smoked ham hock
1   tablespoon salt
1½ cups chopped celery, cut into ½-inch pieces
1½ cups chopped onion, cut into ½-inch pieces
2   cloves garlic, minced
½   teaspoon Tabasco sauce
3   tablespoons minced fresh parsley

8 servings

Place cayenne pepper, black pepper, bay leaves and cumin in center of 6-inch square of cheesecloth. Pull edges together, making a ball of the spices. Twist and tie with heavy thread.

Rinse beans and put them in large kettle with spice ball, water, ham hock, salt, celery, onion and garlic. Heat to boiling, reduce heat and simmer covered for 3-4 hours or until beans are tender, stirring occasionally. Just before serving, remove spice ball. Stir in Tabasco and parsley. Pass extra Tabasco sauce.

Flavor improves if soup is made 1 day ahead. Try serving this soup over hot rice with **Cornbread Muffins** *on the side for a hearty southern-style meal.*

Soups

Cajun Black Bean Soup

1   pound dry black beans
1½   pounds smoked ham hock
1½   quarts water
¼   cup dried minced onion
2   tablespoons paprika
½   teaspoon cayenne pepper
¼   cup minced green bell pepper
2   tablespoons chili powder
1   teaspoon salt
½   teaspoon ground cumin

Garnish:
shredded Monterey Jack cheese
sour cream
minced chives
chopped hard cooked eggs

8 servings

In large kettle, combine beans, ham hock and water. Heat to boiling, reduce heat and simmer covered for 2-2½ hours. Stir frequently and add more water if necessary to cover beans. To test for doneness, remove a few beans from kettle with a slotted spoon and blow on them. Skins will pop open when beans are cooked. Remove ham hock. Chop meat from bones, discarding fat and bones. Add meat to soup. Stir in minced onion, paprika, cayenne pepper, green pepper, chili powder, salt and cumin. Cover and simmer for 1 hour. Remove ¾ of soup and purée in blender. Stir purée back into remaining beans. If necessary, add water to obtain desired thickness. Serve garnished with shredded cheese, sour cream, minced chives or chopped eggs.

Make this spicy full-meal soup ahead and reheat for dinner after a day in the mountains.

Hearty Minestrone

2   pounds chuck roast
1   teaspoon salt
4   quarts water
1   cup sliced celery
1   onion, diced
1   carrot, peeled and sliced
3   tomatoes, peeled and chopped
2   tablespoons minced fresh parsley
1   6-ounce can tomato paste
1   tablespoon salt
1   teaspoon dried oregano
½   teaspoon dried basil
1   16-ounce can dark red kidney beans
1   15-ounce can garbanzo beans
1   16-ounce can baked beans
1   10-ounce package frozen chopped
        spinach, thawed
3   small zucchini, sliced
1   pound Italian sweet sausage, sliced
1   8-ounce package kluski (homemade
        style) noodles

Garnish:
freshly grated Parmesan cheese

8 quarts

In large kettle, combine chuck roast, 1 teaspoon salt and water. Cover and simmer for 3 hours or until beef is tender. Remove meat from kettle and set aside. Remove fat from broth by letting kettle cool in refrigerator and then lifting hardened fat off top and discarding. Break meat into 1-inch pieces and combine with broth in a very large stock pot. Stir in celery, onion, carrot, tomatoes, parsley, tomato paste, 1 tablespoon salt, oregano, basil, kidney beans with liquid, garbanzo beans with liquid, baked beans, spinach, zucchini and sliced sausage. Simmer, covered, until vegetables and sausage are tender, about 1 hour. *Soup may be frozen at this point.*

To serve, cook noodles according to package directions. Rinse, drain and add to hot soup. Sprinkle each serving with Parmesan cheese.

This recipe makes 8 quarts of soup. The recipe can be halved, but because of the preparation time involved, it is well worth the effort to make the larger amount and freeze the balance... if there is any left! **Italian Bread Sticks** *complement this soup.*

Soups

Chili Blanco Especial

1	pound dry White Northern beans
5¼	cups chicken broth
2	cloves garlic, minced
1	large white onion, chopped
1	tablespoon ground white pepper
1	teaspoon salt
1	tablespoon dried oregano
1	tablespoon ground cumin
½	teaspoon ground cloves
1	7-ounce can diced green chiles
5	cups diced cooked chicken breast
1¾	cups chicken broth
1	tablespoon diced jalapeño pepper (optional)
8	flour tortillas

Condiments:
shredded Monterey Jack cheese
sliced black olives
chunky salsa
sour cream
diced avocado

8 servings

Soak beans in water to cover for 24 hours; drain.

In crock pot or large kettle, combine beans, 5¼ cups chicken broth, garlic, onion, white pepper, salt, oregano, cumin and cloves. Simmer covered for at least 5 hours until beans are tender, stirring occasionally. Stir in green chiles, diced chicken and 1¾ cups chicken broth. For hotter taste, add jalapeño. Cover and simmer for 1 hour. To serve, line each bowl with 1 flour tortilla. Spoon in chili and serve with all condiments for a very special chili.

Flavors are enhanced when this chili is made 1 day ahead.

Skiers' Sweet and Sour Stew

3	tablespoons vegetable oil
2	pounds round steak, cut into 1-inch cubes
1	15-ounce can tomato sauce
2	teaspoons chili powder
2	teaspoons paprika
¼	cup packed light brown sugar
1	teaspoon salt
½	cup cider vinegar
½	cup light corn syrup
2	cups peeled and sliced carrots
2	cups chopped onions
1	large green bell pepper, cut into 1-inch squares
1	4-ounce can pineapple chunks, drained
6	small round loaves sourdough bread (optional)

6 servings

Heat oil in skillet and brown round steak. Transfer to crock pot or large kettle. Stir in tomato sauce, chili powder, paprika, brown sugar, salt, vinegar, corn syrup, carrots, onions, green pepper and pineapple. Cover and simmer for 6 hours or until meat is tender. Serve in individual bowls or hollowed-out rounds of bread.

Served with a tossed green salad, this is a hearty meal after a day on the slopes!

Soups

Chili Primero

- 1 pound smoked bacon, cut into ⅜-inch pieces
- 4 pounds round steak, cut into ¼-inch cubes
- 2 28-ounce cans tomatoes
- 1 15-ounce can tomato sauce
- 1 6-ounce can tomato paste
- 1 7-ounce can diced green chiles
- 2 tablespoons diced jalapeño peppers (optional)
- 1 4-ounce can diced, pickled cactus, drained (optional)
- 2 cups chopped onions
- 2 cups chopped green bell pepper
- 1 cup minced fresh parsley
- 2 teaspoons ground coriander
- 3 cloves garlic, minced
- 8 teaspoons ground cumin
- 1 teaspoon cayenne pepper
- ¼ teaspoon dried oregano
- ¼ teaspoon paprika
- 2 teaspoons salt
- 1 teaspoon freshly ground black pepper
- 1 tablespoon fresh lemon juice
- 2 tablespoons mild chili powder
- ½ teaspoon medium-hot chili powder
- ½ cup masa harina (corn flour)

Garnish:
sour cream
shredded Cheddar cheese or
shredded Monterey Jack cheese

10 servings

In large skillet, brown bacon; drain and set aside, reserving grease. In same skillet, brown round steak. Put browned round steak and bacon pieces in large stockpot. Stir in tomatoes with liquid, tomato sauce, tomato paste, green chiles, jalapeños and cactus. Heat to simmering. In same skillet, sauté onions in ½ reserved bacon grease until transparent. Add to stockpot. Repeat with green peppers. Stir in parsley, coriander, garlic, cumin, cayenne pepper, oregano, paprika, salt, pepper, lemon juice and chili powders. Cook over low heat for 1 hour, stirring occasionally to prevent sticking. Sprinkle masa harina over soup and stir. Simmer covered for 4 hours. Garnish each serving with sour cream and shredded cheese.

*Serve with **Cornbread Muffins** and pinto beans. This chili is best when made 1 day ahead; its flavor improves with age.*

Salads

Salads

Colorado Pine Nut Salad

¼   **cup pine nuts**
2   **cloves garlic**
1   **cup water**
¼   **teaspoon salt**
1   **teaspoon Dijon mustard**
2   **tablespoons white wine vinegar**
½   **cup virgin olive oil**
1   **large head romaine lettuce, torn into pieces**
    freshly ground black pepper to taste
¼   **cup coarsely shredded Parmesan cheese**

6 servings

Toast pine nuts under broiler until golden brown; watch carefully. Set aside.

In small saucepan, boil garlic in water for 10 minutes; drain. In large salad bowl, mash garlic and salt to a paste. Whisk in mustard and vinegar. Add oil in a stream, whisking dressing until oil is emulsified. Add romaine; toss well and season with pepper. Sprinkle Parmesan and pine nuts over salad and serve.

Cool, crisp and green, an excellent year-around salad. Pine nuts are also sold under the name pinon nuts.

A Caesar to Love

3   **anchovy fillets**
¼   **cup virgin olive oil**
    juice of ½ lemon
¼   **teaspoon salt**
¼   **teaspoon freshly ground black pepper**
¼   **teaspoon dry mustard**
1   **egg**
1   **head romaine lettuce, torn into pieces**
⅓   **cup freshly grated Parmesan cheese**
1½   **cups Garlic Croutons**

4-6 servings

Mash anchovies in wooden salad bowl. Add olive oil and mix well. Add lemon juice, salt, pepper and dry mustard; mix well. Whisk egg into mixture. Add romaine and toss well. Sprinkle with Parmesan and croutons.

Garlic Croutons:

2   **cloves garlic**
½   **cup virgin olive oil**
1½   **cups cubed French bread**

Soak garlic in olive oil overnight.

Discard garlic. In medium skillet, heat olive oil. Add bread cubes, turning to coat, and brown lightly; set aside.

A classic version of a traditional favorite, this recipe does not double well.

Salads

Curried Fruit and Nut Salad

½ cup slivered almonds
1 head iceberg lettuce, torn into
pieces
1 cup spinach, rinsed, stemmed and
torn into pieces
1 11-ounce can mandarin oranges,
chilled and drained
1 cup seedless grapes, halved
1 avocado, peeled, pitted and diced

Curry Vinaigrette Dressing:
½ cup vegetable oil
½ cup white vinegar
1 clove garlic, minced
2 tablespoons packed light brown
sugar
2 tablespoons minced fresh chives
1 tablespoon curry powder
1 teaspoon soy sauce

10-12 servings

Toast almonds under broiler until golden, watching carefully. In salad bowl, combine lettuce, spinach, mandarin oranges, grapes, avocado and almonds. Prepare *Curry Vinaigrette Dressing.* Pour dressing over salad and toss gently.

Combine all ingredients in lidded jar. Shake well.

*Serve this picture-perfect salad with **Raspberry Muffins.***

Mixed Greens with Watercress Dressing

6 leaves Bibb lettuce
6 leaves Belgian endive
6 leaves curly endive
12 cherry tomatoes, halved
1 red bell pepper, sliced

Watercress Dressing:
⅓ cup mayonnaise
1 tablespoon fresh lemon juice
1 tablespoon milk
1 tablespoon Dijon mustard
¼ teaspoon dried tarragon
2 tablespoons finely chopped
watercress

6 servings

Tear lettuce leaves into pieces and put on salad plates. Divide cherry tomatoes and red pepper slices among the plates and drizzle with *Watercress Dressing.*

In small bowl, combine all ingredients and mix well.

Easy but elegant, an exceptional choice for a dinner salad.

Salads

Sweet and Sour Cole Slaw

1   head cabbage, cored and thinly
      sliced
2   green onions, sliced
2   carrots, grated
½   cup green bell pepper, chopped
1   teaspoon celery seed
⅓   cup vegetable oil
¾   cup cider vinegar
½   cup sugar
1   teaspoon salt
½   teaspoon freshly ground black
      pepper

8-10 servings

In large bowl, combine cabbage, onions, carrots, green pepper and celery seed. In saucepan, heat oil, vinegar, sugar, salt and pepper to boiling. Pour over salad, toss well and refrigerate for 24 hours.

A deliciously different version of an all-American favorite.

Splendid Raspberry Spinach

2   tablespoons raspberry vinegar
2   tablespoons raspberry jam
⅓   cup vegetable oil
8   cups spinach, rinsed, stemmed and
      torn into pieces
¾   cup coarsely chopped macadamia
      nuts
1   cup fresh raspberries
3   kiwis, peeled and sliced

8 servings

To prepare dressing, combine vinegar and jam in blender or small bowl. Add oil in a thin stream, blending well. Toss spinach, ½ of nuts, ½ of raspberries and ½ of kiwis with dressing on a platter or in a flat salad bowl. Top with remaining nuts, raspberries and kiwis. Serve immediately.

An outstanding salad which delights the palate and excites the eye — equally as splendid with strawberries, strawberry jam and strawberry vinegar.

Salads

Exotic Spinach Salad

8 cups spinach, rinsed, stemmed and torn into pieces
1 papaya, peeled and cut into ½-inch pieces
1 mango, peeled and cut into ½-inch pieces
1 kiwi, peeled and sliced
1 cup sliced strawberries

Sesame and Poppy Dressing:
⅓ cup sugar
2 tablespoons sesame seeds
1 tablespoon poppy seeds
1½ teaspoons grated onion
¼ teaspoon Worcestershire sauce
¼ teaspoon paprika
½ cup vegetable oil
¼ cup cider vinegar

8 servings

Combine spinach with papaya, mango, kiwi and strawberries. Toss with **Sesame and Poppy Dressing** and serve.

In a blender, combine sugar, sesame seeds, poppy seeds, onion, Worcestershire, paprika and oil. Slowly add vinegar until dressing is moderately thick.

An unusual salad, as good to eat as it is beautiful to look at. Enjoy this delicious dressing with your favorite fruit salad.

Silverglade Spinach Salad

6 cups spinach, rinsed, stemmed and torn into pieces
6 ounces Swiss cheese, cut into julienne strips
6 ounces Cheddar cheese, cut into julienne strips
2 cups seedless grapes, halved

Dressing:
¼ cup cider vinegar
½ cup vegetable oil
2 teaspoons Dijon mustard
2 teaspoons packed light brown sugar
4 slices bacon, fried crisp, drained and crumbled
2 tablespoons sliced green onions

6 servings

To prepare dressing, whisk together vinegar, oil, mustard and brown sugar. Stir in bacon pieces and onion. Refrigerate.

In a large bowl combine spinach, cheeses and grapes. Toss with dressing.

A very appealing contrast of colors, textures and tastes.

Salads

Spinach, Bacon and Apple Salad

5 slices bacon
¼ cup sliced almonds
8 cups spinach, rinsed, stemmed and torn into pieces
1 Red Delicious apple, unpeeled, cored and chopped
3 green onions, sliced

Dressing:
¼ cup vegetable oil
3 tablespoons red wine vinegar
1 teaspoon sugar
½ teaspoon prepared mustard
salt and freshly ground black pepper to taste

6-8 servings

In lidded jar, combine all dressing ingredients. Shake well and refrigerate.

In skillet, cook bacon until crisp. Drain on paper towel; crumble. In same skillet, cook almonds in 1 tablespoon bacon grease. Shake over high heat until almonds are browned. In large salad bowl, combine spinach with bacon, almonds, apple and onions. Toss with dressing.

*Team this colorful salad with **Cheese and Wine Bread**.*

Country Spinach Salad

½ cup mayonnaise
½ cup sour cream
10 ounces spinach, rinsed, stemmed and torn into pieces
2 hard cooked eggs, diced
1 Red Delicious apple, unpeeled, cored and diced
½ small red onion, sliced into thin rings
¼ pound blue cheese, crumbled

6-8 servings

In salad bowl, combine mayonnaise and sour cream; mix well. Add spinach, eggs, apple, onion and blue cheese. Toss well.

Varied in flavors and colors, this salad is perfect for blue cheese lovers.

Salads

Spinach Salad with Creamy Mustard Dressing

1	pound spinach, rinsed, stemmed and torn into pieces
½	pound bacon, fried crisp, drained and crumbled
¼	pound mushrooms sliced
1	cup sliced water chestnuts
½	cup black olives, sliced

Creamy Mustard Dressing:

2	hard cooked eggs, mashed with fork while still warm
½	teaspoon salt
1½	teaspoons sugar
1	tablespoon coarsely ground black pepper
1	clove garlic, crushed
½	cup virgin olive oil
1	tablespoon Dijon mustard
5	tablespoons heavy cream
¼	cup red wine vinegar

8-10 servings

In large bowl, combine all ingredients and toss well with *Creamy Mustard Dressing.*

One at a time and in order, thoroughly blend all other ingredients into mashed eggs. Do not substitute. When blended, whisk until smooth.

A beautiful, elegant introduction to an evening meal.

Artichoke Salad

2	14-ounce cans artichoke hearts, drained and halved
2	cups thinly sliced mushrooms
1⅓	cups snow peas, trimmed
8	large lettuce leaves
	sliced blanched almonds (optional)

Dressing:

¼	cup red wine vinegar
¼	cup vegetable oil
2	teaspoons Dijon mustard
1	teaspoon minced garlic
1	teaspoon dried dill weed
	salt and freshly ground black pepper to taste
1	cup heavy cream

8 servings

In medium non-metal bowl, combine artichoke hearts, mushrooms and snow peas. In separate bowl, combine all dressing ingredients except cream; mix well. Slowly add cream, whisking until well combined. Pour dressing over vegetables and toss well. Serve on lettuce leaves. Sprinkle with almonds if desired.

In a word, sensational!

Salads

Surprising Broccoli Salad

3	cups broccoli flowerets
6	slices bacon, fried crisp, drained and crumbled
1	cup chopped red onion
½	cup shredded Cheddar cheese

Dressing:

1	cup mayonnaise
2	tablespoons white vinegar
¼	cup sugar

6 servings

Cut flowerets off broccoli stalks. Discard stalks. Toss together broccoli flowerets, bacon, onion and cheese. In small bowl, combine dressing ingredients and mix well. Pour dressing over salad and toss thoroughly. Cover and refrigerate until ready to serve.

Quick, easy and delicious. Salad will keep several days refrigerated in a tightly-sealed container.

Marinated Fresh Vegetable Medley

1	clove garlic, halved
1½	cups thinly sliced mushrooms
1½	cups cherry tomatoes, halved
1½	cups thinly sliced zucchini
1½	cups thinly sliced carrots
1½	cups thinly sliced green onions, including tops
1½	cups thinly sliced green bell pepper rings
1½	cups broccoli flowerets
1½	cups cauliflower flowerets

Dressing:

1	teaspoon salt
½	teaspoon freshly ground black pepper
½	teaspoon dry mustard
1	teaspoon minced fresh chives
2	tablespoons red wine vinegar
1	tablespoon fresh lemon juice
2	tablespoons virgin olive oil

8-10 servings

Rub a large salad bowl with garlic; discard garlic. Combine dressing ingredients in lidded jar and shake well for 30 seconds. Place vegetables in salad bowl and pour dressing over them. Toss well. Cover bowl and marinate vegetables in refrigerator for 8 hours or overnight.

Use only the freshest of ingredients to create a salad which is nutritious and delicious.

Salads

Apple Salad

1	Red Delicious apple, cored and chopped
1	Golden Delicious or Granny Smith apple, cored and chopped
½	cup seedless raisins
½	cup golden raisins
½	cup chopped celery
½	cup cubed Cheddar cheese
¼	cup chopped macadamia nuts
	juice of 1 orange
8	ounces vanilla yogurt
	ground cinnamon

8 servings

In medium bowl, combine apples, raisins, celery, cheese and nuts. Blend orange juice into yogurt. Pour over salad and toss well. Sprinkle cinnamon on top.

A new and fresh-tasting interpretation of the classic Waldorf salad, especially festive at holidays.

Cranberry Apple Salad

1½	cups cranberries, coarsely chopped
3	tablespoons sugar
2	tablespoons fresh lime juice
2	teaspoons Dijon mustard
½	cup virgin olive oil
1	cup chopped walnuts
2	large Granny Smith apples, cored and coarsely chopped
¼	cup sliced green onions
1	head romaine lettuce

Garnish:

freshly grated lime peel

6-8 servings

In small bowl, combine cranberries and sugar. Cover and refrigerate overnight.

In medium bowl, mix lime juice and mustard. Add oil in slow stream, beating constantly. Marinate walnuts, apples and onions in this dressing for 1-4 hours.

To serve, line a large bowl with romaine leaves. Spoon apple mixture over leaves. Make a well in middle of apple mixture and spoon in cranberry mixture. Garnish with grated lime peel.

A festive, refreshing salad that goes especially well with a holiday turkey. Freeze an extra bag of cranberries to enjoy this salad during the summer months.

Salads

Festival of Fruits

¼ cup raspberries
2 teaspoons fresh lime juice
1 tablespoon honey, or to taste
1 pint strawberries, hulled and halved
1 papaya, peeled and sliced into
    ½-inch pieces

4 servings

In blender or food processor, purée raspberries with lime juice and honey. In serving bowl, mix sliced strawberries and papaya. Pour dressing over fruit, toss gently and serve immediately.

Papaya halves make lovely edible salad bowls. A splendid summer salad when fruits are plentiful.

Fresh Fruit Mélange

1 pint sliced strawberries
1 pint blueberries
3 kiwis, peeled and thinly sliced
1 medium cantalope, cut into balls
1 medium honeydew, cut into balls
1 cup chopped mint leaves

Garnish:
whole mint leaves

Dressing:
½ cup fresh orange juice
¼ cup fresh lemon juice
3 tablespoons sugar

10-12 servings

Toss strawberries, blueberries, kiwis, cantalope and honeydew together gently. Sprinkle mint over fruit. Combine dressing ingredients and pour over fruit mixture. Serve chilled, garnished with fresh mint leaves.

Show off this beautiful salad in a crystal bowl or trifle dish.

Salads

Nutty Wild Rice Salad

½ cup wild rice
2 cups canned beef bouillon, undiluted
1 cup frozen peas, thawed
2 stalks celery, thinly sliced on the diagonal
4 green onions, sliced
¼ cup slivered almonds, toasted
lettuce cups (optional)

Dressing:
2 tablespoons red wine vinegar
1 tablespoon soy sauce
1 teaspoon sugar
¼ cup vegetable oil
2 teaspoons sesame oil

4 servings

In medium saucepan, cover rice with cold water to a depth of 1 inch above rice. Heat to boiling. Drain water from rice and add bouillon. Simmer covered until liquid is absorbed, about 1 hour. Combine all dressing ingredients and mix well. While rice is still warm, toss with dressing; cool. In medium bowl, combine rice with peas, celery, green onions and almonds. Toss well. Refrigerate. Serve in small lettuce cups or a lettuce-lined bowl.

Wild rice, one of America's most distinguished native foods, tastes sensational in this salad. Recipe can be doubled, but any larger amounts should be made in separate batches.

Elegant Wild Rice Salad

2 quarts plus 1 cup water
3 cups wild rice
2 6-ounce jars marinated artichoke hearts
1 10-ounce package frozen peas
1 green bell pepper, chopped
1 bunch green onions, chopped
1 pint cherry tomatoes, halved
toasted slivered almonds

Dressing:
1⅓ cups vegetable oil
½ cup white vinegar
¼ cup freshly grated Parmesan cheese
1 tablespoon sugar
2 teaspoons salt
1 teaspoon celery salt
½ teaspoon ground white pepper
½ teaspoon dry mustard
¼ teaspoon paprika
1 clove garlic, minced

10-12 servings

Combine all dressing ingredients in lidded jar and shake well. Refrigerate until ready to use.

In large saucepan, heat water and rice to boiling. Reduce heat to low, cover and simmer for 45 minutes. Drain excess liquid from rice. Drain artichoke hearts, reserving marinade. Halve artichoke hearts and add to rice with peas, green pepper, green onions, tomatoes, reserved marinade and half the dressing. Toss well. Cover and chill. Just before serving, toss again and taste. Add some of remaining dressing, if desired. Sprinkle with almonds and serve.

Colorful ingredients highlight this spectacular salad, which is delicious served with grilled meats or seafood.

Salads

Pasta Verde Salad

8   ounces spinach linguini, cooked al dente and drained
¾   cup peeled julienne strips of carrot
1   large tomato, diced
¼   cup sliced green onions
¼-½   cup freshly grated Parmesan cheese
2   tablespoons sliced black olives

Dressing:

15-20   fresh basil leaves
4   cloves garlic, minced
½   cup white wine vinegar
1¼   cups virgin olive oil
    freshly ground black pepper to taste

8-10 servings

In large bowl, mix linguini, carrot, tomato, green onions, Parmesan cheese and olives.

Combine basil and garlic in food processor and process until finely minced. With processor running, add vinegar, oil and pepper. Toss salad with dressing and serve.

This colorful salad is perfect for picnics and barbecues, and a welcomed change from the usual.

Fusilli Salad

¾   pound feta cheese
1   pound spinach fusilli, cooked al dente and drained
¼   cup chopped red onion
½   cup drained and chopped sundried tomatoes
1   cup Kalamata olives, pitted
3   cups thinly sliced spinach

Dressing:

½   cup virgin olive oil
3   tablespoons red wine vinegar
1   clove garlic, crushed
½   teaspoon salt
    freshly ground black pepper to taste

8-10 servings

Crumble feta cheese over pasta. Add red onion, sundried tomatoes, olives and spinach; toss. Combine dressing ingredients and mix well. Pour dressing over pasta, toss well and serve.

This salad may be made the day ahead. Do not substitute for any of the ingredients. The unique combination of flavors is worth the extra effort required to locate these items in a deli or specialty market.

Salads

Pesto Pasta Salad

1 cup packed fresh basil leaves, washed, patted dry and slivered
2 large cloves garlic, minced
½ teaspoon salt
2 tablespoons pine nuts
¼ cup virgin olive oil
¼ cup freshly grated Parmesan cheese
½ cup dry white wine
2 tablespoons lemon juice
   salt and freshly ground black pepper to taste
1 pound bay scallops
12 ounces spaghetti, cooked al dente and drained

4-6 servings

In blender or food processor, combine basil, garlic, salt and nuts. With motor running, gradually add oil, blending the mixture to a smooth paste. Add Parmesan and process until ingredients are thoroughly combined. Transfer pesto to a large bowl.

In small saucepan, bring wine, lemon juice, salt and pepper to a boil. Add scallops and cook for 2-3 minutes. Drain, reserving cooking liquid.

Combine warm pasta and pesto, tossing to coat pasta. Gradually add reserved scallop cooking liquid and toss well. Add scallops and toss again. Refrigerate 1 hour or longer before serving.

Pesto and bay scallops complement each other perfectly!

Tortellini Salad

10 ounces fresh cheese tortellini, cooked al dente and drained
¼ cup minced fresh parsley
¼ pound salami, cubed
¼ pound Havarti cheese, cubed
1 red or green bell pepper, chopped
½ cup black olives, sliced
2 green onions including tops, sliced

Dressing:
3 tablespoons red wine vinegar
1 teaspoon dried basil
1 teaspoon Dijon mustard
¼ teaspoon salt
¼ teaspoon coarsely ground black pepper
1 clove garlic, minced
½ cup virgin olive oil

4-6 servings

In large bowl, combine tortellini, parsley, salami, cheese, bell pepper, olives and green onions. In blender or food processor, combine all dressing ingredients and blend well. Pour dressing over salad and toss thoroughly. Cover and refrigerate at least I hour.

If making more than 3 hours ahead, reserve half the dressing and toss with salad just before serving.

Salads

Seafood and Pasta with Basil Dressing

1	pound bay scallops, rinsed
1	cup dry white wine
½	pound fusilli, cooked al dente and drained
1	teaspoon garlic powder
1	pound medium shrimp, cooked, peeled and deveined
1	cup frozen peas, thawed
½	cup chopped red bell pepper
½	cup diced red onion
1	cup Kalamata olives, sliced

Basil Dressing:

1	cup packed fresh basil leaves
2	tablespoons virgin olive oil
2-3	cloves garlic, crushed
½	cup virgin olive oil
3-4	tablespoons fresh lemon juice
	salt and freshly ground black pepper to taste

8-10 servings

Simmer scallops in wine until opaque; drain well. Toss fusilli with garlic powder. Add scallops and shrimp; toss again. Add peas, red pepper and onion. Pour **Basil Dressing** over salad and toss thoroughly. Serve or refrigerate. *If made ahead, salad will need extra dressing, so double the dressing ingredients.* Scatter olives around salad before serving.

In food processor, purée basil leaves, 2 tablespoons olive oil and garlic to a paste. Add ½ cup olive oil, lemon juice, salt and pepper. Process until well blended.

Perfect summer fare, casual but dramatic. Serve with wine and crusty French bread.

Seafood in Artichokes

1½	teaspoons minced green onions
½	teaspoon salt
¼	teaspoon dried tarragon
1	egg yolk
1	teaspoon Dijon mustard
1	tablespoon fresh lemon juice
1	tablespoon red wine vinegar
6	tablespoons virgin olive oil
	freshly ground black pepper to taste
	Tabasco sauce to taste
3	large artichokes
¾	pound cooked seafood: a combination of shrimp, scallops and crab

6 servings

In small bowl, mash together green onions, salt and tarragon. Beat in egg yolk, mustard, lemon juice and vinegar. Gradually beat in oil. Season to taste with pepper and Tabasco; set aside.

Cut stems off artichokes close to leaves and pull off tough outer leaves. Cut off prickly tops with scissors. In deep saucepan, cook artichokes in 1½ inches of water, covered, for 25-45 minutes. Artichokes are cooked when an outer leaf can be easily pulled off. Drain artichokes upside down. Chill. Cut artichokes in half lengthwise. With a teaspoon, scoop out central core of thin purple leaves; discard.

If dressing mixture has separated, whisk again until it is pale yellow and of a smooth consistency. Combine the seafood and dressing and toss well. Spoon into artichokes and serve at room temperature.

This combination of seafood and vegetable in a main-course salad is light eating at its best.

Salads

Parmesan Pasta Salad

2   cups cubed cooked chicken
¼   pound fettucini, cooked al dente
      and drained
¼   cup virgin olive oil
½   cup freshly grated Parmesan
      cheese
¼   teaspoon garlic powder
¼   cup chopped celery
¼   cup chopped green bell pepper
¼   cup sliced green onions
¼   cup sliced mushrooms
½   cup small broccoli flowerets
½   cup sliced black olives
½   cup sliced carrots
1   cup frozen peas, thawed
¼   cup slivered almonds

Dressing:
¼   cup red wine vinegar
⅛   teaspoon freshly ground black
      pepper
¼   teaspoon salt
¼   teaspoon garlic powder
¾   teaspoon dried tarragon
½   teaspoon dried basil
½   teaspoon dried oregano
1   teaspoon Worcestershire sauce
1½   tablespoons Dijon mustard
      juice of ¼ lemon
¼   cup virgin olive oil
¼   cup water

6-8 servings

Toss chicken and fettucini with olive oil and cool. Add Parmesan and garlic powder and toss well. Refrigerate 1 hour or as long as overnight.

To serve, add celery, green pepper, green onions, mushrooms, broccoli, olives, carrots, peas and almonds. Combine all dressing ingredients except water in lidded jar and shake well; add water and shake again. Pour over salad and toss thoroughly.

*A zesty pasta salad that is perfect teamed with **Italian Cheese Sticks.***

Salads

First Course Salmon Salad

6	tablespoons sherry wine vinegar
2	tablespoons fresh lemon juice
1	tablespoon coarse-grained mustard
1	tablespoon minced green onions
1½	teaspoons minced garlic
1	cup vegetable oil
	salt and freshly ground black pepper to taste
6	cups mixed greens (radicchio, red leaf lettuce, Belgian endive and green leaf lettuce), torn into pieces
1	pound salmon fillet, cut on diagonal into 6 pieces and boned
¼	cup butter

Garnish:

golden caviar
nasturtium flowers

6 servings

In large bowl, blend vinegar, lemon juice, mustard, green onions and garlic. Gradually whisk in oil. Season with salt and pepper. Add mixed greens, tossing well. Arrange salad on 6 plates.

Pat salmon dry. Season with salt and pepper. Heat butter in large skillet over medium-high heat. Add salmon and sear quickly on both sides. Set 1 salmon piece atop each salad. Garnish with caviar and nasturtiums.

Nasturtiums, an edible garnish, have a pleasant peppery flavor.

Fresh Scallop Salad

½	cup dry white wine
¼	pound bay scallops
1	medium tomato, chopped
1	small cucumber, chopped
2	stalks celery, chopped
1	small head red leaf lettuce
1	head Bibb lettuce, torn into pieces

Dressing:

6	tablespoons virgin olive oil
1	tablespoon red wine vinegar
1	tablespoon balsamic vinegar
1	tablespoon fresh lemon juice
1	tablespoon minced fresh parsley
1	teaspoon sugar
½	teaspoon salt
½	teaspoon freshly ground black pepper
1	clove garlic, minced

4 servings

In small saucepan, bring wine to a slow boil. Add scallops and cook until no longer transparent; drain. Combine all dressing ingredients in lidded jar and shake well. Pour ⅓ of dressing over scallops; chill.

In separate bowl, marinate tomato, cucumber and celery in another ⅓ of dressing; chill.

To serve, line 4 plates with red leaf lettuce. Top with Bibb lettuce. Divide marinated vegetables among the 4 plates. Arrange scallops on vegetables and drizzle with remaining ⅓ of dressing.

Light and elegant; perfect for special occasions.

Salads

Papaya, Shrimp and Avocado Salad

Marinade:
- ¼ cup virgin olive oil
- ¼ cup dry white wine
- 2 teaspoons fresh lemon juice
- 2 tablespoons chopped onion

- 30 large shrimp, cooked, peeled and deveined
- 1 small head red leaf lettuce
- 1 small head Bibb lettuce
- 10 ounces fresh spinach, rinsed and stemmed
- 2 ripe papayas, peeled, halved, seeded and sliced lengthwise
- 2 avocados, peeled, pitted and sliced
- 1 small cucumber, halved lengthwise, seeded and thinly sliced
- ¼ cup toasted walnuts

Dressing:
- 2 green onions including tops, sliced
- 2 tablespoons honey
- ¼ cup fresh lime juice
- ⅔ cup virgin olive oil

Garnish:
- sprigs of watercress
- nasturtium flowers

6 servings

Combine marinade ingredients. Marinate shrimp, refrigerated, for two hours.

Mix all dressing ingredients in blender or food processor. Chill.

Arrange lettuce and spinach leaves on 6 individual plates. Remove shrimp from marinade and arrange on top of leaves with alternating slices of papaya, avocado and cucumber in a pinwheel design. Sprinkle with walnuts and drizzle with dressing. Garnish and serve.

An imaginative combination of flavors and colors. Very nice for special occasions.

Salads

Seafood with Curried Chutney Dressing

1 head lettuce, torn into pieces
4 stalks celery, chopped
4 green onions, chopped
1 pound lump crabmeat
1 pound shrimp, cooked, peeled and deveined

Condiments:
1 cup cashews, toasted
1 cup coconut, toasted
1 cup raisins

Curried Chutney Dressing:
2 tablespoons peach or mango chutney
1 cup mayonnaise
2 tablespoons tarragon vinegar
2 tablespoons vegetable oil
2 teaspoons curry powder
¼ cup half and half

8 servings

Combine lettuce with celery and green onions; toss well. Arrange seafood on top of lettuce and drizzle with *Curried Chutney Dressing.* Sprinkle condiments to taste over salad.

Combine dressing ingredients. Mix well and refrigerate for 1 day before using.

The condiments add crunch and pizzaz to this refreshing summer salad.

Seafood Monterey Salad

¼ cup vegetable oil
3 tablespoons red wine vinegar
1 tablespoon fresh lemon juice
2 teaspoons Dijon mustard
1 teaspoon anchovy paste
¼ teaspoon freshly ground black pepper
1 pound cooked tiny shrimp, bay scallops or a combination of both
4 teaspoons freshly grated Parmesan cheese
3 medium avocados, peeled and halved
12 ounces Monterey Jack cheese, shredded

6 servings

Combine oil, vinegar, lemon juice, mustard, anchovy paste and pepper in a lidded jar and shake well. Pour dressing over seafood and add Parmesan cheese; mix well. Marinate for 1 hour.

Place 1 avocado half in each of 6 individual ramekins. Divide seafood evenly among avocados. Sprinkle with Monterey Jack cheese. Place ramekins under heated broiler until cheese melts. Serve immediately.

A sensational salad for seafood lovers!

Salads

Bronco Beef Salad

Marinade:

½ cup virgin olive oil
¼ cup red wine vinegar
2 teaspoons Dijon mustard
1 clove garlic, crushed
1 teaspoon salt
  freshly ground black pepper to taste
½ teaspoon sugar

12 small mushrooms, sliced
1-1½ pounds cooked roast beef or steak, sliced into strips
12 cherry tomatoes, halved
1 14-ounce can artichoke hearts, drained and halved
1 head iceberg lettuce, sliced
2 tablespoons minced fresh parsley
3 tablespoons blue cheese, crumbled

4-5 servings

In lidded jar, combine marinade ingredients and shake well. In medium bowl, combine mushrooms, beef, tomatoes and artichokes; pour marinade over beef mixture and refrigerate overnight.

To serve, arrange beef mixture with marinade on bed of lettuce on individual plates or in salad bowl. Sprinkle with parsley and blue cheese.

A salad guaranteed to please a beef lover on a warm summer night.

Cold Beef Salad with Caper Vinaigrette

1½ pounds rare roast beef, sliced into strips
¾ pound fresh string beans, trimmed, blanched and sliced
½ red onion, sliced
½ pound mushrooms, sliced
3 tomatoes, cut into wedges
1 14-ounce can hearts of palm, cut into rings
1 bunch watercress, washed and stems removed
1 head Bibb lettuce
1 tablespoon minced fresh oregano
1 tablespoon minced fresh thyme

Caper Vinaigrette:

4 teaspoons capers
3 tablespoons fresh lemon juice
½ cup red wine vinegar
4 teaspoons Dijon mustard
1 cup vegetable oil
¾ teaspoon salt
¼ teaspoon freshly ground black pepper
2 teaspoons sugar

6-8 servings

Prepare **Caper Vinaigrette.** Pour ⅓ of vinaigrette over roast beef. Marinate, refrigerated, for at least 3 hours.

Add string beans, red onion, mushrooms, tomatoes, hearts of palm and watercress. Toss with additional dressing as needed. Arrange on lettuce leaves and sprinkle with oregano and thyme.

Combine all ingredients and mix well.

This hearty salad is substantial enough for an entrée. Use remaining dressing on any mixed greens salad.

Salads

Antipasto Salad

1	head lettuce, torn into pieces
3	Italian tomatoes, sliced
½	pound provolone cheese, cut into ½-inch cubes
1	cup pitted black olives
¼	pound pepperoni, thinly sliced
1	small green bell pepper, thinly sliced
½	cup garbanzo beans
6	medium mushrooms, sliced
1½	cups artichoke hearts, halved
½	cup freshly grated Parmesan cheese

Hearty Italian Vinaigrette:

6	tablespoons virgin olive oil
2½	tablespoons red wine vinegar
2	tablespoons chili sauce
1½	teaspoons Worcestershire sauce
1	clove garlic, minced
1½	teaspoons minced fresh parsley
1	teaspoon Italian Herb Seasoning
½	teaspoon sugar
¼	teaspoon salt
½	teaspoon freshly ground black pepper
1	tablespoon freshly grated Parmesan cheese

6 main course servings
12 first course servings

In large salad bowl, combine lettuce, tomatoes, cheese, olives, pepperoni, green pepper, garbanzo beans, mushrooms and artichoke hearts. Prepare **Hearty Italian Vinaigrette** and pour over salad until all ingredients are lightly coated; toss well. Sprinkle with Parmesan cheese.

In blender, mix all ingredients until well combined.

An excellent main-course salad served with wine and bread. The dressing is excellent on any pasta salad or fresh vegetable combination.

Salads

Turkey Bowl

½ head romaine lettuce
½ head iceberg lettuce
1 large tomato, diced
2 cups cubed, cooked turkey breast
1 large avocado, peeled, pitted and
    cubed
3 ounces blue cheese, crumbled
6 slices bacon, fried crisp, drained
    and crumbled
8 large ripe olives, pitted and sliced

Dressing:
¾ cup vegetable oil
¼ cup white vinegar
1 clove garlic, minced
1 teaspoon salt
2 teaspoons sugar
    freshly ground black pepper to
    taste

4-6 servings

Tear lettuce into pieces and place in large bowl. Add tomato, turkey, avocado, blue cheese and bacon. Combine all dressing ingredients in lidded jar and shake well. Pour dressing over salad and toss well. Top with olive slices.

A delicious luncheon salad, offering a wonderful combination of flavors. Substitute chicken for turkey, if desired.

Turkey Chutney Salad

2 cups diced cooked turkey or
    chicken
1 13 ¼-ounce can pineapple tidbits,
    drained
1 cup chopped celery
¼ cup salted peanuts
½ cup sliced green onions
¾ cup chopped unpeeled apple
    lettuce leaves (optional)

Dressing:
1 cup mayonnaise
3 tablespoons chopped chutney
½ teaspoon freshly grated lime peel
2 tablespoons fresh lime juice
1 teaspoon ground ginger
½ teaspoon curry powder
¼ teaspoon salt

6-8 servings

In a large bowl, toss turkey, pineapple, celery, peanuts, green onions and apple. Combine dressing ingredients in lidded jar and shake well. Pour dressing over salad and mix well.

Arrange individual servings on beds of lettuce or in pineapple boats.

Salads

Maifun Salad

Marinade:
  1   dried Chinese hot red pepper
  3   tablespoons sugar
  1   tablespoon soy sauce
  ½   cup corn oil
  6   tablespoons white vinegar

  2   whole chicken breasts, cooked, skinned and shredded
  1   cup drained and sliced water chestnuts
  1   head iceberg lettuce, shredded
  4   green onions, sliced
  2   tablespoons sesame seeds, lightly toasted
  2   ounces Maifun Chinese rice noodles, deep fried according to package directions

8-10 servings

Break red pepper in half; shake out and discard all seeds. Crush red pepper. In medium bowl, combine red pepper with all other marinade ingredients; mix well. Stir in chicken and water chestnuts. Marinate, refrigerated, overnight.

In large salad bowl, mix together lettuce and green onions; refrigerate. Just before serving, add marinated chicken mixture, toasted sesame seeds and maifun noodles. Toss gently and serve immediately.

The secrets to cooking Chinese rice noodles are to make sure the oil is hot enough (Test by adding a few noodles they should puff instantly.) and to cook the noodles in small batches.

Overnight Chicken Salad

  6   cups shredded iceberg lettuce
  ¼   pound bean sprouts
  1   cup sliced water chestnuts
  ½   cup thinly sliced green onions
  1   medium cucumber, thinly sliced
  4   cups cooked chicken, sliced into 2-inch strips
  2   6-ounce packages frozen snow pea pods, thawed and patted dry
  1   cup Spanish peanuts
  24   cherry tomatoes, sliced

Dressing:
  4   cups mayonnaise
  4   teaspoons curry powder
  2   tablespoons sugar
  1   teaspoon ground ginger

10-12 servings

In shallow 4-quart serving dish, distribute shredded lettuce in an even layer. Top with layers of bean sprouts, water chestnuts, green onions, cucumber, chicken and pea pods.

In small bowl, stir together all dressing ingredients. Spread dressing evenly over pea pods, cover dish and refrigerate for as long as 24 hours.

To serve, add layers of peanuts and cherry tomato slices. Let each guest help himself to the salad, scooping down to the bottom of the dish and lifting out a portion of all the layers.

Use a glass serving dish so the layers of this beautiful salad can be seen and appreciated.

Salads

Lemon-Ginger Chicken Salad

½ cup mayonnaise
¼ cup sour cream
1 tablespoon sugar
½ teaspoon freshly grated lemon peel
1 tablespoon fresh lemon juice
½ teaspoon ground ginger
¼ teaspoon salt
2 cups cubed, cooked chicken
1 cup seedless green grapes
1 cup sliced celery
2 cantalopes or honeydew melons, halved (optional)
 slivered almonds, toasted (optional)

4 servings

In mixing bowl, combine mayonnaise, sour cream, sugar, lemon peel, lemon juice, ginger and salt, stirring well. Add chicken, grapes and celery. Toss salad to coat well. Cover and chill at least two hours before serving. If desired, serve salad in melon halves and sprinkle with toasted slivered almonds.

Tart and tasty, a delicious chicken salad destined to become a favorite.

Oriental Salad

1 head iceberg lettuce, sliced
1 cup shredded, cooked chicken
4 green onions, chopped
2 tablespoons sesame seeds, toasted

Dressing:
4 tablespoons sugar
1 teaspoon salt
2 teaspoons soy sauce
½ cup vegetable oil
6 tablespoons white vinegar

6 servings

Arrange lettuce on 6 salad plates. Top with chicken. Sprinkle with onions and sesame seeds. Combine all dressing ingredients in lidded jar and shake well. Drizzle dressing over salad and serve immediately.

A main-course salad offering wonderful Oriental flavors.

Breads

Breads

Creamy Banana Coffee Cake

6	ounces cream cheese, softened
1/3	cup sugar
1	tablespoon all-purpose flour
1/2	teaspoon ground nutmeg
1	egg
1/2	cup butter, softened
1½	cups sugar
2	eggs
1	teaspoon baking soda
3	tablespoons hot water
3	cups all-purpose flour
1	teaspoon baking powder
1/2	teaspoon salt
1/2	teaspoon ground nutmeg
1	teaspoon ground cinnamon
1/3	cup fresh orange juice
1	teaspoon pure vanilla extract
3	medium, ripe bananas, mashed
1	cup chopped pecans
1	tablespoon butter, melted
1	tablespoon sugar
1/4	teaspoon ground cinnamon

12-16 servings

Combine cream cheese, 1/3 cup sugar, 1 tablespoon flour and 1/2 teaspoon nutmeg, beating until smooth. Add 1 egg and beat again. Set mixture aside.

Cream 1/2 cup butter, gradually adding 1½ cups sugar; beat well. Add 2 eggs, one at a time, beating well after each. Combine soda and hot water and add to creamed mixture, stirring until well blended.

In separate mixing bowl, combine 3 cups flour, baking powder, salt, 1/2 teaspoon nutmeg and 1 teaspoon cinnamon. Add flour mixture to butter mixture alternately with orange juice. Stir in vanilla, bananas and pecans. Spoon 1½ cups of banana batter into lightly greased 10-inch tube pan. Spread cream cheese mixture evenly over batter. Spoon remaining banana batter over cream cheese. Bake at 350 degrees for 50-55 minutes or until a wooden pick inserted in center comes out clean. Cool 15 minutes in pan before removing to a rack to finish cooling. Brush with melted butter and sprinkle with 1 tablespoon sugar combined with 1/4 teaspoon cinnamon.

Garnish this rich coffee cake with whole pecans for an artistic flair.

Cocoa Swirl Coffee Cake

1/2	cup sugar
4½	teaspoons unsweetened cocoa powder
2	tablespoons ground cinnamon
1	cup unsalted butter, softened
8	ounces cream cheese
1½	cups sugar
1½	teaspoons pure vanilla extract
4	eggs
2¼	cups all-purpose flour
1½	teaspoons baking powder
3/4	cup raisins (optional)
3/4	cup chopped pecans

12-16 servings

Preheat oven to 325 degrees. In small bowl, combine 1/2 cup sugar, cocoa and cinnamon; set aside. In large mixing bowl, cream butter. Beat in cream cheese, 1½ cups sugar and vanilla. Add eggs, 1 at a time, beating well after each. Add flour, baking powder and raisins, stirring until smooth. Generously grease a 10-inch tube pan and sprinkle pecans over bottom. Spoon 1/2 batter into pan. Cover with 1/2 cinnamon-cocoa mixture. Spoon remaining batter into pan. Top with remaining cinnamon-cocoa mixture. Bake at 325 degrees for 65-75 minutes or until a wooden pick inserted in center comes out clean. Cool in pan for 15 minutes. Invert cake onto wire rack to finish cooling.

The pronounced cinnamon flavor with a hint of chocolate makes this an exceptional coffee cake!

Breads

Sweet Bishop's Bread

2½ cups sifted all-purpose flour
2 cups packed light brown sugar
½ teaspoon salt
½ cup butter
1 teaspoon baking powder
¼ teaspoon baking soda
1½ teaspoons ground cinnamon
1 egg
1 cup buttermilk or sour milk (add 1 tablespoon lemon juice to 1 cup milk; let stand 5 minutes)

9-12 servings

Mix together flour, sugar, salt and butter until crumbly. Measure and set aside ¾ cup of this mixture. To the remaining mixture add the baking powder, soda, cinnamon, egg and buttermilk. Beat until batter is smooth. Spread batter in greased 8-inch square pan. Sprinkle ¾ cup reserved mixture on top. Bake at 350 degrees for 50-60 minutes or until wooden pick inserted in center comes out clean. Cool ten minutes. Cut and serve warm.

Don't let the name fool you. This is a melt-in-your-mouth coffee cake!

Blueberry Streusel

¼ cup butter
¾ cup sugar
1 egg
2 cups all-purpose flour
½ teaspoon salt
2 teaspoons baking powder
½ cup milk
2 cups blueberries, fresh or frozen

Topping:
½ cup packed light brown sugar
3 tablespoons all-purpose flour
2 teaspoons ground cinnamon
3 tablespoons butter
½ cup chopped pecans

8 servings

Cream together butter, sugar and egg. Add flour, salt, baking powder and milk, stirring until well blended. Carefully fold in berries. Spoon into greased 10-inch springform pan. Mix together topping ingredients of brown sugar, flour, cinnamon, butter and chopped pecans, using a pastry cutter or fork to blend. Sprinkle topping mixture over batter. Bake at 375 degrees for 40-50 minutes or until a wooden pick inserted in center comes out clean.

Serve this ''blue ribbon'' blueberry streusel warm for its flavorful best.

Breads

Apple Raisin Braid

1	cup warm milk (105-115 degrees)
1	tablespoon dry yeast (1½ packages)
¼	cup sugar
1	egg
¼	cup butter, softened
½	teaspoon salt
2½-2¾	cups all-purpose flour
2	tablespoons milk

Filling:

4	cups peeled, cored and chopped apples
¾	cup raisins
¼	cup packed light brown sugar
½	teaspoon ground cinnamon

12 servings

In large bowl, combine 1 cup warm milk, yeast and sugar. Let mixture stand for 2 minutes. Add egg, butter, salt and 1¼ cups of the flour, mixing until smooth. Beat mixture for 2 minutes. Add enough of remaining flour to make a soft dough. Knead on a well-floured surface for 6-8 minutes until dough is smooth and elastic. A bit more flour may be added to keep dough from sticking. Place dough in a greased bowl; cover with plastic wrap. Let rise until doubled in bulk. Punch down.

In medium saucepan, mix filling ingredients together. Cook for 10-15 minutes until soft. Cool completely. Roll out dough into a 8x14-inch rectangle. Spread filling down the center, covering about a 3-inch width. On each side of filling, make cuts 2 inches long at 1-inch intervals. Take strips from each side, alternately crossing them over the filling to form a braid. Tuck ends under. Cover and let rise until doubled, about 1½-2 hours. Bake at 350 degrees for 30-40 minutes. Brush with 2 tablespoons milk when removed from the oven.

For a special breakfast treat, add a glaze to this bread. Beat together ½ cup sifted powdered sugar, 2 teaspoons hot milk and ¼ teaspoon pure vanilla extract and drizzle over cooled bread.

Cherry Nut Coffee Cake

1	cup sugar
2	cups all-purpose flour
1	teaspoon baking powder
1	teaspoon baking soda
¼	teaspoon salt
½	cup butter, melted
2	eggs
1	cup sour cream

Topping:

⅓	cup sugar
½	cup chopped pecans
1	16-ounce jar Maraschino cherries, drained and cut into small pieces
1½	teaspoons ground cinnamon

10-12 servings

Grease and flour a flat-bottomed tube pan. In a large bowl, mix together sugar, flour, baking powder, baking soda, salt, butter and eggs. Fold in sour cream. Pour ½ batter into pan. Mix topping ingredients of sugar, pecans, cherries and cinnamon; sprinkle ½ topping mixture over batter in pan. Pour remaining batter into pan. Sprinkle with remaining topping. Bake at 375 degrees for 30-45 minutes or until a wooden pick inserted in center comes out clean.

This luscious coffee cake will typically have a cracked top and a delicate pink color.

Breads

Gooey Rolls

1	package dry yeast
2	tablespoons sugar
¼	cup warm water (105-115 degrees)
1	tablespoon salt
¼	cup sugar
2	cups hot water
⅓	cup lard
1	egg, lightly beaten
6	cups all-purpose-flour, divided

Sauce:
¾	cup butter
1½	cups packed light brown sugar
3	tablespoons half and half
1½	cups chopped pecans

Filling:
½	cup butter, melted
½	cup sugar
¼	cup ground cinnamon

24 rolls

Dissolve yeast and 2 tablespoons sugar in ¼ cup warm water and let stand for 5 minutes. Dissolve salt and ¼ cup sugar in 2 cups hot water. Add lard and beat until smooth. Add egg, 2 cups flour and yeast mixture to lard mixture and beat until smooth. Add 2 more cups flour and beat again. Add remaining 2 cups flour, working dough until all flour is moistened. Place dough in greased bowl, turning to coat all sides. Cover with plastic wrap and let rise in refrigerator overnight.

In large saucepan, melt butter. Add brown sugar and half and half; bring sauce to a simmer. Pour sauce into 2 9x12-inch pans and sprinkle with nuts. Remove dough from refrigerator and divide into 2 parts. Roll each part into a long rectangle about 12x18 inches. Spread with melted butter. Mix sugar with cinnamon and sprinkle over dough. Roll up dough from the long side like a jellyroll. Slice into 1-inch slices. Place on end in prepared pans, cover, and let rise until doubled in bulk, about 1 hour. Bake at 375 degrees for 20-25 minutes or until golden brown. Remove from oven and immediately invert onto cookie sheet. Cool.

A classic version of a traditional favorite.

Baking Powder Cinnamon Rolls

2	cups all-purpose flour
¼	cup sugar
4	teaspoons baking powder
½	teaspoon salt
½	teaspoon cream of tartar
½	cup margarine, softened
⅔	cup milk

Filling:
2	tablespoons butter, melted
½	cup sugar
2	tablespoons ground cinnamon
¼	teaspoon ground nutmeg

16 rolls

In large bowl, combine flour, sugar, baking powder, salt and cream of tartar. Using pastry blender, cut margarine into dry ingredients. Add milk, mixing with a fork. Roll out dough onto floured board in large rectangle.

In a separate bowl, combine the filling ingredients and spread over dough. Roll up dough and cut into 16 sections. Place sections in greased muffin tins and bake at 425 degrees for 15 minutes or until a light golden color.

Old-fashioned cinnamon rolls the quick and easy way.

Breads

Sweet Bread Rollups

12 ounces cream cheese, softened
½ cup sugar
1 teaspoon pure vanilla extract
1 egg
2 loaves white sandwich bread
¾ cup butter, melted
¾ cup sugar
2 teaspoons ground cinnamon

78 2-inch rolls

In medium bowl, beat together cream cheese, sugar, vanilla and egg; set aside. Trim crusts off bread. Using a rolling pin, roll each slice until flat. Keep flattened slices under damp towel to prevent drying. Spread cream cheese mixture on rolled bread slices. Roll up each slice like a jelly roll. Cut each roll in half. *At this point, rollups may be frozen.* Dip each roll in melted butter, then in mixture of sugar and cinnamon. Bake at 400 degrees for 15 minutes. Serve immediately.

An ideal make-ahead treat.

Surprise Muffins

2 cups all-purpose flour
¼ cup sugar
1 tablespoon baking powder
½ teaspoon baking soda
½ teaspoon salt
¼ cup butter
1 cup plain yogurt
¼ cup milk
1 egg
½ teaspoon pure vanilla extract
¼ cup jam or preserves
powdered sugar (optional)

12 muffins

Preheat oven to 425 degrees. In large bowl, mix flour, sugar, baking powder, soda and salt, stirring until well blended. Set aside. Melt butter and pour into small mixing bowl. Add yogurt and milk, stirring until smooth. Beat in egg and vanilla. Add butter mixture to dry ingredients and stir well. Batter will be heavy, like a biscuit dough. Spoon half the batter into buttered muffin tins. Place about one teaspoon of jam on batter in each tin and top with remaining batter. Bake 15 to 20 minutes or until golden. Let stand 5 minutes before removing muffins from tins. Sift powdered sugar over each muffin before serving, if desired.

A delicious surprise in the center with every delectable bite.

Breads

Poppy Seed Poundcake Muffins

2	cups all-purpose flour
3	teaspoons poppy seeds
½	teaspoon salt
¼	teaspoon baking soda
1	cup sugar
½	cup butter
2	eggs
1	cup plain yogurt
1	teaspoon pure vanilla extract

12 muffins

In small bowl, stir together flour, poppy seeds, salt and baking soda. In large bowl, cream together sugar and butter. Beat in eggs, one at a time. Beat in yogurt and vanilla until well blended. Stir in flour mixture until moistened thoroughly. Spoon batter into greased muffin tins and bake at 400 degrees for 15-20 minutes or until a wooden pick inserted in center comes out clean. Cool muffins on wire rack for 5 minutes before serving.

Rich, moist and delicious. These will disappear fast.

Raspberry Muffins

1½	cups all-purpose flour
½	teaspoon baking soda
½	teaspoon salt
1½	teaspoons ground cinnamon
1	cup sugar
1	12-ounce package frozen unsweetened raspberries, thawed
2	eggs, well beaten
⅔	cup vegetable oil
½	cup chopped pecans

12 muffins or 1 loaf

Preheat oven to 400 degrees. In medium bowl, mix flour, soda, salt, cinnamon and sugar. Make a well in the center and stir in undrained raspberries and eggs. Thoroughly mix in oil and pecans. Spoon batter into lightly greased muffin tins. Muffin cups will be full. Batter is heavy and will not overflow. Bake 15-20 minutes. Cool 5 minutes before removing from pan.

This recipe can also be baked in a greased and floured 9x5-inch loaf pan at 350 degrees for 1 hour or until a wooden pick inserted in center comes out clean.

Breads

Chocolate Chip Banana Muffins

½ cup butter, softened
1 cup packed light brown sugar
2 eggs, lightly beaten
2 cups all-purpose flour
½ teaspoon salt
½ teaspoon baking powder
2 cups mashed ripe bananas (about 3 medium bananas)
¾ cup chopped nuts
¾ cup mini chocolate chips

12 muffins

Cream together butter and brown sugar. Add beaten eggs and mix well. Sift flour with salt and baking powder and add to brown sugar mixture, stirring until well blended. Add bananas and beat until mixture is smooth. Fold in nuts and chocolate chips. Spoon batter into greased muffin tins. Bake at 350 degrees for 35-45 minutes or until golden brown.

Chocolate and banana lovers rejoice! A winning combination of flavors.

Strawberry Bread

1¼ cups vegetable oil
4 eggs
20 ounces fresh strawberries or unsweetened frozen strawberries, thawed, undrained
3 cups all-purpose flour
1 teaspoon baking soda
1 teaspoon salt
1½ teaspoons ground cinnamon
2 cups sugar
1½ cups chopped pecans

2 loaves

Beat oil and eggs until fluffy. Add strawberries and mix well. Combine flour, soda, salt, cinnamon and sugar and add to egg mixture, stirring until well blended. Stir in chopped pecans. Pour batter into 2 greased and lightly floured 9x5-inch loaf pans. Bake at 325 degrees for 1 hour and 15 minutes or until a wooden pick inserted in center comes out clean.

Blend together cream cheese and strawberry jam and spread between two pieces of this bread to make delightful tea sandwiches.

Breads

Very Lemon Bread

⅓ cup butter, melted
1 cup sugar
3 tablespoons lemon extract
2 eggs, lightly beaten
1½ cups sifted all-purpose flour
1 teaspoon baking powder
1 teaspoon salt
½ cup milk
2 tablespoons freshly grated lemon
peel
½ cup chopped pecans

Lemon Glaze:
¼ cup fresh lemon juice
½ cup sugar

1 loaf

In large bowl, mix butter with sugar, lemon extract and eggs. In separate bowl, sift flour with baking powder and salt. To butter mixture, add flour mixture alternately with milk, stirring just enough to blend. Fold in lemon peel and pecans. Pour batter into greased and floured 9x5-inch loaf pan and bake at 350 degrees for 1 hour or until a wooden pick inserted in center comes out clean. Remove bread from pan and with a wooden pick poke holes at 1-inch intervals on all sides. While loaf is still warm, drizzle lemon glaze mixture over top and sides. Wrap in foil and store for 1 day before slicing to serve.

A distinctive lemon flavor perfect for coffee, a morning meeting or an afternoon tea.

Pumpkin Fruit Bread

2 cups sugar
1 cup vegetable oil
3 eggs
1 16-ounce can cooked pumpkin
3 cups all-purpose flour
1 teaspoon baking soda
½ teaspoon salt
½ teaspoon baking powder
1 teaspoon ground cinnamon
1 teaspoon ground cloves
1 teaspoon ground nutmeg
1 cup chopped nuts
1 cup raisins
1 cup chopped dates

2 loaves

In large mixing bowl, beat together sugar and oil. Beat in eggs and continue beating until light and fluffy. Add pumpkin and mix well. Sift together flour, soda, salt, baking powder, cinnamon, cloves and nutmeg and add to pumpkin mixture. Stir until dry ingredients are moistened. Fold in nuts, raisins and dates, and pour into 2 9x5-inch loaf pans greased with vegetable cooking spray. Bake at 325 degrees for 60-70 minutes or until a wooden pick inserted in center comes out clean. Leave loaves in pans for 10 minutes before removing; cool on wire racks.

The blend of pumpkin and fruits creates a delectably moist bread.

Breads

Mountain Bran Bread

1	cup All-Bran cereal
1	cup buttermilk
⅛	teaspoon salt
1	teaspoon baking soda
1	egg, lightly beaten
1	cup packed light brown sugar
1	cup golden raisins
1	cup walnuts
1	cup all-purpose flour

1 loaf

Mix All-Bran with buttermilk, salt and soda. Add egg, brown sugar, raisins, walnuts and flour, stirring until well blended. Pour batter into well-greased and floured 9x5-inch loaf pan and bake at 350 degrees for 60-70 minutes or until a wooden pick inserted in center comes out clean. Cool on wire rack.

Enhance the flavor of this delicious bread by spreading it with cream cheese.

Braided Sweet Bread

1	package dry yeast
¼	cup warm water (105-115 degrees)
1	cup milk, scalded and cooled (105-115 degrees)
½	cup sugar
½	teaspoon salt
1	teaspoon ground cardamom or 1½ teaspoons anise seeds
2	eggs, lightly beaten
4-4½	cups all-purpose flour
¼	cup butter, melted
1	egg, beaten
1	teaspoon sugar

1 loaf

Dissolve yeast in water and set aside for 5 minutes. Add milk, sugar, salt, cardamom, 2 eggs and 2 cups flour, beating well. Add 1½ cups flour and butter, then beat again. Add remaining flour , mixing until well blended. Turn dough onto lightly floured board, cover and let sit for 15 minutes. Knead dough until smooth and elastic. Place dough in greased bowl, turning it to coat all sides. Cover with damp towel and let rise in a warm place for 1 hour.

Punch dough down, cover and let rise again for 30 minutes. Divide into 3 balls, rolling each ball into a 20-inch long strip. Braid 3 strips, pinching the ends together. Place on a greased baking sheet and let rise for 30 minutes. Glaze with beaten egg and sprinkle with sugar. Bake at 400 degrees for 25-35 minutes.

For uniform braids, place dough ropes side by side. Start braiding from the middle of the ropes and braid to one end. Pinch ends together to seal, then continue braiding from middle to other end.

Whole Wheat Raisin Bread

1	package dry yeast
¼	cup warm water (105-115 degrees)
¼	cup honey
1½	cups buttermilk
3	tablespoons butter
2	teaspoons salt
3½	cups whole wheat flour
½	teaspoon baking soda
½	cup raisins

1 loaf

Dissolve yeast in water and honey and let sit until frothy. Heat buttermilk and butter just until butter melts. Stir into yeast mixture. In separate bowl, mix together salt, flour and soda. Stir raisins into dry ingredients. Combine flour mixture with buttermilk mixture and beat until smooth. Set the bowl in a pan of warm water. Cover with towel and let rise until doubled in bulk, about 1 hour.

Beat dough for 3 minutes and put in greased 9x5-inch loaf pan. Set pan in warm water, cover and let rise until rounding over pan. Put pan in cold oven. Set oven to 400 degrees and bake for 15 minutes. Reduce heat to 325 degrees and continue baking for another 30-35 minutes. Turn out onto a board to cool, covered loosely with a towel.

Omit the raisins and you have a nourishing, traditional whole wheat bread.

Quick and Easy Coors Beer Bread

½	cup butter
3	cups self-rising flour
2	tablespoons sugar
1	12-ounce can Coors beer

1 loaf

Melt butter and pour enough into a 9x5-inch loaf pan to coat the bottom. In large bowl, mix together flour, sugar and beer. Spoon dough into loaf pan. Pour remaining butter over the top. Bake at 350 degrees for 50-60 minutes or until bread is a light golden color. Let stand 10 minutes before cutting with a serrated knife.

Great big taste with very little effort. Serve warm.

Breads

Cheese and Wine Bread

1	cup plus 2 tablespoons all-purpose flour
½	teaspoon baking powder
¼	teaspoon cream of tartar
½	teaspoon salt
⅛	teaspoon baking soda
¼	cup instant nonfat dry milk
⅓	cup vegetable shortening
1	tablespoon sugar
1	tablespoon minced onion
1	egg, beaten
¼	cup milk
¼	cup white wine
½	teaspoon dried oregano
¼	cup freshly grated Parmesan cheese

8 servings

Sift together flour, baking powder, cream of tartar, salt, soda and dry milk. Cut in shortening until the mixture resembles coarse meal. Add sugar, minced onion, egg, milk, wine and oregano. Mix thoroughly. Spread mixture in greased 8 or 9-inch round pan and sprinkle with cheese. Bake at 425 degrees for 15-20 minutes or until a wooden pick inserted in center comes out clean.

*Serve this flavorful bread with **Spinach, Bacon and Apple Salad** for a real taste treat.*

Monkey Bread

1	package dry yeast
½	cup warm water (105-115 degrees)
½	cup butter
¼	cup sugar
1	teaspoon salt
½	cup evaporated milk
3½	cups sifted all-purpose flour
½	cup butter, melted

1 loaf

In large bowl, dissolve yeast in warm water; set aside. In small saucepan, melt ½ cup butter with sugar, salt and evaporated milk. Cool to lukewarm and stir into yeast mixture. Add sifted flour and knead until smooth and elastic. Place dough in greased bowl, turning to coat all sides. Cover and let rise until doubled in bulk.

Punch down dough and roll out on lightly floured board into a 12x18-inch rectangle. Cut into diamond shapes or squares, about 3 inches in size. Dip each piece into melted butter. Place in overlapping layers in ungreased tube pan. Cover and let rise until doubled in bulk. Bake at 350 degrees for 45 minutes or until golden brown. Remove from mold and serve while bread is warm.

This buttery, pull-apart showpiece will become a favorite of your family and guests.

Breads

Light Rye Bread

1¾	cups skim milk
¼	cup unsalted butter
2	tablespoons light molasses
1	package dry yeast
¼	cup warm water (105-115 degrees)
1	tablespoon light molasses
1	teaspoon salt
1	teaspoon caraway seeds
2	cups all-purpose flour
2	cups rye flour
1	cup all-purpose flour

2 loaves

In medium saucepan, combine milk, butter and 2 tablespoons molasses and cook over low heat until butter melts; set aside to cool. Dissolve yeast in warm water with 1 tablespoon molasses and let stand 5 minutes. To yeast mixture add cooled milk mixture, salt, caraway seeds and 2 cups all-purpose flour, stirring until well blended. Add rye flour and stir until all flour is moistened. Add remaining 1 cup all-purpose flour and work until the dough is smooth. Turn dough out onto lightly floured board and knead for about 5 minutes. Place dough in greased bowl, turning to coat all sides. Cover with damp towel and let rise until doubled in bulk, about 1 hour. Punch dough down and divide in half. Pat each piece into a 9x9-inch square and roll up. Place rolls seam side down in two greased 9x5-inch loaf pans. Cover and let rise for 45 minutes. Bake at 375 degrees for 30-35 minutes. Remove and cool on racks.

Wonderful flavor with a subtle hint of rye.

Herb Bread

1	package dry yeast
¼	cup warm water (105-115 degrees)
1	teaspoon sugar
1	cup creamed cottage cheese, warmed
1	egg, lightly beaten
2	tablespoons sugar
1	tablespoon minced onion
1	tablespoon butter, melted
2	teaspoons dill seed
½	teaspoon dill weed
1	teaspoon salt
¼	teaspoon baking soda
2¼	cups all-purpose flour

Glaze:

2	tablespoons butter, melted
¼	teaspoon salt (optional)

1 loaf

Dissolve yeast in warm water with 1 teaspoon sugar. Let stand for 10 minutes. Combine cottage cheese with egg, sugar, onion, butter, dill seed, dill weed, salt, soda and yeast mixture, stirring until well blended. Stir in flour, working dough until all flour is moistened. Beat well. Cover with damp towel and let rise in warm place until doubled in bulk, about 1 hour. Punch down and turn dough into well-greased 2-quart casserole dish. Let rise until doubled in bulk, about 30 minutes. Bake at 375 degrees for 15 minutes; lower temperature to 300 degrees and bake for another 25 minutes or until golden brown. Brush with melted butter and sprinkle with salt, if desired.

*Try substituting 2 teaspoons crumbled dried sage for dill seed and weed. Either herb provides outstanding flavor. Serve warm with **Garden Cheddar Soup** for a satisfying meal.*

Breads

Mustard Cheese Bread

2	packages fast-rising dry yeast
1	teaspoon sugar
½	cup warm water (105-115 degrees)
2-2¼	cups all-purpose flour
5	ounces sharp Cheddar cheese, shredded (about 1¼ cups)
¼	cup minced fresh chives
1	egg, lightly beaten
1	tablespoon prepared spicy mustard
¾	teaspoon salt
2	teaspoons mustard seeds

1 loaf

In large mixing bowl, mix together yeast, sugar and warm water. Let stand for 5 minutes. To this add flour, cheese, chives, egg, mustard and salt, stirring until will blended (dough will be stiff). Knead dough for 3 minutes on lightly floured board. Place dough in lightly greased bowl, turning to coat all sides. Cover with damp towel and place in warm location until doubled in bulk, about 30 minutes. Punch down and place dough on lightly floured board, forming 9-inch square. Roll up dough and place in lightly greased 9x5-inch loaf pan, seam side down. Cover with damp towel and let rise in warm place until doubled. Using pastry brush, lightly coat surface of loaf with water and sprinkle mustard seeds on top. Bake at 325 degrees for 40-50 minutes or until golden brown.

An intriguing, compatible blend of flavors.

Cornbread Muffins

1	cup yellow cornmeal
1	cup all-purpose flour
3	tablespoons sugar
	pinch of salt
4	teaspoons baking powder
4	tablespoons butter, melted
1	cup milk
1	egg, lightly beaten

12 muffins

Preheat oven to 400 degrees. Mix together cornmeal, flour, sugar, salt and baking powder. Add melted butter, milk and egg, stirring until well blended. Spoon batter into greased muffin tins. Bake 10-12 minutes or until a light golden brown.

For perfect browning, heat muffin tins before spooning in batter.

Buttermilk Biscuits

2	cups all-purpose flour
2	teaspoons baking powder
1	teaspoon salt
½	teaspoon baking soda
¼	teaspoon cream of tartar
¼	cup vegetable shortening
1	cup buttermilk

10 2 ½-inch biscuits

Sift together flour, baking powder, salt, soda and cream of tartar. Add shortening and mix well. Stir in buttermilk and beat until smooth. Turn out dough onto lightly floured board and knead for 1 minute. Using a lightly floured rolling pin, roll out dough to a thickness of ½ inch. Cut biscuits and place 1 inch apart on greased baking sheet. Bake at 450 degrees for 12-15 minutes or until light golden brown.

A snap to prepare! To make even, uniform biscuits, press a floured cutter straight down without twisting it.

Breads

Crescent Rolls

½ cup milk
2 tablespoons sugar
½ teaspoon salt
¼ cup vegetable oil
1 egg, beaten
1 package dry yeast
2 cups sifted all-purpose flour
2 tablespoons butter, melted

16 rolls

Scald milk and set aside. Place sugar, salt and oil in mixing bowl and stir until blended. Stir in cooled (105-115 degrees) milk and beaten egg. Dissolve yeast in milk mixture. Add flour and mix well. Cover and let rise 2 hours. Place dough on a lightly floured board and roll into a 15-inch circle. Brush with melted butter. Cut into 16 pie-shaped wedges and roll each from the wide end to the narrow end. Place rolls on a baking sheet and let rise 2 hours. Bake at 400 degrees for 6-8 minutes. Watch closely as these rolls can burn easily.

A beautiful, buttery roll for your next dinner party.

Overnight Potato Rolls

1 package dry yeast
1 teaspoon sugar
1½ cups warm water (105-115 degrees)
1¼ teaspoons salt
⅔ cup sugar
⅔ cup vegetable shortening
1 cup mashed potatoes
2 eggs, lightly beaten
7 cups all-purpose flour

30 3-inch rolls

In large bowl, dissolve yeast and 1 teaspoon sugar in warm water. Add salt, sugar, shortening, potatoes and eggs, stirring until well blended. Add ½ of the flour, stirring until smooth. Gradually add remaining flour, stirring after each addition. Knead dough on a lightly floured board for 3-5 minutes. Return dough to large bowl, covering loosely with plastic wrap to allow for expansion. Refrigerate dough for 12-24 hours. Punch down dough. Roll out dough on lightly floured board to ¾-inch thickness. Cut out rolls and place on baking sheet. Cover and let rise for 2 hours. Bake at 400 degrees for 10-13 minutes or until light golden brown.

Mile High Biscuits

2 cups all-purpose flour
1 cup whole wheat flour
4½ teaspoons baking powder
2 tablespoons sugar
¼ teaspoon salt
¾ teaspoon cream of tartar
¾ cup butter, softened and cut into pats
1 egg, lightly beaten
1 cup milk

20 biscuits

In large bowl, combine flours, baking powder, sugar, salt and cream of tartar. Using pastry blender, cut butter into dry ingredients until mixture resembles coarse meal. Add egg and milk, stirring with fork until smooth. Knead dough on lightly floured board. Roll dough out to 1-inch thickness and cut into 2-inch biscuits. Place in greased, 9-inch square pan and bake at 450 degrees for 12-15 minutes or until golden brown.

Breads

Onion Biscuits

3 medium onions, diced
2 tablespoons water
2½ cups all-purpose flour
1 tablespoon baking powder
1 teaspoon salt
½ teaspoon dried thyme
½ cup butter
¾ cup milk

12 2-inch biscuits

In a covered saucepan, steam onions in water for 5 minutes. Drain and cool. In mixing bowl, combine flour, baking powder, salt and thyme. Using a pastry blender, cut butter into flour mixture. Add milk and mix well. Stir in onion.

Place dough on lightly floured board and knead for 1 minute. Roll dough with floured rolling pin to a thickness of 1 inch. Cut out biscuits and place on an ungreased baking sheet. Bake at 375 degrees for 30 minutes or until lightly browned. Serve warm.

*These biscuits double in height when baked, and are especially good served with **Cajun Black Bean Soup**.*

Italian Cheese Sticks

1 cup all-purpose flour
2 tablespoons freshly grated Parmesan cheese
½ teaspoon garlic powder
½ teaspoon onion powder
¼ teaspoon dried basil
¼ teaspoon dried oregano
¼ teaspoon dried rosemary
¼ teaspoon salt
½ cup butter, cut into small pats
1 cup shredded sharp Cheddar cheese
3 tablespoons cold water

2 dozen bread sticks

Preheat oven to 425 degrees. In large bowl, mix together flour, Parmesan cheese, garlic powder, onion powder, basil, oregano, rosemary and salt. Using pastry blender, cut butter into flour mixture until mixture resembles coarse meal. Add Cheddar cheese and mix until well blended. Add water one tablespoon at a time, mixing well after each addition. Roll portions of dough into strips ½ inch wide and 5-6 inches long. Repeat until all dough is rolled out in this manner. Place cheese sticks ½ inch apart on an ungreased baking sheet. Bake 12-15 minutes.

Wonderfully flavorful! You'll never eat plain bread sticks again.

Fondue Bread

1 pound Swiss Cheese, shredded
1 cup butter, melted
2 cloves garlic, minced
¼ cup minced fresh parsley
2 loaves French bread

2 loaves

Mix cheese with butter, garlic and parsley. Slice loaves lengthwise and spread halves with topping. Bake at 350 degrees for 20 minutes or until bubbly. Serve warm.

This fabulous melted topping oozes with sensational flavor.

Breads

Parmesan Bread Sticks

4   ½-inch thick slices of white bread,
      frozen
6   tablespoons butter, melted
1¼ cups freshly grated Parmesan
      cheese

16 bread sticks

Trim crusts from bread. Slice each piece into ½-inch strips. Dip in melted butter, coating all sides. Then dip each piece in Parmesan cheese and pat the cheese to help it adhere. Bake strips on a lightly greased baking sheet at 375 degrees for 5-7 minutes. Turn strips over and continue baking for 5 minutes longer or until golden brown. Watch carefully. Serve warm.

These can also be cut into ½-inch cubes for tasty homemade croutons for soups or salads. They freeze beautifully, so keep some on hand for an instant gourmet touch.

Arapahoe Fry Bread

1   package dry yeast
1½   cups warm water (110-115 degrees)
½   cup sugar
1   teaspoon salt
2   eggs, lightly beaten
1   cup evaporated milk
7   cups all-purpose flour, divided
¼   cup vegetable shortening
      vegetable oil for frying
      powdered sugar

4 dozen

In large bowl, stir together yeast and water until yeast is dissolved. Add sugar, salt, eggs and evaporated milk and mix well. Stir in 4 cups flour, 1 cup at a time. Add shortening and beat until well blended. Add remaining 3 cups flour, ½ cup at a time. Dough will be stiff, so last amounts of flour will have to be worked in by hand. Cover bowl with plastic wrap and refrigerate overnight or up to 5 days.

When ready to fry, roll dough out to ⅛-inch thickness and cut into 3x4-inch rectangles. Heat oil in deep fryer to 360 degrees and fry 3 or 4 pieces at a time, turning once or twice during cooking. Fry for 3-4 minutes per batch or until golden brown. Drain on paper towels. Keep warm in a 250-degree oven until ready to serve. Serve sprinkled with powdered sugar.

No matter how many you make, you'll never have enough!

Breads

Cheesy Bread

½ cup butter, softened
¼ cup mayonnaise
1½ cups shredded Cheddar cheese
¼ cup minced onion
½ teaspoon Worcestershire sauce
1 loaf of French bread

1 loaf

Mix together butter, mayonnaise, cheese, onion and Worcestershire. Slice loaf of French bread in half lengthwise. Cut slices at 2-inch intervals but not quite through the bread. Spread cheese mixture over both halves of loaf. Place on aluminum foil and bake at 350 degrees for 10-15 minutes until cheese begins to bubble, or broil bread until cheese bubbles and browns.

*For a **Mexican Cheesy Bread,** substitute Monterey Jack for the Cheddar cheese and 3-4 drops Tabasco for the Worcestershire in the main recipe. Stir in ¼ cup chopped green chiles and proceed with the recipe.*

Pizza Bread

2 packages dry yeast
2 teaspoons sugar
⅛ teaspoon ground ginger
½ cup warm water (105-115 degrees)
1½ cups water
¼ cup powdered nonfat milk
1½ teaspoons salt
2 tablespoons sugar
¼ cup vegetable oil
6 cups all-purpose flour
vegetable cooking spray
¼ cup butter, melted

Filling:
1 pound bulk Italian sausage
1 green bell pepper, finely chopped
1 onion, finely chopped
½ pound pepperoni, coarsely ground
½ pound mozzarella cheese, shredded
½ cup freshly grated Parmesan cheese

2 loaves

Dissolve yeast, 2 teaspoons sugar and ginger in ½ cup warm water; set aside for 5 minutes. In saucepan, combine 1½ cups water, powdered milk, salt, 2 tablespoons sugar and oil and heat to lukewarm. In large bowl, add yeast and milk mixtures to flour. Stir until blended and then beat for 3-5 minutes. Turn dough out onto floured board and knead for 10 minutes. Lightly coat a bowl with vegetable cooking spray and place dough in it, turning to coat all sides. Cover with damp towel and let rise in warm place for 1 hour. Punch down, cover and let rise for another hour.

In skillet, cook sausage and drain fat. Add green pepper and onion and cook for 3 minutes. Combine with pepperoni, mozzarella and Parmesan and mix well. Divide dough into 2 parts; cover 1 and set aside. On floured board, roll dough portion into 12x14-inch rectangle. Spread with ½ filling and roll up like a jelly roll. Place seam side down on greased baking sheet. Repeat with other portion of dough. Cut slits across tops of rolls at 1-inch intervals. Cover with towel and let rise for ½ hour. Bake at 350 degrees for 25-35 minutes or until golden brown. Brush tops with melted butter.

Typical pizza ingredients are baked together in a loaf of bread. Not surprisingly, it makes a satisfying meal with a green salad.

Breads

Coors Reuben Braid

3	tablespoons yellow corn meal
1	12-ounce can Coors beer
1	tablespoon butter
1	tablespoon salt
1	package dry yeast
1	tablespoon sugar
1	tablespoon honey
2	cups bread flour
1½	cups rye flour
1½	teaspoons caraway seeds
¼	cup bread flour

Filling:

½	cup Thousand Island dressing
1	16-ounce can sauerkraut, drained
½	pound corned beef, thinly sliced
½	pound Swiss cheese, thinly sliced

16-20 servings

In medium saucepan, combine corn meal and beer. Heat to boiling and simmer for 2 minutes. Stir in butter and salt. Cool to 105-115 degrees. Stir in yeast, sugar and honey and let stand for 5 minutes. Pour mixture into large mixing bowl and add 2 cups of bread flour, stirring until well blended. Add rye flour and caraway seeds and mix thoroughly. Place dough on a lightly floured board and work in enough of remaining ¼ cup bread flour to reduce stickiness and make dough workable. Place dough in oiled bowl and turn to coat all sides. Let rise until doubled in bulk.

Punch dough down and let rest for 10 minutes. Divide dough in half, covering one piece. On a floured surface, roll other piece into rectangle not longer than baking sheet. Trim dough so that rectangle is a true shape. Lightly score dough into thirds lengthwise. Spread ½ dressing over the center third, leaving 1 inch at top and bottom of section uncovered. Cover dressing with ½ sauerkraut, ½ corned beef and ½ cheese. Fold 1 inch at top and bottom over filling and pinch to seal. On each side of filling, make cuts at 1-inch intervals. Cuts begin ½ inch from filling and go to outer edges. Beginning on right, pull top strip across middle and seal end on other side of filling. Pull top left strip across middle and seal; alternate in braiding fashion until all strips are secured. Repeat with other ball of dough. Cover and let rest for 30 minutes. Place on greased baking sheet and bake at 350 degrees for 30 minutes. Slice to serve.

A delicious interpretation of the classic sandwich.

Ham and Cheese Loaf

6	eggs
¾	cup milk
1½	cups all-purpose flour
2½	teaspoons baking powder
½	teaspoon salt
6	slices bacon, fried crisp, drained and crumbled
1	cup diced cooked ham
1	cup shredded Monterey Jack cheese
1	cup shredded Swiss cheese
1	cup shredded sharp Cheddar cheese

1 loaf

In large bowl, beat eggs until foamy; add milk, flour, baking powder and salt, stirring until well blended. Add bacon, ham and cheeses and mix well. Bake in greased and floured 9x5-inch loaf pan at 350 degrees for 55-65 minutes or until wooden pick inserted in center comes out clean.

This delicious blend of flavors is easy to prepare.

Brunch

Brunch

Caramel Fruit Dip

¼ cup sugar
¾ cup packed light brown sugar
1 teaspoon pure vanilla extract
8 ounces cream cheese, softened
fresh fruit for dipping

1¼ cups

Put sugars, vanilla and cream cheese in blender or food processor and blend until smooth. Serve with a colorful assortment of seasonal fruit such as apple slices, pear slices and strawberries.

For morning coffees or afternoon teas, this yummy dip is perfect for entertaining.

Orange Cream Fruit Dip

8 ounces cream cheese, softened
7 ounces marshmallow creme
2 tablespoons fresh orange juice
½ teaspoon pure orange extract
strawberries for dipping

1¾ cups

In food processor or blender, mix all ingredients. Chill until ready to serve.

Created especially for strawberries.

Strawberry Banana Fruit Cups

1 cup sour cream
½ cup fresh strawberries
1 medium banana
2 tablespoons chopped crystallized ginger
1 tablespoon packed light brown sugar
1 tablespoon rum
3 cups sliced bananas
2 cups fresh strawberries, halved
2 cups seedless green grapes
sprigs of fresh mint (optional)

8 servings

Combine sour cream, ½ cup stawberries, medium banana, crystallized ginger, brown sugar and rum in blender or food processor. Blend until smooth. *Refrigerate overnight.*

In a large bowl, combine bananas, strawberries and grapes. Toss fruit with dressing, garnish with mint and serve.

This wonderful fruit dish looks elegant served in crystal bowls and garnished with mint.

Brunch

Cheesy Baked Apples

4	medium baking apples, peeled, cored and cut into eighths
¼	cup water
2	teaspoons fresh lemon juice
2	tablespoons sugar
1	tablespoon all-purpose flour
¼	teaspoon ground cinnamon
⅛	teaspoon salt
½	cup shredded Cheddar cheese

6 servings

In shallow dish, arrange apple slices. Sprinkle with water and lemon juice. In small bowl, combine sugar, flour, cinnamon and salt. Sprinkle over apples. Bake at 350 degrees for 45 minutes or until apples are tender. Uncover. Top with shredded cheese. Bake for 5 more minutes or until cheese melts.

Cheese and apples are as all-American as Sunday brunch.

Sautéed Fruit

2	Golden Delicious apples, peeled, cored and cut into thick slices
1	Anjou pear, peeled, cored and cut into thick slices
1½	tablespoons fresh lemon juice
2	tablespoons butter
¼	cup orange marmalade
1	tablespoon Grand Marnier liqueur
1	tablespoon butter
2	navel oranges, peeled and sectioned
	sprigs of fresh mint (optional)

4 servings

In small bowl, toss apple and pear slices with lemon juice. In large skillet, melt 2 tablespoons butter. Add fruit and sauté over medium-high heat until apples are tender, stirring gently. With slotted spoon, transfer fruit mixture to bowl. To same skillet, add marmalade, Grand Marnier and 1 tablespoon butter. Stir until melted. Pour sauce over fruit. Add oranges and toss gently. Garnish with sprigs of mint.

This is a delicious and especially attractive warm winter fruit dish.

Brunch

Curried Fruit Stacks

1	20-ounce can pineapple slices
1	29-ounce can pear halves
1	29-ounce can cling peach halves
8	Maraschino cherries
½	cup butter
¾	cup packed light brown sugar
1-2	teaspoons curry powder

8 servings

Drain fruits and pat dry with paper towels. Make fruit stacks by placing a pineapple slice on the bottom, topping it with a pear half, then a peach half and a cherry. Secure stacks with wooden picks and place in shallow baking dish. In small saucepan, melt butter. Stir in brown sugar and curry. Spoon mixture over fruit. Bake covered at 350 degrees for 1 hour. *Refrigerate overnight or several days. To serve, reheat covered fruit at 350 degrees for 30 minutes.*

Vary the amount of curry to suit your taste. Since the flavors continue to blend for several days, this is a good do-ahead brunch dish.

Marzipan Apricots

1	1-pound 14-ounce can whole apricots (12-14 apricots)
1	8-ounce can almond paste
12-14	blanched whole almonds
1	tablespoon cornstarch
1	cup coarsely chopped orange sections
¼	cup sliced almonds, toasted
½	teaspoon freshly grated orange peel
2	teaspoons Cointreau liqueur

6-7 servings

Drain apricots, reserving liquid. If necessary, slit each apricot on one side only to remove pit. Divide almond paste evenly into 12-14 pieces. Insert one whole almond into each piece of almond paste. Roll into ball, being careful to cover almond completely. Put 1 ball inside each apricot. Arrange apricots in 6x10-inch baking dish. Bake at 325 degrees for 25 minutes, or until apricots are heated through and almond paste is slightly browned. Measure apricot liquid and add water, if necessary, to make 2 cups. In small saucepan, combine liquid with cornstarch. Heat to boiling over medium heat, stirring constantly. Add oranges; reduce heat and simmer for 2 minutes, stirring. Stir in toasted almonds, orange peel and Cointreau. Pour over apricots. Serve warm.

Your guests will be in for a pleasant surprise as they bite into the warm apricots.

Brunch

Palisade Poached Pears

2	pounds large, firm, ripe pears, peeled, halved and cored
¼	cup dry vermouth
¼	cup apricot preserves, pressed through a sieve
¼	cup fine macaroon crumbs
3	tablespoons butter

4-6 servings

Cut pears into ⅜-inch slices. Arrange slices in buttered 8-inch round baking dish, overlapping slices in concentric circles. In small bowl, beat together vermouth and apricot preserves; pour over pears. Sprinkle with macaroon crumbs and dot with butter. Bake at 350 degrees for 20-25 minutes. Serve hot.

A spectacular fruit dish which may be served in individual dishes with the sauce spooned over the pears. Garnish with mint or edible flowers such as nasturtiums or violets.

Sausage Kabobs

½	cup apricot preserves
1	tablespoon Grand Marnier liqueur
¼	teaspoon freshly grated orange peel
12	ounces precooked pork sausage links
3	apricots, cut into 1-inch pieces

6 servings

In small saucepan, combine preserves, Grand Marnier and grated orange peel. Heat to boiling. Boil, stirring, for 1 minute. Set aside to cool. Heat sausage. Cut into 1-inch pieces. Alternate sausage with apricots on 8-inch skewers. Glaze sausage and fruit with sauce. Broil for 1-2 minutes or until sauce is bubbly. Serve immediately.

Try substituting peaches or nectarines for the apricots, or using a combination of fruits.

Ham Torte

2	cups ground cooked ham (10 ounces)
1	cup sour cream
2	tablespoons minced green onions
¼	teaspoon Dijon mustard
	dash freshly ground black pepper
8	*Basic Crêpes*
	sour cream (optional)

6-8 servings

In large bowl, mix together ham, sour cream, green onions, mustard and pepper until smooth. Center crêpe on lightly greased ovenproof plate. Spread ⅛ of ham mixture on crêpe. Alternate layers of crêpe and filling, ending with filling on top. Bake at 350 degrees for 30 minutes. Using a very sharp knife, cut into wedges. Serve each wedge with a dollop of sour cream.

A stunning presentation that is very easy and can be made ahead.

Brunch

Fresh Salmon Hash

1	medium russet or Idaho potato, peeled and sliced
3	tablespoons unsalted butter
2	tablespoons safflower oil
1	large clove garlic, minced
½	cup minced onion
⅓	cup finely chopped celery
2	tablespoons chopped pimiento
2	tablespoons diced green bell pepper
6	tablespoons heavy cream
½	teaspoon salt
¼	teaspoon ground white pepper
¼	cup minced fresh parsley
1½	cups cooked, flaked salmon (10 ounces)

6 servings

Cook sliced potato in boiling water until just tender, 5-6 minutes. Drain, rinse under cold water and pat dry. Dice cooked potato slices. In a heavy, 8-inch skillet over high heat, melt 1 tablespoon butter with 1 tablespoon oil. Add the diced potatoes and cook until crisp and golden, 2-3 minutes, stirring frequently. Transfer potatoes to medium bowl and set aside. In the same skillet, over medium-low heat, melt 1 tablespoon butter. Add garlic, onion, celery, pimiento and green pepper. Cook until soft, about 6 minutes, stirring occasionally. Add this mixture to the potatoes. Stir cream, salt and white pepper into potato mixture. Cool to room temperature. Mix parsley and salmon into potato mixture. *Cover and refrigerate up to 24 hours if made ahead.* Sauté salmon hash until crisp and golden, about 4 minutes. Serve immediately.

Complement this hearty dish with eggs and **Fresh Fruit Mélange.**

Breakfast Pizza

	pastry for single-crust 9-inch pie
½	pound bacon, fried crisp, drained and crumbled
2	cups shredded Swiss cheese (8 ounces)
4	eggs
1⅓	cups sour cream
2	tablespoons minced fresh parsley

4-6 servings

On lightly floured board, roll out pastry to fit a 12-inch pizza pan. Fit pastry into pan, pressing edges against pan sides and trimming even with top. Bake on lower rack of oven at 425 degrees for 5 minutes. Gently press down any bubbles in crust; cool before filling.

Sprinkle bacon and cheese over crust. In medium bowl, beat eggs with sour cream and parsley until smooth; pour over pizza. Bake on lower rack of oven at 425 degrees for 20-25 minutes. Let pizza stand 5 minutes before serving.

This pizza is similar to a quiche, and is a big hit with kids the morning after a slumber party.

Brunch

Turkey and Stuffing Quiche

2½-3	cups leftover stuffing or 6-ounce package chicken stuffing
1	cup chopped, cooked turkey
1	cup shredded Swiss cheese
4	eggs, beaten
1	5 ½-ounce can evaporated milk
½	teaspoon freshly ground black pepper

6 servings

If using stuffing mix, prepare according to package directions. Press stuffing into greased 9-inch pie plate or quiche pan, forming a crust. Bake at 400 degrees for 10 minutes. Remove from oven. In small bowl, combine turkey and Swiss cheese; set aside. In separate bowl, beat eggs, milk and pepper. Sprinkle turkey and cheese mixture over hot crust. Pour egg mixture over turkey. Lower oven temperature to 350 degrees and bake quiche for 30-35 minutes or until knife inserted in center comes out clean. Let quiche stand 10 minutes before serving.

A unique variation on an all-American classic.

Crispy Potato Quiche

1	24-ounce package frozen shredded hash browns, thawed
⅓	cup melted butter
1	cup shredded hot pepper cheese
1	cup shredded Swiss cheese
1	cup diced cooked ham
½	cup half and half
2	eggs
¼	teaspoon seasoned salt

6 servings

Press thawed hash browns between paper towels to remove moisture. Fit hash browns into greased 10-inch pie plate, forming a solid crust. Brush crust with melted butter, making certain to brush top edges. Bake at 425 degrees for 25 minutes. Remove from oven. Sprinkle cheeses and ham evenly over bottom of crust. Beat half and half with eggs and seasoned salt. Pour over cheeses and ham. Bake uncovered at 350 degrees for 30-40 minutes or until knife inserted in center comes out clean.

Frozen hash browns cut the preparation time for this spicy quiche.

Mushroom Crust Quiche

3 tablespoons butter
½ pound mushrooms, coarsely chopped
½ cup finely crushed saltine crackers
2 tablespoons butter
¾ cup finely chopped green onions
2 cups shredded Swiss cheese
1 cup cottage cheese
3 eggs
¼ teaspoon ground cayenne
¼ teaspoon paprika

4-6 servings

In skillet, melt 3 tablespoons butter over medium heat; add mushrooms and cook until limp. Stir in crushed crackers. Turn mixture into well-greased 9-inch pie pan, pressing mixture evenly over pan bottom and up sides. In same skillet, melt remaining 2 tablespoons butter over medium heat; add onion and cook until transparent. Spread onions over mushroom crust, then sprinkle evenly with shredded cheese. In food processor, whirl cottage cheese, eggs and cayenne pepper until smooth. Pour mixture into crust and sprinkle with paprika. Bake at 350 degrees for 20-25 minutes or until knife inserted just off center comes out clean. Let stand for 10-15 minutes before serving.

The earthy taste of mushrooms makes this quiche special.

Italian Scrambled Eggs

2 tablespoons butter
1¼ cups sliced mushrooms
¼ pound prosciutto or ham, diced or slivered
¾ teaspoon minced garlic
½ medium green bell pepper, diced
½ pound asparagus, trimmed and cut into 1-inch lengths
10 eggs
1½ tablespoons minced fresh basil or 1 teaspoon dried basil
1 teaspoon ground oregano
¼ teaspoon salt
¾ teaspoon freshly ground black pepper
¾ teaspoon crushed red pepper flakes
6 ounces cream cheese, softened
1½ cups shredded mozzarella cheese
⅓ cup freshly grated Parmesan cheese
4 tablespoons butter

6 servings

In a large skillet, heat 2 tablespoons butter; add mushrooms, prosciutto, garlic and green pepper. Sauté over medium heat until vegetables are tender. Remove with a slotted spoon and set aside. Blanch asparagus in boiling salted water for 1-2 minutes until crisp-tender. Drain well and set aside. Whisk together eggs, herbs and seasonings. Cut cream cheese into bits and add to egg mixture.

Heat remaining 4 tablespoons butter in skillet. Add egg mixture. Cook over medium heat while folding mixture with a spatula to blend in cream cheese. When eggs are half set, add warm vegetable-prosciutto mixture, mozzarella, Parmesan and warm asparagus. Continue to cook while gently folding in cheeses with a spatula. When eggs are just done, serve immediately.

These scrambled eggs are better than an omelet. If asparagus is not available, broccoli is a good substitute.

Brunch

Dillon Scrambled Eggs

12	eggs
¼	cup water
½	teaspoon salt
½	teaspoon freshly ground black pepper
1-2	tablespoons butter
1½	ounces cream cheese, softened and cut into small chunks
2	tablespoons diced pimientos
1	tablespoon minced fresh parsley
1	tablespoon minced fresh chives

6-8 servings

In a large bowl, beat together eggs, water, salt and pepper. Melt butter in skillet. Pour egg mixture into skillet and stir until it begins to thicken. Immediately add small chunks of cream cheese, pimiento, parsley and chives. Continue stirring until eggs are soft and creamy. Serve at once.

Cream cheese helps to hold eggs and keeps them from weeping.

Eggs Taos

1	large clove garlic, minced
½	onion, chopped
¼	cup butter
¼	cup all-purpose flour
2	cups milk, heated
1	7-ounce can chopped green chiles
½	teaspoon salt
¼	teaspoon freshly ground black pepper
10	eggs
2	avocados
8	flour tortillas
3	cups shredded Cheddar and/or Monterey Jack cheese
1	cup sour cream
2	tomatoes, chopped

8 servings

In large skillet, sauté garlic and onion in butter over high heat. Stir in flour. Add heated milk and whisk constantly until thick. Add green chiles, salt and pepper. Remove sauce from heat and set aside.

In large skillet, scramble eggs; set aside. In small bowl, mash avocados. Spoon 2 tablespoons of sauce, ⅛ of eggs, and ⅛ of avocado on each tortilla. Roll up and place seam side down in 9x13-inch baking dish. Spoon remaining sauce over tortillas. Sprinkle with cheese. Bake at 350 degrees 15-20 minutes or until hot. Top with sour cream and chopped tomato.

Wake up to a hearty Mexican breakfast!

Brunch

Egg Baskets

2	packages Pepperidge Farm frozen puffed pastry shells (12 shells)
12	eggs
12	slices tomato
12	slices Canadian bacon, heated

Garnishes:

pimiento strips
sliced black olives
sprigs of fresh parsley

Hollandaise Sauce:

1	cup butter
6	egg yolks
¼	cup fresh lemon juice
¼	teaspoon cayenne pepper

6 servings

Bake pastry shells according to directions, but undercook slightly so shells are light brown. Cool. Cut off tops and scoop out middle dough, being careful not to make holes in shell. Place shells on large cookie sheet. Carefully crack 1 raw egg into each shell. Bake at 325 degrees until egg is set, about 20-25 minutes. Remove from oven. To serve, place tomato slice on slice of heated Canadian bacon, top with cooked shell. Spoon **Hollandaise Sauce** over egg baskets and garnish with crossed strips of pimientos, black olives and sprigs of parsley.

1¼ cups

Heat butter until almost boiling. Remove from heat and let rest for 5 minutes. Place egg yolks, lemon juice and cayenne pepper in blender or food processor. With blender on high speed, slowly pour in butter. Blend for 30 seconds or until thick. Place in double boiler over warm, not boiling, water until ready to serve.

Perfect for an Easter brunch or spring buffet.

Eggs with Shrimp and Dill Sauce

¼	cup butter
1	bunch green onions, thinly sliced, including 1 inch of tops
½	cup cold water
5	tablespoons all-purpose flour
½	cup clam juice
½	cup dry white wine
1	cup heavy cream
¼	cup minced fresh dill or 2 teaspoons dried dill weed
¾	cup freshly grated Parmesan cheese
16	hard cooked eggs
1½	pounds shrimp, boiled with dill sprigs, peeled and deveined
1	cup dry bread crumbs
⅓	cup butter, melted
¾	cup freshly grated Parmesan cheese
	sprigs of fresh dill (optional)

8-10 servings

In medium saucepan, melt butter; add green onions and water. Heat to boiling. Reduce heat to medium and cook until water has boiled away. Stir in flour and cook for 3 minutes. Do not brown. Add clam juice, wine, cream and dill. Cook, whisking constantly, until sauce boils. Stir in ¾ cup Parmesan cheese. Remove from heat and set aside. Cut eggs in half lengthwise. Place eggs, yolk side up, in flat 3-quart pyrex baking dish. Cover with shrimp. Pour sauce on top of shrimp. In small bowl, mix bread crumbs, melted butter and ¾ cup Parmesan. Sprinkle on top of sauce. *Refrigerate until ready to bake. Let stand at room temperature for 30 minutes.*

Bake uncovered at 400 degrees for 20 minutes or until hot and bubbly. Garnish with sprigs of fresh dill.

An easy way to cook eggs for a large crowd.

Brunch

Ham and Egg Bundles

3	tablespoons butter
1	tablespoon minced onion
3	tablespoons all-purpose flour
½	teaspoon salt
2¼	cups milk, heated
2	tablespoons dry sherry
3	cups shredded sharp Cheddar cheese
3	10-ounce packages frozen chopped spinach, thawed and squeezed dry
8	hard cooked eggs
1	tablespoon minced onion
1	teaspoon Dijon mustard
3	tablespoons mayonnaise
1	teaspoon Worcestershire sauce
½	teaspoon salt
8	thin slices baked ham (6-inch diameter)

8 servings

In a 2-quart saucepan, melt 3 tablespoons butter. Sauté 1 tablespoon minced onion until transparent. Blend in flour and salt. Remove from heat and add warmed milk, all at once, while beating with a whisk. Return saucepan to heat and bring mixture to a boil, stirring constantly. Boil and stir 1 minute. Stir in sherry and cheese. Cook over low heat, stirring occasionally, until cheese is melted. Stir 1½ cups cheese sauce into the spinach. Arrange spinach evenly in 7x11-inch glass baking dish.

Slice hard cooked eggs in half lengthwise. Scoop out yolks. In a small bowl mash yolks with 1 tablespoon minced onion, mustard, mayonnaise, Worcestershire and salt. Fill whites with mashed yolk mixture. Place two halves together to make whole eggs. Wrap a ham slice around each egg; fold ends under. Arrange wrapped eggs over spinach, pressing down slightly. Pour remaining cheese sauce over eggs. *May be refrigerated, covered, up to 24 hours.* Bake uncovered at 350 degrees for 35-45 minutes or until bubbly.

A well-balanced flavor combination of cheese, spinach, ham and eggs makes this a classic. For a special brunch presentation, prepare in 8 individual ramekins.

Crab Strata

2	tablespoons bread crumbs
8	slices white bread
½	pound mushrooms, sliced
¼	cup sliced green onions
¼	cup Madeira
8	ounces crabmeat
2½	cups milk
4	eggs
2	cups shredded Cheddar cheese
½	teaspoon salt
½	teaspoon dry mustard
	freshly ground black pepper to taste

6-8 servings

Butter a 2-quart soufflé dish or 6 x 10-inch baking dish and dust with bread crumbs. Set aside. Remove crusts from bread and cut bread into cubes. Set aside. In skillet, sauté mushrooms and onions in Maderia over medium heat. Stir in crabmeat. In prepared soufflé dish alternate layers of bread cubes and crab mixture, ending with bread cubes. In food processor or blender, whirl milk, eggs, cheese, salt, mustard and pepper until thoroughly blended. Slowly pour this mixture over bread cubes. Cover and refrigerate overnight.

Bake uncovered at 325 degrees for 1 hour 30 minutes if using soufflé dish or 1 hour if using 6 x 10-inch dish. Strata is done when knife inserted just off center comes out clean.

A shellfish version of the classic egg and cheese strata.

Smoked Salmon Soufflé

5	tablespoons butter
6	tablespoons all-purpose flour
1¼	cups milk, warmed
3	ounces cream cheese with chives
6	egg yolks
	dash of dill weed
3	ounces smoked salmon, diced
2	teaspoons fresh lemon juice
6	egg whites
½	teaspoon salt
¼	teaspoon cream of tartar

4-6 servings

Make a 2-inch collar with waxed paper around a 2-quart soufflé dish. Butter the collar. In a 2-quart saucepan, melt butter. Add flour and stir over medium heat for 2 minutes. Remove saucepan from heat; add warmed milk all at once, while beating with a whisk. Return saucepan to heat and continue stirring until sauce boils. Remove from heat and stir in cream cheese, mixing until thoroughly combined. Whisk egg yolks, one at a time, into the sauce. Add dill, salmon and lemon juice to sauce, stirring to combine thoroughly and separate pieces of salmon.

In large bowl, beat egg whites with salt and cream of tartar until stiff. Thoroughly fold ¼ of egg whites into sauce to lighten it. Then pour sauce over rest of beaten whites and fold until barely combined. Pour mixture into prepared soufflé dish. *At this point, soufflé may be covered and refrigerated for up to 4 hours.* To bake, set soufflé in larger pan and add boiling water half way up sides of soufflé dish. Bake at 350 degrees for 40 minutes *(or 55 minutes if refrigerated).* Remove collar and serve at once.

*A most luxurious brunch entrée. Serve with **Chilled Lemon Asparagus,** fresh berries and champagne. Leftovers reheat well, which is remarkable for a soufflé.*

Brunch

Cheese Soufflé
with Broccoli Sauce

6   tablespoons butter
⅓   cup all-purpose flour
2   cups milk, heated
3   cups shredded processed
      American cheese (12 ounces)
6   egg yolks
6   egg whites
½   teaspoon cream of tartar

8 individual soufflés

In saucepan, melt butter over medium heat. Blend in flour. Add heated milk all at once. Cook and stir until thick and bubbly. Add cheese, stirring until melted. Remove from heat. In medium bowl, beat egg yolks until thick and lemon colored. Slowly add cheese mixture to yolks, stirring constantly. Cool slightly. In large bowl, beat egg whites and cream of tartar until stiff peaks form. Gradually pour yolk mixture over whites; fold together well. Pour into 8 ungreased individual 1-cup soufflé dishes. *Cover tightly with freezer wrap or foil and freeze until needed.*

To bake, set dishes in shallow pan filled with boiling water to depth of ½-inch. Bake at 300 degrees for 20 minutes *(or for 1 hour 15 minutes if frozen).* Soufflés are cooked when knife inserted just off center comes out clean. Serve immediately with **Broccoli Sauce.**

Broccoli Sauce:

¼   cup chopped onion
2   tablespoons butter
3   tablespoons all-purpose flour
1   chicken bouillon cube
¼   cup boiling water
¾   cup milk, heated
1   10-ounce package frozen chopped
      broccoli, cooked and well
      drained
1   teaspoon dried dill weed
1   teaspoon herbed pepper

In saucepan, sauté onions in butter over medium heat until transparent. Blend in flour. Dissolve bouillon cube in boiling water. Add to saucepan together with heated milk. Cook and stir until thick and bubbly. Stir in broccoli, dill and herbed pepper and cook until heated thoroughly.

A soufflé that can be made ahead and frozen until needed. After the soufflé is in the oven, prepare the sauce. What could be easier?

Brunch

Soufflé Roll with Variations

Soufflé Roll:

4	tablespoons butter
⅓	cup all-purpose flour
1½	cups milk, warmed
⅛	teaspoon freshly ground black pepper
	dash of ground nutmeg
¼	teaspoon salt
6	large egg yolks
6	large egg whites, room temperature
¼	teaspoon cream of tartar
⅛	teaspoon salt
1	cup (4 ounces) shredded Swiss or Cheddar cheese (depending on filling)
2	tablespoons freshly grated Parmesan cheese
⅓	cup buttered, toasted white breadcrumbs

8 servings

Butter a jelly roll pan and line with waxed paper, leaving about 2 inches overhanging at each end. Butter and flour waxed paper.

In 3-quart saucepan, melt butter. Add flour and stir over moderate heat for 2-3 minutes, until foamy but not browned. Remove from heat and add warmed milk all at once, whisking until blended. Return to heat and bring to boil, stirring. Beat in pepper, nutmeg and ¼ teaspoon salt. Let cool 5 minutes.

Whisk egg yolks one at a time into cream sauce. Put egg whites into large mixing bowl. Beat whites until foamy; add cream of tartar and ⅛ teaspoon salt and beat until stiff. Fold ¼ of whites into cream sauce, then fold in rest. Fold in cheeses. Spread soufflé mixture over waxed paper, making a rectangle about 12x17 inches. Bake at 425 degrees on rack in middle of oven for 12-15 minutes until puffed and set. Remove from oven and sprinkle with breadcrumbs. Lay waxed paper, then aluminum foil over top and invert onto cookie sheet. Let stand 5 minutes. Remove pan and carefully remove waxed paper. Some soufflé will stick to the paper. If paper does not remove fairly easily, return soufflé to pan and place in oven for additional 3-4 minutes. *Can be made ahead up to this point. Wrap airtight and refrigerate or freeze. Bring to room temperature before continuing.*

Prepare filling of your choice and spread over soufflé. Roll from long side, using waxed paper and aluminum foil to help roll. Slide onto cookie sheet or ovenproof serving platter. If desired, top with additional slices of cheese used to make soufflé. *Refrigerate, covered, if made ahead.* Bake at 350 degrees until heated through and cheese melts, about 15 minutes *(or 40 minutes for refrigerated soufflé roll)*. Cut into slices and serve.

Spinach Filling:

2	tablespoons butter
¼	cup minced onion
2	10-ounce packages frozen chopped spinach, thawed and squeezed dry
¼	teaspoon salt
¼	cup shredded sharp Cheddar cheese (1 ounce)
¾	cup sour cream
¼	pound sharp Cheddar cheese, sliced

Make soufflé with Cheddar cheese. In large skillet, melt butter and sauté onion until transparent. Turn off heat. Add spinach, salt, ¼ cup shredded Cheddar and sour cream. Stir until thoroughly combined. *Cover and refrigerate if made ahead. Warm to room temperature before filling and rolling soufflé.* Arrange cheese slices over top before baking.

Brunch

Onion and Chile Filling:
- 2 tablespoons vegetable oil
- 2½ cups chopped onions
- 1 clove garlic, minced
- 1 7-ounce can diced green chiles
- 2 tablespoons all-purpose flour
- ½ cup milk
- guacamole
- salsa

Make soufflé with Cheddar cheese. In large skillet, heat oil. Add onions and garlic and sauté until transparent. Stir in chiles. Add flour and stir for 2-3 minutes. Gradually add milk, stirring constantly, and cook until sauce thickens. *Cover and refrigerate if made ahead. Warm to room temperature before filling and rolling soufflé.* Serve baked soufflé roll with salsa and/or guacamole to spoon on top.

Curried Filling:
- 2 tablespoons butter
- 1 tablespoon curry powder
- 1½ tablespoons all-purpose flour
- ¾ cup hot chicken broth
- 1 teaspoon fresh lemon juice
- 1 cup slivered cooked chicken, shrimp or crab
- ¼ cup heavy cream
- salt and freshly ground black pepper to taste
- chutney (optional)

Make soufflé roll with Swiss cheese. In 3-quart saucepan, melt butter. Add curry powder and cook, stirring, over low heat for 1-2 minutes. Add flour and stir 2 minutes more. Add chicken broth and lemon juice and whisk until sauce thickens. Stir in chicken or shellfish, then cream. Add salt and pepper to taste. *Cover and refrigerate if made ahead. Warm to room temperature before filling and rolling soufflé.* Serve baked soufflé roll with chutney, if desired.

Zucchini and Pepper Filling:
- 1 pound zucchini, grated unpeeled
- ½ teaspoon salt
- 1½ cups chopped onion
- 3 tablespoons butter
- 1 large green bell pepper, chopped
- 1 large red bell pepper or 4-ounce jar pimiento, chopped
- ½ teaspoon freshly ground black pepper
- ¼ teaspoon dried oregano
- 1 large tomato, chopped and drained
- 2 tablespoons all-purpose flour
- ½ cup milk
- salt and freshly ground black pepper to taste

Make soufflé with Swiss cheese. Put grated zucchini in colander. Sprinkle with ½ teaspoon salt and place in sink to macerate for 20 minutes. In large skillet, sauté onion in butter until transparent. Squeeze moisture from zucchini and add to skillet. Stir in green and red bell peppers, pepper, oregano and tomato. Cook, stirring frequently, until bell pepper is tender. If necessary, increase heat to boil off excess moisture. Stir in flour and cook, stirring, for 2-3 minutes. Add milk gradually, stirring constantly, and cook until sauce thickens. Season to taste with additional salt and pepper. *Cover and refrigerate if made ahead. Warm to room temperature before filling and rolling soufflé.*

A soufflé roll is an airy egg sponge, baked, covered with filling and rolled jelly roll fashion while warm. A spectacular presentation that's much easier than it looks.

Brunch

Chorizo Omelet Picnic Loaf

1 **round loaf sourdough French bread**
   (10-12-inch diameter)
1 **tablespoon olive oil**
10 **ounces chorizo sausage**
1 **large new potato, cooked**
1 **tablespoon olive oil**
1 **cup finely chopped onion**
1 **clove garlic, minced**
1 **cup chopped green bell peppers**
1 **4-ounce jar chopped pimiento**
9 **eggs**
¾ **teaspoon salt**
¼ **teaspoon freshly ground black**
   pepper
2 **tablespoons olive oil, divided**

6 servings

With long, serrated knife, split bread in half horizontally. Partially hollow out centers of halves, leaving a 1-inch border. Brush cut surfaces with 1 tablespoon olive oil. Reassemble loaf, wrap in foil, and keep warm in 300 degree oven while preparing omelet.

In 10-inch skillet, crumble chorizo and sauté until lightly browned. Remove sausage with slotted spoon and drain; discard drippings. Peel and thinly slice potato. In same skillet heat 1 tablespoon olive oil over medium-high heat. Add potato, onions and garlic. Cook, turning often, until browned, about 3 minutes. Add green pepper and pimiento and cook 1 minute longer; stir in sausage and set aside.

In large bowl, beat eggs with salt and pepper. Return skillet to medium heat and push potato mixture to one side. Drizzle 1 tablespoon olive oil over bottom of pan. Redistribute vegetables in pan and pour in eggs. As edges begin to set, push toward center and shake pan vigorously to allow uncooked egg to flow underneath. Cook omelet until top is just set but appears moist and bottom is lightly browned, about 5 minutes.

To turn omelet, run a wide spatula around edge and under it to loosen. Invert plate over omelet, and with one hand on the plate and the other hand gripping the pan handle, quickly invert pan, turning omelet out onto plate. Add remaining tablespoon olive oil to pan, return to medium heat and gently slide omelet back into pan. Cook until lightly browned on second side, about 2 minutes. Set off heat.

Remove bread from oven and open. Invert bottom half of loaf over top of omelet, trimming omelet to fit size of bread. Then quickly invert pan, turning omelet out onto loaf. Replace top of bread and wrap in several thicknesses of foil to keep warm up to 4 hours. *Or refrigerate wrapped loaf and reheat at 400 degrees for 25-30 minutes or until omelet is hot and steamy.*

Great for picnics, cross country skiing or tailgate parties as the wrapped loaf stays warm up to 4 hours.

Brunch

Crab Croissants

½	cup mayonnaise
¼	teaspoon dried dill weed
2	cloves garlic, minced
¼	cup minced fresh parsley
⅛	teaspoon cayenne pepper
⅔	pound crabmeat
1	cup shredded Cheddar cheese
1	cup shredded Monterey Jack cheese
1	2 ¼-ounce can sliced ripe black olives
1	10-ounce package frozen artichoke hearts, cooked and quartered
4	large croissants

8 servings

In a medium bowl, combine mayonnaise, dill, garlic, parsley, cayenne pepper, crabmeat, cheeses, sliced olives and artichoke hearts. *Cover and refrigerate until ready to use.* Split croissants horizontally. Spread each croissant half with crab mixture. Place croissants on baking sheet and broil 5 inches from heat for 3-4 minutes or until heated through.

The perfect Sunday supper served with fresh fruit or a green salad.

Savory Gruyère Cheesecake

1⅓	cups fine toasted breadcrumbs
5	tablespoons unsalted butter, melted
24	ounces cream cheese, softened
¼	cup heavy cream
½	teaspoon salt
¼	teaspoon ground nutmeg
¼	teaspoon cayenne pepper
4	eggs
1	cup shredded Gruyère cheese
1	10-ounce package frozen chopped spinach, thawed and squeezed dry
2½	tablespoons minced green onions
3	tablespoons unsalted butter
½	pound mushrooms, finely chopped salt and freshly ground black pepper to taste
	Marinara Sauce

12 servings

In small bowl, combine breadcrumbs and melted butter. Butter a 9-inch springform pan. Press crumbs onto bottom and sides of pan. Bake at 350 degrees for 8-10 minutes; set aside to cool.

In large bowl, beat cream cheese, cream, salt, nutmeg and cayenne pepper together until smooth. Beat in eggs, one at a time. Divide cheese mixture between 2 bowls. Stir Gruyère cheese into one. Stir spinach and green onions into the other. Pour spinach filling into cooled crust.

In medium skillet, melt 3 tablespoons butter and sauté mushrooms over medium-high heat until all moisture evaporates, stirring frequently. Season to taste with salt and pepper. Spoon mushrooms over spinach filling. Carefully pour Gruyère filling over mushrooms. Set pan on baking sheet. Bake at 325 degrees for 1¼ hours. Turn oven off and cool cheesecake for 1 hour with door ajar, then cool on rack until room temperature. Serve in wedges topped with warm **Marinara Sauce.**

This savory cheesecake is a fabulous choice for brunch or lunch. Beautiful to serve and scrumptious!

Brunch

Basic Crêpes

1 cup cold water
1 cup cold milk
4 eggs
½ teaspoon salt
2 cups all-purpose flour
4 tablespoons butter, melted

16 crêpes

Put ingredients into blender in order listed. Whirl 1 minute. Scrape down sides and blend another minute. Refrigerate batter at least 2 hours.

Heat a 7-inch crêpe pan or iron skillet over medium-high heat until very hot. Pour in a scant ¼ cup of batter. Tilt pan in all directions so batter runs over bottom. Pour out any excess batter. Return pan to heat for 1 minute. Turn crêpe when bottom is lightly browned. Cook 30 seconds on second side. Slide out of pan onto waxed paper. Repeat with remaining batter.

Crêpes may be used immediately, refrigerated overnight, or frozen. To freeze, stack cooled crêpes between waxed paper. Wrap in aluminum foil, label and freeze no longer than 3 months. Thaw wrapped crêpes at room temperature about 1 hour.

Mushroom Crêpes

3 pounds mushrooms
4 tablespoons butter
1 cup chopped onion
2 cloves garlic, minced
¾ teaspoon dried marjoram
½ teaspoon dried thyme
¼ cup all-purpose flour
¾ cup milk, warmed
3 tablespoons dry sherry
½ cup freshly grated Parmesan cheese
¼ cup minced fresh parsley
salt and freshly ground black pepper to taste
16 *Basic Crêpes*

Sauce:
3 tablespoons butter
3 tablespoons all-purpose flour
dash ground cayenne pepper
1½ cups half and half, warmed
¼ cup dry white wine
½ cup shredded Gruyère cheese
2 tablespoons butter
1 cup sliced mushrooms
pinch nutmeg
1 cup shredded Gruyère cheese
⅓ cup freshly grated Parmesan cheese

8 servings

Chop mushroom stems; slice caps and reserve. In large skillet over medium heat, melt 2 tablespoons butter. Add mushroom stems, onions and garlic. Sauté, stirring, until onions are transparent. Add remaining 2 tablespoons butter, sliced caps, marjoram and thyme. Cook, stirring, until mushrooms are limp. Sprinkle flour over mushrooms. Cook, stirring, until bubbly. Gradually stir in warmed milk and stir until sauce thickens. Remove from heat. Add sherry, Parmesan and parsley. Cool; season to taste with salt and pepper. Divide filling evenly among crêpes, fold in both sides and roll to close. Place crêpes seam side down in greased, shallow baking dish. *If made ahead, cover and refrigerate or freeze.*

In 2-quart saucepan, melt 3 tablespoons butter. Stir in flour and cook until bubbly. Add cayenne. Remove from heat and gradually blend in warmed half and half and wine. Return to heat and cook, stirring constantly, until thickened. Add ½ cup Gruyère cheese, stirring until melted. In skillet, sauté mushrooms in 2 tablespoons butter. Stir sautéed mushrooms into sauce. Add a pinch of nutmeg.

Pour sauce over crêpes. Sprinkle remaining 1 cup Gruyère cheese and Parmesan cheese evenly over crêpes. Bake uncovered at 400 degrees for 30-35 minutes (45 minutes if crêpes were refrigerated) until crêpes are heated through and lightly browned.

Brunch

Scallop Crêpes

1½ cups chicken broth
1½ cups dry white wine
3 green onions, sliced
3 celery stalks with leaves, cut into chunks
1 bay leaf
10 whole white peppercorns
2 pounds bay scallops, or sea scallops cut into fourths
¾ pound mushrooms, sliced
4 tablespoons butter, melted
5 tablespoons all-purpose flour
¾ cup milk
2 egg yolks, lightly beaten
½ cup heavy cream
¼ teaspoon fresh lemon juice
1 teaspoon salt
1 cup shredded Swiss cheese
12 *Basic Crêpes*

6 servings

In 3-quart saucepan, combine chicken broth, wine, green onions, celery, bay leaf and peppercorns. Heat to boiling and boil for 10 minutes. Pour stock through strainer into 12-inch skillet. Discard vegetables. Bring stock to simmer and add scallops and mushrooms. Simmer covered for 5 minutes. Remove scallops and mushrooms with slotted spoon and set aside. Boil stock rapidly until reduced to 1 cup.

In 3-quart saucepan, melt butter and stir in flour. Cook, stirring, for 2 minutes. Remove pan from heat. Whisking constantly, stir in milk and reduced stock. Return pan to medium-high heat and cook, stirring, until sauce thickens and comes to a boil. In small bowl, beat together egg yolks and cream. Stir in a spoonful of hot sauce. Stir in another spoonful of hot sauce, then stir yolk mixture into remaining sauce. Bring to a boil over moderate heat. Remove from heat and stir in lemon juice and salt.

Drain any juices that have accumulated in bowl with mushrooms and scallops. Pour in ⅔ sauce and ½ cheese. Mix together and cool slightly. Lightly butter 2 9x13-inch glass pans or 1 very large baking dish. Spoon ¹⁄₁₂ filling onto each crêpe and roll to enclose. Place crêpes, seam side down, in baking dish. *Cover and refrigerate if made ahead.* Spread remaining sauce over crêpes and sprinkle with remaining cheese. Bake uncovered at 425 degrees for 10 minutes (*or 18 minutes if refrigerated*). Place briefly under broiler to brown top, if desired.

Flavors of scallops, mushrooms and a rich cream sauce create a delicious crêpe filling.

Brunch

Cranberry Blintzes

8	ounces cream cheese
⅓	cup sugar
4	cups cream-style cottage cheese
2	teaspoons pure vanilla extract
12	*Basic Crêpes*

Cranberry Sauce:

12	ounces fresh or frozen cranberries
⅓	cup sugar
2	tablespoons cornstarch
1	cup water

Garnish:

3	ripe bananas
½	cup hazelnuts, toasted and chopped

6 servings

In large bowl, beat cream cheese with sugar. Blend in cottage cheese and vanilla. *If made ahead, cover and refrigerate for up to 2 days.* Spread 3 tablespoons cheese filling over ½ of each crêpe. Fold crêpe in half, then in half again to form a triangle. Repeat for all the crêpes. Set them side-by-side in a shallow baking dish. Heat at 350 degrees for 15 minutes.

While crêpes are heating, prepare **Cranberry Sauce.** In 3-quart saucepan, combine cranberries, sugar and cornstarch. Stir in water. Heat to boiling, stirring constantly. Lower heat and cook for 5 minutes, stirring occasionally. *Do not make ahead because sauce will congeal.*

To serve, place 2 crêpes on each plate. Peel bananas, halve lengthwise and arrange alongside crêpes. Pass warm **Cranberry Sauce** and nuts.

The contrast of flavors is outstanding in this colorful recipe. These crêpes may be served at room temperature, but are best when served warm.

Whole Wheat Pancakes

1	egg
1	cup buttermilk
2	tablespoons vegetable oil
¾	cup whole wheat flour
1	tablespoon packed light brown sugar
1	teaspoon baking powder
½	teaspoon baking soda
½	teaspoon salt

Banana Blueberry Pancakes:

1	ripe banana, mashed
¾	cup blueberries
½	cup chopped walnuts

Cinnamon Raisin Pancakes:

½	cup seedless raisins
1½	cups boiling water
1	teaspoon ground cinnamon

10 4-inch pancakes

In large bowl, beat egg; add buttermilk, oil, whole wheat flour, brown sugar, baking powder, baking soda and salt. Beat until smooth. Pour pancakes onto lightly greased pan or griddle. Turn as soon as they are puffed and edges begin to dry slightly. Cook other side until golden brown.

Stir mashed banana, blueberries and walnuts into the whole wheat batter.

Soak raisins in boiling water for 1 hour or overnight; drain. Stir raisins and cinnamon into whole wheat batter.

Try this recipe and both of the variations. Your family will never want plain pancakes again!

Brunch

Wholesome Waffles

3 egg whites
2 cups buttermilk
1 cup all-purpose flour
1 cup whole wheat flour
¼ cup wheat germ
2 teaspoons baking powder
1 teaspoon baking soda
1 teaspoon pure vanilla extract
⅓ cup safflower or corn oil

4-6 servings

Spray waffle iron with vegetable cooking spray and heat on high. In large bowl, beat egg whites until frothy. Set aside. In separate large bowl, combine buttermilk, flours, wheat germ, baking powder, baking soda, vanilla and oil. Fold dry ingredients into egg whites until smooth. Pour batter onto center of hot waffle iron. Bake about 5 minutes or until steaming stops. Do not over-bake or waffles will be dry.

These low fat, high fiber waffles are surprisingly light!

Sour Cream Waffles

1 cup all-purpose flour, sifted 5 times
1 teaspoon baking powder
⅛ teaspoon salt
1½ teaspoons sugar
1 teaspoon baking soda
3 eggs, separated
2 cups sour cream
3 tablespoons butter, melted

4-6 servings

Spray waffle iron with vegetable cooking spray and heat on high. Sift flour, baking powder, salt, sugar and baking soda together. In a medium bowl, beat egg yolks thoroughly and add sour cream and melted butter. Stir yolk mixture into dry ingredients as quickly as possible. In a medium bowl beat egg whites until stiff peaks form. Fold egg whites lightly and carefully into batter. Spoon batter onto waffle iron. Bake 2½ minutes or until steaming stops.

These light waffles will soak up syrup very quickly. Pass the syrup separately.

Buckwheat Pecan Waffles

1 cup buckwheat flour
1 cup all-purpose flour
¾ teaspoon salt
2½ teaspoons baking powder
2 eggs
1¾ cups milk
½ cup butter, melted
1½ cups pecans, finely chopped

4-6 servings

Spray waffle iron with vegetable cooking spray and heat on high. In large bowl, sift together buckwheat flour, all-purpose flour, salt and baking powder. Set aside. In separate bowl, beat eggs until foamy and add milk. Mix liquid ingredients into dry ingredients with a few quick strokes. Stir in melted butter and pecans. Pour batter onto center of hot waffle iron. Bake waffles until browned and crisp. Keep baked, uncovered waffles warm in oven heated to 200 degrees. Serve waffles hot.

Brunch

Grand Marnier French Toast

1	1-pound loaf unsliced white bread
4	eggs
1	cup milk
2	tablespoons Grand Marnier liqueur
1	tablespoon sugar
½	teaspoon pure vanilla extract
¼	teaspoon salt
¼	teaspoon freshly grated orange peel
	vegetable oil
3	tablespoons butter, melted
	powdered sugar
1	orange, thinly sliced (optional)

4 servings

Slice bread into eight ¾-inch slices. In medium bowl, beat eggs with milk, Grand Marnier, sugar, vanilla, salt and orange peel until well blended. Dip each piece of bread into liquid mixture until well saturated. Place in a flat baking dish. Pour remaining liquid over bread. Cover and refrigerate overnight.

In skillet, heat oil and sauté bread until golden on both sides. Brush with butter and sprinkle with powdered sugar. Top with orange slice and serve immediately with maple syrup.

The delicate orange flavor gives this French toast a new twist.

French Toast Fondue

	vegetable oil
1	teaspoon salt
2	eggs, beaten
½	cup milk
¼	teaspoon salt
1	baguette French bread, cubed

Maple Butter:
1½	cups powdered sugar
½	cup butter
½	cup maple syrup
1	egg white, stiffly beaten

4-6 servings

Heat oil and 1 teaspoon salt in fondue pot. In medium bowl, beat together eggs, milk and ¼ teaspoon salt. When oil in fondue pot is very hot, dip bread cubes into egg mixture, then into oil to cook. Bread is done when it is crispy and golden brown. Remove from fondue pot and dip into **Maple Butter.**

Cream together powdered sugar, butter and maple syrup. Fold in beaten egg white.

Oil must be very hot to insure adequate frying of bread. Perfect for a wintry morning breakfast, and fun for the whole family.

Brunch

Honey Pecan Butter

½ cup well-chilled, unsalted butter,
    cut into 4 pieces
¼ cup honey
⅓ cup pecans, toasted

¾ cup

Blend butter, honey and pecans in food processor until smooth. Serve at room temperature. *May be made up to 1 week in advance if covered and refrigerated.*

A delicious spread for your favorite waffle, pancake or muffin.

Apple Cider Syrup

1½ cups clear apple cider
1   cup packed light brown sugar
1   cup corn syrup
4   tablespoons butter
2   tablespoons fresh lemon juice
⅛   teaspoon ground cinnamon
⅛   teaspoon ground nutmeg
2   teaspoons freshly grated lemon
    peel
2   Granny Smith apples, peeled,
    cored and thinly sliced

3 cups

In a saucepan, heat to boiling all ingredients except apple slices. Reduce heat and simmer uncovered for 20-25 minutes or until mixture is the consistency of maple syrup. *Syrup can be made up to two weeks in advance and refrigerated.* Just before serving, add apple slices and heat several minutes.

Ladle onto pancakes or waffles topped with whipped cream.

Cranberry Maple Syrup

1   cup apple juice
1   cup fresh cranberries
1   cinnamon stick
¼   teaspoon ground cloves
1   cup maple syrup

2 cups

In medium saucepan, combine juice, cranberries, cinnamon stick and cloves. Simmer for 15 minutes or until cranberries pop. Add maple syrup and simmer for an additional 5 minutes. Serve warm.

Delicious and colorful on **Whole Wheat Pancakes.**

Pasta

Pasta

Pasta Fresca

2   eggs, lightly beaten
1¼   cups all-purpose flour
⅛   teaspoon salt

1 pound pasta

In medium bowl, thoroughly mix eggs, flour and salt. Knead for 2-3 minutes. Continue to add small amounts of flour until dough is no longer sticky. Roll dough through pasta machine and cut into desired shapes.

Homemade pasta is the best of fresh. Fresh pasta is readily available in stores everywhere, and was used in testing the recipes in this section.

Marinara Sauce

¼   cup olive oil
2   tablespoons minced garlic
2   tablespoons minced fresh basil or
     ½ teaspoon dried basil
2   tablespoons minced fresh parsley
     or ½ teaspoon dried parsley
2   16-ounce cans stewed Italian
     tomatoes, crushed
¼   teaspoon salt
¼   teaspoon freshly ground black
     pepper

4-6 servings

In 3-quart saucepan, heat olive oil and sauté garlic until golden brown. Stir in basil, parsley and tomatoes. Add salt and pepper and simmer for 20 minutes.

Delicious and easy; perfect with a traditional sprinkling of grated Parmesan cheese.

Ponderosa Pesto

2   cups fresh basil
2   teaspoons minced garlic
1   teaspoon salt
¼   cup pine nuts
1   cup olive oil
½   cup freshly grated Parmesan
     cheese
2   tablespoons freshly grated
     Romano cheese
12   ounces vermicelli, cooked al dente
     and drained
     freshly grated Parmesan cheese

8-10 side dish servings

Place basil, garlic, salt and nuts in blender. Blend at high speed until finely chopped. Add oil in a slow, steady stream. *Can be frozen at this point.* Add cheeses and blend until smooth. *Refrigerate if made ahead.*

In heated serving dish, toss warm vermicelli with basil mixture until thoroughly coated. Sprinkle with Parmesan and serve immediately.

A smooth and rich basil sauce that will add simple elegance to any pasta! Walnuts may be substituted for pine nuts.

Pasta

Sensational Spaghetti

1	medium onion, diced (about ½ cup)
2	cloves garlic, minced
¼	cup butter
1	tablespoon olive oil
½	pound ground beef
½	pound ground pork
½	pound ground veal
½	green bell pepper, chopped
½	pound mushrooms, chopped
2	6-ounce cans tomato paste
1	28-ounce can stewed Italian tomatoes
1½	teaspoons Worcestershire sauce
1½	teaspoons angostura bitters
1	tablespoon sugar
½	cup dry red wine
½	teaspoon salt
¼	teaspoon freshly ground black pepper
½	teaspoon celery salt
2	bay leaves
	dash of cayenne pepper
1	pound spaghetti, cooked al dente and drained
	freshly grated Parmesan cheese

6-8 main dish servings

In large, heavy kettle, sauté onion and garlic in butter and oil until transparent. Add beef, pork and veal, and brown over medium heat. Add green pepper, mushrooms, tomato paste, tomatoes, Worcestershire, bitters, sugar, wine, salt, pepper, celery salt, bay leaves and cayenne pepper. Simmer over low heat for 3 hours. Divide warm spaghetti among warmed individual plates and top with sauce. Sprinkle with Parmesan and serve immediately.

A classic dish. This is the best of all meat sauces, and should be made at least once every few months to sharpen and maintain sauce-making skills.

Mostaccioli with Mint Sauce

1	pound sweet Italian sausage, casings removed
2	large cloves garlic, minced
2	cups chopped fresh mint
1	16-ounce can peeled tomatoes, coarsely chopped
1	cup water
1	teaspoon salt
1	pound mostaccioli, cooked al dente and drained
	freshly grated Parmesan cheese

6-8 servings

In large skillet, cook sausage, garlic and mint over medium-high heat until sausage is brown. Drain off grease. Transfer mixture to blender or food processor and process for 15 seconds or until sausage is coarsely chopped. Do not over process. Return mixture to skillet. Stir in tomatoes, water and salt. Cook over medium heat for 1-1½ hours, or until sauce thickens. Place mostaccioli in heated serving dish and spoon sauce on top. Serve with freshly grated Parmesan cheese.

The pairing of sausage and mint provides the perfect balance of delicacy and savoriness.

Pasta

Spaghetti alla Bacon

2	cloves garlic, minced
½	cup butter
12	ounces spaghetti, cooked al dente and drained
1	cup freshly grated Parmesan cheese
2	cups heavy cream
½	teaspoon freshly ground black pepper
12-15	strips bacon, fried crisp and drained

6-8 servings

In large skillet, brown garlic in butter. Stir in cooked spaghetti, Parmesan cheese, cream and pepper, and simmer over low heat until thick. Place in heated serving dish, crumble bacon over top and serve immediately.

A sensational variation of spaghetti carbonara without eggs!

Proscuitto Delight

¼	cup unsalted butter
¼	cup minced green onions
¼	pound mushrooms, sliced
½	pound proscuitto, cut into ¼-inch julienne strips
1½	cups heavy cream
½	teaspoon freshly ground black pepper
12	ounces penne pasta, cooked al dente and drained
¾	cup freshly grated Parmesan cheese
	freshly grated Parmesan cheese

6 main dish servings
8-10 side dish servings

In large skillet, melt butter and sauté onions, mushrooms and proscuitto for 3-5 minutes. Stir in cream and pepper. Heat to boiling; lower heat and simmer for 6-8 minutes or until sauce thickens slightly. Remove from heat. In heated serving dish, toss warm pasta with Parmesan. Pour proscuitto mixture over pasta and toss until evenly mixed. Serve immediately, sprinkled with additional Parmesan.

Julienned proscuitto and cream combine to make this simple but delicious sauce.

Pasta Bellissima

¼	cup butter
8	ounces Canadian bacon, cut into ¼-inch julienne strips
1	8-ounce jar roasted red bell peppers, drained and chopped
¼	pound snow pea pods, cut in half diagonally
1	cup heavy cream
½	teaspoon salt
¼	teaspoon freshly ground black pepper
1	cup freshly grated Parmesan cheese
1	pound fettucine, cooked al dente and drained

6-8 main dish servings

In large skillet, melt butter. Add bacon and cook, stirring for 1 minute. Add peppers and pea pods. Cook for 1 minute, stirring to coat with butter. Stir in cream, salt and pepper; heat to boiling. Lower heat and simmer, stirring occasionally, until sauce thickens slightly, about 3 minutes. Add Parmesan to sauce and mix until well blended. Toss with warm fettucine and serve immediately.

This dish is a bountiful merger of color and unforgettable flavor.

Pasta

Pasta with Sausage and Cream Sauce

¼ cup butter
1½ pounds sweet Italian sausage, casings removed
2 cups heavy cream
1 cup dry white wine
1 tablespoon minced fresh parsley
½ teaspoon nutmeg
½ cup freshly grated Parmesan cheese
12 ounces pasta, cooked al dente and drained
½ cup freshly grated Parmesan cheese
1 tablespoon minced fresh parsley

6 servings

In large skillet, melt butter. Stir in sausage and fry until brown. Remove sausage and drain grease. Return sausage to skillet and stir in cream, wine, 1 tablespoon parsley, nutmeg and ½ cup Parmesan. Simmer for 3-4 minutes. Place pasta in heated serving dish and stir in 2 tablespoons of sausage mixture and remaining ½ cup Parmesan. Toss until pasta is coated. Pour remaining sausage mixture over pasta. Sprinkle with 1 tablespoon parsley.

Here is a dish that is so sweet and fresh it can never fail to please.

West 38th Street Pasta Special

½ pound sweet Italian sausage, casings removed
½ pound hot Italian sausage, casings removed
½ cup olive oil
½ cup butter
12 large mushrooms, sliced
2 cloves garlic, minced
1 large green bell pepper, seeded and chopped
1 cup chopped green onions
¼ cup minced fresh parsley
¼ cup minced fresh basil or 2 teaspoons dried basil
12 ounces spinach fettucine, cooked al dente and drained
⅔ cup freshly grated Parmesan cheese
1 cup sour cream

6 servings

In large skillet, cook sausages over medium-high heat until brown. Remove sausage and set aside. Drain grease. Add olive oil and butter to skillet and sauté mushrooms, garlic, green pepper, green onions, parsley and basil until tender. Stir in sausage. Place fettucine in heated serving dish. Add sausage mixture, Parmesan and sour cream. Toss gently and serve immediately.

The sour cream brings to life the savory and sweet combination of sausage, mushrooms and peppers!

Pasta

Marinated Chicken Breasts in Pepper Sauce

Marinade:

½	cup olive oil
¼	cup minced fresh basil
3	tablespoons fresh lemon juice
1	tablespoon crushed red pepper flakes
2	teaspoons minced garlic
2	pounds boneless chicken breast
3	tablespoons unsalted butter
1	medium red bell pepper, cut into julienne strips
1	medium yellow bell pepper, cut into julienne strips
½	cup dry white wine
½	cup chicken broth
2	cups heavy cream
1	cup sliced mushrooms
2	tablespoons unsalted butter
½	teaspoon salt
¾	cup freshly grated Parmesan cheese
¼	cup minced fresh basil
12	ounces spinach fettucine, cooked al dente and drained

6-8 main dish servings

In shallow dish, mix marinade ingredients. Add chicken, turning to coat. Cover and refrigerate overnight.

In large skillet, melt 3 tablespoons butter and sauté peppers for 2 minutes. Remove peppers; reserve. Stir in wine and chicken broth. Increase heat to high and boil until sauce is reduced to 2 tablespoons, about 5 minutes. Add cream and cook until sauce is reduced by half, about 4 minutes. In another skillet, sauté mushrooms in 2 tablespoons butter over medium-high heat until slightly browned. Add peppers, cream sauce and salt. *At this point pepper sauce can be refrigerated for up to 24 hours.*

Drain chicken, discarding marinade. Broil chicken 4 inches from heat, turning once, cooking until tender and juices run clear. (Chicken may also be grilled.) Discard skin and cut chicken into ½-inch strips.

Stir Parmesan and ¼ cup basil into heated pepper sauce. On heated serving platter, arrange chicken attractively on top of warm fettucine and pour sauce over top to cover. Serve immediately.

The combination of chicken and red and yellow peppers is as much fun for the eye as it is for the palate.

Pasta

Belvedere's Pasta Seafood Extraordinaire

Tomato Sauce:

6	cloves garlic, minced
3	tablespoons olive oil
4	28-ounce cans stewed Italian tomatoes, crushed
2	tablespoons sugar
1	cup minced fresh basil
¼	teaspoon ground white pepper

4	cloves garlic, minced
3	tablespoons olive oil
1	pound large fresh shrimp, peeled and deveined
1	pound sea scallops, muscle removed
1	pound vermicelli, cooked al dente and drained
	freshly grated Parmesan cheese (optional)

6-8 main dish servings
10-12 side dish servings

In 8-quart saucepan, sauté 6 cloves garlic in oil until golden. Add tomatoes, sugar, basil and pepper and simmer uncovered over low heat for 1-1½ hours.

In large skillet, sauté 4 cloves garlic in oil over medium heat for 2 minutes. Add shrimp and scallops and sauté for 3 minutes or until shrimp are pink and scallops opaque. Do not overcook. Add seafood to tomato sauce. Heat through, about 1-2 minutes. Pour sauce over pasta and serve with Parmesan cheese.

The combination of shrimp and scallops provides a delectable flavor in this light tomato sauce.

Linguine alla Shrimp

2	cups mushrooms, sliced
4	shallots, finely chopped
½	cup butter
1	cup dry white wine
1	tablespoon minced fresh tarragon or I teaspoon dried tarragon, crushed
¼	teaspoon salt
⅛	teaspoon ground white pepper
1	pound large shrimp, peeled and deveined
2	medium tomatoes, peeled, seeded and chopped
12	ounces linguine, cooked al dente and drained
¼	cup butter, melted
½	cup freshly grated Parmesan cheese
¼	cup minced fresh parsley
	freshly grated Parmesan cheese

6-8 servings

In large skillet, sauté mushrooms and shallots in butter over medium-high heat for 3-5 minutes, or until tender but not brown. Stir in wine, tarragon, salt, and pepper. Heat to boiling and reduce heat. Simmer uncovered for 12-15 minutes, or until about ⅔ of the liquid is evaporated. Add shrimp to wine mixture. Simmer covered for 2 minutes until shrimp is tender. Stir in tomatoes and heat through. In heated serving dish, toss cooked linguine with ¼ cup melted butter. Add shrimp mixture, Parmesan and parsley. Toss gently until pasta is coated. Sprinkle with additional Parmesan cheese and serve immediately.

This recipe exemplifies the classic simplicity of an exceptional pasta sauce.

Pasta

Angel Hair Pasta with Basil and Crab

½ pound butter
2 tablespoons chopped shallots
2 tablespoons minced fresh basil or
    1 teaspoon dried basil
2 tablespoons minced fresh parsley
3 16-ounce cans peeled and chopped
    tomatoes, drained
½ cup dry white wine
1½ pounds crabmeat or 1 pound mock
    crabmeat
1 pound angel hair pasta, cooked
    al dente and drained
    freshly grated Parmesan cheese

6 main dish servings
8-10 side dish servings

In large skillet, melt butter and sauté shallots, basil and parsley for 2-3 minutes. Stir in tomatoes and heat to boiling. Cook sauce until reduced by half. Add wine and simmer 5 minutes. Add crabmeat and simmer 2-3 minutes. Remove from heat. Place warm pasta in heated serving dish. Top with sauce. Serve with Parmesan.

The delicate angel hair pasta is a wonderful match for the tender crabmeat!

Spinach Trenette Agata (Strings Restaurant)

4 tablespoons butter
1 pound large shrimp, peeled and
    deveined
8 Roma tomatoes, peeled and diced
    (about 2 ½ cups)
½ pound mushrooms, sliced
¼ cup brandy
2 tablespoons minced fresh basil or
    1 teaspoon dried basil
½ teaspoon salt
½ teaspoon freshly ground black
    pepper
1½ cups heavy cream
1 cup freshly grated Parmesan
    cheese
12 ounces fresh spinach trenette
    pasta (similar to linguine),
    cooked al dente and drained

4-6 main dish servings
8-10 side dish servings

In large skillet, melt butter over medium-high heat and sauté shrimp for 2-3 minutes or until shrimp are firm and opaque. Remove shrimp; set aside. Add tomatoes and mushrooms to skillet and sauté for 5 minutes. Stir in brandy, basil, salt and pepper. Add cream and cook until sauce is reduced by ⅓, about 5-7 minutes. Stir in Parmesan. Reduce heat to low and add shrimp to sauce. Stir for 1-2 minutes to heat shrimp. In heated serving dish, pour sauce over warm pasta, toss gently and serve.

A wonderfully smooth and flavorful shrimp dish that family and friends will rave about!

Pasta

Linguine with White Clam Sauce

1	clove garlic, minced
4	tablespoons butter
2	tablespoons all-purpose flour
2	cups bottled clam juice
¼	cup minced fresh parsley or 1 tablespoon dried parsley
1½	teaspoons dried thyme
¼	teaspoon salt
¼	teaspoon freshly ground black pepper
2	cups fresh minced clams or 3 6¼-ounce cans minced clams
12	ounces linguine, cooked al dente and drained

4-6 main dish servings
8-10 side dish servings

In large skillet, sauté garlic in butter over medium-high heat for 1 minute. Whisk in flour until smooth and add clam juice. Whisk until mixed. Add parsley, thyme, salt and pepper. Reduce heat and simmer for 10 minutes or until sauce is reduced by ⅓. Add clams and heat through. Place warm linguine in heated serving dish. Pour sauce over linguine and toss gently. Serve immediately.

The secret of this sauce is reducing the clam juice so the flavor is intensified.

Avocado and Shrimp Fettucine

1	tablespoon butter
1	teaspoon minced garlic
2	tablespoons minced fresh parsley
½	pound shrimp, peeled and deveined
2	tablespoons dry vermouth or white wine
3	tablespoons butter
½	cup heavy cream
¼	cup freshly grated Parmesan cheese
	pinch of crushed red pepper flakes
¼	teaspoon salt
⅛	teaspoon freshly ground black pepper
9	ounces fettucine, cooked al dente and drained
1	avocado, peeled, pitted and cubed

4 servings

In large skillet, heat 1 tablespoon butter over medium-high heat; add minced garlic and cook for 1 minute. Add parsley, shrimp and vermouth and cook for 2 minutes, stirring constantly, until shrimp turn pink. Do not overcook. Transfer shrimp mixture to small bowl.

In same skillet, heat 3 tablespoons butter until melted. Reduce heat to low and add cream, Parmesan and red pepper flakes; cook for 3 minutes, stirring constantly, until cheese melts and sauce is smooth. Stir in salt and pepper.

To serve, place warm fettucine in serving dish, add shrimp mixture and avocado and toss gently to coat thoroughly.

Undoubtedly, a gastronomic treat!

Pasta

Shrimp Alfredo

½ cup butter
1 pound medium shrimp, peeled and
   deveined
1 tablespoon minced green onions
½ teaspoon minced garlic
9 ounces fettucine, cooked al dente
   and drained
4 egg yolks
1 cup half and half
1 cup freshly grated Parmesan
   cheese
2 teaspoons minced fresh parsley
½ teaspoon salt
¼ teaspoon freshly ground black
   pepper

4 main dish servings

In large skillet, melt butter and sauté shrimp, green onions and garlic over moderate heat for 3-4 minutes, or until shrimp are firm and opaque. Remove pan from heat. Stir warm fettucine into shrimp mixture. In medium bowl, beat egg yolks, half and half and Parmesan. Add egg yolk mixture to shrimp mixture and cook over moderate heat until sauce thickens, about 3-4 minutes. Do not boil. Stir in parsley, salt and pepper. Serve immediately.

An astonishingly simple and tantalizing variation of a classic pasta dish.

Scallops with Spinach and Cucumbers

3 tablespoons unsalted butter
4 large shallots, minced
1 10-ounce package frozen chopped
   spinach, thawed and squeezed
   dry
½ teaspoon salt
1 medium cucumber, peeled, seeded
   and chopped (about 1 cup)
1 cup heavy cream
½ teaspoon salt
¼ teaspoon ground nutmeg
¼ teaspoon crushed red pepper
   flakes
8 ounces sea scallops, cut
   horizontally into thirds
9 ounces linguine, cooked al dente
   and drained
¼ cup freshly grated Parmesan
   cheese

4-6 main dish servings
8-10 side dish servings

In large skillet, melt butter over medium heat. Sauté shallots for 3 minutes. Add spinach and ½ teaspoon salt and cook, stirring frequently, until wilted, about 2 minutes. Add cucumber and cook over medium heat until cucumber begins to soften, about 2 minutes. Stir in cream, ½ teaspoon salt, nutmeg and red pepper flakes. Heat to boiling. Reduce heat and simmer until sauce thickens, 5-6 minutes. *Can be made ahead to this point and refrigerated for 6-24 hours.*

Gently mix scallops into heated sauce and cook until just opaque, about 30 seconds; do not overcook. In large, heated serving dish, toss warm linguine with scallop mixture. Sprinkle with Parmesan and serve immediately.

A dish that will be well received as a dinner or luncheon entrée.

Pasta

Spinach Pasta with Scallops

2	tablespoons butter
2	tablespoons olive oil
¾	pound bay scallops
½	green bell pepper, seeded and diced
1	large tomato, seeded and diced
4	green onions, chopped
10	mushrooms, sliced
2	cups heavy cream
¼	cup freshly grated Parmesan cheese
9	ounces spinach fettucine, cooked al dente and drained
5	ounces Boursin garlic cheese
	salt and freshly ground black pepper to taste

4-6 main dish servings
8-10 side dish servings

In large skillet over moderate heat, melt butter with oil. Add scallops and sauté 2-3 minutes or until opaque. Stir in green pepper, tomato, green onions and mushrooms. Sauté for 4 minutes. Add cream and Parmesan cheese and stir until well blended. Reduce heat and simmer until sauce thickens, about 8-10 minutes. Add Boursin cheese and stir until blended. In heated serving dish, toss warm fettucine with scallop mixture. Add salt and pepper to taste. Serve immediately.

The Boursin cheese adds a savory flavor to the tender scallops.

Linguine Imperial

¼	pound butter
1	tablespoon olive oil
2	cloves garlic, minced
¼	cup minced fresh parsley
2	tablespoons minced fresh basil or 2 teaspoons dried basil
1½	pounds fresh crabmeat or 1 pound mock crabmeat
4	egg yolks, lightly beaten
½	cup freshly grated Parmesan cheese
1	cup heavy cream
½	teaspoon salt
9	ounces linguine, cooked al dente and drained

4 main dish servings
6-8 side dish servings

In large skillet, heat together butter and oil. Sauté garlic, parsley and basil over low heat for 5 minutes. Stir in crabmeat and cook for 2 minutes. Remove from heat. In small bowl, combine egg yolks, Parmesan, cream and salt. In heated serving dish, toss warm linguine with egg mixture. Add crabmeat mixture and toss gently until combined. Serve immediately.

A seafood lover's delight! This rich entrée has a succulent and unique flavor.

Pasta

Pasta col Cavalfiore

1	cup golden raisins
1	cup warm water
2-3	cups small cauliflower flowerets (the smaller the better)
1	cup chopped onion
¼	cup olive oil
1	28-ounce can stewed tomatoes, chopped
¼	teaspoon salt
⅛	teaspoon freshly ground black pepper
1	pound medium pasta shells, cooked al dente and drained
1	cup freshly grated Romano cheese
¼	cup chopped fresh basil salt and freshly ground black pepper to taste

8-10 side dish servings

Soak raisins in water for 20 minutes. Blanch cauliflower in boiling water for 2 minutes; drain. In large skillet, sauté onion in olive oil until transparent. Add tomatoes, salt and pepper and simmer covered for 20 minutes. Drain raisins and stir into cauliflower mixture. Simmer 10 minutes.

In large, heated serving dish, toss warm pasta with sauce, Romano cheese and basil. Season with salt and pepper. Serve immediately.

An exquisite dish. The tastes of tomatoes and raisins come through transparently sweet and fresh, complementing the cauliflower.

Fettucine with Zucchini Sauce

½	cup chopped onion
3	tablespoons minced fresh parsley
2-3	cloves garlic, minced
¼	cup olive oil
6	small zucchini, finely diced (about 4 cups)
2	cups tomato sauce
2	tablespoons minced fresh basil or 1 teaspoon dried basil
1	bay leaf
½	teaspoon salt
¼	teaspoon freshly ground black pepper
½	pound lean ground beef
1	pound fettucine, cooked al dente and drained
3	tablespoons freshly grated Parmesan cheese

4 main dish servings

In large skillet, sauté onion, parsley and garlic in oil for 10 minutes. Stir in zucchini and simmer for 5 minutes. Add tomato sauce, basil, bay leaf, salt and pepper. Cook over low heat for 30 minutes. Remove bay leaf. In separate skillet, cook beef until brown; pour off grease. Add beef to vegetable sauce. Put warm pasta into large, heated serving dish. Pour sauce over pasta, sprinkle with Parmesan and serve immediately.

The coupling of ground beef and zucchini makes a tasty entrée.

Pasta

Spinach Linguine
with Eggplant Sauce Sala

1	medium eggplant, peeled and diced (about 1 pound)
½	teaspoon salt
2	tablespoons olive oil
2	cloves garlic, crushed
3	shallots, chopped
¼	teaspoon crushed red pepper flakes
1	28-ounce can Italian plum tomatoes with juice, coarsely chopped
¼	cup minced fresh parsley
12	ounces spinach linguine, cooked al dente and drained
3	tablespoons freshly grated Parmesan cheese

6-8 servings

Soak eggplant in salted cold water for 30 minutes. Rinse and pat dry. In large skillet, heat oil and sauté garlic, shallots, red pepper flakes and eggplant for 8-10 minutes. Add tomatoes and parsley and cook for another 10-15 minutes. Pour 1 cup of sauce into heated serving dish and add pasta. Sprinkle with Parmesan and toss. Add remaining sauce, toss gently and serve.

Soaking the eggplant eliminates any lingering sharpness and lets a sweeter and milder flavor emerge.

Primavera Pie

9	ounces angel hair pasta, cooked al dente and drained
2	tablespoons butter
2	eggs, beaten
⅓	cup freshly grated Parmesan cheese
1	medium red bell pepper, cut into julienne strips
1	medium onion, thinly sliced and separated into rings
1	clove garlic, minced
¼	cup minced fresh basil or 2 teaspoons dried basil
2	tablespoons butter
2	cups broccoli flowerets, cooked and drained
1½	cups cooked and cubed chicken or turkey
⅓	cup freshly grated Parmesan cheese
⅓	cup heavy cream
1	egg
	freshly grated Parmesan cheese

6 servings

In large bowl, mix hot pasta with 2 tablespoons butter, 2 eggs and ⅓ cup Parmesan cheese. Pour into well-greased 9-inch deep dish pie plate and form a crust. Set aside.

In medium skillet, sauté pepper, onion, garlic and basil in 2 tablespoons butter for 5 minutes, or until pepper is tender. Stir in broccoli, chicken and ⅓ cup Parmesan. Remove from heat.

In small bowl, whisk together cream and 1 egg. Stir into vegetable mixture. Spoon vegetable mixture into pasta crust. Cover with greased foil. Bake at 350 degrees for 25 minutes. Remove and let stand 5 minutes before serving. Sprinkle with additional Parmesan.

An aesthetically pleasing dish and a great use for leftover chicken or turkey.

Pasta

Garden Linguine

2	tablespoons olive oil
½	cup butter
¾	cup chopped green onions
2	cloves garlic, minced
½	pound mushrooms, sliced
1	medium zucchini, sliced
2	medium carrots, cut into julienne strips
1	cup snow pea pods, sliced in half diagonally
1	pound asparagus, trimmed and sliced
½	cup chicken broth
1	cup heavy cream
2	tablespoons minced fresh basil, or 1 teaspoon dried basil
2	tablespoons minced fresh parsley
¼	teaspoon salt
¼	teaspoon freshly ground black pepper
9	ounces linguine, cooked al dente and drained
1	cup freshly grated Parmesan cheese

4 main dish servings
6-8 side dish servings

In large skillet, heat olive oil and butter. Stir in green onions, garlic, mushrooms, zucchini, carrots, snow peas and asparagus, and simmer until tender. Stir in broth, cream, basil, parsley, salt and pepper. Simmer for 3-4 minutes. In heated serving dish, toss linguine with vegetable mixture and Parmesan. Serve immediately.

There is a rich garden color and flavor to this dish!

Fettucine Primavera

4	medium zucchini, sliced (3-4 cups)
2	cups small broccoli flowerets
⅓	cup pine nuts
¼	cup olive oil
1	tablespoon minced garlic
4	large tomatoes, skinned and chopped (about 4 cups)
1	cup snow pea pods, cut in half diagonally
¼	teaspoon salt
¼	teaspoon freshly ground black pepper
8-10	ounces fettucine, cooked al dente and drained
4	tablespoons butter
½	cup heavy cream
1	cup freshly grated Parmesan cheese
¼	cup minced fresh basil or 1 teaspoon dried basil

6-8 servings

Blanch zucchini in boiling water for 1 minute and drain. Blanch broccoli for 3-4 minutes in boiling water and drain. On cookie sheet, toast pine nuts about 2-3 minutes under broiler until light brown. In a large skillet, heat olive oil. Add garlic, tomatoes, zucchini, broccoli, snow pea pods, salt and pepper. Sauté briefly, about 2-3 minutes. Add fettucine to skillet along with butter, cream, Parmesan, pine nuts and basil. Toss gently and serve.

A colorful side dish that will enhance the flavor of poultry, fish and beef.

Pasta

Pasta with Broccoli

1	pound broccoli
¼	cup olive oil
3	cloves garlic, halved
1	tablespoon minced fresh parsley
½	teaspoon salt
¼	teaspoon freshly ground black pepper
1	pound penne pasta, cooked al dente and drained
¼	cup freshly grated Parmesan cheese

6-8 servings

Trim off and discard ends of broccoli stems. Cut off flowerets and chop stems. Cook broccoli in boiling, salted water until tender, about 8-10 minutes. Drain well. In large skillet, heat olive oil and sauté garlic until golden. Discard garlic. Add broccoli, parsley, salt and pepper. Sauté for 2 minutes. In heated serving dish, toss warm pasta with broccoli mixture. Sprinkle with Parmesan and serve immediately.

An easy to prepare side dish that is extremely tasty.

Linguine in Broccoli Cream Sauce

1½	pounds fresh broccoli
¼	cup butter
½	teaspoon salt
⅛	teaspoon freshly ground black pepper
⅛	teaspoon ground nutmeg
2	cloves garlic, sliced in half
1	cup heavy cream
½	cup freshly grated Parmesan cheese, divided
1	pound linguine, cooked al dente and drained

8-10 side dish servings

Trim off and discard ends of broccoli stems, leaving 6-inch stalks. Cut off flowerets and slice stems. In large saucepan, cook broccoli in 1 quart boiling, salted water for 8-10 minutes. Drain, reserving ¼ cup liquid. Set aside liquid and 1 cup flowerets.

In food processor with steel blade, combine remaining broccoli, reserved liquid, butter, salt, pepper and nutmeg. Turn on processor and drop garlic through feed tube. Process until smooth. *Can be made ahead to this point. Cover and let stand at room temperature for up to 2 hours.*

In saucepan, heat cream over medium heat and stir in broccoli sauce. Add ¼ cup Parmesan and heat to simmering. In heated serving dish, toss warm pasta with remaining ¼ cup Parmesan. Pour broccoli sauce over pasta and mix thoroughly. Garnish with reserved flowerets and serve immediately.

One of the simplest and yet most impressive pasta dishes to present.

Pasta

Spinach Pasta with Mushrooms and Artichokes

2	cloves garlic, minced
1	pound mushrooms, sliced
½	cup butter
2	tablespoons flour
⅓	cup dry white wine
1	14-ounce can artichoke hearts, drained and quartered
½	cup freshly grated Parmesan cheese
2	cups half and half
¼	teaspoon salt
½	teaspoon freshly ground black pepper
12	ounces spinach fettucine, cooked al dente and drained

6 main dish servings

In large saucepan, sauté garlic and mushrooms in butter until tender, about 3-5 minutes. Remove from pan with slotted spoon; reserve. Add flour and wine to pan and cook until thickened, about 4 minutes. Add reserved mushrooms, artichokes, Parmesan and half and half. Stir in salt and pepper. Heat thoroughly, but do not boil. In heated serving dish, gently toss fettucine with mushroom and artichoke mixture. Serve immediately.

In this combination, artichokes supply most of the flavor, mushrooms impart texture, and the cream sauce provides sweetness.

Lodestone Lasagne

Sauce:

1	cup chopped onion
2	cloves garlic, crushed
1	28-ounce can crushed tomatoes
1	16-ounce can crushed tomatoes
1	6-ounce can tomato paste
¼	cup minced fresh parsley
1	tablespoon packed light brown sugar
1	teaspoon salt
1½	teaspoons dried oregano
¼	teaspoon dried thyme
1	bay leaf
1	whole stalk celery, leaves removed
2	cups water
1½-2	pounds Italian sausage in casings
1	cup water
8	ounces lasagne noodles, cooked al dente and drained
1	pound ricotta cheese
1½	pounds mozzarella cheese, sliced

10-12 servings

In large saucepan, combine all sauce ingredients and simmer for 3 hours, stirring occasionally. Remove bay leaf and celery stalk.

In large skillet, cook sausage in water over moderate heat. Cook until water evaporates. Reduce heat to low and brown sausage for 5 minutes. Cut into ½-inch pieces. Add sausage to sauce. In a 9x13-inch pan, layer half of noodles, sauce, ricotta and mozzarella. Repeat layers a second time. Cover with greased foil. Bake at 350 degrees for 1 hour.

A hearty lasagne that family and friends will savor.

Pasta

Veal and Broccoli Lasagne

1	pound ground veal
¼	cup chopped onion
2	cloves garlic, minced
2	tablespoons olive oil
¼	pound mushrooms, chopped
½	green bell pepper, chopped
2	6-ounce cans tomato paste
1	teaspoon dried tarragon
2	tablespoons minced fresh basil or 1 teaspoon dried basil
¼	teaspoon dried oregano
½	teaspoon salt
¼	teaspoon freshly ground black pepper
3	cups water
4	sheets uncooked fresh spinach lasagne or 16 ounces spinach lasagne noodles, cooked al dente and drained
1	cup thinly sliced broccoli flowerets
1½	pounds cottage cheese
1½	pounds mozzarella cheese, shredded
½	cup freshly grated Parmesan cheese

9-12 servings

In large saucepan, brown veal over medium heat and drain. Set aside. In same pan, sauté onion and garlic in oil until transparent. Add veal, mushrooms and green pepper. Cook for 5 minutes. Stir in tomato paste, tarragon, basil, oregano, salt, pepper and water. Simmer over low heat for 10-15 minutes. Spread ¼ cup of sauce on bottom of 9x13-inch pan. Layer the following ingredients at least twice: lasagne noodles, sauce, broccoli, cottage cheese, mozzarella and Parmesan. Top with remaining sauce. Cover with greased foil. Bake at 375 degrees for 1 hour. Remove from oven and let stand for 10 minutes before serving.

An intriguing departure from the usual lasagne, the flavors of veal and broccoli are set off by the spinach noodles.

Three Cheese Pasta

White Sauce:

3	tablespoons butter
3	tablespoons all-purpose flour
¾	teaspoon salt
⅜	teaspoon freshly ground black pepper
3	cups milk, warmed
1	tablespoon butter
½	cup fine bread crumbs
12	ounces egg noodles, cooked al dente and drained
2	tablespoons butter
1	cup freshly grated Parmesan cheese
1	cup diced Swiss cheese
1	cup diced mozzarella cheese
½	cup fine bread crumbs

6-8 servings

To prepare white sauce, melt butter in saucepan over medium heat and stir in flour. Add salt and pepper and heat for 1 minute. Stir in milk. Continue to stir until mixture boils. Remove from heat; set aside.

Coat 3-quart baking dish with 1 tablespoon butter and ½ cup bread crumbs. In medium bowl, toss warm noodles with 2 tablespoons butter. Add cheeses and toss again. Layer ½ noodles in baking dish and cover with ½ white sauce. Repeat layers. Sprinkle with ½ cup bread crumbs. Bake at 350 degrees for 30 minutes or until golden brown. Serve immediately.

A creamy melting pot of extraordinary cheese flavors.

Pasta

VERY GOOD LASAGNE WAS DONE IN 30 MINUTES

Lasagne Verdi e Bianco

2 medium onions, finely chopped
¼ cup butter
3 cloves garlic, minced
½ cup chopped almonds
5 10-ounce packages frozen spinach,
   thawed and squeezed dry
¼ teaspoon salt
⅛ teaspoon freshly ground black
   pepper
¼ teaspoon ground nutmeg
⅓ cup raisins
16 ounces ricotta cheese
4 green onions, minced
1 egg yolk, lightly beaten
3 tablespoons minced fresh parsley
3 tablespoons minced fresh basil or
   1 teaspoon dried basil
2 cups shredded mozzarella cheese
1½ cups freshly grated Parmesan
   cheese
¾ cup shredded Swiss cheese
8 ounces lasagne noodles, cooked
   al dente and drained

Herbed Tomato Béchamel Sauce:
¼ cup butter
¼ cup all-purpose flour
3 tablespoons minced fresh basil or
   1 teaspoon dried basil
⅛ teaspoon dried thyme
   pinch dried oregano
2 cups milk
1 10½-ounce can tomato purée
3 egg yolks
¼ teaspoon salt
⅛ teaspoon freshly ground black
   pepper
¼ teaspoon ground nutmeg
1 tablespoon butter, softened

10-12 servings

Prepare **Herbed Tomato Béchamel Sauce;** set aside.

In large skillet, sauté onion in butter until brown and caramelized, about 25 minutes. Stir in garlic and almonds and cook about 30 seconds. Mix in spinach and cook, stirring frequently, until dry. Remove from heat and add salt, pepper and nutmeg. Blend in raisins and set aside.

In medium bowl, combine ricotta, green onions, egg yolk, parsley and basil and blend well. In another medium bowl, combine mozzarella, Parmesan and Swiss cheeses. Set aside 1¼ cup of shredded cheese mixture for topping.

Whisk through béchamel sauce several times to lighten. Spread thin layer of sauce over bottom of generously greased 9x13-inch baking dish. Layer the following ingredients in order at least 3 times: pasta, spinach mixture, ricotta-herb mixture and cheese mixture. Finish with layer of lasagne noodles. Pour remaining sauce over lasagne and sprinkle with reserved cheese. Bake at 375 degrees for 45-60 minutes or until bubbly and lightly browned. Turn off heat; let lasagne sit in oven for 20 minutes before cutting.

3½ cups

In large saucepan, melt butter over medium-low heat until bubbly. Remove from heat and whisk in flour, basil, thyme and oregano. Cook, stirring constantly, about 3-5 minutes. Do not let flour brown. Gradually whisk in milk. Increase heat to medium-high and cook, stirring constantly, until sauce thickens. Stir in tomato purée. Remove from heat and let cool for 5 minutes. Whisk in egg yolks, salt, pepper and nutmeg. Transfer to bowl and spread softened butter over sauce to prevent skin from forming.

This variation of a classic dish maintains its own clearly established character. It is richly laced with tomato béchamel, spinach and a creamy cheese mixture.

Pasta

Marvelous Manicotti

Sauce:
- 2   28-ounce cans crushed tomatoes
- ½   cup olive oil
- ¼   cup diced onion
- 2   cloves garlic, minced

Filling:
- 2   pounds ricotta cheese
- 2   cups shredded mozzarella cheese
- ½   cup freshly grated Parmesan cheese
- 2   eggs, beaten
- ½   teaspoon salt
- ⅛   teaspoon freshly ground black pepper
- 1   tablespoon minced fresh parsley

Crêpes:
- 3   eggs
- ½   cup milk
- ½   cup chicken broth
- 3   tablespoons butter, melted
- ¾   cup all-purpose flour
- ¼   teaspoon salt
- freshly grated Parmesan cheese

8-10 servings

In 3-quart saucepan combine all sauce ingredients and simmer for 30-45 minutes.

In large bowl, combine ricotta, mozzarella, Parmesan and eggs. Beat until fluffy, about 2 minutes. Stir in salt, pepper and parsley. Set aside.

In food processor or blender, combine all crêpe ingredients and mix until smooth, about 2 minutes. Heat 8 or 10-inch crêpe pan over medium-high heat until just hot enough to sizzle a drop of water. For each crêpe, pour just enough batter to cover bottom of pan, tipping and tilting pan to move batter quickly over bottom. Cook until lightly browned on bottom and dry on top. Remove from pan and stack between layers of waxed paper until ready to fill.

Spread ¼ cup filling on each crêpe. Fold up bottom, fold in sides, and roll to close. Place seam-side down in 9x13-inch baking dish. (Two pans may be needed for entire recipe.) Place filled crêpes side by side, 5 or 6 per pan.

Pour sauce over crêpes. Sprinkle with additional Parmesan. Bake uncovered at 350 degrees for 30-45 minutes or until bubbly.

Crêpes enhance the lightness of the cheese filling and add a delicate flavor. However, manicotti pasta may be substituted for crêpes. Filling can also be used to stuff large shells.

Spinach Cabrini

- 9   ounces spaghetti, broken into pieces, cooked al dente and drained
- ½   cup butter, melted
- 2   10-ounce packages frozen cut leaf spinach, cooked and drained
- 4   cups shredded Monterey Jack cheese
- ¼   pound mushrooms, sliced
- 2   cups sour cream
- ¼   cup diced onion
- dash of dried oregano
- ¼   teaspoon salt
- ¼   teaspoon freshly ground black pepper

8-10 servings

In large bowl, stir together all ingredients. Place in 9x13-inch casserole dish. Bake uncovered at 350 degrees for 45 minutes.

A delightful meatless dish that is a satisfying answer to the call of hunger.

Fish & Seafood

Fish & Seafood

Mussels Bonito

Mussels:
- 2 pounds mussels
- 1 cup dry white wine
- 2 bay leaves

Relish:
- 3 bacon slices
- 1 small red bell pepper, finely diced
- 1 small white onion, finely diced
- 1 jalapeño chile, seeded and finely diced
- 2 cloves garlic, minced
- 2½ cups fresh corn kernels (about 3 ears)
- 3 tablespoons chopped fresh cilantro
- 3 tablespoons balsamic vinegar
- salt and freshly ground black pepper to taste

Mayonnaise:
- 4 egg yolks
- 2 large Anaheim chiles, peeled, seeded and coarsely chopped
- 1 tablespoon fresh lemon juice
- 1 cup corn oil

Garnish:
- lemon slices
- sprigs of cilantro

6-8 servings

Scrub and debeard mussels. In large stockpot, combine mussels, wine and bay leaves; cover and steam over medium-high heat, shaking pot occasionally for 3-4 minutes, until mussels open. Remove opened mussels. Steam remaining mussels for 3 more minutes; discard any that do not open. Ladle liquid through strainer lined with several layers of dampened cheesecloth. Reserve liquid. Remove mussels from shells. Reserve half of each mussel shell. Cool mussels completely.

In heavy skillet over medium-high heat, fry bacon until very crisp. Remove bacon and drain on paper towels. Add bell pepper, onion, jalapeño and garlic to skillet and cook, stirring frequently, until soft and lightly caramelized, about 8 minutes. Stir in corn and cilantro. Crumble in bacon. Transfer mixture to bowl. Stir in 2 tablespoons mussel liquid and vinegar. Season with salt and pepper. Cool relish completely.

To make mayonnaise, purée yolks, Anaheim chiles and lemon juice in blender. With machine running, add oil in slow stream. Transfer to another bowl and season with salt and pepper.

To serve, arrange shell halves on platter. Place 1 teaspoon relish in each shell. Top with mussels, then mayonnaise. Garnish with lemon slices and sprigs of cilantro. Pass remaining relish separately.

This makes a delicious first course or a unique cold hors d'oeuvre.

Fish & Seafood

Mussels Dijon
(The Fish Market
Restaurant & Oyster Bar)

2	pounds mussels
2	tablespoons finely chopped green onions
2	cloves garlic, minced
1	teaspoon finely chopped shallots freshly ground black pepper to taste
½	cup dry white wine
1	cup Dijon mustard
2	cups heavy cream
3	tablespoons minced fresh parsley French bread

2 main course servings
4 first course servings

Scrub and debeard mussels. In large stockpot, combine green onions, garlic, shallots, pepper, wine and mussels. Heat to boiling, cover and steam covered for 3-5 minutes or until mussels open. With slotted spoon, transfer mussels to a heated dish. Discard any unopened mussels.

Stir mustard and cream into liquid remaining in kettle. Boil mixture, stirring constantly, for 3-5 minutes or until sauce is reduced by half and thickened. Return mussels to stockpot and add parsley. Stir to coat mussels with sauce. Serve with French bread to soak up sauce.

Perfect for supper served with a crisp green salad, a chilled Muscadet and crusty French bread.

Mussels with Garlic,
Basil and Tomatoes

1-1¼	pounds mussels per serving
¼	cup dry vermouth per serving
1	clove garlic, crushed, per serving
¼	teaspoon dried basil per serving
¼	cup chopped tomatoes

1 serving

Scrub and debeard mussels. Discard any that are open. In a large stockpot, combine vermouth, garlic and basil. Place stockpot over high heat; add mussels. Cover and steam until mussels open, about 5-6 minutes. Shake pot frequently. When mussels are open, remove to heated serving dish, using a slotted spoon. Discard any that do not open. Add tomatoes to remaining stock and simmer for a few minutes. Pour stock over mussels.

*Mussels are more popular and available now than ever before. Serve as a first course or as a light main course with a salad and **Parmesan Bread Sticks.***

Fish & Seafood

Finger-Licking Good Spicy Shrimp

2-3	pounds large shrimp in shell (have fishmonger split and devein)
2	lemons, thinly sliced
1	pound butter
¾	teaspoon dried rosemary
¾	teaspoon dried basil
½	cup Worcestershire sauce
2	teaspoons salt
3	tablespoons freshly ground black pepper
¾	teaspoon Tabasco sauce
3	cloves garlic, peeled and lightly crushed

4-6 servings

In large, shallow, glass baking dish, place shrimp in single layer. Cover with sliced lemons. In saucepan, heat remaining ingredients to boiling. Pour over shrimp and lemons, cover and marinate overnight in refrigerator.

Bring shrimp to room temperature before cooking. Bake shrimp in preheated oven at 450 degrees for 20 minutes.

Relax and enjoy the fun of peeling while you eat! The perfect meal after a game of tennis or round of golf on a warm summer night. Serve with a California Chardonnay and lots of warm crusty French bread for dipping in the sauce.

Clams Casino

6	fresh clams in the shell or 6 ounces fresh clam meat
8	ounces fresh clam meat, diced
1	small green bell pepper, finely chopped
1	small onion, finely chopped
1	teaspoon minced garlic
½	cup butter
1½	cups fine bread crumbs
¼	cup dry white wine
¼	cup fresh lemon juice
2	ounces diced pimiento
½	teaspoon cayenne pepper
½	teaspoon Tabasco sauce
1	teaspoon salt
5	strips thinly sliced bacon

6 servings

Scrub clams and steam open. Remove meat, reserving shells. Dice meat and add to 8 ounces clam meat. Rinse meat extremely well under cold running water to remove any grit; drain well. Wash shells; set aside.

In medium skillet, sauté green pepper, onion and garlic in butter; cool. Add diced clam meat, bread crumbs, wine, lemon juice, pimiento, cayenne pepper, Tabasco sauce and salt; mix well. Divide mixture equally among shells or shell-shaped baking dishes. Cut bacon into narrow strips and place on top of stuffed shells. Place shells on cookie sheet and bake in preheated oven at 350 degrees for 15-20 minutes or until sizzling. Bacon will be brown, but not crispy.

Delicious as a luncheon entrée or an obvious choice for first course fare.

Fish & Seafood

Fish Marinated in Lime Juice and Onions

2   pounds halibut or tuna steaks,
    1½-inch thick, skinned and
    boned
1   cup fresh lime juice, strained
½   cup coarsely chopped onion
2   teaspoons salt
3   medium tomatoes, firm and ripe,
    peeled and chopped
¼   cup coarsely chopped green
    bell pepper
½   cup coarsely chopped green
    onions, including tops
2   hard cooked eggs, chopped
1   cup fresh coconut milk, chilled
    (Have the produce department
    show you how to milk a coconut.)
    lettuce

4-6 servings

Chill steaks briefly in freezer to facilitate cutting. Do not let freeze! With sharp knife, cut steaks lengthwise into ¼-inch slices; cut slices into 1½-inch squares. In deep, glass bowl, combine lime juice, onion and salt. Add fish and stir slowly until evenly coated. Cover and marinate overnight in refrigerator, stirring occasionally. Fish will "cook" in this marinade, and be "done" when firm and opaque.

To serve, drain fish and squeeze slightly to remove excess moisture. Place fish in serving bowl, add tomatoes, green peppers, green onions, eggs and coconut milk. Toss lightly until well combined. Serve on individual plates lined with lettuce leaves.

It is imperative that a glass bowl is used to marinate the fish. Fish will not "cook" properly in plastic or metal.

Oven Poached Whole Salmon

1   whole boned salmon, 6-8 pounds
2   lemons, sliced
2   onions, sliced
12   whole peppercorns
2   cups dry white wine

8 servings

In large roasting pan such as a turkey roaster, place a large piece of cheesecloth that extends over the edge of the pan to provide handles to lift fish from the pan. Place whole fish on top of the cheesecloth and add lemon, onions and peppercorns. Pour wine over the fish. Poach at 350 degrees for 45-60 minutes or until fish flakes easily with a fork. Skin salmon after poaching for a prettier presentation. Serve warm or chilled. (This poaching method can also be used to poach salmon steaks. Reduce recipe by ½ if poaching 4 steaks, and cook for 15-20 minutes or until steaks flake when tested with a fork.)

*Serve with **Cucumber Sauce, Horseradish Sauce** or **Green Sauce.***

Smoked Trout

Brine:

2	large onions, unpeeled, quartered
2	large bunches fresh dill or 2 tablespoons dried dill weed
2	bunches parsley
6	cloves garlic, unpeeled
3	large shallots, unpeeled
1	4-inch piece ginger root, unpeeled
1¼	cups soy sauce
1	cup red or white wine
½	cup liquid brown sugar
2	tablespoons coarse salt
2	tablespoons onion powder
4	whole cloves
3	bay leaves
1	teaspoon garlic powder
¼	teaspoon mace

10	trout, 8-10 ounces each
½	bag hickory or other wood chips (4 pints)
	charcoal briquets
	vegetable cooking spray

Condiments:

2	heads Bibb lettuce
2	large onions, chopped
3	eggs, hard cooked, chopped
¾	cup capers, drained
3	lemons, cut into thin wedges
	Horseradish Sauce

20 servings

To make brine, combine onions, dill, parsley, garlic, shallots and ginger in food processor and purée. Turn into glass or enamel dish just large enough to hold fish. Add soy sauce, wine, liquid brown sugar, salt, onion powder, cloves, bay leaves, garlic powder and mace; mix well. Add enough cold water (about 2 cups) to raise depth of brine 3-inches and stir thoroughly. Add fish and just enough water to cover. Refrigerate 24 hours, turning several times.

Soak hickory chips in water overnight.

To smoke fish, prepare barbecue grill by heaping briquets on one side of grill (start with about 30 for large grill). Ignite and burn until coals glow and gray ash forms.

Set drip pan opposite briquets. Remove fish from brine and wipe dry.

Pile hickory chips over briquets. Set grill rack in place and coat side over drip pan with vegetable cooking spray. Immediately set fish over drip pan and tightly cover barbecue. Leave one or two vents open to allow smoke to escape. Smoke until fish flakes when tested with fork, about 8 minutes per pound. (Time will depend on weather; if temperature is quite cold, it can take 45-60 minutes or longer). Add coals as necessary if briquets begin to burn down.

Transfer fish to large platter and let cool. Cover and refrigerate until 1 hour before serving. *Can be made 3 days ahead.*

To serve, separate lettuce leaves carefully, using only those that form a perfect cup. Place chopped onions in sieve lined with paper towel to dry slightly. Place fish on serving platter and surround with lettuce cups alternately filled with onions, eggs, capers and lemon wedges. Pass **Horseradish Sauce** separately.

A 10-12 pound salmon trout may be substitued for the smaller trout; allow 2-3 days marinating time and 8 minutes per pound cooking time. This is a terrific first course or a delicious light dinner and is sure to please your favorite fisherman.

Fish & Seafood

Fillet of Sole Stuffed with Shrimp

10	ounces large shrimp, cooked, peeled and deveined
8	ounces feta cheese, room temperature
2	tablespoons water
2	cups finely chopped spinach
8	ounces whole water chestnuts, quartered and drained
3	green onions, including tops, chopped
3	leaves fresh basil, chopped
6	sole fillets, 4-ounces each salt and freshly ground black pepper, to taste
½	cup dry white wine
6	tomato slices, ½-inch thick
6	leaves fresh basil

6 servings

Set aside 3 shrimp and chop remainder. In medium bowl, crumble cheese and blend in water. Add chopped shrimp, spinach, water chestnuts and ¼ of the green onions. Rinse sole under cold water, pat dry and sprinkle with salt and pepper. Divide shrimp mixture among fillets, spreading evenly. Starting at narrow end, roll up fillets, secure with wooden picks, and arrange in baking dish. Pour wine into dish. Sprinkle with any remaining filling, cover and bake in preheated oven at 325 degrees until sole is opaque and filling is heated through, about 15-20 minutes.

While fish is cooking, arrange tomato slices on baking sheet. Sprinkle with salt and pepper. Set basil leaf on each tomato. Bake until heated through. Transfer sole and tomato to heated plates. Slice reserved shrimp in half. Top each portion with shrimp half. Sprinkle with remaining onions. Serve immediately.

*Serve with **Creamy Lemon Rice.***

Shrimp and Scallops in Orange Sauce

	fresh lemon juice
12	jumbo shrimp, peeled and deveined
16	sea scallops, cleaned all-purpose flour
4	tablespoons margarine
2	shallots, finely chopped
2	cloves garlic, minced
2	tablespoons margarine
¼	cup dry vermouth
⅔	cup fresh orange juice
1	cup heavy cream
4	leaves fresh basil, chopped
1	cup mandarin orange slices

4 servings

Squeeze a little lemon juice on shrimp and scallops; toss them lightly in flour. In large skillet, sauté shrimp and scallops in 4 tablespoons margarine; set aside. In another skillet, sauté shallots and garlic in 2 tablespoons margarine. Pour vermouth over shallots and reduce by ⅓. Add orange juice and reduce by ⅓-½. Add heavy cream and cook mixture about 10 minutes. Add basil, shrimp and scallops. Heat quickly and serve. Sprinkle orange slices over each serving.

A delicious combination of flavors and colors which is good served with plain rice.

Fish & Seafood

Fish Broccoli Roll Ups

1   bunch fresh broccoli or 1 10-ounce
      package frozen broccoli
4   fish fillets (orange roughy,
      flounder or sole)
    salt and freshly ground
      black pepper to taste
    juice of 1 lemon
2   tablespoons butter
2   tablespoons all-purpose flour
1   cup half and half
1   tablespoon dry sherry
    grated peel of 1 lemon
½   cup slivered almonds

4 servings

Steam broccoli until tender. Arrange steamed broccoli spears into four bundles with flowerets at both ends. Wrap one fillet around each bundle. Arrange seam side down in 9-inch square glass baking dish. Sprinkle with salt, pepper and lemon juice. In medium saucepan, melt butter and stir in flour. Add half and half and heat to boiling. Stir in sherry and lemon peel. Pour over fillets and sprinkle with almonds. Bake at 350 degrees for 20-25 minutes, until fish flakes when tested with a fork.

This entrée is so pretty that it is worthy of company, but too easy to save for special occasions. Serve with rice and a fresh fruit salad.

Sole with Grapes in Avocado Sauce

1   cup plain yogurt
1   small avocado, peeled, pitted
      and chopped
2   cloves garlic
½   teaspoon dried basil
    juice of one lemon
¾   cup green grapes
½   cup wheat germ
½   cup whole wheat flour
    salt and ground white pepper
      to taste
4   large sole fillets
1   tablespoon vegetable oil
    lemon wedges

4 servings

Place yogurt, avocado, garlic, basil and lemon juice in blender. Process until smooth. Transfer to medium saucepan. Add grapes and set aside for no longer than 2 hours.

Combine wheat germ, flour, salt and pepper on large plate. Dredge fish in flour mixture to coat well. Heat oil in large non-stick skillet. Add fish and sauté until lightly brown, about 3 minutes on each side. Heat avocado mixture over low heat until just warm; pour mixture over fish and serve immediately.

*The avocado sauce tastes rich and creamy, but don't be fooled, yogurt is the main ingredient. This is especially good served with **Garden Rice Pilaf.***

Fish & Seafood

Greek Style Shrimp with Feta Cheese

1	teaspoon finely chopped garlic
¼	cup olive oil
3	tablespoons butter
1	pound medium shrimp, peeled and deveined
3	cups Del Monte tomato wedges, drained
¼	cup bottled clam juice
1	teaspoon dried oregano
1	teaspoon crushed red pepper flakes
3	tablespoons capers, drained
	salt and freshly ground black pepper to taste
¼	pound feta cheese

2-4 servings

In large skillet, sauté garlic in olive oil and butter; remove and discard garlic. Sauté shrimp until pink; remove from pan. Add tomatoes and reduce by ⅓. Add clam juice, oregano, pepper flakes, capers, salt and pepper. Mix well. Divide ½ of sauce among individual baking dishes. Divide shrimp evenly among dishes, and spoon remaining sauce over shrimp. Crumble feta cheese over top and bake in preheated oven at 350 degrees for 10-15 minutes.

Feta cheese will brown but not melt in this recipe.

Fisherman's Fantasy

2	cups thinly sliced leeks, including 1-inch of green stalks
2	cloves garlic, minced
3	boiling potatoes, peeled, quartered lengthwise, and cut into ½-inch pieces
¼	cup olive oil
¼	cup chopped oil-cured black olives
½	cup dry white wine
¼	cup minced fresh parsley
2	tomatoes, peeled and chopped
1	teaspoon dried basil
1½	pounds fish fillets (cod, bass or halibut), cut into 6 portions with thinner tail sections folded under for even thickness
½	pound shrimp, peeled and deveined
½	pound bay scallops
	fresh lemon juice
	salt and ground white pepper to taste
½	cup fine fresh bread crumbs
½	cup shredded Gruyère cheese
2	tablespoons unsalted butter, melted

4 servings

In large skillet, cook leeks, garlic and potatoes in oil over moderate heat, turning frequently, for 20 minutes or until potatoes are just tender. Stir in olives, wine, parsley, tomatoes and basil. Spoon mixture into a shallow baking dish large enough to hold fish in one layer. Arrange fish in single layer over the mixture and add shrimp and scallops, slightly pressing them down between the fish fillets. Sprinkle with lemon juice, salt and white pepper.

In small bowl combine bread crumbs and Gruyère cheese. Sprinkle mixture over seafood, and drizzle seafood with the butter. Bake in preheated oven at 350 degrees for 30-40 minutes or until the top is golden brown and fish flakes easily.

This is a hearty and different fish casserole to serve on a cold winter night. Oil-cured olives are available in the deli section of major supermarkets.

Fish & Seafood

Shrimp Victoria

1	pound medium shrimp, peeled and deveined
¼	cup minced onion
4	tablespoons butter
½	pound mushrooms, quartered
1	tablespoon butter
1	tablespoon all-purpose flour
	salt and freshly ground black pepper to taste
1	cup sour cream
	red bell pepper strips
	yellow bell pepper strips

4-6 servings

In skillet, sauté shrimp and onion in 4 tablespoons butter until shrimp are pink. Add mushrooms and cook 5 minutes. Stir in remaining butter, flour, salt and pepper. Cook for 1 minute. Slowly stir in sour cream, blending until hot and smooth. Arrange red and yellow pepper strips around shrimp.

This is a terrific luncheon entrée and is beautiful when presented in a chafing dish for a buffet. Serve with a simple lemon rice, made by adding lemon peel and lemon juice to rice while cooking.

Orange Roughy Parmesan

2	pounds orange roughy
2	tablespoons fresh lemon juice
½	cup freshly grated Parmesan cheese
4	tablespoons butter, softened
3	tablespoons mayonnaise
3	tablespoons chopped green onions
¼	teaspoon salt
	freshly ground black pepper to taste
	dash of Tabasco sauce

4 servings

In a buttered baking dish, place fillets in a single layer. Brush with lemon juice. Let stand for 10 minutes. In a small bowl, combine cheese, butter, mayonnaise, green onions, salt, pepper and Tabasco sauce. Broil fillets 3-4 inches under preheated broiler for 5 minutes. Spread with cheese mixture and broil for an additional 2-3 minutes. Watch closely!

Delicious and easy, this will become a family favorite! Sole or any other fresh, skinless, white fish can be substituted for orange roughy.

Island Grilled Halibut

Marinade:

2	cloves garlic
¼	teaspoon ground white pepper
2	tablespoons sugar
⅓	cup soy sauce
6	tablespoons corn oil
3	green onions, chopped
1	tablespoon sesame seeds
6	halibut steaks, 1 inch thick

6 servings

Combine marinade ingredients and pour over halibut steaks. Cover and marinate in refrigerator overnight.

Place steaks on grill and cook 7 minutes per side or until fish flakes easily.

Super simple supper.

Fish & Seafood

Hallelujah Halibut

2	pounds halibut steaks, 1-inch thick
½	cup mayonnaise
½	cup sour cream
2	teaspoons all-purpose flour
1½	teaspoons fresh lemon juice
1	tablespoon minced onion
⅛	teaspoon cayenne pepper
½	cup shredded Cheddar cheese

4-6 servings

Rinse halibut and pat dry. Arrange steaks side by side in greased 8x12-inch baking dish. In small bowl, combine mayonnaise, sour cream and flour, stirring until smooth. Stir in lemon juice, onion and cayenne. Spoon mixture evenly over fish to cover completely. Bake uncovered in preheated oven at 425 degrees for 20-25 minutes, or until fish is opaque in center of thickest part. Sprinkle cheese over fish and continue to bake until cheese is just melted, about 2 minutes. Lift steaks onto warmed platter and serve at once.

Even children who do not like fish will love this!

Red Snapper Florentine

2	10-ounce packages frozen chopped spinach, thawed
¼	cup mayonnaise
¼	cup sour cream
¼	cup freshly grated Parmesan cheese
4	Pacific red snapper fillets, about 1¼ pounds total
2	tablespoons fresh lemon juice
½	teaspoon freshly ground black pepper
	lemon wedges

4 servings

Squeeze spinach to remove as much liquid as possible. In ungreased 9x13-inch baking dish, mix spinach with mayonnaise, sour cream and ½ the Parmesan. Spread evenly in pan. Rinse fish, pat dry and arrange in single layer on top of spinach, overlapping thinner edge of fillets if necessary. *Can be made ahead up to this point. Cover and refrigerate for up to 6 hours.*

Brush lemon juice over fish; sprinkle with pepper and remaining Parmesan. Bake uncovered at 350 degrees for 20-25 minutes or until fish flakes when tested with a fork. Garnish with lemon wedges.

Firm-textured, juicy and flavorful, red snapper stars in this recipe.

Fish & Seafood

Red Snapper with Tomato and Black Olive Vinaigrette

8   red snapper fillets, 3 ounces each
     salt and freshly ground
       black pepper to taste
1   cup peeled and diced tomato
½   cup diced black olives
⅓   cup sliced green onions
1   clove garlic, minced
6   tablespoons olive oil
2   tablespoons rice vinegar
1   pound snow peas, trimmed

8 servings

Preheat broiler. Rinse fish and pat dry. Sprinkle with salt and pepper. Broil, turning once, 9 minutes per 1-inch thickness of fish or until opaque.

While fish is broiling, cook tomato, olives, green onions, garlic, oil and vinegar in double boiler over gently simmering water until heated through, stirring occasionally. Blanch peas in rapidly boiling water until crisp-tender, about 1 minute. Arrange snapper on plates and spoon sauce over fish. Top with peas and serve.

With such glorious colors, this dish needs no garnish.

Puerto Vallarta Red Snapper

6   red snapper fillets
1   teaspoon salt
2   cloves garlic, crushed
½   cup fresh lime juice
3   tablespoons olive oil
2   medium onions, thinly sliced
2   fresh Anaheim chiles (mild
     peppers) OR 2 fresh jalapeño
     chiles (hot peppers), seeded and
     minced
3   pounds fresh tomatoes, peeled, or
     1 28-ounce can stewed tomatoes
2   tablespoons tomato paste
2   bay leaves
¼   teaspoon dried oregano
¼   teaspoon dried thyme
2   tablespoons chopped fresh cilantro
3   tablespoons butter

6 servings

Place fillets in shallow glass dish. In small bowl, combine salt, garlic and lime juice; pour over fillets. Marinate the fillets, covered and refrigerated, for two hours.

Heat olive oil in 2 skillets. Divide onions between the pans and sauté until transparent. Divide chiles, tomatoes, tomato paste, bay leaves, oregano, thyme and cilantro between the two skillets. Simmer for ten minutes. Set aside. Reheat gently before serving.

Ten minutes before serving, heat butter in 2 skillets over medium-high heat. Discard marinade and sauté fillets in skillets for 2-3 minutes per side. Fish will begin to flake when done. Place fillets on warm platter and cover with warm sauce.

This is a colorful and deliciously flavorful dish that can be either medium spicy or hot depending upon which chiles are used.

Fish & Seafood

Tuna Steaks with Tarragon Mustard Sauce

2   ounces macadamia nuts
1   cup dry bread crumbs
    salt and ground white pepper
      to taste
4   tuna steaks, 6-8 ounces each
1   egg, beaten
½   cup water
¾   cup vegetable oil
    whole macadamia nuts, toasted

Tarragon Mustard Sauce:
3   tablespoons unsalted butter
½   cup dry white wine
1   teaspoon dried tarragon
2   teaspoons Dijon mustard
¼   cup heavy cream
    salt and ground white pepper
      to taste

4 servings

Chop 2 ounces macadamia nuts and mix with bread crumbs, salt and pepper. Dredge tuna steaks in crumbs. Mix beaten egg and water. Dip tuna into egg/water mixture and dredge in crumbs again. Set aside. In large skillet, heat oil. Fry tuna steaks for 10 minutes per inch of thickness. Do not crowd. Drain on paper towels and place on warm platter. Serve with *Tarragon Mustard Sauce* and garnish with toasted whole macadamia nuts.

In medium saucepan, melt butter. Add wine, tarragon and mustard. Simmer until reduced by ⅓ to ½. Stirring constantly, pour in cream. Simmer for 1 minute. Season with salt and pepper and serve over tuna.

In this recipe, macadamia nuts beautifully complement the mild flavor of tuna. The mustard sauce adds zest.

Broiled Tuna Steaks with Japanese Sauce

4   yellow fin tuna steaks, 1 inch thick
    sesame oil
1   rounded teaspoon cornstarch
⅓   cup rice vinegar
⅓   cup mirin
⅓   cup soy sauce
1   pound spinach leaves, rinsed,
      stemmed and dried
1   6-ounce box Wagner's Saffron Rice,
      cooked according to directions
3   tablespoons minced crystallized
      ginger

4 servings

Rinse tuna steaks in cold water and pat dry. Rub with sesame oil. Grill over hot coals for 5-7 minutes per side.

Dissolve cornstarch in vinegar. In saucepan, combine vinegar mixture, mirin and soy sauce. Stir and simmer until mixture is a clear, dark brown color and slightly thickened. Remove from heat, but keep warm. Steam spinach leaves for only 2 minutes.

To serve, arrange a bed of spinach on each plate. Place tuna steak on top of spinach, spoon a ring of yellow rice around edge of plate, spoon sauce over tuna, and sprinkle with minced, crystallized ginger.

This may sound complicated, but it is really very easy to do and provides a complete meal on 1 dinner plate. Preparation is easiest if these steps are followed in sequence: start coals, start rice, make sauce, grill fish, steam spinach and assemble.

Fish & Seafood

Grilled Salmon with Ginger Marinade

4	salmon steaks, 6-8 ounces each
	juice of 1 lemon
¼	cup Chinese soy sauce
	salt and freshly ground black pepper to taste
¼	cup sesame oil
2	teaspoons ground ginger
	hickory chips, soaked
	lemon wedges

4 servings

Rinse salmon in cold water and pat dry. In flat dish, sprinkle salmon with lemon juice, soy sauce, salt and pepper, sesame oil and ginger. Cover and refrigerate for at least 2 hours but preferably overnight.

Cook over a gas or charcoal grill, adding hickory chips that have been soaked in water. The hotter the fire, the denser the smoke; use a moderate fire for a mild smoke flavor. Grill, covered, for 5-8 minutes per side until fish is cooked. Remove from grill to heated serving platter and garnish with lemon wedges.

*Eating light means enjoying fish! Serve with **Moroccan Dilled Rice.***

Grilled Swordfish with Avocado Butter

8	small swordfish steaks, or 4 large steaks cut in half
½	cup vegetable oil
⅓	cup soy sauce
¼	cup fresh lemon juice
1	teaspoon grated lemon peel
1	clove garlic, crushed
	sprigs of parsley (extra tasty if marinated with fish)
	lemon wedges

8 servings

Pierce fish on both sides with fork and place in shallow baking dish. In small bowl, combine oil, soy sauce, lemon juice, lemon peel and garlic; pour over fish. Marinate in refrigerator a minimum of 6 hours but preferably overnight, turning occasionally.

Drain fish, reserving marinade. Grill fish over hot coals for 9 minutes per inch of thickness, turning once and brushing often with marinade. Transfer cooked fish to warmed plates and top each steak with dollop of ***Avocado Butter.*** Garnish with sprigs of parsley and lemon wedges.

Avocado Butter:

½	cup butter, softened
½	cup mashed ripe avocado
5	tablespoons fresh lemon juice
2	tablespoons minced fresh parsley
2	cloves garlic, minced
	salt to taste

1 cup

Beat butter until soft and creamy. Beat in avocado, lemon juice, parsley and garlic. Season with salt. Cover and refrigerate.

*Serve with **Couscous and Chanterelles** for a truly special dinner.*

Fish & Seafood

Swordfish Steaks with Mushroom Sauce

3	tablespoons dry white wine
3	tablespoons fresh lemon juice
1	clove garlic, minced
½	teaspoon salt
½	teaspoon freshly ground black pepper
½	teaspoon dried thyme
½	teaspoon dried oregano
2	pounds swordfish steaks, 1 inch thick
3	tablespoons olive oil
½	pound mushrooms, sliced

4 servings

In small bowl, combine wine, lemon juice, garlic, salt, pepper, thyme and oregano. Place fish in plastic bag and add the wine mixture. Marinate in refrigerator at least 2 hours, but preferably overnight. Turn the bag occasionally.

Preheat broiler or grill. Remove fish from bag, reserving marinade. Broil or grill until fish turns opaque, about 4-6 minutes per side (allow about 9 minutes per inch of thickness).

While fish is cooking, heat oil in medium skillet over medium-high heat. Add mushrooms and sauté until tender, about 5 minutes. Stir in marinade and continue cooking until sauce is heated through. Transfer cooked fish to warm platter and pour sauce over steaks.

Serve with steamed asparagus bundles in lemon rings. Remove pulp from sliced lemons to make rings of lemon peel and stuff asparagus spears inside to make bundles.

Grilled Swordfish Steaks

4	swordfish steaks, 6 ounces each
½	cup vegetable oil
3	tablespoons soy sauce
2	tablespoons dry sherry
1½	teaspoons peeled and grated fresh ginger root
1	teaspoon freshly grated orange peel
	freshly ground black pepper to taste
	vegetable oil for brushing grill

4 servings

In large dish, arrange swordfish in single layer. In small bowl, combine oil, soy sauce, sherry, ginger root, orange peel and pepper. Pour marinade over fish and marinate in refrigerator overnight, turning occasionally. Cook over glowing coals, basting with marinade, for 4-5 minutes per side or until firm to touch.

*Grilled swordfish is meaty, moist and especially delicious served with **Spiced Rice.***

Fish & Seafood

Fried Catfish
with Walnuts and Bacon

8	thick slices hickory-smoked bacon
½	cup coarsely chopped walnuts
1	egg
½	cup milk
1	cup all-purpose flour
1	cup yellow corn meal
4	catfish, 1 pound each, skinned and cleaned with heads removed
½	teaspoon salt
½	teaspoon freshly ground black pepper
2	tablespoons fresh lemon juice
4	tablespoons unsalted butter
¼	cup vegetable oil
4	tablespoons unsalted butter
2	tablespoons fresh lemon juice lemon halves

4 servings

Preheat oven to 350 degrees. On baking sheet with sides, cook bacon for 20 minutes, or until crisp. Drain on paper towels and cut into ½-inch pieces.

On cookie sheet, roast walnuts in oven until lightly browned, about 15 minutes; set aside. Leave oven on.

In medium bowl, beat together egg and milk until blended. In shallow pan, mix together flour and cornmeal. Rinse catfish under cold running water; pat dry. Sprinkle fish inside and out with salt, pepper and 2 tablespoons lemon juice.

In large skillet, melt 4 tablespoons butter with oil over medium-high heat. Dip fish into cornmeal-flour mixture to coat lightly. When butter and oil are sizzling, add fish and cook, turning once, until golden brown on each side, about 5 minutes total. Transfer fish to baking pan large enough to hold them in single layer. Bake at 350 degrees for 8-10 minutes, until fish have lost their pink color next to bone.

While fish is baking, cook 4 tablespoons butter in small saucepan over high heat until it foams and turns nut brown. Add 2 tablespoons lemon juice. Place fish on warmed plates and sprinkle with bacon pieces and toasted walnuts. Pour browned butter over fish and garnish with lemon halves.

A spectacular way to serve fried catfish!

Fish & Seafood

Turban of Sole

½ pound fillet of sole
½ cup clam or chicken broth
½ cup long grain rice
1 cup minced fresh parsley
1 teaspoon salt
1 teaspoon freshly grated lemon peel
¼ teaspoon ground mace or ground nutmeg
¼ teaspoon freshly ground black pepper
2 tablespoons butter
1 tablespoon fresh lemon juice
2 pounds fillet of sole
1½ pounds baby carrots
1½ pounds asparagus, cut diagonally into 2-inch pieces
2 tablespoons butter
Hollandaise Sauce

6-8 servings

Place ½ pound fillet of sole (1 large fillet) in lightly greased skillet. Add broth. Cover and simmer over low heat for 6-8 minutes or until fish is fork-tender. Drain well. Cool and flake fish medium fine to measure 1 cup. Set aside.

In medium saucepan, cook rice according to package directions. When rice is cooked, add flaked fish, parsley, salt, lemon peel, mace and pepper. Add 2 tablespoons butter and lemon juice. Toss gently and cook over low heat to warm filling, stirring gently with rubber spatula to prevent sticking.

Grease 5-cup ring mold well. Line with 2 pounds fish fillets, placing whitest sides of fillets against mold. Tail ends of fillets should overhang center of mold. Widest parts of fillets should overhang outer edge. Overlap each fillet slightly. If fillets are thick, press with broad blade of knife to flatten. Gently press warm filling into mold, filling completely. Fold tails of fillets from center of mold over filling. Fold widest parts of fillets from outer edge to cover filling. With a small spatula, tuck ends of fillets into inner side of mold. Finished raw dish will mound slightly above rim of mold.

Cover a 12-inch square of aluminum foil with same size waxed paper. Grease waxed paper well. Holding squares together, place waxed paper greased side down over mold. Twist to seal or tie with string. Set mold in baking pan. Add 1 inch hot water. Bake in preheated oven at 400 degrees for 20 minutes.

Cook baby carrots in boiling salted water for 10-15 minutes. Cook asparagus in boiling salted water until tender, about 5 minutes. Drain vegetables well. Combine vegetables and toss with 2 tablespoons butter. Keep warm while unmolding fish.

Remove mold from water bath. Remove foil and waxed paper and drain liquid from surface. Invert serving platter over mold. Holding platter and mold together, turn right side up. Gently remove mold from fish. Surround and fill center of mold with cooked vegetables. Serve with **Hollandaise Sauce.**

A beautiful combination of fish, asparagus and carrots in a main course... light eating at its best.

Fish & Seafood

Poisson en Croûte

Buttery Pastry:
3	cups all-purpose flour
½	teaspoon salt
1	cup butter
¾	cup cold water

Filling:
1½	pounds lean, mild fish fillets, cut 1 inch thick
½	teaspoon salt
2	tablespoons fresh lemon juice
4	tablespoons butter
1	medium onion, chopped
¾	cup long grain rice
½	cup minced fresh parsley

Shrimp and Clam Sauce:
2	tablespoons butter
2	tablespoons all-purpose flour
¼	cup bottled clam juice
1¼	cups half and half dash of ground nutmeg
6	ounces chopped clams
8	ounces tiny shrimp, cooked salt to taste
1	egg, beaten

8-10 servings

To prepare pastry, combine flour, salt and butter and blend with fork or pastry blender until mixture is consistency of coarse meal. Add water, tossing mixture with fork until pastry clings together. Press firmly into 2 balls. Wrap well and chill for at least 1 hour or as long as overnight.

To prepare filling, arrange fish fillets in single layer in shallow baking pan, overlapping thin edges. Sprinkle with salt and lemon juice. Cover and bake in preheated oven at 450 degrees for 10-15 minutes or until fish is opaque. Cool; pour off all juices and reserve. Cover fish and refrigerate until ready to complete preparations.

In 2-quart saucepan, melt butter and cook onion over medium heat until transparent. Add rice and stir to coat. Add water to reserved fish juice to make 1½ cups. Pour over rice. Simmer covered until rice is tender, about 20 minutes. Stir in parsley; cool. Cover and refrigerate until ready to complete preparations.

To prepare shrimp and clam sauce, melt butter in small saucepan and stir in flour. Cook over medium heat until mixture bubbles. Remove from heat and gradually stir in clam juice and half and half. Cook over medium heat until thickened, stirring constantly. Stir in nutmeg, clams and shrimp. Add salt to taste; cool.

TO ASSEMBLE: Remove pastry from refrigerator. Cut out cardboard pattern in shape of a fish, about 16 inches long and 9 inches wide. On floured board using well-floured rolling pin, roll out 1 pastry ball to form large oval, approximately 10x20 inches and ⅛-inch thick. Set fish pattern onto pastry and cut around pattern with small, sharp knife. Lift off scraps and transfer fish-shaped pastry onto large, lightly greased cookie sheet. (Using a cookie sheet with only two sides will make it easier to slide the finished fish onto a platter.) Roll out remaining pastry ball and scraps into large oval, approximately 15x23 inches. Set aside until ready to assemble fish.

Spread ⅔ of rice mixture over fish-shaped pastry within 1 inch of edges. Arrange fillets over rice. Spoon **Shrimp and Clam Sauce** over fillets. Cover with remaining rice. Brush edges of pastry with beaten egg. Drape 15x23-inch piece of pastry over filling. Trim edges to extend ½ inch beyond bottom pastry. Tuck top pastry under bottom. Seal all edges with tines of fork. If desired, roll out remaining pastry scraps and cut 2 fin-shaped pieces. Attach fins to fish by brushing 1 edge with beaten egg, placing edge underneath fish and sealing with tines of fork. With tips of kitchen scissors, snip through top pastry to make scales and other decorative details. *Cover and refrigerate for up to 24 hours.*

Brush entire pastry with beaten egg. Bake uncovered in preheated oven at 425 degrees for 10 minutes. Reduce heat to 375 degrees and bake for an additional 40-50 minutes. If fins and tail brown too quickly, cover with aluminum foil. Fish is done when pastry is golden and fish is heated through; insert tip of knife through slit in pastry at thickest part to test for doneness. Cut into thick slices to serve.

Fish & Seafood

Scallops in Phyllo

4	tablespoons unsalted butter
¾	pound mushrooms, cut into ¼-inch slices
6	tablespoons dry white wine
8	ounces cream cheese, softened
2	teaspoons all-purpose flour, combined with 2 teaspoons butter
	salt and ground white pepper to taste
2	eggs, lightly beaten
2	pounds bay scallops, chilled and patted dry
¾	cup unsalted butter, melted
16	sheets (¾ pound) phyllo dough, covered with plastic wrap to prevent drying

40 pieces

In large skillet over medium-high heat, melt 4 tablespoons butter. Add mushrooms and sauté for 4-5 minutes. Remove mushrooms with slotted spoon. Add wine to skillet, increase heat to high, and cook until liquid is reduced by half. Reduce heat to low and add cream cheese, stirring until melted. Bring mixture to gentle simmer. Gradually whisk in flour-butter mixture, blending until smooth. Season with salt and pepper. Let cool. Blend in eggs. Fold in mushrooms and scallops.

Butter a baking sheet or line with parchment paper. Lay one sheet phyllo on work surface. Brush with melted butter. Top with second phyllo sheet. Spoon ⅛ of scallop mixture in strip along short end of phyllo, leaving a 2 to 3-inch margin at each end of scallops. Roll up short end tightly, enclosing scallops, until ⅔ rolled. Fold in sides of phyllo. Brush remaining ⅓ of dough with butter and finish rolling. Place seam side down on prepared baking sheet and brush with butter. Repeat with remaining phyllo. *Can be made to this point 1 day in advance, tightly covered and refrigerated. Let come to room temperature before baking.*

To serve, bake in preheated oven at 400 degrees until golden brown, approximately 15-20 minutes. Slice each roll into 5 pieces and serve immediately.

This dish is a perfect first course. In larger portions it makes a delicious luncheon entrée.

Fish & Seafood

Cumin-Sauced Salmon with Deep Fried Celery Leaves

½   **cup club soda**
⅓   **cup all-purpose flour**
½   **teaspoon salt**
½   **cup firmly packed celery leaves**
      vegetable oil for deep frying
4   **center cut salmon fillets,**
      6 ounces each
1   **tablespoon unsalted butter,**
      softened
      salt and freshly ground
      black pepper to taste
¼   **cup minced shallots or onion**
2   **teaspoons ground cumin**
1   **teaspoon celery seeds**
3   **large plum tomatoes, finely**
      chopped (fresh or canned)
⅔   **cup dry white wine**
½   **cup water**
⅔   **cup heavy cream**
      salt and freshly ground
      black pepper to taste

4 servings

In medium bowl, whisk together club soda, flour and salt until just combined. Dip celery leaves in mixture and fry in batches in 1½-inches hot oil at 375 degrees for about 30 seconds, turning once. Remove from oil with slotted spoon and drain on paper towels. *Keep warm and covered.*

Rinse salmon and pat dry. Spread butter on bottom of shallow flame-proof baking dish just large enough to hold salmon in a single layer. Place salmon in dish and sprinkle with salt and pepper. Add shallots, cumin, celery seeds and tomatoes. Pour wine and water over salmon. Heat liquid to boiling over moderate heat. Cover salmon with buttered waxed paper and aluminum foil, and poach in oven preheated to 350 degrees for 10-12 minutes, turning once. Fish is done when it flakes. Transfer fish to a heated platter; keep warm and covered.

Pour poaching liquid into a saucepan and boil until reduced to about ¾ cup. Add cream, salt and pepper to taste, and any salmon juices that may have accumulated on the platter, and boil the mixture until it is thickened. Strain sauce over salmon and top with deep fried celery leaves. Serve immediately.

Beautiful, delicious and sophisticated. Perfect for a very important dinner. Serve with **Million Dollar Rice.**

Fish & Seafood

Salmon with Red Radish Dill Sauce

½ cup dry white wine
½ cup heavy cream
1 shallot, finely chopped
1 cup unsalted butter
¼ teaspoon ground white pepper
½ teaspoon salt
8 large red radishes, washed and trimmed
3 tablespoons chopped fresh dill
1 tablespoon prepared white horseradish, drained
1 tablespoon unsalted butter
1 tablespoon vegetable oil
4 salmon fillets, 8 ounces each
1 cup milk
½ cup all-purpose flour
¼ teaspoon salt
4 sprigs of fresh dill

4 servings

In medium saucepan, combine wine, cream and shallot. Heat to boiling and cook over medium heat until reduced to ½ cup, about 10 minutes. Reduce heat to low and whisk in 1 cup butter, 1-2 tablespoons at a time. Season with white pepper and ½ teaspoon salt. Remove sauce from heat.

Cut 12 thin slices from radishes for garnish; set aside in bowl of cold water. Finely chop remaining radishes and add to sauce. Stir in chopped dill and horseradish; set aside.

In large skillet, melt 1 tablespoon butter with oil over medium-high heat. When oil begins to sizzle, dip each piece of salmon in milk, dust with flour, shake off excess and add to skillet. Sauté, turning once, until lightly browned, about 3 minutes per side. Reduce heat to moderate and continue cooking, turning once or twice, until fish has almost lost its translucency in thickest part, 1-2 minutes longer depending on thickness of fish. Season with ¼ teaspoon salt.

Warm sauce over low heat and divide among 4 heated plates. Place salmon on top of sauce and garnish with reserved radish slices and sprigs of dill.

Enjoy the bounty of the sea accompanied by a unique sauce blending the extraordinary flavors of radishes and dill.

Fish & Seafood

Salmon with Seafood Mousse

4	salmon steaks, 8 ounces each, 1 inch thick
¼	pound sole fillet
¼	pound medium shrimp, peeled and deveined
½	cup heavy cream, chilled
1	egg yolk
	pinch of freshly grated nutmeg
¼	teaspoon salt
⅛	teaspoon freshly ground black pepper
3	egg whites
2	tablespoons unsalted butter
1	large shallot, minced
2	tablespoons fresh lemon juice
¼	teaspoon salt
⅛	teaspoon freshly ground black pepper
1	cup Alsatian Riesling
1	cup bottled clam juice
1	cup *Crème Fraîche*
6	tablespoons unsalted butter

4 servings

Prepare **Crème Fraîche** at least 8 hours ahead.

Cut salmon steaks in half lengthwise along central bone. Remove and discard bones. Cut off skins and discard. Re-form steaks to original shape and pin together with 2 wooden picks.

In food processor, combine sole and shrimp. Purée until smooth. With processor running, add heavy cream and egg yolk and process until blended. Scrape fish purée into stainless steel bowl and set in larger bowl half-filled with ice and water. Add nutmeg, ¼ teaspoon salt and ⅛ teaspoon pepper. Using a wooden spoon, stir mixture until completely chilled. In medium bowl, beat egg whites until soft peaks form. Gently fold beaten whites into chilled fish purée; set aside.

In large ovenproof skillet, melt 2 tablespoons butter over moderately high heat. Add shallot and cook, stirring occasionally, until softened, about 5 minutes; remove from heat.

Season salmon with lemon juice, ¼ teaspoon salt and ⅛ teaspoon pepper; set aside. Mound ½ cup seafood mousse on top of each salmon steak, smoothing with a wet spatula. Place steaks in skillet and pour Riesling and clam juice around fish. Bake in preheated oven at 400 degrees until mousse is firm, about 10 minutes. Transfer to broiler and lightly brown tops. Remove steaks to heated platter and place in warm oven.

In same skillet, bring **Crème Fraîche** to boil over high heat. Cook until liquid is reduced to 1 cup, about 12 minutes. Reduce heat to low and whisk in 6 tablespoons butter, 1 tablespoon at a time. Adjust seasoning if necessary and strain sauce through a fine-mesh sieve.
To serve, place salmon steaks on warmed plates and surround each with ⅓ cup sauce.

Crème Fraîche:

1	cup heavy cream
2½	teaspoons buttermilk

1 cup

In tightly covered jar, shake cream and buttermilk at least 1 minute. Let mixture stand at room temperature for at least 8 hours, until thick. Store in refrigerator. *Will keep for 4-6 weeks.*

For those times when you want an impressive main course, try this elegant salmon entrée.

Palace Trout

3	pounds trout
1	tablespoon butter
⅓	cup milk
⅓	cup water
	salt and freshly ground black pepper to taste
3	bay leaves
4	cups cooked angel hair pasta, tossed with butter and pepper
½	cup butter
¾	pound mushrooms, sliced
2	cloves garlic, pressed
4	green onions including tops, finely chopped
¼	pound shrimp, cooked
¼	pound lobster, cooked
2	tablespoons all-purpose flour
1	cup milk
1	cup heavy cream
	salt and freshly ground black pepper to taste
	freshly grated Parmesan cheese
	paprika
	sprigs of parsley
	fresh lemon juice
	lemon slices

4 servings

Skin and bone trout and place side-by-side in non-stick skillet with 1 tablespoon of butter. Add just enough milk and water to come halfway up fish. Sprinkle with salt and pepper and add bay leaves. Cover pan and heat liquid to boiling. Reduce heat and cook for 15 minutes or until fish flakes easily, but is still firm. Remove fish from skillet with pancake spatula and place on bed of hot angel hair pasta. Remove bay leaves and discard. Reduce remaining poaching liquid to ½ cup and set aside.

In medium skillet, melt ½ cup butter and sauté mushrooms and garlic for 5 minutes, stirring occasionally. Add green onions and cook for additional 5 minutes. Add shrimp and lobster; heat thoroughly. Stirring constantly, sprinkle with flour and cook for 2 minutes. Gradually add milk, cream and reduced poaching liquid and simmer for 10 minutes over low heat until smooth and thickened. Season with salt and pepper.

Reheat fish in microwave for 1½ minutes. Pour sauce around edge of fish and sprinkle liberally with Parmesan cheese and paprika. Add sprigs of parsley and squeeze lemon juice over top. Serve with lemon slices, additional Parmesan cheese and freshly ground black pepper.

This can be prepared over an open fire for those romantics who travel prepared. Be sure to keep trout warm. Serve with champagne and firelight.

Slumgullion Curry

½ **pound beef tenderloin, sliced
⅛-inch thick and cut into
1½-inch squares**
½ **pound pork tenderloin, sliced
⅛-inch thick and cut into
1½-inch squares**
  **salt and freshly ground
black pepper to taste**
  curry powder
1 **pound large shrimp, peeled
and deveined**
½ **pound bay scallops
fresh lemon juice**

Curry Sauce:
1 **tablespoon butter**
1 **cup minced onion**
6 **¼-inch thick slices fresh
ginger root**
2 **bay leaves**
1 **tablespoon curry powder**
¼ **teaspoon whole coriander seeds**
⅔ **cup dry vermouth**
1 **cup heavy cream**

½ **cup vegetable oil, divided
all-purpose flour**
½ **cup butter**
1 **cup diced banana**
1 **cup diced fresh pineapple**
1 **cup chopped green onions**
½ **cup diced pimientos**
¼ **cup fresh lemon juice**
4-6 **cups cooked rice**

Condiments:
½ **cup sliced almonds, toasted**
½ **cup shredded coconut
Mango chutney**

4-6 servings

In medium bowl, lightly season beef and pork with salt, pepper and curry powder. Place shrimp and scallops in separate bowls and lightly sprinkle with salt, pepper, curry powder and lemon juice. Cover meats and seafood and refrigerate for 30 minutes.

In heavy saucepan, melt 1 tablespoon butter over medium heat. Add onion and ginger and cook until onion begins to soften, about 5 minutes. Add bay leaves, curry powder and coriander, and stir for 3 minutes. Add vermouth and heat to boiling, stirring constantly. Boil until reduced to ½ cup, stirring occasionally. Add cream and boil until reduced by ⅓, about 10 minutes. Strain sauce; return to saucepan. Keep warm.

In large, heavy skillet, heat ¼ cup oil over high heat. Add shrimp and stir just until pink, about 2 minutes. Transfer to platter. Wipe out skillet. Add remaining ¼ cup oil and heat over high heat. Dust meat with flour. Cook meat, stirring until no longer pink, about 2 minutes. Transfer to platter with shrimp. Wipe out skillet. Add ½ cup butter and melt over high heat. Cook scallops, stirring until almost opaque, about 1 minute. Using slotted spoon, transfer scallops to platter with meat. In same skillet, cook banana, pineapple, green onions, pimientos and ¼ cup lemon juice, stirring until heated through, about 1 minute. Return meat and seafood to skillet and stir until heated through, about 1 minute.

Spoon mixture onto plates. Arrange rice on side. Spoon sauce over all and top with sliced almonds and shredded coconut. Serve curry immediately, passing chutney separately.

An intriguing departure from usual curry dishes, this entrée is rich, complex and worthy of an important celebration.

Fish & Seafood

Cucumber Sauce

1   **cucumber, peeled and seeded**
2   **tablespoons mayonnaise**
½   **cup sour cream**
1   **tablespoon fresh lemon juice**
    salt and ground white pepper
       to taste
    dried dill weed to taste

1 cup

Shred cucumber in food processor and drain on paper towels. Mix together with remaining ingredients. Serve with salmon.

Horseradish Sauce

3   **tablespoons finely chopped fresh dill or 1 tablespoon dried dill weed**
1   **tablespoon green peppercorns, drained and crushed**
1   **teaspoon onion powder**
    dash of cayenne pepper
    dash of ground mace
2   **cups sour cream**
½   **cup freshly grated horseradish or horseradish in vinegar, drained (or more to taste)**
    paprika

2 cups

Combine dill, peppercorns, onion powder, cayenne pepper and mace in bowl and mix. Add sour cream and stir lightly. Blend in horseradish. Do not beat or sour cream will thin. Transfer to serving bowl. Cover and refrigerate. Sprinkle with paprika and serve chilled.

Green Sauce for Poached Salmon

2   **cups sprigs of fresh parsley**
3   **green onions including tops, sliced**
½   **cup fresh dill**
3   **anchovy fillets, drained**
3   **cloves garlic, coarsely chopped**
1   **tablespoon capers, drained**
6   **tablespoons fresh lemon juice**
⅓-¾   **cup olive oil (⅓ cup produces a pesto-like consistency, while ¾ cup will yield a creamy-textured sauce)**
    salt and freshly ground black pepper to taste
2   **hard cooked eggs, finely chopped**

2 cups

Purée parsley, onions and dill in food processor. Add anchovies, garlic, capers and lemon juice, and process until smooth. With machine running, add oil in a thin, steady stream. Season with salt and pepper. Place in serving bowl and stir in eggs. Serve at room temperature with cold poached salmon.

The fresh dill, parsley and green onions give this sauce both its green color and its fresh taste.

Poultry

Poultry

Chicken Amandine

1   cup toasted almonds, ground
⅔   cup minced fresh parsley
1   cup fresh bread crumbs
4   whole chicken breasts, halved,
      boned, skinned and pounded thin
3   egg whites, beaten with ½
      teaspoon water until frothy
½   cup butter
¾   cup freshly grated
      Parmesan cheese
2-3 tablespoons butter
2-3 tablespoons slivered almonds
1   clove garlic
¼   cup dry white wine
      juice of ½ lemon
2   tablespoons sour cream or
      Crème Fraîche

4-6 servings

Combine ground almonds, parsley and bread crumbs. Dip chicken breasts into egg whites, then into almond-parsley mixture, coating both sides. Chill several hours to set coating.

Melt butter over medium-high heat. Sauté breasts until brown and crisp on each side. About 30 seconds before removing from pan, sprinkle 1 tablespoon Parmesan on each chicken breast. Remove from pan and keep warm. In same pan, melt 2-3 tablespoons butter and stir to loosen any particles remaining on bottom. Add slivered almonds and whole garlic clove. Sauté until almonds are brown. Add wine and lemon juice, cooking until liquids are reduced by half. Lower heat and blend in sour cream. Pour sauce over chicken.

The delicious combination of chicken, almonds and cream is a tempting trilogy.

Drunken Chicken

4   whole chicken breasts, halved,
      boned and skinned
      salt and freshly ground black
      pepper to taste
1   cup all-purpose flour
2   tablespoons olive oil
2   tablespoons butter
1   large onion, finely chopped
2   tablespoons freshly minced parsley
1   16-ounce can tomato wedges
½   teaspoon ground cinnamon
¼   teaspoon ground cloves
¼   cup packed light brown sugar
1   cup dry sherry or vermouth
½   cup golden raisins
½   cup slivered almonds

6 servings

Season chicken with salt and pepper and dredge with flour. In large skillet, brown chicken in oil and butter. Place browned chicken in shallow 3-quart casserole. In same pan, cook onions until transparent. Add parsley, tomatoes with liquid, cinnamon, cloves, brown sugar, sherry and raisins and simmer uncovered for 15-20 minutes, stirring occasionally. Pour over chicken and sprinkle with almonds. Bake at 375 degrees for 30 minutes.

Easy and delicious. Boneless chicken breasts are ideal for today's overscheduled cook.

Poultry

Chicken Scampi

½ cup butter
¼ cup olive oil
¼ cup finely chopped green onions
1 tablespoon minced garlic
 juice of 1 lemon
2 pounds chicken breasts, boned, skinned and cut into ½-inch pieces
1 teaspoon salt
½ teaspoon freshly ground black pepper
¼ cup minced fresh parsley
1 tomato, chopped
 buttered noodles or cooked rice

4-6 servings

In skillet, heat together butter and olive oil and sauté green onions and garlic. Add lemon juice, chicken, salt, pepper and parsley. Continue cooking, stirring constantly, for 5-8 minutes or until chicken is done. Add tomatoes and heat through. Serve over buttered noodles or hot rice.

Fresh-tasting goodness and easy preparation will make this a regular favorite.

Tarragon Chicken

2 whole chicken breasts, boned, skinned and pounded to ¼-inch thickness
 all-purpose flour
4 tablespoons butter, divided
½ pound sliced mushrooms
2 tablespoons all-purpose flour
1 cup chicken broth
1¼ teaspoons minced fresh tarragon or ¼ teaspoon dried tarragon
½ cup half and half
 salt and freshly ground black pepper to taste

2-4 servings

Dredge chicken breasts in flour and brown in 2 tablespoons butter. Remove chicken to warm platter. Add remaining 2 tablespoons butter and sauté mushrooms. Sprinkle mushrooms with 2 tablespoons flour and blend well. Gradually add chicken broth, then tarragon. Cook until thickened. Slowly add half and half, and season with salt and pepper. Return chicken to pan and heat through. Sauce should be only slightly thick.

Arrange over a bed of noodles and sprinkle with fresh tarragon.

Poultry

Zesty Lemon Chicken

6   whole chicken breasts, boned and
     skinned
2   cups fresh lemon juice
     (9-10 lemons)
1   cup all-purpose flour
1½   teaspoons salt
2   teaspoons paprika
1   teaspoon freshly ground
     black pepper
½   cup safflower oil
2   tablespoons grated lemon peel
⅓   cup packed light brown sugar
¼   cup chicken broth
2   lemons, sliced
     minced fresh parsley

6 servings

In large zip-lock bag, combine chicken breasts and lemon juice. Squeeze out air and seal. Refrigerate overnight, turning once.

Remove chicken, reserving 2 tablespoons of marinade, and pat dry. Put flour, salt, paprika and pepper in a plastic bag. Shake until well mixed. Put chicken breasts in bag, one at a time, and shake to coat evenly. In large skillet, heat oil and fry breasts, a few at a time, until well browned, about 10 minutes. Arrange chicken in a single layer in large baking dish. Sprinkle evenly with lemon peel and brown sugar. Mix chicken broth with reserved 2 tablespoons of marinade and pour around chicken. Place a thin lemon slice on top of each breast and sprinkle with minced parsley. Bake at 350 degrees for 20-30 minutes or until tender.

Excellent hot and terrific cold, this is a treat for al fresco dining on your patio or in the mountains. And yes, you really do need 10 lemons!

Chicken Fruita

1   large white onion, chopped
2   tablespoons vegetable oil
1   pound chicken breasts, boned,
     skinned and cut into
     1-inch cubes
2   tablespoons all-purpose flour
2   cups water
¼   teaspoon garlic powder
1   teaspoon salt
¼   teaspoon freshly ground
     black pepper
1½   teaspoons curry powder
1   teaspoon chicken bouillon granules
1   cup sliced bananas
1   cup sliced peaches
1   cup sliced kiwis
2   tablespoons butter
     cooked rice
½   cup heavy cream, whipped

6 servings

In large skillet, sauté onion in oil. Add chicken cubes and brown. Slowly add flour and blend into pan juices. Add water, stirring constantly until thickened. Add garlic powder, salt, pepper, curry powder and chicken granules, and cook over medium-low heat for 15-20 minutes. In separate skillet, sauté fruit in butter until warm and soft. To serve, place rice on a round platter, top with chicken mixture, encircle with fruit and mound whipped cream in center.

A luscious combination of chicken and fruit in a rich curry sauce. A beautiful dish.

Poultry

Mandarin Chicken

2	whole chicken breasts, boned, skinned and pounded lightly
3	tablespoons butter
1½	cups sliced mushrooms
2	teaspoons all-purpose flour
⅔	cup water
¼	cup frozen orange juice concentrate, thawed
2	packages instant chicken broth and seasoning mix
1	11-ounce can of Mandarin orange sections, drained
½	cup thinly sliced green onions cooked rice

2 servings

In large skillet, brown chicken in butter and set aside. In same skillet, cook mushrooms over high heat until liquid evaporates, about 1-2 minutes. Remove from heat. Sprinkle mushrooms with flour and stir quickly to combine. Gradually stir in water. Add orange juice and dry seasoning mix. Heat to boiling, stirring constantly. Reduce heat, add chicken and simmer about 3 minutes. Add orange sections and sprinkle with green onions. Serve over a bed of rice.

A subtle citrus flavor enhances this light entrée.

Szechwan Chicken and Cashews

2	whole chicken breasts, boned, skinned and cut into ¾-inch cubes
1	tablespoon soy sauce
1	tablespoon Chinese rice wine or dry Sherry
2	tablespoons soy sauce
1	tablespoon cornstarch
2	teaspoons sugar
1	teaspoon white vinegar
¼	cup vegetable oil
½-1	teaspoon crushed red pepper flakes
3	green onions, sliced diagonally
1	tablespoon minced fresh ginger
½	cup unsalted cashews cooked rice

4 servings

Marinate chicken in 1 tablespoon soy sauce and rice wine for 30 minutes.

Combine 2 tablespoons soy sauce, cornstarch, sugar and vinegar and set aside. Heat oil in wok or skillet. Add red pepper to taste and cook until black. Add chicken and stir fry for 2 minutes. Remove chicken. Add green onions and ginger and stir fry for 1 minute. Return chicken to wok. Cook 2 minutes. Stirring constantly, add soy sauce mixture and any remaining chicken marinade. Add cashews. Serve over cooked rice.

*Serve this spicy entrée with **Steamboat Stirfry** for a complete Szechwan meal.*

Chicken Kashmir

Yogurt Sauce:

- 2 tablespoons corn oil
- 1 tablespoon minced fresh ginger
- 2 teaspoons curry powder
- 2 teaspoons ground fennel seed
- ½ teaspoon ground cumin
- ½ teaspoon ground coriander
- 2 cups plain yogurt
- 1¼ teaspoons salt
- ¼ teaspoon freshly ground black pepper
- 1 teaspoon fresh lemon juice
- 1 tablespoon minced fresh cilantro or parsley

- ¾ cup all-purpose flour
- 1 teaspoon salt
- 2 teaspoons freshly ground black pepper
- ¾ teaspoon curry powder
- ¾ teaspoon ground coriander
- ¼ teaspoon ground cumin
- ¼ teaspoon ground cinnamon
- ¼ teaspoon ground nutmeg
- ¼ teaspoon ground cardamom
- 3 eggs, beaten
- 2 teaspoons ground turmeric
- 16 tomato slices, each ¼-inch thick
- ½ cup unsalted butter
- 8 chicken breasts, halved, boned and skinned
- 1 tablespoon minced fresh cilantro or parsley

8 servings

Combine all sauce ingredients; set aside. Serve at room temperature.

Sift together flour, salt, pepper, curry powder, coriander, cumin, cinnamon, nutmeg and cardamom in wide, shallow dish. In another shallow dish, beat eggs and turmeric. Heat the tomato slices in a rimmed tray in a 350 degree oven for 5 minutes. Heat unsalted butter until hot in a skillet large enough to hold the chicken in a single layer. Pound each halved chicken breast between 2 pieces of waxed paper until ¼-inch thick. Dip each chicken breast first in flour mixture, shaking off excess, then coat with egg, letting the excess drip off. Sauté chicken for 2 minutes on each side over medium heat. Serve at once topped with a warm tomato slice drizzled with some sauce and sprinkled with minced cilantro or parsley. Pass the remaining sauce.

*The tangy **Yogurt Sauce** is a delicious accompaniment to this mild, curried chicken and creates a memorable dish.*

Poultry

Oriental Pistachio Chicken

8	chicken breasts, halved, boned and skinned
1	teaspoon garlic powder
1	teaspoon paprika
	salt and freshly ground black pepper to taste
3	tablespoons safflower oil
2	cups beef broth
2	teaspoons cornstarch
⅓	cup dry red wine
2	tablespoons oyster sauce
4	green onions, including tops, chopped
¼	cup pistachio nuts, shelled
	Chinese rice noodles
	pistachio nuts (optional)

8 servings

Season chicken breasts with garlic powder, paprika, salt and pepper. Sauté chicken in oil over medium-high heat. In saucepan, combine beef broth, cornstarch, wine and oyster sauce. Heat to boiling and simmer for 10 minutes. Add green onions and ¼ cup pistachios. Prepare rice noodles according to package directions. Place noodles on heated serving dish, top with chicken breasts and pour sauce over all. Garnish with additional pistachios.

An outstanding chicken entrée that demonstrates that easy need not be boring.

Chicken Italiano

½	cup freshly grated Parmesan cheese
2	tablespoons minced fresh parsley
1	teaspoon dried oregano
1	clove garlic, minced
½	teaspoon freshly ground black pepper
2	whole chicken breasts, boned and skinned
3	tablespoons butter, melted

4 servings

Combine Parmesan, parsley, oregano, garlic and pepper. Dip chicken in melted butter, then in cheese mixture. Place in shallow baking dish. Drizzle remaining butter over chicken. Bake at 375 degrees for 25 minutes or until tender.

A perfect weeknight dinner, ready in ½ hour. Delicious either hot or cold.

Poultry

Greek Lemon Chicken

Marinade:

1	cup fruity white wine
¼	cup olive oil
¼	cup fresh lemon juice
1	teaspoon freshly grated lemon peel
1	teaspoon salt
1	teaspoon freshly ground black pepper
3	cloves garlic, crushed
6	whole large chicken breasts, boned and skinned
3	tablespoons olive oil
2	tablespoons butter
2	tablespoons all-purpose flour
½	teaspoon salt
2	teaspoons prepared mustard
1	cup milk
2	egg yolks
	freshly grated peel of 1 lemon
1	teaspoon fresh lemon juice
1	teaspoon dried dill weed
¼	cup minced fresh parsley
1	cup sour cream
¼	cup butter, melted
½	cup crumbled feta cheese
1	pound angel hair pasta, cooked al dente and kept warm
½	cup shredded Muenster cheese

6-8 servings

In a bowl, combine all marinade ingredients. Pound chicken breasts slightly and place in shallow casserole or in plastic zip-lock bag, and cover with marinade. Refrigerate for up to 12 hours.

Discard marinade. Heat oil in skillet and sauté chicken until tender. Slice and set aside.

In saucepan, melt 2 tablespoons butter; blend in flour and salt to create a roux. Add mustard and slowly add milk, stirring constantly until thick and smooth. In small bowl, mix egg yolk, lemon peel and lemon juice together. Whisk a small amount of roux into egg mixture. Then whisk egg mixture into roux and bring to a gentle boil. Remove from heat and add dill and parsley. When parsley wilts, stir in sour cream.

Add ¼ cup butter, ¾ cup of the egg sauce and feta cheese to cooked pasta; stir well. Place in greased 9x13-inch casserole, and top with sliced chicken breasts, remaining sauce and Muenster cheese. Broil until cheese is golden.

This is a wonderful entrée for a luncheon or dinner buffet.

Chicken Étouffée

Creole Spice:
- 1 teaspoon freshly ground black pepper
- 1 teaspoon ground white pepper
- 1 teaspoon cayenne pepper
- ½ teaspoon dried thyme
- ¼ teaspoon dry mustard
- ¼ teaspoon ground mace
- 1 bay leaf, finely crumbled

- ⅓ cup vegetable oil
- ⅓ cup all-purpose flour
- ½ cup chopped onion
- ¼ cup chopped celery
- ¼ cup chopped green bell pepper
- 2 teaspoons minced garlic
- 1 16-ounce can tomatoes, chopped
- 8 ounces clam juice
- 1¾ teaspoons *Creole Spice*
- 1 teaspoon salt
- 3 chicken breasts, boned, skinned and cubed
- ¼ cup minced fresh parsley
- 1½ cups rice

6 servings

In small bowl, combine all **Creole Spice** ingredients; set aside.

In heavy, 4-quart kettle over medium heat, heat oil. Stir in flour and cook stirring constantly until dark red-brown, about 10 minutes. Add onion, celery, green pepper and garlic; cook 5 minutes. Stir in tomatoes, clam juice, 1 teaspoon **Creole Spice,** salt and cubed chicken. Heat to boiling. Reduce heat and simmer uncovered, stirring occasionally, for 10-15 minutes. Remove from heat and let stand 3 minutes. Add parsley.

Cook rice according to package directions, adding ¾ teaspoon **Creole Spice** to the water. Serve rice with étouffée.

A wonderful spicy chicken entrée featuring the best of Creole cooking.

Poultry

Shanghai Smoked Chicken

1 3-4 pound whole chicken
1 medium cooking bag

Marinade:
1 green onion, chopped
6 tablespoons soy sauce
2 tablespoons hoisin sauce
2 tablespoons dry white wine
1 teaspoon packed dark brown sugar
1 teaspoon minced fresh ginger
1 teaspoon salt
1 teaspoon Liquid Smoke

Garnish:
sprigs of parsley
minced green onions

4-6 servings

Tie wings close to chicken and place in cooking bag. Combine all marinade ingredients in a small bowl. Pour marinade into bag. Tie bag and rotate so marinade coats chicken. Refrigerate several hours or overnight.

Slit steam vents in top of cooking bag. Bake chicken at 350 degrees for 1½ hours or until well browned. Cool slightly. Slice chicken into serving portions, arrange on platter, and pour liquid from bag over chicken. Garnish with parsley and green onions.

Expect the most wonderful results — a very moist, deliciously-flavored chicken. Serve with fried rice as an accompaniment.

Clay Pot Chicken with Spring Vegetables

1 3-4 pound chicken
2 tablespoons butter
1 teaspoon salt
½ teaspoon freshly ground black pepper
2 cups sliced red onion
20 cloves garlic, peeled
14 tiny new potatoes
12 ounces tiny carrots, scrubbed
½ teaspoon dried rosemary, crumbled
¼ teaspoon dried thyme
1 teaspoon dried basil
3 tablespoons diced green onions
½ cup chicken broth
3 tablespoons Spanish sherry vinegar
2 cups fresh snow peas (optional)

4 servings

Soak clay pot according to manufacturer's directions. Rub chicken with butter, salt and pepper. Place onions and garlic in bottom of pot. Add chicken, breast down, and surround with potatoes, carrots, rosemary, thyme, basil, green onions, broth and vinegar. Cover and roast according to manufacturer's suggested temperature and time (generally about 1 hour). Add peas about 20 minutes before end of cooking time. Serve hot.

A sensational light recipe with an emphasis on fresh vegetables and great attention to color. You must use a large clay pot to preserve the natural juices of the bird.

Poultry

Herb-Roasted Chicken with Shallots

1   5-pound roasting chicken
    kosher salt and freshly ground
       black pepper to taste
    juice of 1 lemon
10 sprigs of fresh thyme
6   sprigs of fresh rosemary
6   sprigs of fresh sage
16 shallots, peeled
6   cloves garlic, unpeeled
½   cup dry white wine

4 servings

Rub inside of chicken with salt, pepper and lemon juice. Fill cavity with half of fresh herbs. Truss chicken firmly with cotton twine. Place chicken, breast side up, in shallow roasting pan. Roast at 400 degrees for 15 minutes. Place whole shallots and garlic cloves around chicken. Add remaining herbs to pan, reserving a few for garnish. Pour white wine over shallots and garlic, and return to oven. Roast for another 45 minutes. To test for doneness, pierce thickest part of thigh . Juices should run clear. Place chicken on heated serving platter and arrange shallots and garlic around it. Garnish with reserved herbs.

Fresh herbs give this roast chicken a new and exciting flavor. Enjoy the subtle taste of the shallots and feast on the sweetness of the roasted garlic.

Microwave Honey Chicken

1   3-pound fryer
1   oven cooking bag
¼   cup soy sauce
⅓   cup honey
⅓   cup sherry
1   tablespoon water
2   tablespoons cornstarch

4 servings

Place whole fryer on its side in oven cooking bag set in an 8x12-inch baking dish. Combine soy sauce, honey and sherry. Pour over chicken. Close bag and marinate in refrigerator for 2 hours, turning chicken to other side after 1 hour.

Slit cooking bag near closure. Insert temperature probe into chicken and microwave at medium high to a temperature of 190 degrees, or for 25-30 minutes. After chicken is cooked, combine water and cornstarch in 2-cup glass measuring cup. Cut corner off cooking bag and drain juices from bag into cornstarch mixture. Stir to blend. Microwave sauce on high for 2-3 minutes or until thick and clear. Remove chicken from bag, pour sauce over chicken, and serve.

Easy, delicious chicken, prepared quickly on those busy days.

Poultry

Mustard Chicken in Phyllo Pastry

¼ cup unsalted butter
3 whole large chicken breasts, boned, skinned and cut into 1-inch cubes
 salt and ground white pepper to taste
¼ cup Dijon mustard
2 tablespoons minced fresh tarragon
1½ cups heavy cream
¾ cup unsalted butter, melted
10 phyllo pastry sheets

6-8 servings

In large skillet, melt ¼ cup butter over medium heat. Sprinkle chicken pieces with salt and pepper to taste. Sauté chicken until no longer pink, about 5 minutes. Do not overcook. Transfer to platter; keep warm. Whisk mustard into chicken drippings. Add tarragon and reduce slightly. Whisk in cream, blending thoroughly. Reduce heat to low and simmer until sauce is slightly thickened and reduced by about ¼. Pour sauce over chicken pieces and toss to coat completely.

Brush shallow, 2-quart casserole with melted butter. Lay one phyllo sheet in casserole, patting to fit sides. (Do not trim excess that overlaps edge of dish.) Brush with melted butter. Repeat with 4 more sheets of phyllo. Fill casserole with chicken mixture. Layer 5 more phyllo sheets on top of chicken mixture, buttering between each layer. Trim excess phyllo to within 1 inch of casserole edge. Tuck edges neatly under and brush once more with melted butter. Bake at 425 degrees for 15 minutes or until heated through and crisply golden brown on top.

A very special main course. The rich flavors of mustard and tarragon are mellowed by heavy cream.

Skillet Chicken, Vegetables and Bulgar

2 cups chopped onion
1½ cups chicken broth
1 cup water
1 cup Bulgar wheat
1 teaspoon minced garlic
1 teaspoon curry powder
3 pounds chicken parts, skinned
¼ teaspoon freshly ground black pepper
1½ cups peeled, sliced carrot
1½ cups zucchini, halved lengthwise and cut into ½-inch slices
1 large green bell pepper, cut into 1-inch pieces

4 servings

In a deep, 12-inch skillet mix onion, broth, water, Bulgar wheat, garlic and curry powder. Sprinkle chicken with pepper and add to skillet. Heat to boiling, cover and simmer 10 minutes over moderate heat. Turn chicken, add carrots, cover and simmer 15 minutes more. Add zucchini and green pepper, cover and simmer 5-15 minutes longer or until vegetables are tender and chicken is cooked through.

Bright and colorful. A meal in itself!

Silver Bullet Chicken

Marinade:

1	teaspoon dried oregano
½	teaspoon dried thyme
4	cloves garlic, minced
1	bay leaf
¼	teaspoon freshly ground black pepper
¼	cup wine vinegar
1	cup stuffed olives, rinsed and drained
¼	cup capers, rinsed and drained
2	chicken bouillon cubes
½	cup olive oil
2	sprigs of fresh cilantro or parsley, minced

1	5-pound chicken, skinned and cut into pieces
2	cups short grain rice
1	tablespoon olive oil
2	chorizo or Italian sausages, sliced, and/or 8 strips bacon, chopped
2	green bell peppers, chopped
2	large onions, chopped
2	28-ounce cans tomatoes
1	cup dry red wine
3	12-ounce cans *Coors*LIGHT beer
	salt and freshly ground black pepper to taste
1	4-ounce jar sliced pimientos
1	10-ounce package frozen peas, thawed
1	10-ounce package frozen asparagus, thawed

12 servings

Combine all marinade ingredients. Add chicken and marinate, refrigerated, overnight. *Chicken and marinade may be frozen until ready to use.*

Wash and rinse rice well. Cover with water and let sit for 45 minutes. In large kettle, heat oil and brown sausage and/or bacon. Add peppers and onions and sauté until limp. Add chicken with marinade mixture and brown well. Add tomatoes with liquid, wine and beer. Cook 10 minutes. Add well-drained rice, cover and cook for 25 minutes or until rice is tender. Season with salt and pepper. If mixture is too thick, add more bouillon or water. Ten minutes before serving add pimientos, peas and asparagus.

With such glorious colors, this dish needs little garnish.

Chicken Artichoke Casserole

4   whole chicken breasts
1   10-ounce package frozen artichoke hearts
⅓   cup butter
⅓   cup all-purpose flour
2½   cups chicken broth
¼   cup dry white wine or vermouth
4   cups shredded sharp Cheddar cheese
2   tablespoons chopped green onions
¼   cup freshly grated Parmesan cheese
1   cup dry bread crumbs
1   teaspoon dried thyme
2   tablespoons freshly grated Parmesan cheese

6 servings

Place chicken breasts in large pot, cover with water, bring to boil, and simmer 30 minutes. Remove chicken. Cool, bone, skin and cut into large chunks. Cook artichoke hearts according to package directions, drain well, and pat dry. Layer chicken chunks and artichoke hearts in the bottom of 9x13-inch baking dish.

In medium saucepan, melt butter. Blend in flour, then gradually add chicken broth. Stirring constantly, heat to boiling and cook until thickened. Remove from heat. Add wine, Cheddar cheese, green onions and ¼ cup Parmesan. Blend until smooth. Pour sauce over chicken and artichokes. In small bowl, combine bread crumbs, thyme and 2 tablespoons Parmesan. Sprinkle over sauce. Bake uncovered at 350 degrees for 20-25 minutes or until bubbly.

Here's a delicious chicken entrée perfect for buffet dining.

Adobe Chicken Casserole

2   cups cooked brown rice
2   cups cooked white rice
2   large tomatoes, peeled and chopped, or 1 16-ounce can tomatoes, drained and chopped
1   medium onion, chopped
3   cups cooked chicken, cut into ½-inch cubes
   salt and freshly ground black pepper
2   cups sour cream
1   7-ounce can whole green chiles, seeded and cut into strips
3   cups shredded Monterey Jack cheese (12 ounces)
1   2¼-ounce can sliced ripe olives, drained

6-8 servings

In a large bowl combine brown and white rice, tomatoes, onion and cubed chicken. Season to taste with salt and pepper. Spoon half of the mixture into a shallow, greased 2½-quart casserole. Cover with half the sour cream, chile strips, cheese, and all of the olives. Repeat layering with remaining chicken mixture, sour cream, chiles and cheese. *This much can be done ahead, covered and refrigerated up to 24 hours.* Bake uncovered at 350 degrees for 45 minutes *(1 hour if chilled).* Allow to stand 10 minutes before serving.

*A wonderful casserole offering flavors of Mexico. Serve with **Squash Corn Bread** and a green salad.*

Poultry

Chicken Lasagne

2   whole chicken breasts, boned and
     cut into 1-inch cubes
3   cups sliced mushrooms
2   cloves garlic, minced
1   large onion, chopped
1   teaspoon dried oregano
1   teaspoon dried basil
1   teaspoon dried thyme
2   tablespoons olive oil
1   28-ounce can Italian tomatoes
     with basil
1   15-ounce can tomato sauce
3   tablespoons freshly grated
     Romano cheese
2   cups grated carrots
½   teaspoon salt
1   teaspoon freshly ground
     black pepper
8   ounces lasagne noodles, cooked
     al dente and drained
½   cup freshly grated Romano cheese
6-8 slices mozzarella cheese

8 servings

Sauté chicken, mushrooms, garlic, onion, oregano, basil and thyme in olive oil until chicken is white. Stir in tomatoes, tomato sauce, 3 tablespoons Romano cheese, carrots, salt and pepper. Cook uncovered for 5 minutes.

In oiled, 9x13-inch baking dish, place ½ the lasagne noodles. Top with ½ of sauce, Romano cheese and mozzarella cheese. Repeat layers. Cover and bake at 350 degrees for 20 minutes. Uncover and bake for 10 additional minutes or until bubbly and cheese melts.

A light and fresh-tasting interpretation of a classic lasagne, offering the best flavors of Italian cooking.

Barbecued Chicken

2   whole frying chickens,
     cut into pieces
¾   cup vegetable oil
⅓   cup soy sauce
3   tablespoons Worcestershire sauce
¼   cup red wine vinegar
     juice of 1 lemon
1   tablespoon dry mustard
1   teaspoon salt
2   tablespoons minced fresh parsley
1   clove garlic, crushed

6 servings

In a plastic zip-lock bag, combine all ingredients and marinate for 6-24 hours.

Remove chicken, reserving marinade. Grill over medium-hot coals 15-20 minutes or until chicken is cooked, basting frequently with reserved marinade.

*Barbecued chicken is great for a summer party. Serve with **Cold Pea Confetti** and your favorite potato salad.*

Poultry

Grilled Sesame Chicken

Marinade:

½	**cup olive oil**
½	**cup white wine**
½	**cup soy sauce**
1-2	**tablespoons freshly grated ginger**
1	**tablespoon dry mustard**
1	**teaspoon freshly ground black pepper**
4	**cloves garlic, crushed**
½	**cup chopped green onions**
3	**tablespoons sesame seeds**

2	**whole chickens, quartered**

4-6 servings

Combine all marinade ingredients. Place chicken in large zip-lock bag and pour in marinade. Squeeze out air and seal. Marinate refrigerated for 4-8 hours.

Remove chicken, reserving marinade. Grill over medium-hot coals for 15-20 minutes or until chicken is cooked, basting frequently with reserved marinade.

A snap to prepare. The sesame seeds toast as the chicken grills, imparting a nutty flavor.

Barbecued Chicken on a Bun

1	**whole 4-pound chicken**
1¼	**cups ketchup**
2	**cups water**
1	**onion, finely chopped**
1	**teaspoon salt**
1	**teaspoon celery seed**
1	**teaspoon chili powder or paste**
¼	**cup packed light brown sugar**
¼	**teaspoon Tabasco sauce**
¼	**cup Worcestershire sauce**
¼	**cup red wine vinegar**
6	**Kaiser rolls**

6 servings

Place whole chicken in large kettle, cover with water, heat to boiling and simmer until chicken is cooked, about 1 hour. Remove chicken from pan, cool and shred meat from bones.

In large saucepan, combine ketchup, water, onion, salt, celery seed, chili powder, brown sugar, Tabasco, Worcestershire and vinegar. Add shredded chicken. Simmer chicken in sauce for 1½ hours. Serve warm on rolls.

This is Colorado cooking that pleases children and adults alike. Enjoy at summer picnics or after a day of skiing.

Poultry

Chicken Hero

¾ cup mayonnaise
5 green onions, including tops, thinly sliced
1 8-ounce can water chestnuts, drained and coarsely chopped
4 teaspoons Dijon mustard
1 teaspoon Worcestershire sauce
1 teaspoon salt
5-6 drops Tabasco sauce
4 cups diced, cooked chicken
1 cup shredded Monterey Jack cheese
1 baguette loaf French bread
1 cup chopped tomato
1 cup shredded Monterey Jack cheese

Garnish:
minced fresh parsley
sliced green onions
sliced black olives

6-8 servings

In large bowl, combine mayonnaise, green onions, water chestnuts, mustard, Worcestershire, salt and Tabasco. Stir in chicken and 1 cup cheese. *Up to this point, chicken mixture can be prepared ahead, covered and refrigerated for up to 24 hours.*

Split French loaf in half lengthwise. Trim any uneven crust from bottom so loaf rests evenly. Place bread, cut side up, on baking sheet. Mix tomato into chicken mixture. Spread evenly over each bread half and sprinkle with 1 cup cheese. Bake until cheese is bubbly and lightly browned, about 10 minutes. Transfer to long cutting board. Garnish with parsley, sliced green onions or olives.

A hot chicken salad, served individually, is a welcome variation of a chicken salad sandwich.

Chicken in Pastry Shells

2 whole chicken breasts, halved, boned and skinned
2 cups chicken broth
⅓ cup Dijon mustard
3 tablespoons red wine vinegar
¾ cup vegetable oil
1½ tablespoons dried tarragon, crumbled
1 teaspoon ground celery seed
½ teaspoon salt
freshly ground black pepper to taste
½ cup plus 2 tablespoons light cream
1 8-ounce can water chestnuts, drained and thinly sliced
1 cup thinly sliced green onions
⅓ cup finely chopped pimiento
8 frozen puff pastry shells, cooked according to package directions
¼ pound Gruyère or Swiss cheese, shredded

8 servings

In large pot, combine chicken breasts and broth. Add enough water to cover and simmer for 10 minutes or until chicken is just cooked. Remove chicken, cool slightly and cut into ¾-inch cubes.

In large bowl, combine mustard and vinegar. Slowly add oil, beating constantly, until mixture is smooth and thick. Season with tarragon, celery seed, salt and pepper. Whisk in cream. Add water chestnuts, green onions, pimiento and chicken.

Place cooked pastry shells on baking sheet. Fill shells with chicken mixture and sprinkle with shredded cheese. Heat at 350 degrees for 12-15 minutes or until cheese is melted and filling is hot. Serve immediately.

Elegant for lunch, this recipe delivers a blend of flavors, texture and color.

Poultry

Chicken to Go

½ cup all-purpose flour
1½ tablespoons sesame seeds
½ tablespoon ground thyme
¾ tablespoon ground tarragon
½ tablespoon poppy seeds
1 teaspoon salt
8 chicken thighs
2 egg whites, lightly beaten
4 tablespoons unsalted butter
1 round loaf Sheepherder's bread

Melted Herb Butter:
4 tablespoons butter
3 tablespoons sesame seeds
1½ teaspoons dried tarragon
1 tablespoon ground thyme
1 tablespoon poppy seeds

4 servings

In small mixing bowl, combine flour, sesame seeds, thyme, tarragon, poppy seeds and 1 teaspoon salt. Dip chicken thighs in beaten egg, and coat each piece in flour mixture. In a 10 or 12-inch skillet, melt butter. Brown chicken thoroughly, about 7 minutes per side over medium heat. Place chicken in 3-quart casserole, cover and bake at 350 degrees for 40 minutes.

In small saucepan, combine all herb butter ingredients and heat until melted. Keep warm.

Cut large top off Sheepherder's loaf. Scrape out inside of loaf, leaving about ¾-inch of bread all the way around. Using a pastry brush, spread herb-butter inside loaf and on inside of top. Place loaf and top on cookie sheet. Arrange chicken in loaf. Return to oven and bake uncovered for an additional 20 minutes. Remove loaf from oven, replace top and wrap in several layers of foil, surrounded by several layers of newspaper. Loaf will remain very warm for several hours.

Tastes delicious and travels beautifully for picnic outings and sporting events.

Chicken Mousse

4 pounds split chicken breasts
3 bay leaves
1 onion, quartered
3 hard cooked eggs, chopped
2 cups diced celery
1 cup chopped pecans
1 cup chopped ripe olives
1 tablespoon Worcestershire sauce
1 tablespoon chili sauce
2 cups mayonnaise
1 envelope plain gelatin
¼ cup cold water
1 cup degreased chicken stock
　 salt and freshly ground
　　 black pepper to taste
　 mayonnaise

12 servings

Boil chicken with bay leaves and onion in salted water to cover. Drain, reserving stock. Cool chicken; bone, skin and chop into ½-inch pieces. Add eggs, celery, pecans and olives to chopped chicken. Mix Worcestershire and chili sauce with mayonnaise and fold into chicken mixture. Dissolve gelatin in cold water for 5 minutes. Bring 1 cup chicken stock to a boil and stir into gelatin. Stir gelatin mixture into chicken mixture. Season to taste with salt and pepper. Pour into large ring mold or loaf pan lightly coated with mayonnaise and refrigerate until set.

Wonderful for a luncheon or light summer dinner. Make individual molds for an elegant presentation.

Poultry

Apricot Glazed Game Hens with Fruited Wild Rice

Fruited Wild Rice:
2	cups water
1	chicken bouillon cube
1	cup wild rice
¼	cup sliced green grapes
¼	cup chopped red apple
¼	cup chopped pecans
1½	teaspoons freshly grated orange peel
¼	cup chopped water chestnuts
½	teaspoon dried basil
½	teaspoon dried thyme
	salt and freshly ground black pepper to taste
4	Cornish game hens, rinsed and patted dry
2	tablespoons butter, melted

4 servings

In large saucepan, heat water to boiling. Add bouillon cube and stir to dissolve. Add wild rice and return to boiling. Reduce heat, cover and simmer for 1 hour. Remove from heat; drain. In large mixing bowl, stir together cooked rice, grapes, apple, pecans, orange peel, water chestnuts, basil and thyme. Add salt and pepper to taste.

Fill cavities of hens with rice mixture. Use wooden picks to close. Rub skin of hens with melted butter. Bake at 350 degrees for 1 hour, basting with **Apricot Glaze** several times during the last 20 minutes.

Apricot Glaze:
⅔	cup sugar
¼	teaspoon ground cloves
2	tablespoons cornstarch
2	cups apricot nectar
1	tablespoon fresh lemon juice

In small saucepan, stir together all ingredients. Cook over medium heat for 5-7 minutes or until mixture turns clear and thickens.

Glazed golden brown and filled with flavorful wild rice, these Cornish game hens make a festive meal.

Tipsy Hens

4	Cornish game hens

Marinade:
½	cup soy sauce
¾	cup olive oil
½	cup gin
2	small onions, minced
2	cloves garlic, minced
¼	teaspoon freshly ground black pepper
⅛	teaspoon crushed red pepper flakes
1	teaspoon ground ginger
1	tablespoon sugar or honey
1	tablespoon Worcestershire sauce

4 servings

Place hens in large zip-lock bag. Combine marinade ingredients and pour into bag. Squeeze out air and seal. Marinate, refrigerated, overnight. Remove hens from bag and place in roasting pan. Bake at 350 degrees for 50-60 minutes, basting regularly with the marinade.

*Create a spectacular dinner by serving these game hens with **Million Dollar Rice** and **Broccoli a l'Orange.***

Poultry

Turkey Fontina

8	turkey breast slices
½	cup all-purpose flour
4	tablespoons butter, divided
	salt and freshly ground
	black pepper to taste
1½	cups sliced mushrooms
4	tablespoons butter
¾	cup dry white wine
½	cup chicken broth
	salt and freshly ground
	black pepper to taste
½	cup shredded Fontina cheese
½	cup freshly grated
	Parmesan cheese

8 servings

Place each turkey slice between 2 pieces of waxed paper. Using a meat mallet or rolling pin, flatten slices to ⅛-inch thickness. Dredge turkey lightly in flour. In large skillet, melt 2 tablespoons of butter and cook 4 turkey pieces at a time over low heat for 3-4 minutes per side or until golden brown. Place turkey slices in greased 9x13-inch baking dish, overlapping edges. Sprinkle with salt and pepper to taste. Repeat with remaining 2 tablespoons butter and turkey slices. Reserve drippings in skillet.

In another skillet, sauté mushrooms in 4 tablespoons butter until tender. With slotted spoon, remove mushrooms and sprinkle over turkey. Add wine and chicken broth to skillet with turkey drippings. Simmer for 10 minutes, stirring occasionally. Season with salt and pepper to taste. Pour sauce over mushrooms. Combine cheeses and sprinkle over turkey. Bake at 400 degrees for 8-10 minutes. Place under broiler for 1-2 minutes or until lightly browned.

The combination of turkey, mushrooms and cheeses creates a delicious entrée.

Mexican Turkey Slices

½	cup all-purpose flour
¼	teaspoon chili powder
¼	teaspoon garlic powder
1¼	pounds turkey breast slices,
	⅛-¼ inch thick
2-3	tablespoons vegetable oil
	salt and freshly ground
	black pepper to taste
½	cup salsa
2	tomatoes or red bell peppers,
	sliced
1	cup shredded Monterey Jack or
	Cheddar cheese
	sour cream
	salsa

4 servings

In shallow dish, mix flour, chili powder and garlic powder. Coat turkey slices, shaking off excess flour. Heat oil in large skillet over medium-high heat. Cook turkey until no longer pink, about 2 minutes on each side. Season to taste with salt and pepper. Place turkey slices on rack of broiler pan. Top each slice with salsa, a tomato or red pepper slice and cheese. Broil 4 inches from heat for 1-2 minutes or until cheese is melted. Serve with sour cream and additional salsa.

*Serve with **Mexican Zucchini** and **Frijoles Refritos**.*

Poultry

Smacked Flat Turkey

4 turkey tenderloins
1 teaspoon garlic powder
¼ cup Italian bread crumbs
¼ cup freshly grated
  Parmesan cheese
¼ teaspoon freshly ground
  black pepper
½ teaspoon paprika
¼ cup butter
1 tablespoon olive oil
2 tablespoons butter
  juice of 1 lemon

4 servings

Pound turkey tenderloins lightly between 2 sheets of waxed paper to ¼-inch thickness. In plastic bag, combine garlic powder, bread crumbs, Parmesan, pepper and paprika. Shake to mix well. Place 1 or 2 tenderloins at a time in bag mixture and coat well.

In large skillet, heat butter and olive oil until bubbling. Sauté tenderloins, a few at a time, 2-3 minutes on each side. Do not overcook. Drain and keep warm. Add 2 tablespoons of butter to skillet. When it bubbles, add juice of one lemon and stir rapidly. Continue to cook over high heat, stirring constantly and scraping any brown bits from bottom of skillet as mixture thickens slightly. Pour liquid over tenderloins and serve.

Turkey, no longer just associated with Thanksgiving dinner, makes a quick and satisfying meal. Chicken breasts can be substituted.

Turkey Hash

5 tablespoons butter
½ cup all-purpose flour
5 cups rich chicken broth
1-2 teaspoons crushed red pepper
  flakes
1½ pounds sweet Italian bulk sausage,
  crumbled
1 medium red bell pepper, sliced
1 large yellow onion, peeled and
  sliced
5 cups cooked, boned, skinned and
  cubed turkey
¼ cup dried bread crumbs
  additional bread crumbs

8-10 servings

In large, heavy saucepan, melt butter over medium-low heat. Whisk in flour and stir 3 minutes. Blend in broth and red pepper flakes. Increase heat and boil until liquid is reduced by half. Set sauce aside.

In large, heavy skillet, cook crumbled sausage over medium heat until no longer pink, stirring frequently. Remove using slotted spoon and drain on paper towels. Reduce heat to medium-low. Add bell pepper and onion to skillet and cook, stirring occasionally, for 20 minutes. Return sausage to skillet. Mix in sauce, turkey and ¼ cup bread crumbs. Spoon into 9x13-inch buttered casserole. Sprinkle top with additional bread crumbs. Bake in preheated 400 degree oven for 20-25 minutes until heated thorough.

Colorful and flavorful, this hash will have you cooking turkey more than just once a year.

Poultry

Peppered Duck

1	orange, quartered
1	4-pound duckling,
	halved lengthwise
½	cup dry white wine
2	teaspoons coarsley ground
	black peppercorns
¾	cup fruit chutney
¼	cup Dijon mustard

Garnish:
      sprigs of watercress or parsley

2 servings

Squeeze quartered orange over duck. Place duck halves on rack of roasting pan and put orange quarters under duck. Pierce duck with fork and roast at 350 degrees for 1 hour. Remove from oven and drain drippings from bottom of pan. Pour wine over duck. Return to oven and continue roasting for 30 minutes. Remove orange quarters and discard.

In saucepan, combine pepper, chutney and mustard. Heat thoroughly. Brush duck with sauce, return to oven and roast for an additional 30 minutes. Serve remaining sauce with duck. Garnish with watercress or parsley.

The sweet flavor of chutney blends with the pungent flavor of mustard to create a uniquely delicious sauce for this duck.

Duck à l'Orange

1	4-pound duck, quartered
1	teaspoon salt
¼	teaspoon freshly ground
	black pepper
¼	cup frozen orange juice
	concentrate, thawed
	orange slices

Orange Currant Sauce:

1	10-ounce jar red currant jelly
	(1 cup)
¼	cup canned brown gravy
¼	cup frozen orange juice
	concentrate, thawed
¼	cup chicken broth
1	tablespoon white vinegar
1	teaspoon fresh lemon juice
2	teaspoons Grand Marnier
1	orange
1	cup water

2 servings

Sprinkle duck with salt and pepper and pierce skin in several places. Place duck skin side up on rack in roasting pan. Roast at 325 degrees for 2 hours, basting 2-3 times with orange juice concentrate. Place duck halves on serving platter and top with twisted orange slices. Spoon ¼ cup **Orange Currant Sauce** over duck. Pass remaining sauce.

Melt jelly over medium heat, stirring constantly. Add gravy, orange juice concentrate, chicken broth, vinegar, lemon juice and Grand Marnier. Heat to boiling. Reduce heat to low and simmer for 10 minutes, stirring occasionally. Remove peel from orange, carefully avoiding the white membrane. Cut peel into very thin strips. In small saucepan, heat orange peel and water to boiling. Reduce heat to low and simmer for 3 minutes; drain well. Stir orange peel into sauce.

Add wild rice and a green vegetable for a very special dinner.

Poultry

Holiday Goose

1	9-11 pound goose
1	orange, halved
	salt and freshly ground
	black pepper to taste
1	pound bulk pork sausage
1	large onion, chopped
2	cups chopped celery
½	cup butter
1½	cups dry white wine
1	16-ounce package dried
	herb stuffing
12	ounces fresh cranberries
1	cup chopped Granny Smith apples
1	tablespoon freshly grated
	orange peel
¼	cup minced fresh parsley
¼	cup Cointreau or Grand Marnier
2	eggs, lightly beaten
	salt and freshly ground
	black pepper to taste
1	teaspoon ground allspice
1	teaspoon ground mace
	salt and freshly ground
	black pepper to taste
½	cup honey

6 servings

Rinse goose and pat dry. Rub inside and out with cut orange. Sprinkle cavity with salt and pepper.

In large skillet, sauté sausage until no longer pink, crumbling with a fork. Drain and transfer to large mixing bowl. In same skillet, sauté onions and celery in butter until onions are transparent but celery is still crisp. Stir in wine and cook for 1 minute. Pour vegetable mixture over sausage. Add herb stuffing and stir to combine. Add cranberries, apples, orange peel and parsley to stuffing and toss thoroughly. Stir in Cointreau and eggs. Season to taste with salt and pepper.

Loosely stuff bird and truss. Puncture skin around thighs and on back with a fork. Fill roasting pan with ½-inch water. Place goose on a rack in pan and sprinkle with allspice, mace, salt and pepper. Roast goose at 450 degrees for 20 minutes. Reduce heat to 350 degrees and continue roasting until juices run clear, about 20 minutes per pound. Baste frequently with honey and remove rendered fat from bottom of pan with bulb baster. Extra stuffing can be baked in a greased casserole at 350 degrees for 40 minutes.

Remove goose from oven and let stand for 10 minutes before carving.

Very, very special and destined to become a holiday tradition.

Meats

Meats

Grandma's Boardinghouse Meat Loaf

½ cup minced red onion
¾ cup minced green onions
¾ cup minced celery
½ cup minced carrots
½ cup minced green bell pepper
½ cup minced red bell pepper
1 tablespoon minced garlic
3 tablespoons unsalted butter
1 teaspoon salt
¼ teaspoon cayenne pepper
1 teaspoon freshly ground
   black pepper
½ teaspoon ground white pepper
½ teaspoon ground cumin
½ teaspoon ground nutmeg
½ cup half and half
½ cup ketchup
1½ pounds lean ground beef
½ pound ground pork
3 eggs, beaten
¾ cup freshly toasted dry bread
   crumbs

Shallot Gravy:

1 tablespoon minced shallots
1 tablespoon unsalted butter
¼ teaspoon dried thyme
1 bay leaf, crumbled
¼ teaspoon freshly ground
   black pepper
1 cup beef broth
1 cup chicken broth
1 tablespoon unsalted butter
   salt and freshly ground black
   pepper to taste (optional)

6-8 servings

In large, heavy skillet, sauté red and green onions, celery, carrots, green and red peppers and garlic in butter until softened. Set aside and cool to room temperature. Combine salt, cayenne, black and white peppers, cumin and nutmeg and stir into cooled vegetables. Add half and half, ketchup, ground beef, ground pork, eggs and bread crumbs. Lightly form into a loaf and gently place in large baking dish. Bake at 350 degrees for 45-50 minutes.

Prepare **Shallot Gravy.** Remove cooked meat loaf to cutting surface. Heat remaining pan juices on top of stove and deglaze pan with gravy, scraping any brown bits from bottom of pan. Heat to boiling, stirring constantly so gravy will not stick to pan. Slice meat loaf and arrange on serving platter, spooning gravy over top.

Sauté shallots in 1 tablespoon butter with thyme, bay leaf and pepper until softened. Cook over high heat until reduced to a glaze. Add beef and chicken broths and boil until reduced by half. Add remaining 1 tablespoon butter and mix well. Season with salt and freshly ground black pepper to taste.

Makes a hearty and very special, old-fashioned meal when served with roasted potatoes and fresh broccoli.

Meats

White River Reuben Roll

1½	pounds ground beef
1½	cups fresh caraway rye bread crumbs
1	egg, lightly beaten
½	cup finely chopped onion
1	tablespoon sweet pickle relish
¼	cup Thousand Island dressing
1	tablespoon Worcestershire sauce
1½	teaspoons salt
¼	teaspoon freshly ground black pepper
1	14-ounce can sauerkraut, well drained
1½	cups shredded Swiss cheese

6 servings

In large bowl, combine beef, bread crumbs, egg, onion, sweet pickle relish, Thousand Island dressing, Worcestershire, salt and pepper. Work mixture with hands until blended. Shape mixture into 6x14-inch rectangle on a sheet of waxed paper. Sprinkle with sauerkraut and Swiss cheese, leaving a 1-inch border. Starting with narrow end, carefully roll the mixture, using waxed paper as a guide. Place in shallow pan and bake uncovered at 350 degrees for 45 minutes.

A simple meal, equally appropriate for family or guests. Perfect after a day of skiing.

Burgers Bordelaise

1½	pounds lean ground beef
2	tablespoons beef marrow or softened butter
1¼	teaspoons salt
½	teaspoon freshly ground black pepper
1	teaspoon minced fresh thyme or ¼ teaspoon dried thyme
1	egg
	all-purpose flour for dredging
1	tablespoon butter
1	tablespoon oil

Sauce Bordelaise:

1	4-inch piece of beef marrow
½	cup beef bouillon
⅔	cup red wine
3	tablespoons minced shallots or green onions
1	teaspoon cornstarch blended with 1 teaspoon water
	salt and freshly ground black pepper to taste
3	tablespoons minced fresh parsley

4-5 servings

In large bowl, combine ground beef, beef marrow or butter, salt, pepper, thyme and egg, blending thoroughly. Form ground beef mixture into hamburger steaks. Just before cooking, dredge in flour and shake off excess. Sauté in very hot butter and oil for about 6 minutes total for medium rare, or to desired doneness. Remove to hot platter. Prepare **Sauce Bordelaise** and pour over warm hamburgers.

Dig out marrow from bone with small sharp knife. Chop marrow into small pieces. In small saucepan, heat bouillon and wine to boiling; remove from heat. Add marrow and set aside.

Pour fat out of skillet in which meat was cooked. Add shallots and wine mixture to pan, reserving the marrow. Boil rapidly, scraping up coagulated juices with wooden spoon. When reduced to about ½ cup, remove from heat and stir in cornstarch. Simmer 1 minute; add salt and pepper to taste. Fold in marrow and parsley.

*Inviting company fare served with a full-bodied red wine and **Asparagus with Herb Sauce.***

Meats

Miners' Camp Pie

Quite good

4	tablespoons butter
2	cups minced onions
½	pound mushrooms, coarsely chopped
2	pounds lean ground beef, pork or combination
¼	cup dry red wine
2	slices white bread, crumbled
2	teaspoons salt
½	teaspoon freshly ground black pepper
½	teaspoon dried thyme
8	ounces cream cheese, diced
¾	cup minced fresh parsley

Onion Pastry:

2	cups all-purpose flour
3	tablespoons dried onion flakes
1	teaspoon salt
1	teaspoon sugar
¼	teaspoon freshly ground black pepper
¾	cup well-chilled butter, cut into 12 pieces
1	egg, beaten
4-6	tablespoons ice water

Glaze:

1	egg yolk beaten with 1 teaspoon water

6-8 servings

In large, heavy skillet, melt butter over medium-low heat. Add onions and cook until transparent, stirring frequently. Add mushrooms and meat. Increase heat to high and stir until meat is no longer pink. Add wine and stir for about 8 minutes. Pour off remaining liquid. Stir in bread, salt, pepper and thyme. Blend in cream cheese and parsley. Cool to room temperature. *Can be prepared 1 day ahead and refrigerated. Bring to room temperature before continuing.*

To prepare onion pastry, stir flour, onion flakes, salt, sugar and pepper together in a bowl. Cut in butter until mixture resembles coarse meal. Add egg and 2 tablespoons water; blend until dough begins to stick together. Add remaining water a little at a time if dough is dry. (This may be done in a food processor.) Gather dough together. Divide into 2 balls, 1 of which is 2-inches in diameter. Flatten into discs. Wrap tightly and refrigerate for 30 minutes. *Can be prepared up to 3 days ahead.*

Spoon meat into 10-inch pie plate. Brush upper edge and outer rim of plate with glaze. On lightly floured surface, roll larger piece of onion pastry out into 12-inch circle. Cut small hole in center. Place dough over filling, centering steam hole. Press overhanging dough firmly to edge of plate. Press tines of fork along rim. Roll out small dough ball until ¼-inch thick. Cut out decorative shapes. Brush pie with glaze. Place decorations on crust, pressing gently. Brush again with glaze. Bake at 400 degrees for 40 minutes or until golden brown. Cool meat pie for 10 minutes before serving.

*A Sunday evening family favorite served with **Spinach Salad with Creamy Mustard Dressing.***

Meats

Beef Vindaloo
(The Tandoor Kitchen)

1   onion, coarsely chopped
3   cloves garlic
1   teaspoon ground ginger
½   teaspoon cumin seeds
½   teaspoon black mustard seeds
2   tablespoons coriander seeds
1   tablespoon ground turmeric
2   teaspoons crushed red pepper
    flakes (optional)
½   teaspoon fenugreek seeds
¼   cup red wine vinegar
2   pounds beef stew meat, trimmed
    of all fat
4   tablespoons butter
3   cups cooked rice

6 servings

In blender or food processor, combine onion, garlic, ginger, cumin seeds, mustard seeds, coriander seeds, turmeric, red pepper flakes and fenugreek seeds. With machine running, add vinegar in small amounts to make a thick paste. Thoroughly coat meat with paste. Marinate, refrigerated, for at least 6 hours but preferably overnight.

In wok or large, heavy skillet, brown meat in melted butter over high heat. Lower heat and simmer until tender, about 1-1½ hours. Stir occasionally to prevent sticking. Serve over steamed rice.

A truly ethnic meal at its heartiest. Great fare for a winter party.

Mid-Winter Pot Roast

1   2-ounce can anchovies in olive oil,
      drained, oil reserved
⅓   cup milk
4-5   pounds boneless chuck roast of
      beef or eye of round
½   cup all-purpose flour
1   tablespoon paprika
2   tablespoons olive oil
3   medium onions, thinly sliced
½   cup chopped carrots
2   cups beef bouillon
1   cup burgundy
⅓   cup gin
6   cloves garlic, halved
1   bay leaf
      freshly grated peel of 1 orange
1   tablespoon packed light
      brown sugar
½   teaspoon caraway seeds
      large piece of cheesecloth
1½   cups sour cream
2   tablespoons minced fresh dill
1   tomato, peeled, seeded and
      chopped
½   cup crushed gingersnaps
1   cucumber, peeled and sliced
      cherry tomatoes
      sprigs of fresh parsley

6-8 servings

Remove anchovies from oil and soak in milk for 15 minutes. Drain, pat dry and chop into small pieces. Make small slits all over roast and insert anchovies. Combine flour and paprika and pat onto all sides of roast. Heat reserved anchovy oil in heavy roasting pan and brown meat on all sides. Remove roast from pan. Add olive oil and sauté onions and carrots until lightly browned. Add bouillon, burgundy, gin, garlic, bay leaf, orange peel, brown sugar and caraway seeds to pan. Heat to boiling. Add roast and top with wet cheesecloth. Cover and roast at 275 degrees for 5-7 hours or until tender.

Remove roast to platter; keep warm. Skim fat off drippings. Strain ½ cup of drippings into saucepan. Blend in sour cream, dill and chopped tomato. Strain remaining drippings into saucepan. Add gingersnaps. Cook over low heat for 10-15 minutes. Do not boil. Slice meat thinly and garnish with cucumber, cherry tomatoes and parsley. Serve with sauce.

A tantalizing mixture of spices flavors this dish, a family favorite on a snowy night.

Meats

Coors Country Steak Sandwich

⅔	cup Coors beer
⅓	cup vegetable oil
4	cloves garlic, minced
½	teaspoon freshly ground black pepper
1	teaspoon salt
2	beef flank steaks, 1-1¼ pounds each
4	cups sliced onion rings, about 2-3 large onions
2	tablespoons butter
½	teaspoon paprika
1	large loaf French bread

Horseradish Mayonnaise Sauce:

1¼	cups mayonnaise
¼	cup sour cream
¼	cup prepared horseradish
1½	teaspoons fresh lemon juice
¼	teaspoon Tabasco sauce

6 servings

Combine beer, oil, minced garlic, pepper and salt. Marinate steak in beer mixture overnight. Prepare **Horseradish Mayonnaise Sauce** and refrigerate.

In large skillet, sauté onion rings in butter and paprika until tender, but not brown; keep warm. Cut French bread horizontally, then cut each half into 3 equal pieces; set aside. Drain marinade from steak. Grill for 4 minutes per side about 4 inches from coals. Slice meat diagonally into ¼-inch slices. Spread bread pieces with ½ of the **Horseradish Mayonnaise Sauce.** Top with meat and onions. Serve open-faced accompanied by remaining sauce.

In small bowl, combine all ingredients. Cover and refrigerate. Prepare in advance for fuller flavor.

A perfect football Sunday supper that is full of gusto. Serve with a green salad and ice cold Coors!

Golden Grilled Flank Steak

Marinade:

½	cup vegetable oil
2	tablespoons white wine vinegar
3	tablespoons dry vermouth
2	tablespoons whole-grain mustard
2	tablespoons minced fresh rosemary or 1 tablespoon dried rosemary, crumbled
½	teaspoon ground white pepper
1	teaspoon minced fresh thyme (optional)
½-1	teaspoon dry mustard
1	beef flank steak, about 1½-2 pounds

Garnish:

sprigs of fresh rosemary
sprigs of fresh thyme

4 servings

In small bowl, combine all marinade ingredients and whisk to emulsify. Place steak in 9x13-inch pan and add marinade. Turn to coat each side well. Cover and refrigerate overnight, turning occasionally.

Remove steak, then warm marinade over low heat. Grill steak 4-6 inches above hot coals for 5-7 minutes per side, basting meat occasionally with marinade.

Slice thinly on the diagonal and garnish with sprigs of rosemary and thyme.

*Delicious served with **Spinach Artichoke Supreme.***

Meats

Mesa Verde Stuffed Flank

1½ cups freshly grated Parmesan or
    Romano cheese
½ cup soft bread crumbs
2 6-ounce jars marinated artichoke
    hearts, drained and chopped
    (optional)
2 cups finely chopped green onions
1 pound bacon, chopped, fried crisp
    and drained (optional)
2 cups chopped fresh spinach
½ cup minced fresh parsley
½ cup chopped mushrooms (optional)
2 beef flank steaks, about 1½ pounds
    each (have butcher run through
    tenderizer twice)
    Worcestershire sauce
2-4 cloves garlic, minced
½ cup butter
    cotton twine to tie meat
½ pound mushrooms, sliced
1 large onion, thinly sliced
½ cup minced fresh parsley
2½ cups strong beef broth
    sprigs of fresh parsley

6-8 servings

In large bowl, mix Parmesan, bread crumbs, artichoke hearts, green onions, bacon, spinach, ½ cup parsley and ½ cup mushrooms. Divide mixture in half and pat evenly over the two flank steaks. Carefully roll meat in jelly roll fashion. Tie securely in 6-8 places. Seal ends securely. Rub meat with Worcestershire and minced garlic to taste. In large skillet, sear meat on all sides until brown. Place in roasting pan. In medium bowl, mix sliced mushrooms, onion, ½ cup parsley and broth. Pour mixture over meat rolls. Cover pan and roast at 300 degrees for 45-60 minutes or until fork tender. Remove from pan and allow to stand for 5-10 minutes before slicing. Slice ¾-1-inch thick and arrange slices on platter in pinwheel fashion. Garnish with additional parsley.

Wonderful served with buttered noodles and a tossed green salad with Italian dressing.

Summertime Beef Kabobs

Marinade:
2 large cloves garlic, crushed
1 cup vegetable oil
¼ cup soy sauce
¼ cup Worcestershire sauce
¼ cup Dijon mustard
¼ cup fresh lemon juice
1-2 teaspoons coarsely ground
    black pepper

1 5-pound sirloin tip roast of beef
2 Bermuda onions
1 green bell pepper
1 red bell pepper
1 yellow bell pepper
1 pound mushrooms
2 pints cherry tomatoes

8 servings

In large glass baking dish, mix together all marinade ingredients. Cut beef into 1½-inch cubes and add to marinade, turning to coat all sides. Marinate for 24 hours in refrigerator, stirring occasionally.

Prepare onions and peppers by cutting into large chunks that can be skewered. Cut off large stems of mushrooms. Assemble skewers, alternating meat with tomatoes, onions, peppers and mushrooms.

Grill over hot coals 3 minutes per side, turning and basting often with marinade.

*Vegetables in hues of red, purple, green and yellow provide a striking splash of color. Serve with **Million Dollar Rice** for a spectacular summer meal.*

Meats

Saucy Sirloin

2 tablespoons butter
1 cup finely chopped green onions, including tops
2 tablespoons finely chopped shallots (optional)
½ bay leaf, crumbled
1 teaspoon minced fresh thyme or ½ teaspoon dried thyme
1½ cups dry red wine
1 3½-pound boneless beef sirloin steak, about 1½-inches thick
2 tablespoons butter
3 tablespoons minced fresh parsley
1 tablespoon fresh lemon juice
1 tablespoon all-purpose flour

6 servings

In large, heavy skillet melt 2 tablespoons butter over high heat. Sauté onions, shallots, bay leaf and thyme until onions are transparent, about 2-3 minutes. Add wine and cook until reduced by ⅓. Remove sauce from skillet and reserve. In same skillet over high heat, sear steak for 1½ minutes per side. Turn heat to medium and let skillet cool slightly; add sauce, remaining 2 tablespoons butter, parsley, lemon juice and flour. Cook for an additional 2-4 minutes per side, depending on taste. Cut steak in 2-inch diagonal strips and serve with red wine sauce from skillet.

An excellent choice for a last-minute company meal, elegantly served with a medley of fresh garden vegetables and buttered new potatoes. Try substituting buffalo for the beef.

Positively Pinwheel Steaks

1 beef flank steak, about 1½ pounds

Marinade:
2 cups red burgundy wine
½ cup finely chopped green oinons, including tops
2 bay leaves, crumbled
1 tablespoon Worcestershire sauce
1 clove garlic, crushed
1 teaspoon salt
½ teaspoon freshly ground black pepper

½ pound bacon
2 cloves garlic, minced
1 teaspoon salt
½ teaspoon coarsely ground black pepper
¼ cup minced fresh parsley
¼ cup finely chopped onion

3-4 servings

Pound flank steak to ½-inch thickness. Combine all marinade ingredients and mix well. Place flank steak in 9x13-inch pan and pour marinade over meat. Marinate in refrigerator overnight or up to 72 hours.

Remove steak from marinade. Fry bacon until almost done but not crisp. Score steak on both sides. Sprinkle steak with garlic, salt, pepper, parsley and onion. Place bacon lengthwise on steak. Roll-up steak, starting with narrow end. Skewer with wooden picks at 1-inch intervals. Cut into 1-inch slices. Grill over medium-hot coals for 5-7 minutes, turning once.

Serve your guests this favorite with a full-bodied red wine and a zesty salad.

Fireside Fillets in Mushroom Sauce

Marinade:

2	cups sour cream
1	cup finely chopped chives
2	cups mayonnaise
¼	cup red wine
¾	cup buttermilk
¼-½	pound Roquefort cheese, crumbled, to taste
1	tablespoon Worcestershire sauce
1	teaspoon coarsely ground black pepper
1	tablespoon fresh lemon juice
1	teaspoon white vinegar
½	teaspoon celery seed
½	teaspoon garlic salt
½-1	cup minced onion
	Tabasco sauce to taste
10	8-ounce beef fillet steaks

Mushroom Sauce:

1	pound mushrooms, thickly sliced
½	cup chopped green onions
3	cloves garlic, minced
¼	cup minced fresh parsley
½	cup butter

10 servings

In large bowl, mix together all marinade ingredients. Arrange steaks in 9x13-inch pan and pour marinade over meat. Cover. Marinate in refrigerator overnight or up to 72 hours.

Remove steaks from marinade, taking care to keep as much of mixture on steaks as possible. Grill steaks over hot coals to desired doneness. Sauté mushrooms and green onions, garlic and parsley in butter until tender. Pour sauce over steaks.

*An elegant meal to be served by the fireside. Accompany with **Broiled Tomatoes** and a good bottle of red Bordeaux.*

Meats

Trappers' Peak Tenderloin

1	4-pound whole beef tenderloin
2-4	cloves garlic, minced
4-6	tablespoons coarsely ground black pepper
¾	cup Worcestershire sauce
1½	cups soy sauce
1⅓	cups undiluted beef bouillon

6-8 servings

Wash tenderloin and pat dry. Rub with minced garlic and press black pepper onto sides. Combine Worcestershire and soy in large baking dish and marinate beef for 2-3 hours at room temperature.

Preheat oven to 500 degrees. Drain and discard marinade. Pour bouillon around beef. Put into oven and immediately reduce heat to 350 degrees. Cook for 18 minutes per pound for rare, 20 minutes per pound for medium rare, or until internal temperature reaches 135-140 degrees. Slice and serve with **Mushroom-Roquefort Sauce.**

Mushroom-Roquefort Sauce:

¼	pound Rouquefort cheese
½	cup butter
2-4	cloves garlic, minced
1	tablespoon Worcestershire sauce
¼	teaspoon caraway seeds
½	cup chopped green onions, including tops
½	pound mushrooms, sliced

In medium saucepan over low heat, combine cheese, butter, garlic, Worcestershire and caraway seeds. Stir until cheese and butter melt. Add green onions and mushrooms. Continue cooking for 2-3 minutes.

An impressive yet conservatively elegant presentation for family or guests.

Mushroom Tournedos Bordelaise

4	beef fillet steaks, 1½-2-inches thick
8	slices firm white bread
6	shallots, finely chopped
6	whole black peppercorns
4	whole cloves
4	tablespoons butter
3	tablespoons all-purpose flour
3	cups strong beef broth
1⅓	cups dry red wine
½	pound mushrooms
1	tablespoon minced fresh parsley
2	tablespoons butter, divided

4 servings

Trim all fillets to equal size and save trimmings. Set fillets aside. Trim bread into shape of fillets and toast lightly. Set aside. In large, heavy skillet, sauté shallots, peppercorns and cloves in 4 tablespoons butter until shallots are golden. Add flour, stirring until well blended. Gradually add beef broth and wine to skillet. Heat to boiling, stirring constantly. Reduce to low heat and simmer for 8 minutes, reducing sauce.

Finely chop mushrooms and fillet trimmings. In medium skillet, sauté mushrooms, trimmings and parsley in 1 tablespoon butter until moisture has disappeared. Set aside. Heat remaining 1 tablespoon butter in heavy skillet and sauté fillets for 4-5 minutes per side for medium rare, or until well browned. Stir 2 tablespoons of sauce into mushroom mixture. Divide mixture among 4 pieces of toast and top with remaining 4 pieces of toast. Place on serving platter and top with fillets; keep warm. Pour sauce into skillet used to sauté fillets and heat until sauce begins to bubble, scraping any brown bits from bottom of skillet. Spoon sauce over and around fillets.

Meats

Shiitake Mushroom Steak

Marinade:
½ cup hoisin sauce
½ cup sesame oil
3 tablespoons red wine vinegar
   freshly ground black pepper
    to taste
1 cup chopped green onions,
   including tops
4 medium garlic cloves, crushed

6 New York strip steaks,
   1½-inches thick

Shiitake Sauce:
1 pound fresh shiitake mushrooms,
   stems discarded or 4 ounces
   dried shiitake mushrooms
   soaked in hot water for 30
   minutes, drained, squeezed of
   excess moisture, and hard cores
   discarded
3 tablespoons unsalted butter
3 tablespoons peanut oil
8 teaspoons coarse grained
   Dijon mustard
2½ cups beef broth, divided
½ cup heavy cream
   salt and freshly ground
    black pepper to taste
   minced fresh parsley (optional)

6 servings

In medium bowl, mix hoisin sauce, sesame oil, vinegar and generous amount of freshly ground black pepper. Add onions and garlic. Whisk together. In large glass pan, pour marinade over steaks, turning to coat well. Cover and refrigerate for 24-48 hours, turning occasionally.

Slice mushrooms into ½-inch strips. In large heavy skillet over medium heat, sauté mushrooms in butter and oil for 3 minutes or until tender. Add mustard and 1¼ cups of broth. Increase heat to high and boil until reduced by half. Add remaining 1¼ cups of broth, ¼ cup at a time, boiling until sauce is reduced by half at each addition. (Procedure takes about 10 minutes.) Add cream and boil sauce until it coats a metal spoon. Season to taste with salt and pepper. Keep warm.

Remove steaks from marinade. Grill over hot coals about 5 minutes per side for medium rare. Arrange steaks on platter, sprinkle with minced parsley and serve immediately, accompanied by hot **Shiitake Sauce.**

*A delicious grilled steak with flavors and aromas of the Orient. Serve with **Sesame Asparagus.***

Chutney Pepper Steak
(The Broadmoor)

4 6-ounce center-cut beef fillet
   steaks, about 1¼-inches thick
2 tablespoons unsalted butter
¼ cup Major Grey's Mango Chutney
2 teaspoons cracked black pepper
3 ounces Armagnac

4 servings

In large skillet, sauté fillets in melted butter over medium-high heat. Cook for 3 minutes per side for rare or until desired doneness. Top with chutney, then pepper. Flambé with Armagnac. Use caution when flaming brandy.

*Armagnac should be warmed before flaming, but not boiled. Flame in a large spoon and pour over meat. Complete this elegant company entrée with **Tomatoes Florentine** and **Bacon Almond Potato Balls.***

Meats

Shadow Mountain Tenderloin

Spinach Stuffing:

1¼	pounds fresh spinach, rinsed and stemmed
2	tablespoons butter
½	pound mushrooms, chopped
1½	cups shredded Swiss cheese
2	eggs, beaten
1	teaspoon fennel seeds
1	teaspoon dried sage
	salt and freshly ground black pepper to taste
1	whole beef tenderloin, trimmed of excess fat (8 pounds)
6-8	cloves garlic, minced
1½	teaspoons fennel seeds
1½	teaspoons coarsely ground black pepper
½	cup beef broth
½	cup Madeira or dry Sherry

16 servings

Drain spinach briefly and put in large skillet. Cover and cook over medium heat just until spinach wilts, about 3 minutes, stirring once or twice. Remove from heat. Uncover, let cool and chop coarsely. Squeeze out excess water. (Frozen spinach may be substituted. Thaw and squeeze out excess water. Do not cook.) Using same pan, melt 2 tablespoons butter over medium-high heat. Add mushrooms. Cook, stirring, until mushrooms are limp and all juices evaporate. Remove from heat. Stir in spinach, cheese, eggs, 1 teaspoon fennel seeds, sage, salt and pepper. *This can be covered and refrigerated as long as overnight.*

Cut a lengthwise slash in tenderloin to within ½ inch of each end and opposite side to form a pocket. Spoon spinach filling evenly into pocket; pat in firmly. Sew up tenderloin using a large embroidery needle and strong thread or dental floss, making stitches ½-inch apart.

Blend together garlic, 1½ teaspoons fennel seeds and pepper. Rub mixture all over outside of roast. Place meat in preheated 500-degree oven. Immediately reduce heat to 350 degrees. Roast 18 minutes per pound for medium rare, or to an internal temperature of 135-140 degrees. Let stand 10 minutes.

While meat is standing, pour drippings into 3-quart saucepan. Add broth and Madeira. Boil on high heat until mixture reduces to ½ cup. Serve sauce with meat.

This recipe can be halved by using a smaller tenderloin and adjusting the stuffing ingredients accordingly. A striking buffet entrée glamorous enough for the most sophisticated palate.

Meats

Fall River Rib Roast

½ cup minced fresh parsley
3 tablespoons freshly grated
     lemon peel
4 teaspoons dried thyme, crumbled
8 juniper berries, crushed
6 cloves garlic
1 teaspoon freshly ground
     black pepper
4-8 drops Tabasco sauce
1 cup olive oil
¼ cup fresh lemon juice
1 10-pound standing rib roast of beef

10-12 servings

Combine parsley, lemon peel, thyme, juniper berries, garlic, pepper and Tabasco in blender. Add oil 1 tablespoon at a time, blending until a smooth paste is formed. Add lemon juice and blend. Rub mixture over surface of roast. Cover and refrigerate for at least 24 hours.

Bring roast to room temperature before proceeding. Place roast in large, heavy roasting pan and roast in preheated oven at 500 degrees for 15 minutes. Reduce temperature to 350 degrees and continue roasting for 15 minutes per pound for rare, 20 minutes per pound for medium, or 25 minutes per pound for well done. Let roast rest for 10 minutes before carving. Serve with *Hunters' Horseradish Sauce.*

Hunters' Horseradish Sauce:

6 egg yolks
2 tablespoons fresh lemon juice
    salt and freshly ground
     black pepper to taste
1 cup butter, melted and hot
1½ cups heavy cream, whipped
6-8 tablespoons prepared horseradish
2-4 drops Tabasco sauce
3 tablespoons minced onion
3 tablespoons minced fresh parsley

4 cups

Combine egg yolks, lemon juice, salt and pepper in blender. Mix until well blended. While machine is running, add hot butter in a slow stream. Transfer to large bowl and fold in whipped cream. Add horseradish and Tabasco to taste. Fold in minced onion and parsley and transfer to serving bowl.

The best prime rib recipe ever!

Meats

Claimjumpers' Corned Beef

1	cup salt
¼	cup sugar
2	quarts water
2	bay leaves
4	whole black peppercorns
1	clove garlic, crushed
1	tablespoon pickling spice
1	4-pound beef brisket
2	bay leaves
4	whole black peppercorns
1	clove garlic, minced

Sauce:

¾	cup bourbon
1½	cups firmly packed dark brown sugar
3	tablespoons prepared mustard
¾	cup apple juice

8 servings

Start corning beef 7 days before serving. In large pot, pour salt and sugar into water, stirring to dissolve. Add 2 bay leaves, 4 peppercorns, 1 clove garlic and pickling spice. Place beef in brine. Place weighted plate on beef to keep beef submerged. Cover pot and refrigerate for 7 days. Turn beef at least once every day.

Remove beef from brine and wash well in clear water. Place beef in deep stock pot and cover with fresh water. Add remaining 2 bay leaves, 4 peppercorns and 1 clove garlic. Heat to boiling. Turn heat down immediately and simmer slowly, covered, for at least 3 hours or until tender. Remove corned beef from pot and place on rack in shallow roasting pan, fat side up. Prepare basting sauce by combining bourbon with brown sugar, mustard and apple juice. Pour basting sauce over brisket. Roast at 400 degrees for 30 minutes, basting with pan juices every 10 minutes. Slice thinly on diagonal and serve with remaining sauce.

Absolutely wonderful! Use the fireplace as a focal point for dining on a fall evening and serve corned beef surrounded by a harvest of steamed vegetables.

Tivoli Veal Tarragon

2	tablespoons dried tarragon
3	tablespoons dry white wine
½	cup all-purpose flour
	salt and ground white pepper to taste
4	veal steaks, ¾-inch thick, pounded to ¼-inch thick
4	tablespoons butter
¼	cup finely chopped shallots (optional)
¼	cup chopped green onions, including tops
2	tablespoons butter, softened
1	cup dry white wine
1	teaspoon chicken bouillon granules
2	cups heavy cream

4 servings

Combine tarragon and 3 tablespoons wine; set aside. Season flour with salt and white pepper. Lightly dust veal steaks with flour. In large skillet melt butter and brown steaks on both sides. Remove veal from skillet to warm platter. Brown shallots and green onions in 2 tablespoons butter. Add 1 cup wine and reduce by half. Add chicken granules, wine-soaked tarragon and cream. Heat to boiling; reduce slightly. Add juice from veal platter; mix well. Return veal to skillet and warm. Serve veal topped with tarragon sauce.

A simple delicacy served with vermicelli and green beans.

Meats

Liver Alive with Avocados

½	cup all-purpose flour
1	teaspoon salt
¼	teaspoon freshly ground black pepper
6	avocados
¼	cup fresh lemon juice
12	slices calves' liver, cut very thinly
¾	cup butter, divided
	juice of 3 lemons
½	cup beef broth
1	teaspoon minced fresh thyme or ½ teaspoon dried thyme
½	cup minced fresh parsley
2	tablespoons dry white wine

4 servings

In flat dish, mix together flour, salt and pepper; set aside. Peel avocados and cut into thin slices. Sprinkle with ¼ cup lemon juice; set aside. Thoroughly dry liver slices. Dip slices of liver and avocado into seasoned flour and pat between hands to give them a thin dusting. Heat 4 tablespoons butter in heavy skillet until foam subsides. Sauté liver and avocados quickly, a few at a time, about 1½ minutes per side or until liver is still pink in center. Arrange liver and avocados alternately on heated platter; keep warm.

In same skillet, melt ½ cup butter. Heat until butter just browns. Add juice of 3 lemons, beef broth, thyme, parsley and wine. Stir to mix. When sauce is bubbling, pour over liver and avocados and serve.

A zesty liver dish that is sure to be enjoyed by even those who think they don't like liver. **Lemon Carrots** *are a pleasant addition to this flavorful dish.*

Brandied Peach Veal Steaks

½	cup unsalted butter
4	veal steaks, pounded salt and freshly ground black pepper to taste
½	teaspoon marjoram, crumbled
4	large fresh peaches, peeled, pitted and thickly sliced
⅔	cup peach brandy or dry sherry
2	cups sour cream

4 servings

Melt butter in large skillet. Add veal and sauté over medium heat until browned, about 1½ minutes per side. Remove from heat and season with salt, pepper and marjoram. Brown peaches in remaining butter in skillet. Remove and keep warm. Add brandy to pan and cook over low heat until liquid is reduced by half. Add sour cream slowly and heat. Return veal to pan and warm. To serve, spoon sauce over veal and top with browned peaches.

An elegant late summer meal to serve on your patio. Serve with **Green Bean Bundles.**

Meats

Cognac Medallions of Veal

1½ pounds veal medallions, ⅜-inch
    thick and 2 inches in diameter
1½ cups brown sauce or 1 package
    Knorr Swiss Hunter Sauce mix,
    prepared according to package
    directions
    all-purpose flour
4-6 tablespoons butter
  1 10-ounce package frozen artichoke
    hearts, thawed and halved
  1 tablespoon finely chopped shallots
  1 pound mushrooms, thinly sliced
    salt and freshly ground
    black pepper to taste
  ¼ cup cognac
  6 tablespoons heavy cream

4 servings

Place medallions between sheets of waxed paper and pound with mallet to flatten. Flour veal lightly. In large skillet, sauté veal in butter about 1 minute per side. When veal is bright brown, add artichoke hearts, shallots, mushrooms, salt and pepper. Sauté a few minutes. Add cognac and sauté a few minutes longer, adding butter as needed. Remove veal from pan. Add cream and brown sauce. Cook until sauce is thick and smooth. Return veal to pan and heat thoroughly over low heat.

Enticing served over fresh fettucine and accompanied by **Pistachio'd Carrots.**

Veal Scallops in Velvet Mushroom Sauce

  ¾ cup all-purpose flour
    salt and freshly ground
    black pepper to taste
  8 ½-inch thick slices of veal,
    pounded to ¼-inch thick
2-4 tablespoons butter
  2 cloves garlic, minced
  4 shallots, minced
  ½ cup chopped green onions,
    including tops
  2 tablespoons butter
  1 cup dry white wine
  2 cups heavy cream
  1 teaspoon chicken bouillon granules
  1 pound mushrooms, sliced
  1 bunch spinach, rinsed and
    stemmed

4 servings

Mix flour with salt and pepper to taste. Dust veal lightly. In large skillet, melt 2-4 tablespoons butter and stir in garlic. When butter is very hot, sauté veal 1 minute per side. Remove and keep warm. In same skillet, sauté shallots and green onions in 2 tablespoons butter for 1 minute. Add white wine and boil until reduced to almost nothing. Add cream, chicken bouillon granules and mushrooms. Boil down to serving consistency, stirring constantly. Return veal to skillet and keep warm. Blanch spinach for 2 minutes in boiling water seasoned with salt and pepper. Rinse and drain well. Serve veal on bed of spinach, topped with creamed mushroom sauce.

A fabulous main course, perfect for entertaining.

Meats

Veal Scallops Marsala

1 cup unsalted butter, softened
½ cup minced fresh parsley
2 tablespoons minced fresh sage
3 large cloves garlic, minced
   freshly grated peel of 1 lemon
12 veal scallops, pounded
   (about 2½ pounds)
12 paper-thin slices prosciutto, cut to
   same size as veal
12 paper-thin slices Fontina cheese,
   cut to same size as veal
   olive oil

Garnish:
lemon slices
minced fresh parsley

Mustard Marsala Sauce:
2-4 cloves garlic
½ teaspoon salt
1 tablespoon coarsely ground Dijon
   mustard
½ teaspoon freshly ground black
   pepper
2 egg yolks, room temperature
¾ cup vegetable oil
¾ cup olive oil
2-3 tablespoons fresh lemon juice
1-2 tablespoons dry Marsala

6 servings

In small bowl, blend butter, parsley, sage, garlic and lemon peel. Spread herbed butter evenly over veal scallops. Top each scallop with a prosciutto slice, then a slice of cheese. Cut each scallop in half. Starting at short end, roll up each scallop. Tie with string and thread lengthwise onto 10-inch skewers, about 3 to a skewer. Cover and refrigerate overnight.

Balance ends of skewers on sides of broiler pan. Brush with olive oil. Either broil 8-10 minutes, basting frequently with drippings; or roast at 400 degrees for 10-12 minutes. Remove veal from skewers and remove string. Arrange veal on platter, garnish with lemon slices and parsley, and serve with *Mustard Marsala Sauce.*

2 cups

In food processor, blend together garlic, salt, mustard, pepper and egg yolks. With machine running, pour oils through tube in a slow, steady stream. Sauce will be thick. Blend in lemon juice and Marsala. Refrigerate overnight or until ready to use. *Keeps well for 1 week.*

An entrée typical of Northern Italian cuisine which is a particular favorite of men. An enticing meal for an anniversary dinner.

Kiwi Veal
(The Bay Wolf)

4 fresh kiwis, peeled
⅓ cup kiwi preserves
¼ cup crystallized ginger
2 tablespoons dry white wine
1½ pounds veal, pounded into
   18 medallions
   all-purpose flour
2 tablespoons olive oil
   fresh kiwi slices

6 servings

In food processor, purée 4 kiwis, preserves, ginger and white wine until smooth. In small saucepan, heat mixture over low heat while preparing veal. Lightly dust veal medallions with flour. Sauté veal in hot oil about 2 minutes per side. Pour heated kiwi sauce onto 4 plates. Top with veal scallops. Garnish with kiwi slices.

An exceptionally refreshing veal dish created by one of Denver's finest restaurants.

Meats

Veal Tonnato

4 cloves garlic, minced
1 2-ounce can anchovy fillets, drained
2 tablespoons chopped fresh basil
1 3½-pound loin of veal, boned and tied
6 tablespoons olive oil
3 medium onions, sliced
3 carrots, peeled and cut into 1-inch rounds
1 large leek, white part only, chopped
½ cup minced fresh parsley
1¾ cups dry white wine
1 cup strong chicken broth
salt and freshly ground black pepper to taste

Garnish:
lemon slices
capers
sprigs of fresh parsley

Homemade Mayonnaise:
1 teaspoon sugar
1 teaspoon salt
½ teaspoon dry mustard, or to taste
dash of cayenne pepper
⅛ teaspoon ground white pepper, or to taste
2 egg yolks
1½ tablespoons vinegar
2 cups vegetable oil
2 tablespoons fresh lemon juice

Tonnato Sauce:
1 7-ounce can tuna in oil
6 flat anchovy fillets
2 cloves garlic
3 tablespoons capers
juice of 1 lemon
¾ cup olive oil
jellied veal broth as needed
1½-2 cups *Homemade Mayonnaise*

6-8 servings

In small bowl, mix together garlic, anchovies and basil to form a paste. Make 8-10 ½-inch incisions on all sides of veal. Stuff each pocket with garlic mixture. In large, heavy kettle, heat oil until hot. Add veal and brown on all sides, turning frequently. Add onions, carrots, leek and parsley. Cook for 5-8 minutes or until vegetables are lightly colored. Add wine, broth, salt and pepper and heat to boiling. Cover and transfer to preheated 300-degree oven. Cook slowly for 1½ hours or until meat is fork-tender. Remove to platter and cool to lukewarm. Cover and refrigerate overnight. Strain pan juices into bowl, discarding vegetables. Chill overnight. Skim fat from top of jellied stock; reserve stock for future use.

Slice veal very thinly. On large platter, pour small amount of *Tonnato Sauce* to cover bottom. Arrange veal slices in slightly overlapping pattern on top of sauce. Cover veal with remaining sauce. Cover and refrigerate overnight. To serve, garnish with lemon slices, capers and parsley.

2 cups

In blender or food processor, combine sugar, salt, mustard, cayenne pepper, white pepper and egg yolks. Add vinegar slowly, blending constantly. With machine running, slowly add oil. Continue blending until mixture thickens. Blend in lemon juice. Cover and refrigerate.

In blender or food processor, combine tuna, anchovies, garlic, capers, lemon juice and oil. Process to fine paste. If sauce is too thick, add a few tablespoons of jellied veal broth. Blend in mayonnaise to taste, a small amount at a time, keeping mixture smooth. Mix well, cover and refrigerate until ready to assemble veal.

This dish is best when veal is cooked on day one, sliced and marinated in Tonnato Sauce on day two, and served on day three. An excellent choice for a luncheon or summer buffet, presented on a table decorated with fresh flowers of the season.

Meats

Cattle Creek Glazed Veal Riblets

3   teaspoons finely sliced lemon peel
1   cup plus 1 tablespoon fresh
       lemon juice
6   tablespoons hoisin sauce
6   tablespoons sesame or peanut oil
1   cup honey
¼   cup sesame seeds
2   tablespoons minced garlic
1   cup chopped green onions,
       including tops
1½   inch piece of fresh ginger root,
       peeled and grated
6   pounds veal riblets, 2½-inches
       long, separated and trimmed

6 servings

In large bowl, combine lemon peel and lemon juice, hoisin sauce, oil, honey, sesame seeds, garlic, green onions and ginger. Whisk to emulsify. Add riblets to marinade, turning to coat well. Cover and marinate 6 hours or overnight in refrigerator.

Grill ribs over medium-hot coals, turning and basting frequently until evenly browned, about 15 minutes.

A great alternative to beef or pork ribs.

Fruited Pork Kabobs

Marinade:

½   teaspoon salt
½   teaspoon freshly ground
       black pepper
½   cup sherry
1   cup port
¼   cup olive oil
6   tablespoons honey
2   tablespoons minced fresh thyme
12   whole pitted dried prunes

2   pounds pork tenderloin
3   peaches, peeled, pitted
       and quartered
3   sweet potatoes
1   cup packed dark brown sugar
1   teaspoon ground cloves
1   teaspoon ground ginger
2   tablespoons sherry
1   fresh pineapple, peeled, cored
       and cut into 1½-inch chunks

4 servings

In large bowl, combine all marinade ingredients. Whisk briskly to emulsify. Marinate whole tenderloins and peach quarters for 4 hours.

Boil sweet potatoes in water to cover until barely tender. Peel and cut into 1½-inch chunks. In small bowl, combine brown sugar, cloves, ginger and sherry to make a paste. Roll potato chunks, pineapple chunks and peach quarters in paste to coat evenly. Remove prunes from marinade. Assemble fruit and potatoes alternately on skewers. Brush with remaining paste. Cut pork into 1½-inch pieces and assemble on separate skewers. Grill pork over medium-hot coals for 2 minutes on each of 4 sides. Grill fruit kabobs for 8 minutes total.

An unusual twist for grilled kabobs using fruit for color, texture and sweetness.

Meats

Pitkin County Pork Chops

2   tablespoons butter
½   cup chopped onion
2-3 cloves garlic, minced
1   teaspoon salt
¼   cup prepared mustard
¼   teaspoon cayenne pepper
2   tablespoons cider vinegar
2   tablespoons packed light
      brown sugar
2   tablespoons Worcestershire sauce
6   pork chops, 1½-inches thick
¾   cup ketchup
½   cup chili sauce
⅓   cup water

6 servings

In small bowl, combine butter, onion, garlic, salt, mustard, cayenne pepper, vinegar, brown sugar and Worcestershire to make a paste. Spread over pork chops. Place in large baking dish and broil close to heat for 5 minutes. Remove from oven. In small bowl, combine ketchup, chili sauce and water; blend well. Pour sauce over chops. Cover and bake at 350 degrees for 1 hour or until pork is tender.

A tantalizing mixture of sweet, sour and spice which is excellent served over fresh linguine.

Squaw Point Pork Chops with Lemon Dill Sauce

Lemon Dill Sauce:
6   tablespoons mayonnaise
6   tablespoons sour cream
½   cup Dijon mustard
½   cup fresh lemon juice
1   teaspoon coarsely ground
      black pepper
8   teaspoons minced fresh dill

4   boneless pork loin chops,
      1½-inches thick

4 servings

Combine all sauce ingredients. Pour ½ of sauce over chops, cover and refrigerate for 4-6 hours. Cover and refrigerate remaining sauce.

Remove chops, discarding marinade. Grill chops over medium coals for 9-11 minutes per side or to desired doneness. Brush top side of chops with **Lemon Dill Sauce** one minute prior to removing from grill. Pass remaining sauce.

*Sure to be a hit when served with **Saffron Carrots and Turnips.** This marinade works equally well with veal or lamb chops.*

Meats

Campfire Grilled Spareribs

6	pounds country-style pork spareribs
3	tablespoons olive oil
1/3	cup hoisin sauce
1/3	cup soy sauce
4	teaspoons freshly minced ginger root
3/4	cup whiskey
	freshly grated peel of 1 orange
1/4	cup fresh orange juice
1/4	cup fresh grapefruit juice
1/2	cup packed dark brown sugar
8	cloves garlic, minced

Trading Post Barbecue Sauce:

1	cup double-strength coffee
1 1/2	cups ketchup
1/2	cup corn oil
1/2	cup Worcestershire sauce
1/2	cup packed dark brown sugar
1/3	cup cider vinegar
1	teaspoon chili powder

6 servings

In large kettle, parboil ribs in water to cover for 20 minutes; drain. Combine remaining ingredients to make marinade. Place ribs in shallow baking dish, pour marinade over, cover and refrigerate for 1-2 days, turning occasionally.

Heat **Trading Post Barbecue Sauce** to simmering. Remove meat from marinade; discard marinade. Grill ribs over medium-hot coals for 15 minutes, turning frequently to prevent burning. Baste often with barbecue sauce. Serve remaining sauce warm with ribs.

In medium saucepan, stir together all ingredients. Heat to simmering over medium-high heat and cook for 5 minutes or until desired thickness. Cool, cover and refrigerate.

Sauce is at its fullest flavor when prepared several days in advance. Great for a barbecue in the mountains or a moveable feast.

Cantonese Pork Tenderloin

Marinade:

1/2	cup peanut oil
1/4	cup hoisin sauce
1/4	cup soy sauce
1/2	cup distilled white or rice wine vinegar
1/4	cup dry sherry
1/2	teaspoon hot chili oil (optional)
1	tablespoon dark sesame oil (optional)
4	whole green onions, finely chopped
4	cloves garlic, minced
2	tablespoons minced fresh ginger root

2-4	pork tenderloins, 3 pounds total

4-6 servings

Combine all marinade ingredients and mix well. Pour over pork and marinate 3-4 hours at room temperature or overnight in refrigerator.

Grill over medium-hot coals for 9-11 minutes per side, basting frequently with marinade.

*Even the most discriminating cook will agree that the combination of flavors in this Oriental-inspired pork tenderloin is truly spectacular. Try serving with **Cinnamon Beans with Bacon**.*

Meats

Pork at Its Peak

Marinade:

- ½ cup dry white wine
- ¼ cup vegetable oil
- 6 tablespoons Dijon mustard
- ¼ cup chopped mushrooms
- 2 tablespoons soy sauce
- 2 tablespoons fresh lemon juice
- 2 tablespoons minced onion
- 2 tablespoons butter
- ½ teaspoon celery seed
- ½ teaspoon salt
- ½ teaspoon freshly ground black pepper

- 1 5-pound pork loin roast, boned, rolled and tied

8-10 servings

In large bowl, mix together all marinade ingredients. Place pork roast in rectangular baking pan and pour marinade over meat. Cover and refrigerate 24 hours, turning occasionally.

Drain and reserve marinade. Roast at 350 degrees for 2½ hours or to an internal temperature of 155-160 degrees. Baste frequently with reserved marinade during last 30 minutes of roasting time.

*Serve this succulent pork roast with **Powderhorn Potatoes** and steamed fresh broccoli.*

Orchard Mesa Ham and Pear Crisp Sandwich

- ½ cup unsalted butter, room temperature
- ½ teaspoon freshly grated nutmeg
- ½ teaspoon ground cinnamon
- ½ teaspoon ground coriander
- ½ teaspoon ground ginger
  salt to taste
- 8 slices pumpernickel bread, crusts trimmed
- 4 ¼-inch thick slices Gruyère cheese
- 2 large pears, peeled, cored and thinly sliced lengthwise
- ½-¾ pound thinly sliced smoked ham
- 4 ¼-inch thick slices Fontina cheese sprigs of fresh parsley (optional)

4 servings

In small bowl, cream together butter, nutmeg, cinnamon, coriander, ginger and salt. Spread mixture on 1 side of each slice of bread. On 4 slices of bread, layer 1 slice Gruyère, several thin slices pear, several thin slices ham, and 1 slice Fontina. Repeat pear and ham layers. Top each sandwich with 1 slice bread, buttered side in. Press down on sandwiches to retain shape. Butter top, gently turn over and place in heavy skillet over medium heat. Butter top sides of sandwiches. Cover sandwiches with piece of waxed paper and top with heavy plate. Cook until golden brown on bottom side. Remove plate and gently remove waxed paper. Carefully turn sandwiches to grill other side until golden brown. Arrange any remaining pear slices on top of parsley sprigs on serving plates for garnish.

A wonderful late-night supper in front of a blazing fireplace served with hot spiced wine.

Meats

Pork Tenderloin a la Crème

8	strips bacon
8	slices pork tenderloin, 2-inches thick, butterflied
¼	cup brandy or cognac
2	teaspoons dry mustard
	salt and freshly ground black pepper to taste
¼	cup dry white wine
2-3	tablespoons beef bouillon granules
2	cups heavy cream
2-3	tablespoons all-purpose flour
¼	pound mushrooms, sliced

4-6 servings

Fry bacon until limp. Wrap bacon around outside edge of each butterflied tenderloin, secure with a wooden pick and place in ungreased roasting pan. Using a spoon, drizzle brandy over meat. Sprinkle meat with mustard, salt and pepper. Bake uncovered at 350 degrees for 20-30 minutes. Remove pork. Skim grease from drippings. Add wine and bouillon granules and deglaze roasting pan over medium heat. Whisk together cream and flour until smooth. Whisk into drippings. Stir and boil until thickened and smooth, about 4 minutes. Return meat to pan, turning to coat both sides. Sprinkle with mushrooms. Bake uncovered at 350 degrees for 15 minutes, or until sauce is thickened.

A special weekend meal served with a dry white wine, steamed fresh vegetables and crusty French bread.

Estes Park Pork Loin

1	pound bulk country sausage
1	teaspoon dried sage
½	cup minced fresh parsley
1	medium onion, finely chopped
1	boneless pork loin roast, tied (3-4 pounds)
4	teaspoons dry mustard
2	teaspoons dried sage
1	teaspoon salt
1	teaspoon freshly ground black pepper
	sprigs of fresh parsley

Herbed Sautéed Apples:

4	tablespoons butter
3	cardamom pods, hulls removed, crushed with flat side of knife
1	bay leaf, crumbled
½	teaspoon lemon pepper
½	teaspoon chopped fresh rosemary
½	teaspoon chopped fresh thyme
1	teaspoon fresh lemon juice
3	tablespoons packed dark brown sugar
2	large Granny Smith apples, cored and sliced into rings

6 servings

In medium bowl, mix sausage, 1 teaspoon sage, parsley and onion. Stuff cavity of pork roast with sausage mixture until filled completely. Reserve remaining sausage mixture. In small bowl, mix mustard, 2 teaspoons sage, salt and pepper. Rub mixture over entire roast. Place in roasting pan and cover with foil. Cook at 325 degrees for 30-45 minutes. Remove foil and cook an additional 45 minutes or until meat thermometer registers 155 degrees. Baste often with pan drippings.

In small skillet, crumble and fry remaining sausage mixture. Season to taste with salt and pepper. Keep warm while carving roast into ¼-inch slices. Arrange meat on platter with **Herbed Sautéed Apples** and sprinkle with remaining sausage mixture. Garnish with parsley.

In medium skillet, melt butter over moderately low heat. Add cardamom, bay leaf, lemon pepper, rosemary, thyme, lemon juice and brown sugar. Whisk thoroughly. Add apples and sauté until glaze forms. Remove from heat and serve warm with pork roast.

Oven-roasted potatoes are an easy and delicious accompaniment. Triple the herbed apple recipe if used as a side dish rather than garnish.

Meats

Pinecliffe Roasted Pork

1½ pounds pitted dried prunes
    dry Madeira (enough to
      cover prunes)
3 cups ½-inch cubes of bread
1 cup diced celery
1 small onion, finely chopped
1 small green bell pepper,
    finely chopped
¾ teaspoon salt
¼ teaspoon freshly ground
    black pepper
¾ cup chicken broth
1 6-pound pork loin, butterflied
½ teaspoon ground ginger
½ teaspoon salt
⅛ teaspoon freshly ground
    black pepper
½ cup dry white wine
1 cup heavy cream
½ cup minced onion
¼ cup minced fresh parsley
6 tablespoons all-purpose flour
3 cups chicken broth
1 cup dry white wine
    salt and freshly ground
      black pepper to taste

10-12 servings

In medium bowl, combine prunes with Madeira and let stand at room temperature for 2-3 hours.

Drain prunes, reserving Madeira. Coarsely chop prunes. Mix together prunes, bread cubes, celery, onion, green pepper, ¾ teaspoon salt and ¼ teaspoon pepper. Moisten mixture with ¾ cup chicken broth.

Pound pork loin to an even thickness just under 1 inch. Spread stuffing over pork. Roll up from long side and tie into shape with string. Combine ginger, ½ teaspoon salt and ⅛ teaspoon pepper. Rub onto all sides of roast. Place roast in baking pan and sear in oven preheated to 500 degrees for 15 minutes. Lower temperature to 350 degrees. Mix reserved Madeira with ½ cup wine and pour over roast. Continue roasting, basting frequently with pan juices, for 30 minutes. Add cream and continue roasting, basting frequently, until meat thermometer inserted in thickest part registers 155 degrees, about 45 minutes. Remove roast from pan and keep warm.

Reserve ⅓ cup of pan juices and pour off rest. Heat juices on top of stove over medium heat, scraping any brown bits from bottom of pan. Add minced onion and parsley and cook until onion is transparent, about 4 minutes. Add flour and cook, stirring frequently, for 5 minutes. Add 3 cups broth and 1 cup wine. Cook, stirring occasionally, for 5 minutes. Season to taste with salt and pepper. Remove strings from roast and slice, arranging slices carefully on platter and topping with a small amount of gravy. Pass additional gravy.

An exquisite display when meat is sliced, revealing the fruit stuffing. A truly hearty meal served after a day of hunting in the woods for the perfect Christmas tree!

Apricot Brandied
Crown Roast of Pork

1   8½-pound crown rib roast of pork
      (14-16 ribs)
      salt and freshly ground
        black pepper to taste

Stuffing:
1   pound unseasoned pork sausage
½   cup finely chopped onion
½   cup finely chopped celery
½   cup butter
1   cup finely chopped, unpeeled
      Jonathon or McIntosh apples
1   cup golden raisins
½   cup finely chopped dried apricots
⅓   cup brandy or apricot flavored
      brandy
3   cups whole wheat bread crumbs
¼   teaspoon ground cinnamon
¼   teaspoon ground mace
1   teaspoon salt
¼   teaspoon freshly ground
      black pepper
½   cup chicken broth
      pinch of ground nutmeg
      pinch of dried sage
      pinch of dried thyme

Brandied Apricot Sauce:
1   12-ounce jar apricot preserves
2   tablespoons fresh lemon juice
⅓   cup kirsch
2   tablespoons butter
2-3   tablespoons pan drippings
        from meat

8-10 servings

Set crown roast in large roasting pan. Sprinkle with salt and pepper; set aside.

Cook sausage in skillet; drain and crumble. Sauté onion and celery in butter until soft. In large bowl combine sautéed vegetables and sausage with all other stuffing ingredients and mix well. Mound stuffing high in center of roast. Cover top of stuffing with foil to prevent burning. Bake at 350 degrees for 1¾-2 hours, or until internal temperature reaches 150-155 degrees.

Combine all sauce ingredients in small saucepan. Heat to boiling. Serve separately. *Peaches and peach preserves may be substituted for the apricots and apricot preserves.*

For a festive holiday platter, garnish the roast with fresh parsley and apricot halves filled with fresh cranberry sauce.

Meats

Coors Golden Glazed Ham

1	15-pound precooked ham with bone
1	pound dark brown sugar
8	12-ounce cans *Coors* beer
¼	cup honey
¼	cup Dijon mustard
2	cups packed dark brown sugar
½	cup bourbon

10-12 servings

Place ham in deep roasting pan. Firmly pat 1 pound brown sugar on all sides of ham. Pour beer around ham. Cover and bake at 325 degrees for 3¾ hours (15 minutes per pound). One hour before end of baking time, pour off all but 1½ inches of beer. In small saucepan combine honey, mustard, 2 cups brown sugar and bourbon; heat until sugar melts. Baste ham every 10 minutes with beer mixture from bottom of pan and then bourbon glaze. Use all of bourbon glaze before removing ham from oven. Slice thinly and serve with sauce remaining in pan.

A fine dish for an important dinner or outdoor buffet. Delicious, and relatively quick and simple to prepare.

Grilled Rocky Mountain Lamb Steaks

2	1¼-pound center-cut lamb steaks, 1½-inches thick
2	tablespoons grapeseed or olive oil
¼	teaspoon kosher salt
¼	teaspoon freshly ground black pepper
⅓	cup minced chives
3	cloves garlic, minced
½	cup minced fresh parsley
6	tablespoons unsalted butter, softened
¼	teaspoon freshly ground black pepper
¼	teaspoon kosher salt
½	tablespoon grapeseed or olive oil

4 servings

Rub lamb steaks with 2 tablespoons oil and sprinkle with ¼ teaspoon salt and ¼ teaspoon pepper. Refrigerate until 1 hour before serving. In food processor, combine chives, garlic, parsley, butter, ¼ teaspoon pepper and ¼ teaspoon salt and purée until smooth. *Cover and refrigerate if made in advance.*

Brush broiler rack with ½ tablespoon oil. Set steaks on rack and broil for 3 minutes per side. Remove from broiler, cover loosely with foil tent, and let stand for a minimum of 30 minutes. When ready to serve, place steaks on baking sheet and coat top of each steak with 1 teaspoon butter mixture. Bake, without turning over, at 475 degrees 8 minutes for rare, 9-10 minutes for medium rare. To serve, remove bone from each steak and slice thinly on the diagonal. Serve with remaining butter mixture.

A savory lamb dish complemented by the refreshing taste of mint in **Sautéed Snow Peas and Cucumbers.**

Meats

Telluride Smoked Ham

1	12-14 pound smoked, precooked ham with bone
½	cup bourbon
2	cups chopped green onions, including tops
1	large carrot, chopped
½	cup minced fresh parsley
4	cloves garlic, sliced
2	bay leaves
1	tablespoon minced fresh oregano
1	tablespoon minced fresh thyme
1	tablespoon minced fresh sage

16 servings

In large roasting pan, combine ham, bourbon, green onions, carrot, parsley, garlic, bay leaves, oregano, thyme and sage. Add cold water to cover and heat to boiling. Reduce heat and simmer for 1½ hours. Drain ham. Trim skin and fat. Place ham in shallow roasting pan and baste with **Bourbon Mustard Glaze.** Bake at 350 degrees for 45 minutes, basting every 10 minutes with glaze. Remove ham from oven and carefully pat **Herbed Bread Crumbs** over ham, covering completely. Return ham to oven and bake until bread crumbs are golden brown, about 15-20 minutes.

Bourbon Mustard Glaze:

¾	cup country-style Dijon mustard
1½	cups packed dark brown sugar
½	cup bourbon
1	tablespoon freshly ground black pepper
½	teaspoon salt

Herbed Bread Crumbs:

7-8	cups fresh bread crumbs made from French bread
1½	cups minced fresh parsley
½	cup butter, melted
½	cup minced fresh sage
½	cup minced fresh oregano
1	tablespoon minced fresh rosemary
¼	cup minced fresh thyme
1	teaspoon minced garlic
3-4	tablespoons Bourbon Mustard Glaze

In large bowl combine all ingredients. Toss until well mixed.

A beautiful main dish for a buffet table, served hot or at room temperature.

Meats

Festive Fresh Ham

Marinade:

- 2 cups dry white wine
- 2 cups apple cider
- ½ cup cider vinegar
- ½ cup Calvados or applejack
- ½ teaspoon cardamom pods, crushed
- 2 cinnamon sticks, broken
- ½ cup chopped onion
- 1 tablespoon whole black peppercorns, crushed
- 1 tablespoon whole allspice, crushed
- ½ teaspoon ground ginger
- 5 whole cloves
- 4 cloves garlic, crushed

- ½ fresh ham (5-6 pounds), boned and flattened or 4-5 pounds sirloin pork roast, boned and flattened

Stuffing:

- 4 tablespoons unsalted butter
- 10 green onions, minced
- 3 large cloves garlic, minced
- 1 cup chopped dried apricots
- ½ cup shelled pistachio nuts
- ¾ cup minced fresh parsley
- ½ cup pine nuts, toasted
- 1½ tablespoons finely grated lemon peel
- 1 scant tablespoon cider vinegar freshly ground black pepper to taste

Garnish:

lemon leaves or other greens

8-10 servings

Two days before serving, marinate meat and prepare stuffing.

Combine all marinade ingredients in large baking dish. Add fresh ham, turning to coat well. Cover and refrigerate for 2 days, turning meat every 12 hours.

To prepare stuffing, melt butter in large, heavy skillet over medium-high heat. Add green onions and garlic and sauté 3 minutes. Remove from heat and stir in apricots, pistachio nuts, parsley, pine nuts, lemon peel, vinegar and pepper, blending well. Cover and refrigerate for 2 days. Remove meat from marinade and pat dry with paper towels. Strain marinade; set aside. Set meat on work surface fat side down and flatten slightly. Spread stuffing evenly over meat, leaving 1-inch border all around. Roll up lengthwise and tie at 2-inch intervals with heavy string. *If using ham with skin intact, score skin in diamond pattern before tying.* Set meat skin side down in large, deep roasting pan. Pour 3 cups strained marinade into pan and roast at 400 degrees for 1 hour. Reduce heat to 350 degrees and continue roasting, basting frequently with remaining marinade, until meat thermometer inserted in thickest part registers 155 degrees, about 1¼ hours longer. Transfer meat to heated serving platter and keep warm.

Degrease pan juices. Transfer to saucepan and boil over high heat until thickened and reduced. Surround meat with lemon leaves or other greens and carve meat at table. Pass sauce separately.

Marinated ham can be prepared for 16-24 people. Use a 14-16 pound boned, fresh ham. Double the marinade and increase stuffing by ¼. Roast 1 hour at 400 degrees, then approximately 3 hours longer at 350 degrees. An impressive holiday entrée mixing the richness of fresh ham with the sweet taste of fruit. Excellent served with Beaujolais wine.

Meats

Tandoori Lamb Kabobs (The Tandoor Kitchen)

Marinade:

2	cups plain yogurt
¼	cup heavy cream
¼	teaspoon grated fresh ginger root
3	cloves garlic
½	teaspoon salt
¼	teaspoon ground cloves
¼	teaspoon ground cinnamon
1	teaspoon ground coriander
1	teaspoon ground cumin
½	teaspoon ground turmeric
3	tablespoons white vinegar
2	tablespoons fresh lemon juice
½	teaspoon red chili powder (optional)

2	pounds lamb, cut into 2-inch cubes
2	green bell peppers, cut into 1-inch pieces
2	red bell peppers, cut into 1-inch pieces
2	yellow bell peppers, cut into 1-inch pieces
2	onions, quartered
8-12	ounces small mushrooms

6 servings

Place all marinade ingredients in blender and mix until turned to paste. Thoroughly coat lamb with marinade. Cover and refrigerate for at least 6 hours and preferably overnight.

Arrange meat on skewers alternately with peppers, onions and mushrooms. Grill over hot coals to desired doneness, turning often and basting with marinade.

An excellent alternative to beef kabobs to serve outdoors on a summer evening.

Cajun Lamb Chops

2	teaspoons cayenne pepper
1	teaspoon freshly ground black pepper
1	teaspoon ground white pepper
½	teaspoon garlic powder
1	teaspoon dry mustard
2	teaspoons onion powder
1	teaspoon salt
1	teaspoon dried thyme
8	loin lamb chops, 1¼-1½-inches thick
1	cup unsalted butter, clarified

4 servings

In small bowl, combine peppers, garlic powder, mustard, onion powder, salt and thyme. At high temperature, heat large cast iron skillet at least 10 minutes, until faint ash appears on bottom of skillet. Brush each lamb chop with clarified butter. Press seasoning mixture on both sides of each chop, patting so spices adhere. Fry chops uncovered over high heat, turning once, for 1-2 minutes on each side. Chops should be charred on outside and rare inside.

This recipe should not be prepared indoors without using a fanned vent over the stove. It can be prepared outdoors on a gas or charcoal grill.

Lamb Shanks Florentine

Marinade:

½	cup fresh orange juice
1	tablespoon minced fresh parsley
1	teaspoon salt
½	teaspoon freshly ground black pepper
¼	teaspoon freshly grated orange peel
1	teaspoon dried thyme
3	cloves garlic, sliced

4	small lamb shanks, about 14 ounces each, trimmed of excess fat
8	large cloves garlic, whole and unpeeled
½-1	cup olive oil
4	slices day-old French bread, cut ½-inch thick
2	tablespoons olive oil
2	pounds fresh spinach, rinsed and stemmed
4	tablespoons unsalted butter
3	tablespoons heavy cream
½	teaspoon salt
½	teaspoon freshly ground black pepper
	pinch of ground nutmeg
	pinch of sugar

4 servings

In shallow baking dish, combine all marinade ingredients. Arrange shanks in a single layer, turning to coat well. Cover and refrigerate overnight.

Remove shanks from refrigerator 4 hours before serving and wipe marinade from meat with paper towels. Discard marinade. Place shanks in shallow baking dish with 8 whole cloves garlic. Pour olive oil over shanks and cover dish with foil. Roast in center of preheated 300 degree oven for 3 hours or until tender, turning lamb every hour.

Brush French bread with 2 tablespoons olive oil and toast in oven for about 5 minutes while lamb is baking. Set aside.

Tear spinach into ¼-inch shreds. Place in large cast iron skillet and cook in water remaining on leaves over moderate heat for 2-3 minutes, stirring once or twice. Drain spinach to remove as much water as possible. In medium skillet, melt butter over moderately high heat. Add spinach and cream, stirring until blended, about 1 minute. Season with remaining ½ teaspoon salt, ½ teaspoon pepper, nutmeg and sugar. Transfer creamed spinach to warmed serving platter.

When lamb is cooked, remove cooked garlic cloves from oil. Squeeze pulp from cloves and spread on toasted bread. Remove lamb shanks from baking dish and arrange on spinach. Serve with garlic French bread.

This entrée creates an ambiance of relaxed elegance for family or friends.

Meats

Southwestern Grilled Lamb

1   **5-pound leg of lamb, boned and butterflied**

Marinade:
½   **cup olive oil**
⅓   **cup fresh orange juice**
1   **teaspoon freshly grated orange peel**
2   **large cloves garlic, minced**
1½   **teaspoons minced fresh thyme or ½ teaspoon dried thyme**
1   **bay leaf, crumbled**
1   **tablespoon minced fresh parsley**
½   **teaspoon freshly ground black pepper**
½   **teaspoon salt**

    olive oil

Jalapeño Mint Sauce:
3   **tablespoons water**
⅓   **cup sugar**
¼   **teaspoon unflavored gelatin**
1   **teaspoon hot water**
¼   **cup shredded fresh mint**
2   **large fresh jalapeño peppers, seeded and minced**
¼   **teaspoon crushed red pepper flakes, or to taste**
2   **drops pure vanilla extract**

6 servings

Trim excess fat from lamb. Divide lamb into two pieces, separating thicker piece from thin one. In large bowl, combine all marinade ingredients. Place lamb in marinade, turning to coat well. Cover and refrigerate overnight.

Remove lamb from marinade and bring to room temperature. Prepare grill. When coals are white and hot, position grill 3-inches above coals. Brush grill with oil, and brush each piece of lamb with marinade. Sear lamb on grill for 1 minute each side. Move thinner piece 4-5 inches from heat to prevent charring. Grill, basting frequently with marinade, until internal temperature reaches 135-140 degrees for medium rare, about 20-25 minutes. Slice lamb on diagonal and serve with *Jalapeño Mint Sauce.*

In small saucepan, combine 3 tablespoons water and sugar. Stir over low heat until sugar dissolves. Soften gelatin in 1 teaspoon water and add to saucepan. Increase heat and bring to boil. In small bowl, combine mint, jalapeño peppers and red pepper flakes; add to boiling syrup. Let stand until cool, stirring occasionally. Stir in vanilla. Refrigerate 15 minutes or until chilled before serving.

A dinner combining the fresh taste of herbed lamb with the spicy flavors of the Southwest.

Meats

Hunters' Stuffed Lamb

1   7-8 pound leg of lamb, boned

Marinade:
1   cup red wine
½   cup Worcestershire sauce
1   teaspoon lemon pepper

6   ounces dried apricots,
     finely chopped
1   cup apple brandy
1   teaspoon lemon pepper
1   cup chopped onion
¼   cup minced fresh basil or
     4 teaspoons dried basil
2   teaspoons salt
1   6-ounce package long grain and
     wild rice, cooked according to
     package directions

10-12 servings

Place lamb in large pan. Combine red wine, Worcestershire and 1 teaspoon lemon pepper and pour over lamb, turning to coat well. Cover and marinate lamb in refrigerator for at least 24 hours.

Marinate apricots in brandy for 24 hours.

Remove lamb from marinade; reserve marinade for basting. Combine 1 teaspoon lemon pepper, marinated apricots, onion, basil, salt and cooked rice in large bowl. Blend well. Stuff lamb with rice mixture, packing lightly. Secure opening with skewers or heavy string. Place lamb on rack in shallow roasting pan, stuffed side up. Bake at 325 degress for 20-25 minutes per pound. Baste lamb with reserved marinade 3-4 times during cooking. Remove skewers or string, slice and serve.

A fruited stuffed lamb with a rich blend of flavors. Suited for a feast. Beautiful served with **Vegetarian Shish Kabobs.**

Silverthorne Smoked Lamb Sandwiches

1   cup chopped fresh rosemary
¾   cup chopped fresh basil
6   medium cloves garlic
¼   cup olive oil
6   pounds leg of lamb, boned,
     trimmed and butterflied
     salt and freshly ground
       black pepper to taste
2   cups applewood or cherrywood
     chips, soaked in water to cover
     for 15 minutes and drained
1   large sourdough baguette, cut
     diagonally into ½-inch slices
     olive oil
2   bunches watercress, large stems
     removed

10 servings

In food processor, blend rosemary, basil and garlic until paste forms. With machine running, slowly add oil until paste is smooth. Spread mixture over surface of lamb. Sprinkle with salt and pepper. Cover and refrigerate overnight.

Prepare smoker on low heat with wood chunks. Cover and heat smoker to 160 degrees. Place lamb on rack, cover and smoke until meat thermometer reads 140 degrees for medium rare, approximately 45-60 minutes. Add wood chips as necessary to maintain smoke. Remove and let stand 15-20 minutes. Brush both sides of bread with oil. Grill until golden brown on both sides. Remove and spread one side of each bread slice with **Pesto Mayonnaise.** Top with watercress. Cut lamb thinly on diagonal and layer on top of watercress. Pour **Rosemary Mustard** on top of each sandwich and serve.

Meats

Pesto Mayonnaise:
1	cup packed fresh basil leaves
¼	cup chopped fresh parsley
4	egg yolks, room temperature
¼	cup fresh lemon juice
3	cups olive oil
	salt and ground white pepper to taste
	pinch of cayenne pepper
¾	cup toasted pine nuts

In food processor, blend basil, parsley, egg yolks and lemon juice until smooth. With machine running, slowly add oil and blend until mixture is thick. Season with salt, pepper and cayenne. Transfer to small bowl and stir in pine nuts. Cover and refrigerate until needed.

Rosemary Mustard:
1	cup olive oil
½	cup country-style Dijon mustard
⅓	cup minced fresh rosemary
¼	cup red wine vinegar
	ground white pepper to taste

In medium bowl, combine all ingredients and whisk together until thickened. Cover and refrigerate until needed.

Both mayonnaise and mustard are best when made in advance. A superb dinner after a day of skiing, served with a platter of cheeses, fresh fruit and a light red wine.

Spring Creek Rack of Lamb

4	racks of lamb, about 1½ pounds each, trimmed and patted dry
	peanut oil
¼	cup sesame seeds, toasted
¼	cup Dijon mustard
¼	cup hoisin sauce
3	tablespoons sesame oil
3	tablespoons packed light brown sugar
2	tablespoons soy sauce
2	tablespoons minced garlic
2	tablespoons kosher salt or coarsely ground salt
2	teaspoons freshly ground black pepper
1	cup chopped fresh sage leaves or 6 tablespoons dried sage
1	cup chicken broth
4	tablespoons unsalted butter
4	teaspoons sesame oil
4	teaspoons sesame paste or creamy peanut butter

4 servings

In large skillet over medium-high heat, brown lamb on all sides in thin layer of peanut oil. Remove and cool to room temperature.

In small mixing bowl, blend sesame seeds, mustard, hoisin sauce, 3 tablespoons sesame oil, brown sugar, soy sauce, garlic, salt and pepper. Coat lamb on all sides with mixture and let stand at room temperature for 1 hour.

Preheat oven to 450 degrees. Place lamb in large roasting pan and sprinkle with sage that has been moistened slightly with water. Cover with foil. Place in oven and immediately reduce temperature to 400 degrees. Roast lamb for 25-30 minutes for medium rare or to desired doneness. Remove to platter and let stand for 20 minutes.

Skim fat from roasting pan. Place pan over high heat on stove, stirring in broth while scraping brown bits from bottom of pan. Boil until reduced by ⅓. Whisk in butter, 4 teaspoons sesame oil and sesame paste. Cut racks into chops and serve with sauce.

*For special guests, serve this with **Stir Fried Squash with Chèvre.***

Colorado Wild

Colorado Wild

Colorado Wild is specifically designed for ease of preparation. It will dispell the myth that only gourmet cooks can prepare wild game dishes. If a "gamey taste" is not desired, the following general hints will disguise these wild flavors:

Soak dark meats or fowl in salted water, milk, buttermilk or vinegar to remove blood from the flesh.

Age meat or fowl under refrigeration for three to seven days to enhance tenderness.

Soak meat or fowl in marinades containing wine or vinegar with the heavier flavors of soy or garlic.

Serve wild dishes with sweet or spicy sauces as condiments to temper the wild taste.

Trim fat from game meats to remove a major source of the wild flavor.

General hints for the preparation of game birds:

Dark-meat fowl are better served medium to medium-rare. Those who prefer roast beef at this level of cooking may also prefer fowl the same way.

The tenderness of game birds varies greatly depending on their age, and there is no easy way to determine this fact. One rule of thumb holds: larger game birds of a species are older and hence less tender.

When roasting any fowl to well done, take precautions to keep the meat moist by covering, basting, or roasting with added liquid to prevent dryness of the meat. All game birds contain less muscle fat than domestic equivalents, and so will have a drier taste.

All white-meat game birds (pheasants, quail, chukar) can be substituted in a favorite chicken recipe. Do not be afraid to experiment.

Boning game birds allows serving ease and inspection for unwanted shot pellets. Always inspect the whole game bird for obvious puncture wounds before roasting.

Game birds do not improve with aging in the freezer. Generally they should be consumed within one year's time.

Randall H. Lortscher, M.D., is a physician in Denver, Colorado. He is an avid sportsman who, out of necessity, learned to prepare game dishes as a teenager, when the household rule was, "If you shoot it, you clean it, and you cook it." Most of the selections in the game section were developed by Randy, whose simple-to-prepare recipes yield gourmet results.

Colorado Wild

Piney Creek Pheasant Asparagus

4	pheasant breasts
1	teaspoon salt
1	teaspoon freshly ground black pepper
½	cup butter
4-6	cloves garlic, minced
2-3	tablespoons freshly grated lemon peel
12	juniper berries, crushed
½	cup dry white wine
½	cup minced fresh parsley
½	cup finely chopped onion
1	cup diced celery
¾	pound mushrooms, thinly sliced
2	10 ½-ounce cans cream of asparagus soup, undiluted
1	cup sour cream
½	cup dry white wine
1½	cups freshly grated Parmesan cheese
1	pound whole asparagus spears

4 servings

Wash pheasant breasts and pat dry. Season breasts with salt and pepper. In large skillet, melt butter and add garlic, lemon peel, juniper berries and pheasant breasts. Sauté breasts until golden brown. Remove to large baking dish and keep warm. Deglaze skillet with ½ cup wine. Stir in parsley, onion, celery and mushrooms and sauté until onions are transparent. Add soup, sour cream and remaining ½ cup wine, stirring until well blended. Pour ½ of sauce from skillet over breasts. Sprinkle with ½ of cheese. Pour rest of sauce over cheese. Top with asparagus spears and remaining cheese. Bake at 325 degrees for 1 hour or until breasts are fork-tender.

A blend of herbs imparts marvelous flavor to pheasant and asparagus in this regal treat. Serve with a combination of long grain and wild rice for a sumptious meal.

Wild Pheasant Stroganoff

2	small pheasants, cleaned, boned, skinned and cut into bite-size pieces
4	cups milk
2	tablespoons butter
	salt and freshly ground black pepper to taste
	onion powder to taste
	garlic powder to taste
8	ounces fresh mushrooms, thickly sliced
2	10¾-ounce cans condensed cream of mushroom soup
½	cup dry sherry
1	tablespoon paprika
½	cup dry sherry
½	cup half and half
1	cup sour cream
	buttered noodles

4 servings

Soak pheasant pieces in milk for 4 hours in refrigerator.

Remove pheasant and pat dry; discard milk. In large skillet, melt butter and sauté pheasant pieces until lightly browned. Sprinkle with salt, pepper, onion powder and garlic powder. Add mushrooms and sauté for 2 minutes. Add soup and stir to coat. Pour in ½ cup sherry, making sure all pheasant pieces are covered with sauce. Sprinkle with paprika. Cover and simmer for 1 hour. Add remaining ½ cup sherry and stir well. With slotted spoon, remove pheasant to hot platter. Mix half and half and sour cream into sauce. Stir until well blended. Spoon over top of pheasant and serve immediately, accompanied by buttered noodles.

In this recipe, milk serves as a marinade which can turn an old bird into a "spring chicken" as it tenderizes the meat. The result is delicious; the time required is minimal.

Colorado Wild

Prairie Land Grilled Pheasant Breast

2-3	pheasant breasts, boned and skinned
8-12	slices bacon
3	tablespoons Chinese soy sauce
1	cup dry white wine
	salt and freshly ground black pepper to taste

4-6 servings

Cut each boned pheasant breast into 4 pieces. Wrap 1 bacon slice around each breast piece and secure with string or wooden picks. In large bowl, combine soy sauce, wine, salt and pepper. Add pheasant, turning to coat all sides. Cover and marinate, refrigerated, at least 6 hours or overnight.

Remove pheasant from marinade and grill for 10-12 minutes or until the meat is browned and bacon begins to crisp.

Any meal becomes a festive occasion when game birds are served. For an elegant picnic, serve grilled pheasant and champagne.

Easy Roast Pheasant with Cream Sauce

3	pheasants
	butter
1	cup heavy cream
	salt and freshly ground black pepper to taste
1	teaspoon fresh lemon juice, or more to taste
	sprigs of parsley (optional)

6 servings

Wash pheasants and pat dry. Liberally rub butter all over outside of pheasants. Do not season. In covered roasting pan, cook pheasants at 450 degrees for 45-60 minutes. Baste with pan juices every 10 minutes. Remove birds to heated platter and keep warm. Drain fat from pan and discard. To drippings in pan add heavy cream, salt, pepper and lemon juice. Heat just to boiling, constantly stirring drippings from side and bottom of pan until sauce thickens. Serve over carved pheasant. Garnish with sprigs of parsley.

A delicious way to serve pheasant — appetizing-looking and richly flavorful. Experiment by substituting one game bird for another. In general, 1 pheasant equals 3 chukars. (Decrease cooking time when using smaller birds.)

Colorado Wild

Baked Pheasant with Long Grain and Wild Rice

1	6-ounce box Uncle Ben's Long Grain and Wild Rice
1	10¾-ounce can cream of chicken soup
1	10¾-ounce can cream of celery soup
1¼	cups vermouth
1	package dry onion soup mix
4	pheasant breasts
½	cup flour
3	tablespoons unsalted butter
	salt and freshly ground black pepper to taste

8 servings

In large casserole, mix together rice, soups, vermouth and dry soup mix. Let stand for 2 hours. Bake covered at 325 degrees for 30 minutes.

Wash pheasant breasts and pat dry. Halve if desired. Lightly coat on all sides with flour. In large skillet, melt butter and sauté breasts until lightly browned. Season with salt and pepper. Remove from skillet and place in the rice mixture, coating pheasant pieces. Cover and return to oven for 2 hours.

When you're short on time, here's an astonishingly fine dish that comes out of commercial packages. Assemble and bake — guaranteed success for first time game bird cooks.

Colorado Roast Pheasant

1	young pheasant (2½-3 pounds)
	salt and freshly ground black pepper
1	bay leaf
2-3	celery stalk tops
2	sprigs fresh parsley
1	thick slice lemon
4	slices fatty bacon
4	tablespoons butter, melted
1	cup strong chicken broth
3	small onions, sliced
½	pound whole mushrooms
	flour or cornstarch

4 servings

Wash pheasant and pat dry. Sprinkle inside and out with salt and pepper. Place bay leaf, celery, parsley and lemon in cavity. Tie legs together with string, closing body cavity. Lay bacon slices over breast and fasten with wooden picks. Place pheasant on rack in roasting pan and baste with melted butter. Add chicken broth, onion slices and mushrooms. Roast at 350 degrees for 75 minutes. Baste every 15 minutes. Remove pheasant and place on heated platter; keep warm. Skim fat from pan drippings. Stir flour or cornstarch into drippings to thicken into gravy. Cut pheasant in half, discard cavity contents and serve with gravy.

Simple and super! Dry white wine, wild rice and a sautéed vegetable would be perfect accompaniments.

Colorado Wild

Roasted Canadian Goose with Plum Sauce Windsor

1   large Canadian goose
      (6-8 pounds dressed)
      poultry seasoning to taste
3   oranges, cut into quarters
3   apples, cut into quarters
3   medium red onions,
      cut into quarters
      salt and freshly ground black
      pepper to taste
¼   cup cognac

Plum Sauce Windsor:

4   tablespoons unsalted butter
¼   cup firmly packed light
      brown sugar
1   tablespoon cognac
1   10-ounce jar red plum jelly

6 servings

Wash goose and pat dry. Sprinkle cavity liberally with poultry seasoning. Mix together oranges, apples and onions. Place inside cavity and pack firmly. Truss opening closed. Sprinkle outside of goose with salt, pepper and poultry seasoning. Place in large roasting pan. Roast at 500 degrees for 20 minutes on each side. Reduce heat to 350 degrees and continue roasting for 1 hour and 20 minutes. Baste several times with cognac and pan juices. Remove goose and carve breast against the grain in thin slices. Serve with *Plum Sauce Windsor.*

In small saucepan, melt butter. Add brown sugar, cognac and jelly. Mix well and heat until bubbly.

Wild goose is different from domestic goose. With a domestic goose, it is necessary to release as much fat as possible during cooking. Wild goose has very little fat and requires frequent basting. Wild goose meat is better pink, but may be cooked longer.

Honey Wild Goose

1   goose (4-6 pounds)
4   teaspoons salt
2   teaspoons ground ginger
2   teaspoons dried basil
1   teaspoon freshly ground
        black pepper
1½   cups honey
½   cup butter
2   teaspoons freshly grated
        orange peel
¼   cup fresh orange juice
1   tablespoon fresh lemon juice
¼   teaspoon dry mustard
2   oranges, peeled and quartered

6-8 servings

Wash goose and soak overnight, refrigerated, in salted water to cover.

Pat dry and place in roasting pan. Mix together salt, ginger, basil and pepper. Rub mixture inside cavity and over skin. In double boiler, mix together honey, butter, orange peel, orange juice, lemon juice and dry mustard. Cook until mixture becomes like syrup. Be careful not to carmelize. Coat goose body with 3 tablespoons syrup. Place oranges in cavity. Pour ¼ cup syrup over oranges. Truss opening. Pour remaining syrup over goose. Cover with foil. Bake at 375 degrees for 2 hours. Baste 4-6 times with pan juices. After 2 hours remove foil, reduce heat to 325 degrees, and bake for an additional 30 minutes.

The hearty flavor of goose blends well with other equally distinctive flavors. Serve with chutney or spiced peaches.

Colorado Wild

Bacon-Wrapped Duck Breast Hors d'Oeuvres

2 cups dry red wine
2 teaspoons garlic powder
1 tablespoon soy sauce
   salt and freshly ground black pepper to taste
4-6 duck breasts, boned, skinned and cut into bite-size pieces
½ pound thinly sliced bacon strips, cut in half

8-10 servings

In large bowl, combine red wine, garlic powder, soy sauce, salt and pepper. Add duck pieces and marinate, refrigerated, for 24 hours.

Remove duck pieces from marinade and wrap ½ slice of bacon around each piece. Secure with wooden picks. *Can be prepared ahead to this point, covered and refrigerated.* Roast at 350 degrees for 25-30 minutes or until bacon is cooked. Serve hot.

Serve with a sauce for dipping. Dove breasts can be substituted for duck breasts.

Wild Duck Gumbo

2 mallard ducks or 3 duck breasts, boned, skinned and cut into 1x2-inch pieces
   salt and freshly ground black pepper to taste
   cayenne pepper to taste
½ cup vegetable oil
½ cup all-purpose flour
2 medium onions, chopped
1 cup chopped celery
1 large green bell pepper, chopped
1 bunch green onions, chopped
2 cloves garlic, minced
2 quarts hot water
1 bay leaf
1 tablespoon Worcestershire sauce
   pinch of dried thyme
   Tabasco sauce to taste
   salt and freshly ground black pepper to taste
2 10-ounce packages frozen sliced okra, thawed
⅓ cup tomato paste
1 pound smoked sausage, cut into ¼-inch slices
¼ cup minced fresh parsley
6 cups cooked rice

8 servings

Season duck well with salt, pepper and cayenne pepper. In large, heavy skillet, brown duck pieces in hot oil. Remove and keep warm. Pour off all but ⅓ cup oil. Add flour and stir constantly over low heat until roux is dark brown in color. Add onions, celery, green pepper, green onions and garlic and cook until onions are transparent. Pour in hot water and add bay leaf, Worcestershire, thyme, Tabasco, salt, pepper, okra and tomato paste. Stir well. Add duck and sausage pieces. Simmer uncovered over low heat for 2 hours or until duck is tender. Stir occasionally and add water as needed. Shortly before serving add parsley. Serve in bowls over rice.

Served with a simple green salad, French bread and a full-bodied red wine, this can't be beat! Although created for wild duck, domestic duck and Canadian goose also work well in this recipe. This recipe freezes well, so make plenty.

Colorado Wild

San Luis Valley Duck

Sauce:

- 1½   cups butter
- ⅔   cup sherry
- ½   cup bourbon
- ⅔   cup currant jelly
- ¼   cup Worcestershire sauce

- 4   mallard ducks, cleaned and picked
- 2   large apples, peeled, cored and cut into 1-inch pieces
- 4   stalks celery, chopped
- 2   10¾-ounce cans beef consommé, undiluted
- 1¼   cups water

-   cooked rice
- 6   slices bacon, fried crisp, drained and crumbled

6-8 servings

In small saucepan, combine all sauce ingredients. Heat to simmering. If sauce is too thin, thicken with a small amount of flour.

Wash ducks and pat dry. Toss together apples and celery. Stuff ducks with mixture. Combine consommé and water and pour into large casserole or roaster. Place duck in casserole breast side down. Cover tightly and cook at 350 degrees for 2 hours or until tender. Slice breast and place in greased, shallow casserole.

Pour sauce over duck. Cover and bake at 350 degrees just until hot, about 10-15 minutes. Arrange duck on bed of rice and sprinkle with bacon. Pass any remaining sauce.

Simple and delicious!

Mile High Roast Duck

- 4   mallard ducks
-   salt and freshly ground black pepper to taste
-   poultry seasoning to taste
- 4   red apples, chopped into large pieces
- 4   oranges, chopped into large pieces
- 4   medium onions, chopped into large pieces
- 2   oranges, halved
- 2   ounces cognac

4 servings

Wash ducks and pat dry. Sprinkle cavities liberally with salt, pepper and poultry seasoning. Toss together apples, oranges and onions and fill the cavities tightly so ducks appear to enlarge in size. Use 1 orange half to close opening on each duck. Place on rack in roasting pan and pour cognac over ducks. Sprinkle with poultry seasoning. Roast ducks at 500 degrees for 10 minutes on each side. Reduce heat to 350 degrees, turn ducks on their backs and continue roasting for 10-15 minutes longer.

Serve duck medium rare. Roast longer if you prefer it well done. The flavor of wild duck combines well with apples and cognac. Serve with wild rice and a green vegetable.

Colorado Wild

Grilled Duck Breasts with Red Currant Sauce

4-6   whole duck breasts

Marinade:
2	tablespoons soy sauce
½	teaspoon dry mustard
1	tablespoon Worcestershire sauce
¼	teaspoon garlic powder
¾	cup dry red wine

Red Currant Sauce:
4	tablespoons unsalted butter
1	10-ounce jar red currant jelly
¼	cup ketchup
¼	cup packed light brown sugar

4-6 servings

Remove meat in one piece from both sides of breast bone. Remove skin and trim tendons. In large bowl, combine all marinade ingredients. Add duck, turning to coat all sides. Marinate, refrigerated, for at least 4 hours or overnight.

Grill breasts for 5 minutes per side. Meat should be rare to medium rare. Carve into ¼-inch thick slices, cutting across grain. Serve with **Red Currant Sauce.**

Melt butter in small saucepan. Stir in jelly, ketchup and brown sugar. Heat until jelly melts and mixture boils.

A gala way to serve wild duck!

Canyonland Deep Fried Chukar

6	chukar breasts, boned, skinned and cut into large bite-size pieces
1½	cups whole milk
	poultry seasoning to taste
1	cup all-purpose flour
1	teaspoon salt
1	teaspoon freshly ground black pepper
3-4	cups safflower oil

6 servings

Wash chukar and pat dry. Place milk in large bowl and add chukar. Let soak for 15 minutes. Remove from milk and sprinkle with poultry seasoning. In large plastic bag, combine flour, salt and pepper. Add chukar pieces, a few at a time, and shake until well coated. Heat oil to 300 degrees and deep fry for 2-5 minutes. Chukar should be golden brown.

*Chukar has a very delicate flavor similar to pheasant. Serve with **Sweet and Sour Sauce** and tempura vegetables. Quail or pheasant can be substituted for chukar.*

Colorado Wild

South Platte Broiled Quail

4-6   quail, cleaned and skinned
     salt and freshly ground black
       pepper to taste
1   tablespoon minced fresh parsley
4   tablespoons unsalted butter,
     melted
     melted butter (optional)
     lemon wedges (optional)

2-3 servings

Wash quail and split down the back so birds will lay flat. If necessary, use a cleaver to pound them slightly into a flattened position. Pat dry. Season both sides of birds with salt and pepper. Sprinkle with parsley. Brush generously with melted butter and place under broiler, approximately 3 inches from heat. Broil for 5 minutes per side or until breasts are golden brown. Drizzle with melted butter and garnish with lemon wedges.

Offering the pure and simple flavor of quail, the most delicately flavored game bird.

Potted Quail

4-6   quail, backs removed
     salt and freshly ground black
       pepper to taste
     all-purpose flour
½   cup butter
¼   cup chopped shallots
¾   cup sliced mushrooms
2   tablespoons minced fresh parsley
¾   cup dry white wine or vermouth
1   cup heavy cream

6 servings

Wash quail and pat dry. Rub with salt, pepper and flour. In large skillet, melt butter and sauté birds for 5 minutes per side. With slotted spoon, remove birds to large casserole. In same skillet, sauté shallots, mushrooms and parsley in drippings for 3 minutes or until shallots are transparent. Add wine and cream. Cook until sauce is heated through. Pour over birds. Cover and bake at 325 degrees for 30-45 minutes or until tender.

*The supreme epicurean treat when served with **Million Dollar Rice.** Feel free to substitute dove or chukar for quail in this recipe.*

Grouse Breasts Marsala

4-6   sharptail or blue grouse breasts,
     boned, skinned and halved
¾   cup Marsala wine
½   teaspoon garlic powder
     salt and freshly ground black
       pepper to taste
¼   cup finely chopped shallots

4-6 servings

Wash grouse and pat dry. Place grouse in large casserole. Pour Marsala over birds. Season with garlic powder, salt and pepper. Add chopped shallots. Cover and bake at 325 degrees for 1½ hours or until tender.

Easy and wonderful served with chutney as a condiment.

Colorado Wild

Minted Grouse Breasts

4-6   **sharptail, sage grouse or blue grouse breasts, boned, skinned and halved**
1   **5¾-ounce bottle Crosse & Blackwell mint sauce**
½   **cup dry white wine**
      salt and freshly ground black pepper to taste
¼   **cup chopped shallots**
2   **tablespoons butter**

4-6 servings

Place grouse breasts in large casserole. Add mint sauce, wine, salt and pepper. In small skillet, sauté shallots in butter until transparent. Pour over grouse. Cover and bake at 325 degrees for 1½ hours or until tender.

A delicious dish. Serve with wild rice and chutney.

Gunnison Trapper Game Pie

8-10   **small (quail, chukar) or 2-3 large (pheasant, grouse) game birds or a combination of both**
7   **cups water**
3   **chicken bouillon cubes**
10   **celery leaves**
4   **carrots, halved**
1   **medium onion, cut into thick rings**
½   **clove garlic, minced**
      salt and freshly ground black pepper to taste

Filling:
½   **pound mushrooms, quartered**
2   **tablespoons butter**
⅓   **cup chopped celery**
⅓   **cup chopped green onions**
1   **tablespoon butter**
1   **tablespoon all-purpose flour**
1½   **cups chicken broth**
¼   **teaspoon Worcestershire sauce**
¼   **teaspoon dried basil**
      dash of nutmeg
      salt and freshly ground black pepper to taste
1   **10-ounce package frozen tiny peas, thawed**

1   **recipe *Best Ever Pastry Shell***
      milk

4-5 servings

In large kettle, combine birds, water, chicken bouillon cubes, celery leaves, carrots, onion, garlic, salt and pepper. Heat to boiling and cook until tender, about 1 hour. Remove birds; cool. Discard broth and vegetables. Cut meat from bones, cube and set aside.

In small skillet, sauté mushrooms in 2 tablespoons butter until tender. In large skillet, sauté celery and green onions in 1 tablespoon butter until softened. Add flour and stir. Add chicken broth, stirring until smooth. Add Worcestershire, basil, nutmeg, salt and pepper. Stir thoroughly. Add bird meat, mushrooms and peas; mix well.

Line a 9-inch deep dish pie plate with pastry. Pour in filling mixture. Top with pastry; seal and flute edges. Glaze with milk. Bake at 425 degrees for 35-40 minutes.

A noteworthy recipe offering a wonderful blend of flavors certain to delight your favorite hunter.

Colorado Wild

Noisettes of Venison with Rosemary and Orange

4	tablespoons butter
2	tablespoons olive oil
8	noisettes of venison cut ¾-inch thick from the saddle (4-6 ounces each)
2	tablespoons cognac
1	tablespoon all-purpose flour
2	cups heavy cream
¼	cup Dijon mustard
2	tablespoons freshly grated orange peel
1	tablespoon minced fresh rosemary or 1½ teaspoons dried rosemary, crumbled
½	teaspoon salt
¼	teaspoon freshly ground black pepper

4 servings

In large skillet, melt butter in oil over medium heat. Add venison noisettes and sauté for 3 minutes per side, turning once. Meat should be rare. Remove to warm platter and cover loosely to keep warm.

Add cognac and flour to skillet and deglaze, stirring constantly, for about 3 minutes. Whisk together cream and Dijon mustard until thoroughly blended. Pour into skillet and continue whisking until incorporated. When sauce is heated through, reduce heat and add orange peel and rosemary. Simmer for 5 minutes. Season with salt and pepper. To serve, place 2 noisettes on each plate and coat with sauce.

A succulent venison entrée featuring the pungent flavor of mustard combined with orange and rosemary in a rich cream sauce. Serve with fresh pasta.

Colorado Wild

Rocky Mountain Venison Sauerbraten

Marinade:
- 2 cups dry red wine
- 1 stalk celery, minced
- 1 carrot, finely chopped
- 1 red onion, chopped
- 1 bay leaf
- 2 teaspoons whole black peppercorns
- 1 teaspoon salt
- ¼ teaspoon dried thyme

- 1 3½-pound rack of venison or venison sirloin
- 2 tablespoons butter
- 1-2 tablespoons all-purpose flour
- 1½ tablespoons butter, softened
- ½ cup sour cream

6 servings

In container large enough to hold venison, combine all marinade ingredients, mixing well. Wash venison and carefully trim off all visible fat. Put venison in marinade, turning to coat all sides. Refrigerate for 3 days, turning each morning and evening.

Remove roast and pat dry. Strain marinade and reserve. In large skillet, brown venison on all sides in 2 tablespoons butter. Pour marinade into skillet and cover. Simmer for 1½-2 hours or until tender. Remove meat to warm platter. Add flour, butter and sour cream to skillet. Cook, stirring until thickened. Slice meat and serve with sauce.

In this recipe, the marinade has a dual role. It tenderizes and flavors the meat, them becomes a part of the accompanying sauce. Serve with parsleyed noodles. New Zealand red stag can be substituted for venison.

Mt. Evans Roast Venison with Port Wine Sauce

- 1 3½-pound saddle roast of venison
- 3 cloves garlic, slivered
  salt and freshly ground black pepper to taste
- ½ cup red wine vinegar

4-6 servings

Wash venison and carefully trim off all visible fat. Puncture meat and insert garlic slivers so meat appears dotted. Season with salt and pepper. Place in large casserole. Add vinegar and cover. Marinate in refrigerator for at least 6-8 hours.

Remove from marinade and place in roasting pan. Cook at 350 degrees for 30 minutes per pound or until slightly pink. Serve with **Port Wine Sauce.**

Port Wine Sauce:
- 4 tablespoons unsalted butter
- 2 tablespoons port wine
- 2 tablespoons fresh lemon juice
- ½ cup red currant jelly or more to taste
- 2 tablespoons cornstarch

In small saucepan, melt butter. Stir in remaining ingredients. Heat to boiling, stirring constantly.

*A noble roast full of character for deserving guests. Serve piping hot with **Port Wine Sauce** and buttered new potatoes.*

Colorado Wild

Hunters' Haunch of Venison

1   2¼-pound haunch of venison
      salt and freshly ground black
        pepper to taste
6   juniper berries, crushed
1   tablespoon minced fresh marjoram
1   tablespoon minced fresh thyme
4   tablespoons butter
1   cup finely chopped onion
1   cup dry red wine
2   tablespoons red wine vinegar
      hot water
1   tablespoon red currant jelly
1   tablespoon cider vinegar
1   cup heavy cream

4-6 servings

Wash venison and pat dry. Carefully trim off all visible fat. Season with salt and pepper. Mix together juniper berries, marjoram and thyme. Vigorously rub mixture into venison. In large cast iron skillet, melt butter and brown venison evenly on all sides. When browning last side, add onion. Add red wine and vinegar. Cover and simmer over low heat for 1½ hours, basting every 15 minutes. Add hot water, if necessary, to maintain liquid level. Remove venison to heated platter and keep warm. Strain cooking liquid into a saucepan. Deglaze skillet with hot water, using a wooden spoon to loosen caramelized juices. Add juices to saucepan and cook for 3 minutes. Add jelly and turn off heat. Whisk vinegar into cream and stir into saucepan. Slice meat and serve with sauce.

Juniper berries bring out the excellent flavor of venison in this wonderfully aromatic entrée. Serve with noodles and red cabbage. Easily prepared at hunting camp.

Echo Lake Elk Steaks with Green Peppercorn Sauce

4   8-ounce elk steaks, cut 1-inch thick
2-3   cloves garlic, minced
2   tablespoons virgin olive oil
       salt and freshly ground black
         pepper to taste

4 servings

Wash steaks and pat dry. Carefully trim away all visible fat. Combine garlic and olive oil. Pour over steaks and marinate, refrigerated, for 2-4 hours.

Season steaks with salt and pepper. Broil 5-7 minutes per side or until meat has only a hint of pink. Serve with **Green Peppercorn Sauce.**

In small saucepan, melt butter and stir in remaining ingredients. Heat to boiling, stirring occasionally.

*Simple fare with a touch of elegance. Venison or red stag steaks can be substituted for elk. Serve with **Port Wine Sauce** for a variation.*

Green Peppercorn Sauce:

4   tablespoons unsalted butter
¼   cup whole green peppercorns
      salt and freshly ground black
        pepper to taste
1   tablespoon cognac

Colorado Wild

Pike's Peak Pepperoni

4 pounds ground elk or venison
4 teaspoons ground anise
4 teaspoons mustard seed
4 teaspoons garlic powder
2 teaspoons hickory smoked salt
2 teaspoons freshly ground
    black pepper
2 teaspoons curing salt

4 sausages

Mix ground meat with all seasonings. Cover and refrigerate for at least 24 hours, mixing meat every 8 hours.

Divide meat into 4 parts. Roll each into a log and place on broiler pan to collect excess fat drippings. Bake at 225 degrees for 4 hours. Cool before serving.

The best sausage you'll ever eat! These freeze beautifully, so make lots to use on homemade pizza or serve with crackers on a snack tray.

High Plains Country Fried Antelope Steaks

Marinade:
½ cup red wine
3 cloves garlic, minced
    salt and freshly ground black
      pepper to taste

1 pound antelope steaks,
    cut ½-inch thick
1½ cups milk
½ pound bacon
1 large onion, sliced
½ cup all-purpose flour
    salt and freshly ground black
      pepper to taste
    garlic powder to taste
1-2 tablespoons butter

2 servings

Combine all marinade ingredients; set aside. Wash steaks and pat dry. Remove all visible fat. Pound steaks to flatten and tenderize. Pour marinade over steaks and marinate, refrigerated, for at least 4 hours.

Remove meat and discard marinade. Pour milk into casserole. Add steaks and soak for 10-15 minutes. In large heavy skillet, cook bacon until almost crisp. Drain and set aside. Sauté onions in bacon grease until transparent. Remove and set aside. Dredge steaks in flour and season with salt, pepper and garlic powder. Fry steaks in skillet until tender, adding butter to bacon grease if needed. Just before meat is cooked, return bacon and onions to skillet. Heat through.

Relish the taste of the wild in this recipe — the one and only way to eat antelope! Easily made at hunting camp.

Colorado Wild

Coors Bighorn Sheep Stew

vegetable oil
2 pounds Rocky Mountain bighorn sheep, cut into 1½-inch cubes
all-purpose flour
2 small cloves garlic, minced
1 6-ounce can tomato paste
2¼ cups *Coors* beer
2 bay leaves
1 teaspoon salt
1 teaspoon beef bouillon granules
1½ teaspoons freshly ground black pepper
1 tablespoon sugar
½ teaspoon dried thyme
¾ teaspoon dried oregano
8-10 small boiling onions, peeled
6 carrots, peeled and cut into chunks
6 stalks celery, cut into chunks
½ pound mushrooms, halved
6 small potatoes, peeled and cut into chunks

6 servings

Heat ¼ inch of oil in large skillet. Dredge meat in flour and brown in hot oil. Transfer to large kettle. Add remaining ingredients. Cook over low heat for 3 hours or until meat is tender.

A hearty one-dish meal which pleases everyone. Don't be intimidated by the long list of ingredients, this delicious entrée is easy to make. Lamb can be substituted for sheep.

Marinated Rocky Mountain Bighorn Sheep

1 5-pound butterflied leg of Rocky Mountain bighorn sheep
1 tablespoon bouquet garni
salt and freshly ground black pepper to taste
1 5¾-ounce bottle Crosse & Blackwell mint sauce
1 package dry Good Seasons Italian dressing, prepared according to package directions

4-6 servings

Sprinkle meat with bouquet garni, salt and pepper. Rub spices gently into meat. Place meat in large non-metallic container. Combine mint sauce and prepared dressing. Pour mixture over meat and marinate refrigerated for 24 hours. Turn meat every 6-12 hours.

Meat may be grilled or baked in oven. Grill meat in covered grill for 25 minutes per side, or roast at 350 degrees for 20 minutes per pound. Meat should be pink.

Absolutely delicious! Butterflied leg of domestic lamb can be substituted for sheep.

Colorado Wild

Sautéed Rabbit

3   pounds rabbit, cut into serving pieces
3   sprigs of fresh rosemary, minced, or 1 tablespoon dried rosemary
8   fresh sage, minced, or 1 teaspoon dried sage
4   cloves garlic, minced
12 juniper berries, crushed
    salt and freshly ground black pepper to taste
5   tablespoons white wine vinegar
½ cup olive oil
¾ cup minced onion

4-6 servings

Wash rabbit pieces and pat dry. In small bowl, combine rosemary, sage, garlic and juniper berries. Mix well, mashing spices together. Rub rabbit pieces with spice mixture. Season with salt and pepper. Place rabbit in large bowl. Add vinegar, olive oil and onion. Marinate, refrigerated, for 3-4 hours, turning meat several times.

Place rabbit and marinade in large, heavy kettle. Heat to boiling. Reduce heat and cover kettle. Simmer for 40-50 minutes, stirring occasionally. Increase heat to medium-high. Uncover and cook for 10-15 minutes or until meat is tender and only several tablespoons of sauce remain. Remove rabbit to heated platter. Taste and adjust seasonings in sauce. Spoon sauce over rabbit and serve immediately.

As delicious a way to prepare rabbit as there is. Rabbit is low in cholesterol and is now available in major supermarkets.

Rifle Gap Buffalo Steaks

Marinade:

2   tablespoons freshly grated lemon peel
⅓ cup fresh lemon juice
2   tablespoons sherry wine vinegar
¼ cup tarragon wine vinegar
1⅓ cups extra virgin olive oil
12 juniper berries, crushed
2   teaspoons green peppercorns, crushed
8-10 cloves garlic, minced
½ teaspoon freshly ground black pepper
2   tablespoons minced fresh tarragon or 1 tablespoon dried tarragon
1   cup white zinfandel
2   bay leaves, crumbled
1   teaspoon minced fresh thyme or ½ teaspoon dried thyme
1   teaspoon minced fresh oregano or ½ teaspoon dried oregano
1   teaspoon minced fresh rosemary or ½ teaspoon dried rosemary

2   buffalo sirloin steaks, 1½-2 inches thick

6 servings

In large bowl, combine all marinade ingredients and whisk until emulsified. Pour over buffalo steaks and marinate overnight, refrigerated.

Grill over hot coals for 5-6 minutes per side for medium-rare.

Buffalo meat tastes like beef but is lower in cholesterol. This marinade combines a garden of herbs and would be equally delicious on beef or other game steaks.

Vegetables

Vegetables

Artichokes and Green Beans Romano

⅔ cup onion, finely chopped
1 clove garlic, minced
¼ cup olive oil
½ cup Italian bread crumbs
1 10-ounce package frozen French-style green beans, cooked and drained
1 14-ounce can artichoke hearts, drained and quartered
½ cup freshly grated Romano cheese
salt and freshly ground black pepper to taste

4 servings

In large skillet, sauté onion and garlic in olive oil until transparent. Stir in bread crumbs, blending well to absorb oil. Add green beans, artichoke hearts and cheese. Combine thoroughly, yet gently. Heat slowly to soften cheese. Season to taste with salt and pepper.

Artichokes and green beans combine in a savory mixture flavored with Romano cheese; deliciously simple.

Dilled Artichokes and Peas

¾ cup chicken broth
juice of ½ lemon
1 tablespoon cornstarch
1 tablespoon vegetable oil
2 large green onions, thinly sliced
½ pound snow peas, trimmed
1 14-ounce can artichoke hearts, drained and halved
1 10-ounce package frozen peas, thawed
dill weed to taste
salt and freshly ground black pepper to taste

4 servings

In small bowl, combine broth, lemon juice and cornstarch; set aside. In large skillet, heat oil and stir fry green onions and snow peas over medium-high heat until crisp-tender. Add artichoke hearts and thawed peas, stirring until thoroughly heated. Pour broth mixture over vegetables and cook just until thickened. Add dill, salt and pepper to taste. Serve immediately.

Sesame Asparagus

⅓ cup mayonnaise
3 tablespoons sour cream
¼ teaspoon sesame oil
salt and freshly ground black pepper to taste
1½ pounds asparagus, trimmed and stems peeled
1 tablespoon sesame seeds, lightly toasted

4 servings

In small bowl, stir together mayonnaise, sour cream, sesame oil, salt and pepper. Mix well. In large skillet of boiling salted water, cook asparagus for 3-5 minutes or until barely tender. Drain well and arrange in a row on a shallow serving dish. Spoon mayonnaise mixture across center of asparagus. Sprinkle sesame seeds on top of sauce. Serve warm or at room temperature.

Try this wonderful herbed mayonnaise with steamed artichokes for a springtime first course.

Vegetables

Herbed Asparagus

1¼	pounds fresh asparagus, trimmed
4	tablespoons butter
1	clove garlic, halved
1	teaspoon minced fresh chives
1	tablespoon minced fresh parsley
1	teaspoon fresh lemon juice
¼	teaspoon salt

4 servings

Steam asparagus until tender. Keep warm. In a small skillet, melt butter and sauté garlic over medium heat. Remove garlic. Stir in chives, parsley, lemon juice and salt; heat thoroughly. Place asparagus in serving dish and pour sauce over. Serve immediately.

Choose asparagus that are emerald green with smooth unwrinkled stalks and tightly closed tips.

Chilled Lemon Asparagus

Marinade:

2	tablespoons finely chopped onion
⅓	cup fresh lemon juice
¼	cup water
½	cup Sauterne
⅛	teaspoon garlic salt
¼	teaspoon dried oregano
2	tablespoons vegetable oil
¾	teaspoon salt
2	pounds fresh asparagus, steamed until tender
	salad greens
	lemon slices
	pimiento strips

6 servings

Combine all marinade ingredients. Pour over asparagus and refrigerate, covered, for several hours. Drain and arrange on crisp salad greens. Garnish with lemon slices and pimiento strips.

Asparagus, spring's most aristocratic vegetable, is fabulous cold. For a special presentation, tie asparagus in serving-size bundles with long strips of lemon peel or pimiento.

Asparagus with Oranges and Cashews

3	tablespoons butter, melted
3	tablespoons all-purpose flour
2	cups milk
¾	teaspoon salt
¼	teaspoon ground white pepper
2½	pounds fresh asparagus, steamed
	salt to taste
2	medium oranges, peeled and sectioned
½	cup cashews, chopped

8 servings

In small saucepan, melt butter and stir in flour. When mixture begins to bubble, gradually add milk, stirring constantly. Cook over low heat until mixture thickens. Stir in salt and pepper. Strain sauce through sieve.

Arrange steamed asparagus in serving dish. Sprinkle asparagus with salt. Cut orange sections into large pieces and mix into sauce. Pour sauce over asparagus and sprinkle with cashews.

Vegetables

Green Bean Bundles

2   pounds fresh green beans,
      steamed crisp-tender
6   strips bacon, partially cooked
      garlic salt to taste
4   tablespoons butter, melted
3   tablespoons packed light
      brown sugar

6 servings

Gather 6-10 beans in bundles and wrap ½ piece of bacon around center of each bundle. Place bundles in baking dish. Sprinkle bundles with garlic salt. Pour melted butter over bundles. Sprinkle with brown sugar. Bake at 350 degrees for 15-20 minutes or until bacon is done.

Select the thinnest, most tender beans. They should be bright green and crisp. Present this do-ahead dish with any grilled meat.

Cinnamon Beans with Bacon

1   tablespoon butter
¼   cup chopped onion
¼   teaspoon ground cinnamon
1½ pounds fresh green beans
½   cup chicken broth
⅛   teaspoon salt
      dash of freshly ground
      black pepper
2   tablespoons tomato paste
6   slices bacon, fried crisp and
      crumbled

6 servings

In medium saucepan, melt butter and sauté onion with cinnamon until onion is transparent. Stir in green beans, chicken broth, salt and pepper. Heat to boiling, reduce heat and simmer 20 minutes or until beans are tender. Gently mix in tomato paste and bacon. Serve immediately.

A new twist for an old favorite.

Boulder Beans

1   pound dried lima beans
¼   pound bacon
¾   cup packed light brown sugar
1½ teaspoons sea salt

8-10 servings

Soak beans overnight in 2 inches of water.

Boil beans in water until tender or until skins pop off. Drain, reserving liquid. Cut bacon into small pieces and fry until crisp. Drain, reserving drippings. Put beans in greased 9x9-inch baking dish. Top with bacon and drippings. Sprinkle with brown sugar and sea salt. Barely cover beans with cooking liquid. Cover and bake at 325 degrees for 3 hours. Add more cooking liquid if beans become dry.

A hearty vegetable, simple to prepare.

Vegetables

Broccoli with Orange Sauce

1 pound fresh broccoli,
    cut into spears
2 tablespoons butter
1 tablespoon cornstarch
1 cup fresh orange juice, divided
1 tablespoon minced fresh parsley
1 teaspoon freshly grated
    orange peel
½ teaspoon dried thyme
½ teaspoon dry mustard
⅛ teaspoon lemon pepper
    unsalted chopped cashews
    (optional)

4 servings

Steam broccoli until just tender and place in warmed serving dish. In small saucepan, melt butter over moderate heat. Blend in cornstarch and ½ cup orange juice, stirring until smooth. Mix in remaining ½ cup orange juice, parsley, orange peel, thyme, mustard and lemon pepper. Cook over moderate heat, stirring frequently, until mixture thickens. Pour over broccoli and sprinkle with nuts, if desired.

An easy-to-prepare showstopper which will add a colorful note to poultry, lamb or game dishes.

Brussels Sprouts Supreme

1 pound brussels sprouts,
    trimmed and halved
4 strips bacon
1 tablespoon butter
1 medium yellow onion, chopped
2 small tomatoes, seeded and diced
    salt and freshly ground
        black pepper to taste
    sour cream

6 servings

Steam sprouts until tender and set aside. In medium skillet, cook bacon until crisp; drain and set aside. Discard all but 2 tablespoons drippings. Add butter and onion to skillet and cook until onion is transparent. Crumble bacon and add to onion. Stir in tomatoes. Add salt and pepper. Warm brussels sprouts in mixture and serve. Pass sour cream to spoon over sprouts.

Garnish with tomato roses made by peeling a tomato in one continuous strip and rolling the strip up to resemble a rose.

Broccoli and Blue Cheese

2 tablespoons butter
2 tablespoons flour
1 cup milk
3 ounces cream cheese
⅓ cup crumbled blue cheese
1¼ pounds fresh broccoli, steamed

8 servings

In medium saucepan, melt butter. Stir in flour and heat until bubbly. Slowly add milk, cooking over low heat until mixture thickens. Add cream cheese and blue cheese to sauce. Heat to boiling, stirring constantly. Pour over broccoli and serve.

Arrange broccoli spears on platter, alternating stems and tops. Pour the sauce down through the middle of the stalks.

Vegetables

Red Rocks Cabbage

2	whole allspice
2	whole cloves
6	whole peppercorns
1	bay leaf
1½	cups water
½	cup sugar
1	teaspoon salt
2	medium cooking apples, cored and sliced
1	medium head red cabbage, shredded
1	medium onion, sliced
1	tablespoon bacon fat or vegetable oil
3	tablespoons cornstarch
¾	cup white vinegar

8 servings

Place allspice, cloves, peppercorns and bay leaf in small square of cheesecloth and tie securely. In 5-quart kettle, combine 1½ cups water, spice bag, sugar, salt, apples, cabbage and onion and heat to boiling. Reduce heat and simmer covered for 10-15 minutes, stirring occassionally, until cabbage is crisp-tender. Discard spice bag and stir in fat.

In small bowl, blend cornstarch and vinegar until smooth. Gradually stir mixture into cabbage and cook until thickened, stirring constantly.

Simple country cooking, a traditional American favorite.

Lemon Carrots

2	cups diagonally sliced carrots
¼	cup sugar
2½	tablespoons fresh lemon juice
4	tablespoons butter

4 servings

Boil carrots in salted water until crisp-tender. Drain. In saucepan, mix sugar, lemon juice and butter and heat to boiling. Boil 2-3 minutes or until thickened. Stir in carrots. Coat well. Serve warm.

An excellent way to add texture and color to any meal, year around.

Pistachio'd Carrots

1	pound carrots, sliced diagonally
¾	cup shelled natural pistachios
2	tablespoons butter
	salt and freshly ground black pepper to taste
2	tablespoons brandy

6 servings

Steam carrots until crisp-tender. Put carrots, pistachios, and butter into serving dish. Add salt and pepper to taste. Sprinkle brandy over all. Flame, if desired.

Spectacular when flamed tableside in a chafing dish, this dish is designed for entertaining. Do not use dyed pistachios.

Vegetables

Saffron Carrots and Turnips

½   **pound carrots, peeled and cut into ¼-inch julienne strips**
2   **tablespoons unsalted butter**
¼   **teaspoon crumbled saffron threads or ¹⁄₁₆ teaspoon powdered saffron**
½   **cup chicken broth**
    salt and freshly ground black pepper to taste
¾   **pound turnips, peeled and cut into ¼-inch julienne strips**

6 servings

In large saucepan, combine carrots, butter, saffron, chicken broth, salt and pepper. Heat to boiling. Reduce heat and simmer covered for 5 minutes. Add turnips and continue to simmer uncovered until vegetables are tender and liquid is reduced.

An intriguing and colorful flavor combination.

Cauliflower with Crème Dijon

2   **medium heads cauliflower**

Crème Dijon:
2   **tablespoons butter**
3   **tablespoons all-purpose flour**
1   **cup chicken broth**
1   **cup half and half**
¼   **cup Dijon mustard**
2   **teaspoons fresh lemon juice**
    freshly ground black pepper to taste

8 servings

Break cauliflower into flowerets. Steam until tender; drain.

In medium saucepan, melt butter and stir in flour. Cook stirring for 1 minute. Add chicken broth and half and half. Heat to boiling, stirring constantly. Lower heat and simmer for 5 minutes, stirring occasionally. Remove from heat and whisk in mustard, lemon juice and pepper. Pour over warm cauliflower in serving dish.

Enjoy this zesty cream sauce with any steamed vegetable.

Vegetables

Spicy Chick Peas

2 tablespoons vegetable oil
½ teaspoon whole black mustard seeds
½ teaspoon cumin seed
1 small onion, finely chopped
1 tablespoon ground coriander
½ teaspoon ground turmeric
½ teaspoon paprika
½ teaspoon salt
pinch of ground cinnamon
pinch of freshly ground black pepper
pinch of ground cloves
2 15-ounce cans garbanzo beans
½ cup tomato sauce
2 tablespoons fresh lemon juice
1-2 tablespoons chopped fresh cilantro (optional)

8-10 servings

In large saucepan, heat oil and sauté mustard seeds until they pop. Stir in cumin and onion; cook until onion is lightly browned. Add coriander, turmeric, paprika, salt, cinnamon, pepper and cloves and stir over medium heat until thoroughly blended. Stir in garbanzo beans with liquid and continue cooking until desired consistency. Blend in tomato sauce, lemon juice and cilantro. Heat thoroughly; serve hot.

Avoid vegetable boredom. Try these light and lively garbanzo beans.

Baked Corn in Sour Cream

2 tablespoons butter
2 tablespoons chopped onion
2 tablespoons all-purpose flour
½ teaspoon salt
1 cup sour cream
1½ pounds whole kernel corn
2 tablespoons finely chopped celery
6 slices bacon, cooked crisp, drained and crumbled, divided
1 tablespoon minced fresh parsley

6-8 servings

In large saucepan, melt butter. Stir in onion and sauté until transparent. Blend in flour and salt. Gradually stir in sour cream until mixture is smooth. Add corn and celery, heating thoroughly. Stir in half the crumbled bacon. Pour into greased 2-quart casserole and top with parsley and remaining bacon. Bake at 350 degrees for 30-45 minutes.

A variation on creamed corn, a perennial family favorite.

Fresh Corn Fiesta

8 ears fresh corn
¼ cup butter, melted
1 cup green bell pepper strips
1 medium yellow onion, sliced and separated into rings
1½ teaspoons salt
¼ teaspoon dried oregano
½ cup half and half
2 medium tomatoes, sliced and halved

6 servings

Cut corn from cob. In 10-inch skillet, melt butter over medium heat. Add corn, green pepper and onion. Season with salt and oregano. Cook covered for 6-7 minutes, stirring occasionally. Add half and half and tomato slices. Simmer for 1-2 minutes, until tomatoes are hot but still firm.

Perfect as an accompaniment to a Mexican dinner. Fresh vegetables are always first choice, but when fresh corn is unavailable, substitute 1 pound frozen corn.

Vegetables

Sherried Mushrooms

½ cup tomato sauce
¼ cup olive oil
¼ cup dry sherry
⅛ teaspoon cayenne pepper
2 teaspoons dry mustard
  salt and freshly ground
    black pepper to taste
½ cup heavy cream
1½ pounds mushrooms, quartered

6 servings

In large skillet, combine tomato sauce, olive oil, sherry, cayenne and mustard. Heat thoroughly. Add salt and pepper to taste. Cover and simmer over low heat for 3 minutes. Stir in cream and mushrooms. Heat to boiling. Reduce heat, cover and simmer for an additional 3 minutes. Serve immediately.

The rich earthy flavor of mushrooms dominates this elegant dish. Good with beef, veal or pork.

Golden Onions

6 medium onions, sliced
¾ cup butter, divided
¼ cup all-purpose flour
½ teaspoon salt
¼ teaspoon freshly ground
    black pepper
2 cups milk
2 tablespoons chicken bouillon
    granules
¼ cup Burgundy wine
¾ pound Gruyère or Swiss cheese,
    shredded
1 French bread baguette, sliced into
    ½-inch rounds
4 tablespoons butter, melted

8 servings

In large skillet, sauté onions in ½ cup butter over medium heat, stirring frequently until transparent, about 15 minutes. Transfer onions to buttered 2-quart shallow baking dish. Set aside.

In large saucepan over low heat, melt remaining 4 tablespoons butter. Whisk in flour and stir for 2 minutes. Add salt, pepper, milk and bouillon granules, stirring constantly until thickened. Stir in Burgundy. Pour sauce over onions. Sprinkle with shredded cheese. Dip one side of bread slices in 4 tablespoons melted butter. Place slices, buttered side up, over sauce, covering sauce completely. Bake at 350 degrees for 30 minutes or until bread is completely browned.

Mushrooms Burgundy

6 tablespoons butter
1 medium red bell pepper, cut into
    ¾-inch pieces
1 medium green bell pepper, cut into
    ¾-inch pieces
1 small red Bermuda onion, cut into
    ¾-inch pieces
1 pound mushrooms, halved
⅓ cup Burgundy wine
2 teaspoons garlic salt
¼ teaspoon garlic powder

6 servings

In large skillet, melt butter and sauté peppers over low heat for 10 minutes, stirring frequently. Add onion and cook for 5 more minutes. Stir in mushrooms, Burgundy, garlic salt and garlic powder. Continue cooking for 15-20 minutes. Serve hot.

Wonderful served with grilled or roasted meats.

Vegetables

Hearts of Palm Verde

1   14-ounce can hearts of palm
3   tablespoons vegetable oil
2   tablespoons olive oil
2   tablespoons fresh lemon juice
½   teaspoon dried marjoram
¼   teaspoon dried tarragon
    salt and freshly ground
      black pepper to taste
1   tablespoon chopped pimiento
    (optional)

4 servings

Chill hearts of palm for several hours. Drain and rinse gently with cold water. Slice into ½-inch pieces and place in serving dish. In medium bowl, combine oils, lemon juice, marjoram, tarragon, salt and pepper; mix well. Pour sauce over hearts of palm just before serving. Garnish with pimiento. Do not marinate!

Sauce Verde is also good served over artichoke hearts.

Cold Pea Confetti

1   cup sour cream
1   teaspoon seasoned salt
¼   teaspoon lemon pepper
¼   teaspoon garlic powder
1   20-ounce bag frozen peas, thawed
½   pound bacon, fried crisp, drained
    and crumbled
1   2-ounce jar chopped pimientos
¼   cup minced red onion

6 servings

In medium bowl, combine sour cream, seasoned salt, lemon pepper and garlic powder. Stir in peas, bacon, pimientos and red onion. Mix thoroughly and chill overnight.

Spectacular served in a bowl lined with red leaf lettuce. Fill with chilled peas just before serving.

Denver Mint Peas

1   10-ounce package frozen peas
1   tablespoon butter
1   tablespoon mint jelly
¼   teaspoon dried oregano

4 servings

In saucepan, cook peas until hot; drain. Stir butter, jelly and oregano into hot peas until butter and jelly are melted. Serve immediately.

A simply wonderful vegetable with a hint of mint. Serve as an accompaniment to lamb.

Vegetables

Sautéed Snow Peas and Cucumbers

2   English cucumbers, peeled and
     sliced
½   pound snow peas, washed and
     trimmed
2   tablespoons unsalted butter
1   tablespoon dried mint
     salt and freshly ground
     black pepper to taste

4 servings

Sauté cucumbers and snow peas quickly over high heat in butter. Vegetables should remain crisp and snow peas should be bright green. Season with mint. Add salt and pepper to taste.

White cucumbers and bright green snow peas create a refreshing vegetable combination with great visual appeal. Serve with Grilled Rocky Mountain Lamb Steaks.

Spinach Artichoke Supreme

2   10-ounce packages frozen chopped
     spinach, cooked and drained
8   ounces cream cheese, softened
¼   cup butter, melted
     salt and freshly ground
     black pepper to taste
½   pound artichoke hearts
1   cup seasoned croutons
¼   cup butter, melted

6 servings

In large bowl, mix spinach, cream cheese, ¼ cup butter, salt and pepper. Pour mixture into buttered 1-quart casserole. Arrange artichokes on top. Coat croutons with remaining ¼ cup butter and spread over artichokes. Bake at 350 degrees for 20-30 minutes or until bubbly.

Rich and creamy.

Vegetables

Neptune's Spinach

4	10-ounce packages frozen chopped spinach, cooked and drained
1½	tablespoons all-purpose flour
1½	tablespoons butter, melted
¼	cup bottled clam juice
¼	cup Rhine wine
⅔	cup half and half
1	tablespoon tomato paste
¼	teaspoon salt
	dash of ground white pepper
8	ounces cream cheese, softened
4½-6	ounces tiny shrimp
4	tablespoons butter, melted
3	green onions, chopped
2	tablespoons fresh lemon juice
½	cup seasoned bread crumbs
½	cup freshly grated Parmesan cheese

12 servings

Place spinach in lightly buttered 9x13-inch pan.

In medium saucepan, stir flour into melted butter and cook for 5 minutes on low heat. Stir in clam juice and wine, all at once, and cook for 5 minutes on low heat. Add half and half, tomato paste, salt and pepper and cook for 5-10 minutes on low heat. Mix in cream cheese, shrimp, butter, green onions and lemon juice; heat thoroughly. Pour mixture over spinach. Top with seasoned bread crumbs and sprinkle with Parmesan. Bake at 350 degrees for 30 minutes or until bubbly.

Turn this recipe into an entrée by adding additional shrimp.

Spaghetti Squash Primavera

Basil Tomato Sauce:

2	cups peeled, seeded and chopped tomatoes
⅓	cup olive oil
½	cup firmly packed minced fresh basil leaves
½	cup firmly packed minced fresh parsley
3	tablespoons freshly grated Parmesan cheese
2	cloves garlic, minced
1	teaspoon salt
1	medium spaghetti squash
2	medium carrots, sliced into ½-inch pieces
2	cups broccoli flowerets
1	medium zucchini
½	cup minced green onions
1	tablespoon olive oil
	salt and freshly ground black pepper to taste

6 servings

In medium bowl, combine all sauce ingredients. Cover and let stand at room temperature for 1 hour.

Prick skin of squash. Bake on cookie sheet at 350 degrees for 1½ hours or until tender when pierced. Let cool 15 minutes. Halve lengthwise and carefully remove seeds and any loose membrane. With a fork, scrape spaghetti-like strands of squash away from shell; set aside. Reserve shell.

Separately steam or boil carrots, broccoli and whole zucchini. When each is cooked, transfer to bowl of cold water to cool. Drain. Halve zucchini lengthwise and cut into ½-inch slices. In large skillet, sauté green onions in olive oil until tender. Add drained vegetables and heat thoroughly. Add salt and pepper to taste. Combine hot vegetables, spaghetti squash and sauce. Spoon mixture into reserved squash shells and serve warm or at room temperature.

A colorful medley of fresh vegetables to serve when summer's produce it at its peak.

Vegetables

Zucchini on the Rye

1	pound zucchini, trimmed and sliced
¼	teaspoon minced fresh dill
1	clove garlic
2	cups water
1	teaspoon salt
1	pound mushrooms, sliced
3	tablespoons butter
2	tablespoons all-purpose flour
1	cup sour cream
	salt and freshly ground black pepper to taste
1	cup rye bread croutons
¼	cup butter, melted

8 servings

Add zucchini, dill and garlic to boiling salted water. Reduce heat, cover and simmer gently until zucchini is tender. Do not overcook. Drain, reserving 3 tablespoons of liquid. Discard garlic.

In large skillet, sauté mushrooms in butter for 3 minutes, stirring occasionally. Stir in flour and cook for 2 minutes longer. Add sour cream, zucchini and reserved cooking liquid, stirring constantly. Season with salt and pepper and heat thoroughly, but do not boil.

Pour mixture into 2-quart casserole. Toss croutons in melted butter, and sprinkle on top of casserole. Brown under broiler.

Zucchini and mushrooms are perfect partners. The rye croutons add crunch and pizzaz.

Marinated Vegetables Elegante

Marinade:

⅓	cup white vinegar
⅓	cup balsamic vinegar
⅔	cup vegetable oil
2	cloves garlic, minced
1	teaspoon salt
1	teaspoon sugar
1	teaspoon dried oregano, crumbled
1	teaspoon dried basil, crumbled
¼	teaspoon freshly ground black pepper
1½	cups fresh broccoli flowerets, steamed and drained
¼	cup chopped onion
½	pound mushrooms, halved
1	pound carrots, steamed until just tender, drained and cut into bite-size pieces
1	14-ounce can artichoke hearts, drained and halved
1	cup pitted ripe olives, halved
1	cup sliced celery
1	2-ounce jar sliced pimiento, drained and chopped

6 servings

In medium saucepan, combine all marinade ingredients. Heat to boiling, reduce heat and simmer uncovered for 10 minutes.

In large bowl, combine broccoli, onion, mushrooms, carrots, artichoke hearts, celery, olives and pimiento. Pour hot marinade over vegetables. Stir to coat. Cover and chill several hours, stirring occasionally. Drain vegetables and serve in lettuce-lined bowl.

Marinate the broccoli by itself and add it to the rest of the vegetables before serving, the broccoli will stay a nicer color.

Vegetables

Stir Fried Squash with Chèvre

1   medium onion, cut into thin
       wedges
2   tablespoons olive oil
2   medium yellow summer squash,
       unpeeled, cut into ¼-inch
       julienne strips
2   medium zucchini, unpeeled, cut
       into ¼-inch julienne strips
1   large red bell pepper, cut into
       thin strips
1   large green bell pepper, cut
       into thin strips
1   teaspoon dried oregano
       salt and freshly ground
       black pepper to taste
½   cup pitted Nicoise olives
½   cup finely crumbled soft, mild
       chèvre cheese
1   tablespoon fresh lemon juice

6-8 servings

In large skillet or wok, stir fry onions in oil over medium heat for 5 minutes. Add squash and peppers and continue cooking for 5 minutes, stirring occasionally. Season with oregano, salt and pepper. Add olives and cheese, heating thoroughly. Sprinkle with lemon juice and serve immediately.

The flavor of chèvre cheese is best described as tangy and fresh. It's outstanding in this Mediterranean stir fry.

Souffléd Sweet Potatoes with Brandy Cream Sauce

2   cups sweet potatoes (4-5 potatoes)
1   cup sugar
½   cup butter
8   egg yolks, beaten
       peel and juice of 1 orange
       peel and juice of 1 lemon
¼   teaspoon ground mace
¼   teaspoon ground cinnamon
¼   teaspoon ground allspice
¼   teaspoon ground nutmeg
½   cup dry sherry
8   egg whites, stiffly beaten

10 servings

Peel and quarter sweet potatoes. Cook in boiling water to cover until tender. Drain well and mash. In large mixing bowl, cream together sugar, butter and egg yolks. Stir in mashed potatoes, orange and lemon peels and juices, mace, cinnamon, allspice, nutmeg and sherry. Fold beaten egg whites into potato mixture. Pout into buttered 2-quart soufflé dish. Bake at 350 degrees for 50 minutes or until set. Serve with **Brandy Cream Sauce.**

Vegetables

Brandy Cream Sauce:

    2   tablespoons butter
    2   tablespoons all-purpose flour
    ¾   cup milk
        salt to taste
    2   tablespoons brandy
        juice of 1 orange
    1½ teaspoons powdered sugar
        ground nutmeg

1 cup

In medium saucepan, melt butter and stir in flour. Add milk, whisking constantly. Season to taste with salt. Stir in brandy, orange juice and powdered sugar. Simmer for 2-3 minutes or until sauce thickens slightly. Pour into serving bowl and sprinkle with nutmeg.

Thanksgiving will never be the same without these delicious sweet potatoes!

Herb Broiled Tomatoes

    3   large tomatoes, halved, with stem
            removed
        salt and freshly ground
            black pepper to taste
    ¼   teaspoon dried marjoram
    ⅓   cup soft bread crumbs
    1½ teaspoons butter
    1   tablespoon minced fresh parsley
    6   large mushroom caps
        salt and freshly ground
            black pepper to taste
    1½ teaspoons butter

6 servings

Place tomato halves in shallow baking pan and season with salt, pepper and marjoram. Top with bread crumbs, dot with butter and sprinkle with parsley. Arrange mushroom caps, rounded side down, around tomatoes. Season with remaining salt and pepper and dot with butter. Broil 10 minutes or until golden brown. Invert mushroom caps and place one on each tomato half. Serve immediately.

The best tomato is a home-grown tomato; enjoy this recipe in summer months when local tomatoes are available.

Tomatoes Florentine

    8   thick tomato slices
    1   10-ounce package frozen chopped
            spinach, cooked and drained
    ½   cup soft bread crumbs
    ½   cup seasoned dry bread crumbs
    ½   cup green onions, finely chopped
    3   eggs, lightly beaten
    6   tablespoons butter, melted
    ⅓   cup freshly grated Parmesan
            cheese
    4   strips bacon, fried crisp, drained
            and crumbled
        salt and freshly ground
            black pepper to taste

8 servings

Place tomatoes in a lightly greased 9x9-inch glass baking dish. Combine spinach with bread crumbs, green onions, eggs, melted butter, Parmesan, crumbled bacon, salt and pepper. Spoon spinach mixture over top of each tomato slice. Bake at 350 degrees for 15 minutes, or until lightly browned.

*Easy to manage individual serving portions which are beautiful on a buffet table. Serve with **Chutney Pepper Steak.***

Vegetables

Steamboat Stir Fry

½ cup chicken broth
½ teaspoon ground ginger
1-1½ tablespoons soy sauce
2 teaspoons cornstarch
1 tablespoon vegetable oil
1 tablespoon sesame oil
1 whole dried red pepper
1 yellow summer squash, sliced
1 medium onion, halved and sliced
½ red bell pepper, sliced
½ pound broccoli, cut into bite-size
    pieces
½ cup sliced mushrooms
1 clove garlic, minced
2 tablespoons sesame seeds,
    toasted

4 servings

In small bowl, mix broth, ginger, soy sauce and cornstarch; set aside. In large skillet or wok, heat vegetable and sesame oils and sauté dried pepper for 1 minute over medium-high heat. Add squash, onion, pepper, broccoli, mushrooms and garlic. Stir fry until crisp-tender. Pour in broth mixture, and cook until thickened. Remove dried red pepper. Sprinkle with sesame seeds and serve immediately.

Fresh and light, dazzling with flavor and color.

Winter Vegetable Medley

4 medium carrots, peeled and sliced
2 cups water
½ pound brussels sprouts
½ cup mayonnaise
2 tablespoons chopped onion
1-2 teaspoons prepared horseradish
1 tablespoon Worcestershire sauce
    dash of freshly ground
      black pepper
¼ cup slivered almonds

8 servings

In medium saucepan, cook carrots in boiling water for 10 minutes. Add brussels sprouts and continue cooking for 10 minutes more. Drain, reserving ¼ cup water. Place vegetables and water in 1½-quart baking dish.

In small bowl, combine mayonnaise, onion, horseradish, Worcestershire and pepper. Spoon over vegetables. Sprinkle almonds over sauce. Bake uncovered at 350 degrees for 20-25 minutes or until bubbly.

Vegetables

Bacon Almond Potato Balls

2	large potatoes, peeled, cooked and mashed
5	slices bacon, fried crisp, drained and crumbled
4	tablespoons butter, melted
1	large green onion, finely chopped
½	teaspoon salt
	all-purpose flour
1	egg, beaten
	sliced almonds
	vegetable oil for frying

4 servings

Combine mashed potatoes, bacon, butter, green onion and salt. Chill in refrigerator at least 2 hours. Shape potato mixture into 1-inch balls. Roll in flour, dip in beaten egg and roll in sliced almonds. Deep fry in oil heated to 375 degrees until golden. Drain well and serve immediately.

These will disappear fast! Be sure to make enough.

Crab-Stuffed Potatoes

4	medium baking potatoes
½	cup butter
½	cup heavy cream
¾	teaspoon salt
½	teaspoon ground white pepper
⅓	cup minced green onions
6½	ounces crabmeat
½	cup shredded Cheddar cheese

8 servings

Bake potatoes at 400 degrees for 1 hour. Halve lengthwise and scoop out potato; reserve skins. In large bowl, mash potatoes with butter, cream, salt and pepper. Stir in onions and crab. Fill reserved skins with potato mixture. Sprinkle with cheese. Bake at 350 degrees for 20-30 minutes.

*Add more crab to create a light entrée, and serve with **Spinach, Bacon and Apple Salad** near a cozy fireplace.*

Sweet and Tart New Potatoes

18	new potatoes, unpeeled and quartered
2	small onions, finely chopped
3	tablespoons butter
2	tablespoons sugar
1	tablespoon salt
2	tablespoons all-purpose flour
1½	cups milk
1	cup sour cream
2	tablespoons white vinegar

6 servings

Boil potatoes until tender; drain and set aside. In medium saucepan, sauté onions in butter until transparent. Stir in sugar, salt and flour. Gradually add milk. Simmer until thick, stirring constantly. Add sour cream and vinegar; cook until sauce bubbles. Combine sauce and potatoes. Serve hot.

The Colorado version of a traditional recipe for creamed potatoes. Recipe does not double well.

Vegetables

Pike's Peak Potatoes

1½   pounds new potatoes, unpeeled
       salt and freshly ground
         black pepper to taste
¾   cup heavy cream
½   cup chicken broth
1   cup shredded Swiss cheese

6 servings

Slice potatoes and place in greased 9x9-inch baking dish. Sprinkle with salt and pepper. Mix cream with broth and pour over potatoes. Cover and bake at 350 degrees for 30 minutes. Uncover and bake for another 30 minutes. Sprinkle with cheese and return to oven until cheese is melted.

This will satisfy hungry appetites, and can easily be doubled to feed a crowd.

Powderhorn Potatoes

10   medium potatoes
½   cup butter, melted
8   ounces mild Cheddar cheese, shredded
2   tablespoons chopped green onion tops or chives
2   cups sour cream
      salt and freshly ground
        black pepper to taste

8-10 servings

Bake potatoes in jackets at 400 degrees for 40 minutes or until slightly firm. Cool overnight. Peel and grate potatoes.

Mix together butter, cheese, onion, sour cream, salt and pepper, and stir into potatoes. Pour mixture into lightly greased 2½-quart casserole and bake at 350 degrees for 30-40 minutes or until lightly browned.

Stir in a 7-ounce can of diced green chiles for extra zip.

Spiced Rice

1   cup uncooked white rice
1   inch piece of ginger root, peeled
2   cups boiling salted water
¼   cup seedless raisins
¼   cup currants
¼   cup chopped dried apricots
      freshly ground black pepper to taste
½   teaspoon ground nutmeg
2   teaspoons minced shallots
1   tablespoon fresh lemon juice
½   teaspoon dried coriander
1   tablespoon olive oil
½   cup pine nuts, toasted

6 servings

Cook rice with ginger in boiling salted water until tender, about 25 minutes. While rice cooks, soak raisins, currants and apricots in hot water to cover; drain when plump. Remove ginger from cooked rice, drain any excess liquid and place rice in warm serving casserole. Add pepper, nutmeg, shallots, lemon juice, coriander and olive oil to rice. Gently fold in plumped raisins, currants and apricots. Keep warm until ready to serve. Sprinkle with pine nuts.

An imaginative combination of flavors which is perfect to serve with curry dishes.

Vegetables

Couscous and Chanterelles

5 ounces fresh Chanterelle
    mushrooms, rinsed, trimmed
    and sliced
1 tablespoon vegetable oil
2 tablespoons butter
2 tablespoons minced shallots
1 cup chicken broth
4 tablespoons butter
1 cup couscous
    salt and freshly ground
    black pepper to taste
2 tablespoons butter
¼ cup freshly grated
    Parmesan cheese

4 servings

In medium skillet, sauté Chanterelles in oil and 2 tablespoons butter over moderate heat for 3 minutes or until they give off their liquid. Stir in shallots and sauté mixture for 2-3 minutes, or until Chanterelles are golden and tender.

In medium saucepan, heat chicken broth and 4 tablespoons butter to boiling. Stir in couscous, salt and pepper to taste. Cover pan immediately and let couscous stand off heat for 5 minutes. Dot remaining 2 tablespoons of butter over couscous and let stand for 1 minute. Fluff couscous with fork, tossing until butter is completely melted. Stir in Chanterelle mixture and Parmesan.

Chanterelles are part of a whole new world of exotic mushrooms. Substitute regular mushrooms, if necessary.

Carnival Couscous

1½ cups water
2 teaspoons chicken bouillon
    granules
    dash of Tabasco sauce
1 cup couscous
5 tablespoons butter
1 teaspoon dried dill weed
1 clove garlic, minced
1 cup chopped red bell pepper
    (optional)
8 small mushrooms, thinly sliced
½ cup coarsely shredded carrots
½ cup chopped green onions
½ teaspoon salt

8 servings

In medium saucepan, combine water, bouillon granules and Tabasco. Cover and heat to boiling. Remove from heat, stir in couscous, cover tightly and allow to stand for 30 minutes. In large skillet, melt butter and stir in dill, garlic, pepper, mushrooms and carrots. Sauté until slightly limp. Add green onions and salt, tossing lightly. Stir in couscous and mix thoroughly. Serve immediately or keep warm over low heat for no longer than 30 minutes.

Red, orange, yellow and green — this side dish contains a rainbow of colors.

Vegetables

Vegetarian Shish Kabobs with Garden Rice Pilaf

Marinade:
- ½ cup Tamari sauce
- ¼ cup water
- 1 tablespoon curry powder
- 1 teaspoon ground ginger
- 1 bay leaf
- ½ medium onion, thinly sliced
- 2 cloves garlic, minced

  cherry tomatoes
  mushrooms
  bell peppers, cut into 1-inch pieces
  white onions, cut into 1-inch pieces
  zucchini, cut into thick slices

4-6 servings

Combine all marinade ingredients. In large bowl, toss vegetables with marinade until well coated. Marinate at room temperature for at least 2 hours.

Remove vegetables from marinade and arrange on skewers. Broil or grill until tender. Serve over **Garden Rice Pilaf.**

Garden Rice Pilaf:
- 4 tablespoons butter
- 1 cup diced, peeled eggplant
- 1 cup diced yellow summer squash
- ¼ cup diced mushrooms
- 1 clove garlic, minced
- 2 tomatoes, peeled, seeded and chopped
- 2 tablespoons diced pimientos
- 1 teaspoon salt
- ¼ teaspoon freshly ground black pepper
- 1 cup uncooked white rice
- 2 cups chicken broth

In large saucepan, melt butter and sauté eggplant, squash, mushrooms, garlic, tomatoes, pimientos, salt and pepper over medium heat for 5 minutes. Stir frequently. Stir in rice. Add broth and heat to boiling. Cover and reduce heat to low. Cook for 25-30 minutes or until liquid is absorbed and rice is tender.

A light and lively combination of fresh vegetables served over a colorful rice dish.

Million Dollar Rice

- 3 cups chicken broth
- 1 cup wild rice
- 5 tablespoons butter, divided
- ½ pound fresh Shiitake mushrooms, stems trimmed
  salt and freshly ground black pepper to taste

6 servings

In medium saucepan, heat broth and rice to boiling. Reduce heat to low, cover and simmer 45 minutes. Drain rice well and transfer to 2-quart baking dish. Stir in 2 tablespoons butter and set aside.

In large skillet, melt remaining 3 tablespoons butter over medium-high heat. Add mushrooms and sauté 4 minutes or until tender. Stir mushrooms into rice. Season with salt and pepper. Cover baking dish and bake at 250 degrees for 20 minutes.

Wild rice, like pasta, is best cooked al dente. The earthy taste of mushrooms makes this an outstanding accompaniment to poultry, game birds, meat and fish.

Vegetables

Lemon Pilaf

1 teaspoon freshly grated lemon peel
1 tablespoon fresh lemon juice
2 extra-large egg yolks
¼ cup heavy cream
2 tablespoons butter
1½ cups uncooked long-grain
    white rice
3 cups chicken broth
    salt to taste
3 tablespoons freshly grated
    Parmesan cheese
3 tablespoons minced fresh parsley
    salt and freshly ground
      black pepper to taste

6 servings

In small bowl, combine lemon peel, lemon juice, egg yolks and heavy cream. Whisk until well blended; set aside.

In medium saucepan, melt butter and add rice. Stir and cook briefly, until rice turns opaque. Pour in chicken broth and season with salt. Heat to boiling and reduce heat to a simmer. Cover and cook for 20-25 minutes.

Just before serving, fold lemon-cream sauce into rice. Stir in Parmesan and parsley. Season with salt and pepper. Serve immediately.

This lemony rice is an appetizing accompaniment to lamb, fish or grilled chicken.

Moroccan Dilled Rice

4 cups water
1 tablespoon olive oil
2 cloves garlic, minced
1½ teaspoons salt
2½ tablespoons dried dill weed
2 cups uncooked white rice
½ cup garbanzo beans
½-¾ cup raisins

Mast va Kniar Sauce:
1 cup plain yogurt
½ medium cucumber, diced
3 radishes, diced
1 tablespoon minced fresh parsley
2 tablespoons chopped walnuts
2 green onions, diced
1 tablespoon chopped fresh mint
    raisins to taste

8 servings

In large saucepan, combine water, oil, garlic, salt and dill. Heat to boiling. Stir in rice, beans and raisins; reduce heat to low and simmer covered for 20-25 minutes or until rice is tender. Serve with **Mast va Kniar Sauce.**

In small bowl, combine all ingredients. Cover and refrigerate until ready to serve.

An exotic treatment for white rice. Mound rice on a serving plate, make a well in the center and place a small bowl in the well to hold the sauce. Garnish with fresh mint leaves.

Vegetables

Broccoli Rice Strata with Cashews

1½   cups uncooked brown rice
2   tablespoons vegetable oil
1   large onion, chopped
2   large cloves garlic, minced
½   teaspoon dried dill weed
1   teaspoon dried thyme
1   teaspoon dried oregano
½   bunch parsley, minced
½   pound mushrooms, sliced
1   green bell pepper, thinly sliced
2   pounds broccoli, cut into flowerets with tough stalks discarded
½   cup unsalted cashews
½   pound Gruyère cheese, shredded
¼   cup freshly grated Parmesan cheese
1   pint sour cream, room temperature

10 servings

Cook brown rice according to package directions. In large skillet, heat oil and sauté onion and garlic with dill, thyme and oregano. When vegetables are tender, add parsley, mushrooms and green pepper. Continue cooking for 2 minutes, then stir in broccoli. Sauté until broccoli is crisp-tender. Add nuts and remove from heat.

Spread rice over bottom of 9x13-inch baking dish. Cover with vegetable mixture. Sprinkle with both cheeses and cover with sour cream. *Cover and refrigerate if made ahead.* Bake at 350 degrees for 20 minutes *(30 minutes if refrigerated)* or until mixture is bubbling and cheese is melted.

A well-seasoned vegetable dish which can be made several hours ahead. It will become a favorite for entertaining.

Spinach Phyllo

2   medium onions, finely chopped
½   pound mushrooms, sliced
1   tablespoon butter
3   ounces cream cheese
1   10-ounce package spinach, thawed and squeezed dry
½   teaspoon salt
   juice of ½ lemon
   freshly ground black pepper to taste
2   tablespoons all-purpose flour
1   large egg, lightly beaten
½   cup sour cream
½   pound phyllo pastry, thawed
½   cup unsalted butter, melted
1   pound Swiss cheese, thinly sliced

15 servings

In large saucepan, briefly sauté onions and mushrooms in 1 tablespoon butter. Stir in cream cheese and cook until melted. Add spinach, salt, lemon juice, pepper and flour. Blend and heat thoroughly. In small bowl, mix egg and sour cream; stir into hot spinach mixture. Set aside. When working with phyllo dough, keep it covered with a damp cloth whenever possible. Unroll phyllo dough and lay flat on cutting surface. Place 7x12-inch baking dish on stack of phyllo. Cut around edges of pan with sharp knife. Discard trimmings. Using a pastry brush, brush 6 sheets phyllo with melted butter and layer them in greased baking pan. Spoon ½ spinach mixture over phyllo, spreading evenly to within 1 inch of pan edges. Cover with thin slices of Swiss cheese. Repeat layers of buttered phyllo, spinach and cheese. Brush 4 phyllo sheets with melted butter and place on top. Score top sheets with sharp knife to define serving pieces. Bake uncovered at 375 degrees for 35 minutes or until top is golden brown.

Good for brunch, lunch or an extraordinary vegetable side dish. This is wonderful!

Vegetables

Rolled Eggplant in Tomato Sauce

Tomato Sauce:

½   cup finely chopped carrots
½   cup finely chopped leeks, white part only
1   cup finely chopped onions
3   tablespoons olive oil
2   cloves garlic, minced
1   35-ounce can plum tomatoes, chopped with juice
1   bay leaf
1   teaspoon dried thyme
    salt and freshly ground black pepper to taste

Rolled Eggplant:

2   1½-pound eggplants, peeled and sliced lenthwise ¼-inch thick
    salt
½   pound feta cheese
1   cup whole milk ricotta cheese
1   large egg
½   cup freshly grated Parmesan cheese
1   tablespoon fresh lemon juice
¼   cup minced fresh parsley
½   cup minced green onions
    vegetable oil for brushing eggplant
¼   cup freshly grated Parmesan cheese
2   tablespoons minced fresh parsley

4 servings

In large skillet, sauté carrots, leeks and onions in hot oil until onions are transparent. Stir in garlic and continue cooking for several minutes. Add tomatoes, bay leaf and thyme. Heat to boiling, cover and reduce heat to simmer. Cook sauce for 45 minutes, stirring occasionally. Season with salt and pepper. Discard bay leaf.

Sprinkle both sides of eggplant slices lightly with salt. Let stand 30 minutes, then pat dry. In food processor or blender, combine feta, ricotta, egg, ½ cup Parmesan and lemon juice. Blend until smooth. Add ¼ cup parsley and green onions. Blend 10 seconds to combine.

On jelly roll pan, arrange eggplant slices in single layer. Brush lightly with oil. Broil 4 inches from heat until lightly browned. Turn over, brush with oil and brown other side. Drain on paper towels. Repeat until all eggplant slices are cooked. Place 2 tablespoons of cheese mixture on wide end of each eggplant slice. Roll up each slice to enclose filling.

Spread ¼ cup **Tomato Sauce** on bottom of 7x10-inch baking dish. Place eggplant rolls, seam side down, in single layer on sauce. Pour remaining sauce over rolls. Sprinkle with ¼ cup Parmesan. Bake at 350 degrees for 40 minutes. Sprinkle with parsley before serving.

Although this dish takes a bit of extra preparation, its elegant presentation and outstanding flavor make it well worth the effort.

Desserts

Desserts

Cherry Creek Crisp

¼	cup sugar
1½	tablespoons cornstarch
⅛	teaspoon salt
1	10-ounce package frozen raspberries in syrup, thawed
2	teaspoons fresh lemon juice
1	16-ounce can tart, pitted cherries, drained

Topping:

4	tablespoons butter, softened
¼	cup sugar
½	cup all-purpose flour
⅛	teaspoon salt
	vanilla ice cream

4-6 servings

In small saucepan, combine sugar, cornstarch and salt. Stir in raspberries with syrup and lemon juice. Heat to boiling and cook for 1 minute, stirring constantly. Remove from heat. Press raspberry mixture through sieve, discarding seeds. Stir drained cherries into raspberry mixture and pour into lightly buttered 8x8-inch baking dish.

Cream butter and sugar in small bowl. Blend in flour and salt until crumbly. Sprinkle crumbs over fruit. Bake at 375 degrees for 30-35 minutes or until lightly browned. Serve warm with ice cream.

An interesting interpretation of a heartwarming classic; a winner every time!

Fresh Strawberries with Grand Marnier Cream

1	cup whole milk
1	cup heavy cream
½	teaspoon pure vanilla extract
4	large egg yolks
½	cup sugar
¼	cup Grand Marnier liqueur
1	quart strawberries, hulled and cut into bite-size pieces

6-8 servings

In top of double boiler, scald milk, cream and vanilla. In small bowl, beat egg yolks and sugar until light yellow in color. Add egg mixture to milk mixture very slowly, stirring constantly over low heat until sauce thickens. Stir in liqueur. Pour into a lidded jar and refrigerate. *Can be made 1 week in advance.*

To serve, bring sauce to room temperature and mix with strawberries.

For a delicious finish, serve in stemmed glasses, garnished with a fancy cookie.

Desserts

Fruit with Amaretto Cream

1½	tablespoons Amaretto liqueur
2	tablespoons packed dark brown sugar
½	cup sour cream
2	cups fresh fruit

4 servings

In small mixing bowl, combine Amaretto and brown sugar. Add sour cream and mix well. Prepare at least 2 hours before serving. Stir occasionally to dissolve brown sugar. Put fruit into sherbet glasses or small soufflé dishes. Drizzle with sauce.

Especially good with strawberries, blueberries and green grapes.

A Tart for All Seasons

Crust:

¼	cup ground almonds
½	cup butter, softened
½	cup sugar
1½	cups all-purpose flour
1	large egg yolk
1	teaspoon pure vanilla extract
1	teaspoon pure almond extract

Filling:

8	ounces cream cheese, softened
3	tablespoons sugar
2	tablespoons Amaretto liqueur
1	teaspoon pure vanilla extract
½	teaspoon pure almond extract

Apricot Glaze:

½	cup apricot preserves
1	tablespoon butter
1	tablespoon fresh lemon juice
2	tablespoons Amaretto liqueur

Topping:

3-4	cups fresh or canned fruit (strawberries, kiwis, bananas, mandarin oranges, pineapple, peaches or other favorite fruits) sliced almonds (optional)

12 servings

In food processor or mixing bowl, combine almonds, butter, sugar and flour. Add egg yolk and extracts. Blend until dough holds together. Press onto bottom and sides of 11-inch tart pan with removable bottom. Bake at 375 degrees for 15 minutes or until golden brown. Cool. *Can be made one day ahead.*

Mix all filling ingredients until smooth and spread evenly on cooled tart crust. Chill until firm, about 30 minutes.

In small saucepan, mix all glaze ingredients over low heat until hot. Cool; set aside. Orange marmalade can be substituted for apricot preserves.

Arrange fruits in a circular pattern on filling 1-2 hours before serving. Brush fruit with glaze. Sprinkle sliced almonds on top. Serve slightly chilled or at room temperature.

Beautiful to look at and easy to make, this tart showcases colorful fruit arranged in a sunburst pattern.

Desserts

Crème Brulée

4 cups heavy cream
1 vanilla bean
pinch of salt
¾ cup sugar
8 large egg yolks
½ cup packed light brown sugar

6 servings

In medium saucepan, warm cream with vanilla bean and salt. In large bowl, blend sugar and egg yolks. Remove vanilla bean and pour cream into yolks and mix well. Pour mixture into 6 ramekins or custard cups and place in shallow pan with 1 inch hot water. Bake at 300 degrees for 40 minutes. Let cool for 30 minutes. Sieve brown sugar over tops of ramekins and broil for 15 seconds, watching carefully. Sugar will form a hardened glaze.

All you need are 6 ingredients to create this creamy, delicious dessert.

Colorado Crème

1 tablespoon unflavored gelatin
½ cup sugar
2 cups heavy cream
1½ cups sour cream
1 teaspoon pure vanilla or
   almond extract
fresh berries (strawberries,
   raspberries or blueberries)

6 servings

In medium saucepan, mix gelatin, sugar and heavy cream, stirring until sugar dissolves. Continue stirring over low heat until slightly thickened. Remove from heat and fold in sour cream and extract. Pour into custard cups or pots de creme. Chill for 2-3 hours. Just before serving, spoon fresh berries on top.

The perfect recipe to highlight prize-winning summer fruit.

Old Fashioned Baked Custard

4 cups whole milk
¾ cup sugar
¼ teaspoon salt
5 large eggs, lightly beaten
1 teaspoon pure vanilla extract
½ teaspoon pure lemon extract
ground nutmeg

6-8 servings

In medium saucepan, warm milk; stir in sugar and salt. Add eggs, vanilla and lemon extracts. Pour into 1½-quart baking dish. Sprinkle with nutmeg. Place baking dish in pan with boiling water. Bake at 350 degrees for 1 hour and 10 minutes, or until knife inserted in center comes out clean. Serve warm.

Savor heart-warming childhood memories with every creamy spoonful.

Desserts

Country Apple Pudding

4	large eggs, beaten
1¾	cups packed light brown sugar
⅔	cup all-purpose flour
1¾	teaspoons baking powder
½	teaspoon salt
2	cups chopped walnuts or pecans
2	cups finely chopped, unpeeled Granny Smith apples
2	teaspoons pure vanilla extract sweetened whipped cream

6 servings

In large mixing bowl, mix eggs with brown sugar. Add flour, baking powder and salt. Stir in nuts, apples and vanilla. Pour into buttered 1½-quart baking dish. Bake at 325 degrees for 45 minutes. Serve warm with a dollop of sweetened whipped cream on top.

This moist, delicious dessert will be the "apple of your eye".

Bourbon St. Bread Pudding (Mocha Café)

6	large eggs, beaten
6	cups whole milk
2	cups sugar
10-12	cups 2-inch cubes of day-old French bread
2	tablespoons pure vanilla extract
2	tablespoons brandy
1½	cups raisins

Bourbon Sauce:

½	cup butter
2	cups packed light brown sugar
2	cups half and half
½	cup bourbon or brandy

8-10 servings

Combine all ingredients and let stand in refrigerator overnight.

Butter and flour 10½x14½x2-inch pan. Pour ingredients into pan. Set pan in larger pan; add hot water well up sides. Bake at 350 degrees for 50-60 minutes. Serve warm with **Bourbon Sauce.**

In top of double boiler over boiling water, mix together butter and brown sugar. Stir in half and half. Heat until hot and thick. Add liquor. Serve over bread pudding.

Drench this hearty delight with thick, ultra-rich **Bourbon Sauce.** *One bite and you'll be whistling Dixie.*

Desserts

Grand Marnier Soufflé

3	tablespoons butter
3	tablespoons all-purpose flour
1	cup warm whole milk
4	large egg yolks
¼	cup sugar
	pinch of salt
¼	cup Grand Marnier or Cointreau liqueur
6	large egg whites, room temperature
1	tablespoon sugar

Crème Anglaise:

1¼	cups heavy cream
4	large egg yolks
½	cup sugar
	pinch of salt
3	tablespoons Grand Marnier liqueur

6-8 servings

Butter 2-quart soufflé dish and dust with powdered sugar; set aside. In medium saucepan, melt butter; stir in flour and cook 1 minute. Add milk and stir constantly over medium heat until thickened. Cool slightly. Beat egg yolks with ¼ cup sugar and salt until thick. Beat in liqueur. Stir egg yolk mixture into milk mixture. *Soufflé can be prepared up to this point two hours before serving.*

Beat egg whites with 1 tablespoon sugar until stiff and fold lightly into egg yolk mixture. Pile gently into prepared soufflé dish. Bake at 375 degrees for 30-35 minutes or until puffed and golden brown. Serve immediately, accompanied by **Crème Anglaise.**

Heat cream in saucepan but do not boil. In another saucepan, combine egg yolks, sugar and salt, beating until light yellow in color. Add hot cream to egg yolk mixture and stir until blended. Cook over medium heat until sauce thickens, stirring with a wooden spoon. Cool. Add Grand Marnier just before serving.

A special dessert for special people.

Individual Raspberry Soufflés

1	10-ounce package frozen raspberries in syrup, thawed
4	large egg whites, room temperature
⅔	cup sugar
1	cup heavy cream
1	tablespoon (or to taste) framboise or Grand Marnier liqueur

6 servings

Butter 6 individual soufflé dishes; coat lightly with sugar. In food processor or blender, process raspberries until smooth. (If desired, strain purée through sieve to remove seeds.) In small bowl, beat egg whites until soft peaks form. Add sugar, a little at a time, and continue beating until peaks are stiff and glossy. Gently fold in raspberry purée. Pour batter into soufflé dishes and place in large baking pan. Fill pan with hot water half way up soufflé dishes. Bake at 375 degrees for 14-16 minutes or until puffed and tops are lightly browned. While soufflés are baking, whip cream with liqueur. Serve soufflés hot from oven, passing flavored whipped cream to spoon on top.

Heavenly, light and delicious — raspberries couldn't taste more wonderful.

Desserts

Colorado Peach Soufflé

1 pound peaches, peeled, pitted
  and cut into chunks, or 1 pound
  frozen peaches, thawed, juice
  reserved
¼ cup sugar
1 tablespoon unflavored gelatin
¼ cup sugar
  pinch of salt
4 large egg yolks
¼ teaspoon freshly grated
  lemon peel
2 teaspoons fresh lemon juice
4 large egg whites, room
  temperature
½ cup sugar
1 cup heavy cream, whipped
½ teaspoon pure almond extract

Garnish:
  sliced peaches
  toasted almonds
  sprigs of fresh mint

6-8 servings

Mash peaches. Stir in ¼ cup sugar and let stand
1 hour, stirring occasionally.

In top of double boiler, combine gelatin, ¼ cup sugar
and salt. Drain syrup from peaches and add enough
water to make ½ cup liquid. Blend egg yolks with peach
liquid and add gelatin mixture. Cook over simmering
water 6 minutes, stirring constantly. Remove from heat.
Add lemon peel and juice. Place top of double boiler
over ice. Stir until mixture is thicker than egg whites.
Stir in peaches.

Beat egg whites until soft peaks form. Slowly add
½ cup sugar while beating until stiff peaks form. Fold
into peach mixture. Whip cream with almond extract
and fold into peach mixture. Pour into 2-quart soufflé
dish. Refrigerate overnight. Garnish with sliced
peaches, toasted almonds and/or sprigs of mint, if
desired.

*Chilled soufflés offer the elegance of a soufflé without
the risk.*

Orange Almond Mousse

1 tablespoon unflavored gelatin
¼ cup cold water
1 cup sugar
3 tablespoons freshly grated
  orange peel
½ cup water
1¼ cups fresh orange juice
2 tablespoons fresh lemon juice
1 cup heavy cream, whipped

Garnish:
  toasted almonds
  orange slices

6 servings

Stir gelatin into ¼ cup cold water and set aside
for 15 minutes. In small saucepan, combine sugar,
orange peel and ½ cup water. Heat to boiling and boil
1 minute. Stir softened gelatin into syrup until dissolved. Add juices and mix well. Refrigerate until syrup
thickens to consistency of egg whites, 45 minutes or
more. Do not allow gelatin to set completely. Fold
whipped cream into gelatin mixture. Return to
refrigerator until set. Pile high into stemmed glasses
or serving bowl. Garnish with toasted almonds and
orange slices.

Light and luscious!

Desserts

Mile High Strawberry Squares

Crust:
- ½ cup butter, melted
- ¼ cup packed light brown sugar
- 1 cup all-purpose flour
- ½ cup chopped pecans or walnuts

Filling:
- 1 10-ounce package frozen strawberries in syrup, thawed
- 3 large egg whites, room temperature
- 1 cup sugar
- 1 tablespoon fresh lemon juice
  pinch of salt
- 1 cup heavy cream, whipped

Garnish:
- strawberries
- mint leaves
- chocolate shavings

10-12 servings

Combine all crust ingredients and mix well. Crumble evenly onto ungreased cookie sheet. Bake at 400 degrees until golden brown, approximately 10-12 minutes. Stir to recrumble. Reserve ⅓ cup crumbs for topping. Press remaining crumbs onto bottom and up sides of 9x13-inch glass baking dish. Cool.

Combine berries in syrup, egg whites, sugar, lemon juice and salt in large mixing bowl. Beat at high speed until stiff peaks form, 10-15 minutes. Fold in whipped cream. Spoon evenly over crust. Top with reserved crumbs. Freeze for 6 hours or overnight. Garnish with whole berries, mint leaves and/or chocolate shavings. Serve frozen.

Great light dessert for luncheons or bridge group!

Lemon Baked Alaska

- 1 10-inch deep-dish *Best Ever Pastry Shell*
- 9 tablespoons butter, melted
  freshly grated peel of 1 lemon
- ½ cup fresh lemon juice
- ¼ teaspoon salt
- 1⅔ cups sugar
- 3 large eggs
- 3 large egg yolks (reserve whites)
- 1 quart vanilla ice cream, slightly softened

Meringue Topping:
- 3 large egg whites, room temperature
- ⅓ cup sugar

6-8 servings

Bake and cool pastry shell; set aside.

In top of double boiler over boiling water, combine butter, lemon peel, lemon juice, salt and sugar. Beat together whole eggs and egg yolks. Stir into lemon mixture until smooth and thickened, about 5 minutes. Cool. Spread half of ice cream in bottom of baked pastry shell. Spread half of lemon mixture over ice cream. Freeze. Spread remaining ice cream and lemon mixture over pie and refreeze. *May be frozen up to 1 week without meringue.*

Beat egg whites until soft peaks form. Gradually beat in sugar until stiff peaks form. Top pie with meringue, sealing edges to crust. Brown under broiler, watching carefully. Serve immediately.

An impressive, elegant dessert. For a variation, substitute the crust from Coconut Banana Cream Pie.

Desserts

Frozen Mocha Torte

1	cup crisp macaroon cookie crumbs
2	tablespoons butter, melted
3	cups chocolate ice cream, softened
¼	cup *Hot Fudge Sauce,* cooled
3	cups coffee ice cream, softened
4	ounces chocolate-coated toffee candy bars, coarsely crushed
¼	cup *Hot Fudge Sauce,* cooled

10-12 servings

Stir together cookie crumbs and butter. Lightly press onto bottom of 9 or 10-inch springform pan. Bake at 350 degrees for 8 minutes or until lightly browned. Cool.

Spread chocolate ice cream in an even layer over cooled crust; drizzle evenly with ¼ cup fudge sauce and freeze until firm. Top with layer of coffee ice cream. Sprinkle evenly with crushed candy and drizzle with remaining ¼ cup fudge sauce. Cover and freeze until firm.

Absolutely scrumptious.

Best Ever Pastry Shell

3	cups all-purpose flour
1½	cups Crisco
1	teaspoon salt
1	large egg
1	teaspoon white vinegar
5	tablespoons whole milk

2 10-inch deep-dish pie shells

With pastry blender, combine flour, Crisco and salt until mixture resembles coarse meal. In small bowl, mix egg, vinegar and milk; add to flour mixture, mixing only until dough holds together in a ball. Refrigerate for 1 hour. Roll out on floured waxed paper or pastry cloth. Turn onto lightly-greased pie plate. Trim to a 1-inch overhang and flute edges. *Freezes well.*

To bake, prick all over with fork. Bake at 400 degrees for 11 minutes or until lightly golden brown.

It truly is the best!

Desserts

Lemon Frost Pie with Blueberry Sauce

Crust:
- 1 cup all-purpose flour
- ½ cup margarine, softened
- 2 tablespoons sugar
- ¼ teaspoon salt

Filling:
- 2 large egg whites, room temperature
- ⅔ cup sugar
- 2 teaspoons freshly grated lemon peel
- ¼ cup fresh lemon juice
- 2-3 drops yellow food coloring (optional)
- 1 cup heavy cream, whipped

Blueberry Sauce:
- 2 tablespoons cornstarch
- ⅔ cup cold water
- ⅔ cup sugar
- 1 teaspoon fresh lemon juice
  pinch of salt
- 2 cups blueberries, fresh or frozen

6-8 servings

With pastry blender or fork, combine flour, margarine, sugar and salt until mixture is consistency of coarse meal. Press onto bottom and up sides of 9-inch pie plate. Bake at 375 degrees for 12-15 minutes; cool.

In large bowl, beat egg whites until soft peaks form. Gradually add sugar and beat until stiff peaks form. Gently stir in lemon peel, lemon juice and food coloring. Fold in whipped cream. Pour filling into baked crust. Refrigerate until serving. *Can be made 2 days ahead. Can also be frozen; thaw before serving.* Serve with **Blueberry Sauce.**

In medium saucepan, dissolve cornstarch in cold water. Add sugar, lemon juice and salt. Stir over medium heat until thick. Gently stir in blueberries. Refrigerate sauce until serving. Serve sauce hot or cold over slice of pie.

A feast for the eye as well as the palate!

Snowcap Lemon Pie

- 1 9-inch *Best Ever Pastry Shell*
- 1 cup sugar
- 3 tablespoons cornstarch
- 4 tablespoons butter
- 1 teaspoon freshly grated lemon peel
- ¼ cup fresh lemon juice
- 3 large egg yolks, beaten
- 1 cup whole milk
- 1 cup sour cream
  sweetened whipped cream

Garnish:
- sugared lemon slices
- chopped walnuts

6-8 servings

Bake and cool pastry shell; set aside.

In saucepan, mix sugar, cornstarch, butter, lemon peel, lemon juice, egg yolks and milk; stir and cook until thick, about 5-10 minutes. Cool. Fold in sour cream. Pour into baked pastry shell. Refrigerate at least 12 hours. Serve with sweetened whipped cream, garnished with sugared lemon slices and/or chopped walnuts.

Creamy and delectable.

Desserts

Limelight Pie

1	9-inch *Best Ever Pastry Shell*
1	tablespoon unflavored gelatin
½	cup sugar
¼	teaspoon salt
4	large egg yolks
½	cup fresh lime juice
¼	cup water
1	teaspoon freshly grated lime peel
3	drops green food coloring (optional)
4	large egg whites, room temperature
½	cup sugar
1	cup heavy cream, whipped sweetened whipped cream

6-8 servings

Bake and cool pastry shell. Set aside.

In medium saucepan, combine gelatin, ½ cup sugar and salt. In small bowl, beat egg yolks, lime juice and water; stir into gelatin mixture. Cook over medium heat until mixture boils. Remove from heat. Add lime peel and food coloring. Chill, stirring occasionally, until mixture mounds slightly when dropped from a spoon.

Beat egg whites until soft peaks form. Gradually add remaining ½ cup sugar, beating until stiff peaks form. Fold egg whites into gelatin mixture. Fold in whipped cream. Pour into baked 9-inch pastry shell. Chill until firm. Serve with whipped cream.

Garnish with lime slices and sprinkle curled strips of lime peel over the center for a dazzling finish.

Creamy Fresh Fruit Pie

1	9-inch *Best Ever Pastry Shell*
8	ounces cream cheese, softened
¾-1	cup sugar, depending upon sweetness of fruit
2	teaspoons pure vanilla extract
2	cups heavy cream, whipped
2	cups thinly sliced seasonal fruit

6-8 servings

Bake and cool pastry shell. Set aside.

In small bowl, cream together cream cheese, sugar and vanilla. Fold in whipped cream. Spread into baked pastry shell. Cover and refrigerate. *May be made 1 day in advance.* Just before serving, cover the top with fruit.

Top with glazed strawberries for a truly spectacular presentation. Vary the fruit and you have a pie for all seasons!

Desserts

Peach Pie Supreme

1	10-inch deep dish *Best Ever Pastry Shell*
10-12	medium peaches, peeled, pitted and sliced
1	cup sugar
2	large eggs, lightly beaten
5	tablespoons all-purpose flour
6	tablespoons butter
	sweetened whipped cream

8 servings

Prepare pastry shell. Mound peaches in unbaked shell. In small bowl, mix sugar, eggs and flour until smooth. Pour over peaches. Dot with butter. Bake at 400 degrees for 10 minutes, then at 350 degrees for 45-50 minutes. Let sit before serving. Serve with sweetened whipped cream.

A peach of a pie.

Western Slope Peach Pie

1	9-inch *Best Ever Pastry Shell*
¾	cup sugar
2	tablespoons all-purpose flour
1	teaspoon ground cinnamon
	pinch of salt
6-8	medium peaches, peeled, pitted and thinly sliced

Topping:

½	cup all-purpose flour
¼	cup sugar
¾	cup finely shredded mild Cheddar cheese
4	tablespoons butter, melted

6-8 servings

Prepare pastry shell and set aside. Combine sugar, flour, cinnamon and salt. Gently toss peaches with mixture and put into unbaked pastry shell.

In medium bowl, combine all topping ingredients and mix well. Sprinkle topping mixture over peaches. Bake at 400 degrees for 40 minutes or until brown. Serve warm.

Wonderful flavor with minimal effort!

Desserts

Sour Cream Apple Pie

1	9-inch deep-dish *Best Ever Pastry Shell*
1	cup sour cream
1	large egg, lightly beaten
2	teaspoons pure vanilla extract
¾	cup sugar
⅛	teaspoon salt
¼	cup all-purpose flour
2	pounds Granny Smith apples, peeled, cored and thinly sliced

Topping:

⅓	cup all-purpose flour
¼	cup sugar
¼	cup packed light brown sugar
2½	teaspoons ground cinnamon
¾	cup chopped walnuts
6	tablespoons unsalted butter, chilled and cut into pieces

6-8 servings

Prepare pastry shell and set aside. In large bowl, combine sour cream, egg, vanilla, sugar, salt and flour, stirring until well blended. Stir in apples. Pour into unbaked pastry shell. Bake at 425 degrees for 10 minutes. Reduce heat to 350 degrees and bake an additional 30 minutes.

Combine all topping ingredients, blending until mixture resembles coarse meal. Spoon topping over pie and bake at 350 degrees for an additional 15-20 minutes or until filling is bubbly.

Walnuts add a wonderful crunchy texture to this sensational apple pie.

Pumpkin Fluff Pie

2	8-inch *Best Ever Pastry Shells*
3	large egg yolks (reserve 2 egg whites)
1	cup sugar
1	cup solid pack pumpkin
⅓	cup butter, melted
1	teaspoon ground cinnamon
½	teaspoon ground nutmeg
	pinch of salt
1	teaspoon pure lemon extract
1	teaspoon pure vanilla extract
¾	cup whole milk, scalding hot
¾	cup heavy cream, scalding hot
2	large egg whites, room temperature
	sweetened whipped cream

2 pies, 12-16 servings

Prepare pastry shells and set aside. In large bowl, beat egg yolks and gradually add sugar; beat until light in color. Add pumpkin, melted butter, cinnamon, nutmeg, salt, lemon extract, vanilla, hot milk and cream. Beat until thoroughly mixed. Cool.

Beat egg whites until stiff peaks form. Gently fold into cooled pumpkin mixture. Pour evenly into 2 unbaked pastry shells. Bake at 400 degrees for 10 minutes; reduce heat to 350 degrees and continue baking for an additional 25-30 minutes or until filling is set. Serve with a generous dollop of sweetened whipped cream.

Light as a cloud and just as heavenly.

Desserts

Brandied Walnut Pie

1   9-inch *Best Ever Pastry Shell*
1   cup packed dark brown sugar
2   large eggs
½   cup butter, melted
1   teaspoon pure vanilla extract
3   tablespoons brandy
¼   teaspoon salt
2   cups coarsely chopped walnuts
    sweetened whipped cream

6-8 servings

Prepare pastry shell and set aside. In large bowl, combine brown sugar, eggs, butter, vanilla, brandy and salt. Beat for 2 minutes and stir in walnuts. Pour into unbaked pastry shell. Bake at 350 degrees for 30 minutes or until filling is set . Serve with sweetened whipped cream.

An exciting alternative to pecan pie that is quick, easy and a real show-stopper. Perfect for the holidays.

Coconut Banana Cream Pie

Crust:
2½   cups sweetened flaked coconut
4   tablespoons butter

Filling:
1   cup sugar
5   tablespoons cornstarch
¼   teaspoon salt
3   cups half and half
4   large egg yolks, beaten
2   teaspoons pure vanilla extract
2   large or 3 medium bananas

8-10 servings

To prepare crust, sauté coconut in butter until golden brown. Pour into lightly buttered 10-inch deep dish pie plate and press firmly with back of spoon onto bottom and sides of plate. Chill.

In medium saucepan, combine sugar, cornstarch and salt. Gradually stir in half and half. Cook and stir over medium heat until mixture comes to a boil and thickens. Boil for 2 minutes and remove from heat. Stir ¼ cup of mixture in saucepan into beaten egg yolks, then stir egg mixture into saucepan. Cook 2 more minutes, stirring constantly. Remove from heat and add vanilla. Cool for 10 minutes stirring occasionally. Cover and refrigerate.

Slice bananas and arrange on bottom of crust. Pour cold filling over bananas, refrigerate, covered, at least 2 hours before serving.

Decorate with small rosettes of whipped cream, sliced bananas dipped in lemon juice and chopped cherries.

Desserts

Pecan Praline Cheesecake

Crust:
1	cup vanilla wafer crumbs
2	tablespoons sugar
4	tablespoons butter, melted

Filling:
1⅓	cups chopped pecans
3	tablespoons butter, melted
24	ounces cream cheese, softened
1	cup packed dark brown sugar
2	tablespoons all-purpose flour
3	extra large eggs
1	teaspoon pure vanilla extract

Praline Topping:
1½	teaspoons sugar
¼	cup packed dark brown sugar
2	tablespoons heavy cream
1	tablespoon butter
½	teaspoon pure vanilla extract

12-14 servings

To prepare crust, combine crumbs, sugar and butter in small bowl. Mix thoroughly. Press onto bottom of 9-inch springform pan. Chill.

Combine pecans and butter; spread evenly on baking sheet. Watching carefully, toast at 350 degrees until golden brown. Cool.

In large bowl, combine cream cheese, brown sugar and flour. Beat until light. Add eggs, 1 at a time, blending well after each. Stir in vanilla. Reserving ¼ cup of pecans for topping, add remaining pecans to filling mixture. Pour filling over crust and bake at 325 degrees for 60 minutes. Turn oven off and allow cheesecake to cool in oven for 30 minutes. Loosen cake from rim of pan. When cake has cooled to room temperature, remove the rim.

To prepare topping, combine sugars, cream and butter in small saucepan. Heat to boiling, stirring until sugars dissolve. Cook over low heat to just under the soft ball stage, or approximately 225 degrees on a candy thermometer. Immediately remove from heat and cool slightly. Add vanilla and stir until creamy. Sprinkle reserved pecans on top of cheesecake and drizzle praline mixture over the pecans. Refrigerate at least 8 hours before serving.

The ultimate cheesecake experience!

Desserts

Denver Cheesecake

Crust:

1	12-ounce box vanilla wafers, crushed
6	tablespoons butter, melted

Filling:

40	ounces cream cheese, softened
1¾	cups sugar
3	tablespoons all-purpose flour
¼	teaspoon salt
1	teaspoon freshly grated lemon peel
1	teaspoon pure vanilla extract
6	large eggs
¾	cup heavy cream

12-16 servings

In small bowl, mix together wafer crumbs and butter and press onto bottom and partially up sides of 10-inch springform pan. Chill while preparing filling.

In large mixing bowl, beat cream cheese. Add sugar, flour, salt, lemon peel and vanilla. Beat well. Add eggs, one at a time, beating well after each. Blend in cream. Pour into crust. Bake at 500 degrees for 10 minutes and at 225 degrees for an additional 70-80 minutes. Filling will be almost set. Cool at room temperature. Refrigerate for 8 hours or overnight before serving.

*A fantastic cheesecake — a mile high! Simply elegant adorned with fresh fruit, or try serving with **Pear Sauce, Strawberry Sauce** or **Apricot Glaze.***

Chocolate Glazed Almond Cheesecake

Crust:

2½	cups gingersnap cookie crumbs
⅓	cup butter, melted

Filling:

24	ounces cream cheese, softened
1	cup sugar
3	large eggs, room temperature
2½	teaspoons pure vanilla extract
2½	teaspoons pure almond extract

Chocolate Glaze:

1	cup heavy cream
1⅓	cups semisweet chocolate chips
1	teaspoon pure vanilla extract

8-10 servings

To prepare crust, combine gingersnap crumbs and melted butter. Press crumbs onto bottom of buttered 9-inch springform pan and as far up sides as crumbs allow.

In food processor or large mixing bowl, beat cream cheese until smooth. Blend in sugar, eggs and extracts. Pour into crust. Bake at 350 degrees for 45 minutes. Turn off oven and allow cake to cool with door open. Cool to room temperature. Refrigerate at least 3 hours before cutting.

In small saucepan, scald cream. Add chocolate, stirring until melted. Add vanilla and stir until glaze is smooth. Cool to room temperature. Pour glaze over top of cheesecake and refrigerate until ready to serve.

Easy and tempting dessert fare with a decadent chocolate glaze.

Desserts

Bourbon Pound Cake

2 cups butter, softened
2 cups sugar
8 large egg yolks, room temperature
3 cups all-purpose flour
2½ teaspoons pure vanilla extract
2½ teaspoons pure almond extract
½ cup bourbon
8 large egg whites, room temperature
1 cup sugar
¾ cup chopped pecans
powdered sugar

16-20 servings

In large bowl, cream butter and 2 cups sugar until light and fluffy. Add egg yolks, 1 at a time, beating well after each addition. Add flour alternating with vanilla extract, almond extract and bourbon, mixing thoroughly.

In another bowl, beat egg whites until soft peaks form. Gradually add remaining 1 cup sugar, whipping until stiff peaks form. Fold egg white mixture into egg yolk mixture. Sprinkle half the pecans onto bottom of well-buttered and floured 10-inch tube pan. Gently fold remaining pecans into batter. Pour batter into prepared pan and bake at 350 degrees for 1 hour and 20-30 minutes or until wooden pick inserted in center comes out clean. Cool completely before dusting with powdered sugar. *Keeps well for 1-2 weeks.*

Marvelous for the holidays — makes an excellent holiday gift!

Pumpkin Sheet Cake

4 extra large eggs
1 cup vegetable oil
2 cups sugar
2 cups solid pack pumpkin
2 cups all-purpose flour
2 teaspoons baking powder
1 teaspoon baking soda
½ teaspoon salt
2½ teaspoons ground cinnamon
1 teaspoon ground ginger
1 teaspoon ground cloves
1 teaspoon ground nutmeg

Cream Cheese Frosting:
3 ounces cream cheese, softened
6 tablespoons butter, softened
1 tablespoon whole milk
1 teaspoon pure vanilla extract
3 cups powdered sugar

36 servings

In large bowl, beat eggs, oil and sugar until well blended. Add pumpkin and mix thoroughly. In separate bowl, mix together flour, baking powder, baking soda, salt, cinnamon, ginger, cloves and nutmeg. Gradually add dry ingredients to pumpkin mixture. Mix until smooth. Pour into greased and floured 11x17-inch jelly roll pan. Bake at 375 degrees for 20 minutes or until wooden pick inserted in center comes out clean. Cool before spreading with **Cream Cheese Frosting.**

In medium bowl, beat cream cheese until soft. Add butter, mixing until smooth. Stir in milk and vanilla. Gradually add powdered sugar. Beat until smooth and spread onto cooled cake.

Welcome fall with this moist pumpkin cake.

Desserts

Pumpkin Cake Roll

3	**large eggs**
1	**cup sugar**
⅔	**cup solid pack pumpkin**
1	**teaspoon fresh lemon juice**
¾	**cup all-purpose flour**
1	**teaspoon baking powder**
2	**teaspoons ground cinnamon**
1	**teaspoon ground ginger**
1	**teaspoon ground nutmeg**
¼	**teaspoon salt**
1	**cup finely chopped walnuts or pecans**
	powdered sugar

8-10 servings

In large bowl, beat eggs on high for 5 minutes, gradually adding sugar. Stir in pumpkin and lemon juice. In separate bowl, stir together flour, baking powder, cinnamon, ginger, nutmeg and salt. Fold flour mixture into pumpkin mixture. Spread batter on greased and floured 10x15-inch jelly roll pan. Top with chopped nuts and bake at 375 degrees for 15 minutes. Turn out on a towel which has been liberally sprinkled with powdered sugar. Roll and keep covered.

Filling:

1	**cup powdered sugar**
8	**ounces cream cheese, softened**
4	**tablespoons butter, softened**
½	**teaspoon pure vanilla extract**

In medium bowl, beat all filling ingredients until smooth. Unroll cooled cake and spread with filling. Roll cake up again and chill thoroughly before serving. Serve at room temperature. Sprinkle with additional powdered sugar, if desired.

Serve this delicious treat on a clear glass dessert plate to highlight the pinwheel design.

Apple Cake with Rum Sauce

1	**cup all-purpose flour**
1	**teaspoon baking soda**
1	**teaspoon ground cinnamon**
¾	**teaspoon ground nutmeg**
⅛	**teaspoon salt**
4	**tablespoons butter, softened**
1	**cup sugar**
1	**large egg**
2	**cups grated, unpeeled Granny Smith apples**

6 servings

In small bowl, stir together flour, baking soda, cinnamon, nutmeg and salt. In large bowl, cream butter, sugar and egg until light and fluffy. Stir in grated apples. Blend in flour mixture. Pour into greased 8-inch square pan. Bake at 400 degrees for 30-35 minutes. *May be cooled and stored, covered, in baking pan. Before serving, reheat at 400 degrees for 10 minutes.* Cut into squares and serve with **Rum Sauce.**

Rum Sauce:

½	**cup butter**
1	**cup sugar**
½	**cup half and half**
	dash of ground nutmeg
1	**teaspoon pure vanilla extract**
2-3	**tablespoons rum**

1¼ cups

In top of double boiler, combine butter, sugar and half and half. Cook over boiling water, stirring constantly, until slightly thickened, about 10 minutes. Cool slightly. Add nutmeg, vanilla and rum. Serve warm over heated cake.

This superb dessert may also be served with slices of sharp Cheddar cheese or topped with unsweetened whipped cream.

Rhubarb Cake with Brandy Sauce

¾   **cup buttermilk (or 1 tablespoon white vinegar added to ¾ cup whole milk)**
3   **cups rhubarb, cleaned and cut into ½-inch pieces**
1½   **cups packed light brown sugar**
½   **cup butter, softened**
1   **large egg**
2   **cups all-purpose flour**
1   **teaspoon baking soda**
¼   **teaspoon salt**
2   **tablespoons cognac**

Topping:

½   **cup sugar**
2   **tablespoons butter, softened**
2   **teaspoons ground cinnamon**

Brandy Sauce:

½   **cup packed light brown sugar**
1   **tablespoon cornstarch**
¾   **cup cold water**
1½   **teaspoons butter**
2   **teaspoons brandy or bourbon**

12-16 servings

In small bowl, mix buttermilk with rhubarb and set aside. In another small bowl, cream together brown sugar and butter. Add egg, mixing well. In large bowl, combine flour, baking soda and salt. Add brown sugar mixture and cognac. Mix well. Batter will be thick. Stir in rhubarb mixture until batter is creamy. Pour into greased 9x13-inch pan.

Mix all topping ingredients with fork until well blended. Crumble topping evenly over batter. Bake at 350 degrees for 40 minutes or until a wooden pick inserted in center comes out clean. Serve with **Brandy Sauce.**

In small saucepan, mix brown sugar with cornstarch. Add water and stir over medium-high heat until thick and bubbly, about 5 minutes. Stir in butter and brandy. Serve warm over rhubarb cake.

Served piping hot from the oven and cut into generous squares, this heavenly treat is the perfect ending to a special meal.

Lemon Cheesecake Squares

14   **ounces sweetened condensed milk**
½   **cup fresh lemon juice**
1½   **teaspoons freshly grated lemon peel**
⅔   **cup butter, softened**
1   **cup packed light brown sugar**
1½   **cups all-purpose flour**
1   **teaspoon baking powder**
¼   **teaspoon salt**
1   **cup quick oatmeal**

12-16 squares

In small bowl, mix condensed milk, lemon juice and lemon peel; set aside. In large bowl, cream butter and sugar. Add flour, baking powder, salt and oatmeal. Mix until crumbly. Firmly press half of crumbs onto bottom of buttered 8x12-inch baking dish. Pour condensed milk mixture on top. Cover with remaining crumb mixture and press down gently. Bake at 350 degrees for 25-30 minutes or until brown around edges. Chill before cutting.

Easy and tempting dessert fare with superb lemon flavor.

Desserts

Raspberry Meringue Squares

¾ cup butter, softened
¼ cup sugar
2 large egg yolks, room temperature
1½ cups all-purpose flour
1 cup raspberry preserves
½ cup sweetened flaked coconut
2 large egg whites, room temperature
½ cup sugar
1 cup ground walnuts

24 squares

In large bowl, cream butter with ¼ cup sugar until fluffy. Beat in egg yolks. Stir in flour until well blended. Spread evenly on bottom of greased 9x13-inch pan. Bake at 350 degrees for 15 minutes or until golden.

Spread raspberry preserves over layer in pan. Sprinkle coconut over preserves. Beat egg whites until soft peaks form. Slowly beat in ½ cup sugar until peaks are stiff and glossy. Spoon meringue over coconut and sprinkle with nuts. Bake at 350 degrees for 25 minutes or until lightly golden. Cool thoroughly before cutting into bars. Serve on dessert plates as bars crumble easily.

Ruby red raspberries peaking through baked clouds of meringue — beautiful!

Alpine Apricot Squares

⅔ cup dried apricots
1 cup water
½ cup butter, softened
¼ cup sugar
1 cup all-purpose flour
2 large eggs
1 cup packed light brown sugar
⅓ cup all-purpose flour
½ teaspoon baking powder
¼ teaspoon salt
1 teaspoon pure vanilla extract
1 teaspoon fresh lemon juice
1 cup chopped nuts
¾ cup sweetened flaked coconut (optional)
powdered sugar

24 squares

Rinse apricots. In small saucepan, cook apricots in boiling water for 10 minutes. Drain well and chop; set aside.

In medium bowl, mix together butter, sugar and 1 cup flour. Press onto bottom of 9x13-inch pan. Bake at 325 degrees for 25 minutes.

In medium bowl, beat eggs and gradually add brown sugar. Stir in ⅓ cup flour, baking powder, salt, vanilla and lemon juice. Fold in nuts, chopped apricots and coconut, if desired. Pour over crust and bake at 325 degrees for an additional 20 minutes. Cool. Dust with powdered sugar.

The delectable taste of apricots may be yours any time of the year.

Desserts

Pecan Bars

Crust:
- ½ cup powdered sugar
- 2 cups all-purpose flour
- 1 cup butter, softened

Topping:
- ¾ cup butter
- ¼ cup heavy cream
- ½ cup honey
- 1 cup packed light brown sugar
- 4 cups coarsely chopped pecans

24 bars

Mix sugar and flour together. Blend in butter until crumbly. Firmly pat crumbs onto bottom of greased 9x13-inch pan. Bake at 350 degrees for 20 minutes.

In saucepan over medium heat, melt butter. Add cream, honey and brown sugar, stirring constantly until well mixed. Remove from heat. Stir in pecans and spread over hot crust. Return to oven and bake an additional 30 minutes. As bars are cooling, occasionally run knife around edges of pan to separate caramel from pan. When completely cooled, cut into bars.

Chewy, gooey and thick with pecans!

Macadamia Bars

Crust:
- ½ cup butter, softened
- ¼ cup sugar
- 1 cup all-purpose flour

Filling:
- 2 large eggs, lightly beaten
- ½ cup sweetened flaked coconut
- 1½ cups packed light brown sugar
- 1-1½ cups halved macadamia nuts
- 2 tablespoons all-purpose flour
- 1½ teaspoons pure vanilla extract
- ½ teaspoon baking powder

16-20 bars

In medium bowl, cream together all crust ingredients. Press onto bottom of 9-inch square pan and bake at 350 degrees for 20 minutes.

In medium bowl, stir together all filling ingredients. Pour over hot baked crust and bake at 350 degrees for an additional 20 minutes. Cool completely and cut into squares.

Moist, chewy and absolutely sinful. Great served with vanilla ice cream.

Desserts

Butter Pecan Turtle Bars

2	cups all-purpose flour
¾	cup packed light brown sugar
½	cup butter, softened
1½	cups pecan halves
½	cup packed light brown sugar
⅔	cup butter
1½	cups milk chocolate chips

48 bars

Combine flour, ¾ cup brown sugar and ½ cup butter. Blend until crumbly. Pat firmly onto bottom of ungreased 9x13-inch pan. Sprinkle pecan halves over unbaked crust. Set aside.

In small saucepan, combine ½ cup brown sugar and ⅔ cup butter. Cook over medium heat, stirring constantly, until mixture begins to boil. Boil for one minute, stirring constantly. Drizzle caramel over pecans and crust. Bake at 350 degrees for 18-20 minutes or until caramel layer is bubbly and crust is light brown. Remove from oven and immediately sprinkle with chocolate chips. Spread chips evenly as they melt. Cool completely before cutting.

The heavenly combination of caramel, pecans and chocolate makes these bars irresistible! They disappear fast.

Easy Baklava

Syrup:

½	cup water
1	slice lemon
1	cup sugar
1	cinnamon stick, 2-3 inches long
¼	cup honey

Filling:

2	cups finely chopped walnuts
1¾	cups finely chopped blanched almonds
¼	cup sugar
1	teaspoon ground cinnamon

Pastry:

1	pound phyllo pastry (about 20 sheets)
1	pound butter, melted

24 pieces

In small saucepan, combine water, lemon slice, sugar and cinnamon stick. Heat to boiling. Stir in honey and refrigerate until serving.

In small bowl, mix together all filling ingredients; set aside.

Lay large phyllo sheets flat on cutting board and cut in half, making 40 10x15-inch sheets. Brush butter on bottom of 10x15-inch jelly roll pan. Place 1 phyllo sheet on bottom of pan and brush with butter. Repeat 15 times. Sprinkle the buttered 16th sheet with 2-3 tablespoons filling. Repeat layering with butter and filling until you have 10 phyllo sheets left. Layer last 10 sheets, brushing each with butter. Pour remaining butter over top. Cut on the diagonal into 3-inch diamond-shaped pieces before baking. Bake at 375 degrees for 30 minutes, then at 350 degrees an additional 30 minutes. To serve, pour cold syrup over hot baklava or pour hot syrup over cooled baklava; otherwise pastry turns soggy.

This traditional favorite from Greece is sweet, gooey and flaky — an absolute must for the holidays and special occasions.

Desserts

Fool's Toffee

1	cup butter
1	cup packed dark brown sugar
36	2x2-inch saltine crackers
11½	ounces milk chocolate chips
½	cup chopped pecans or walnuts

3-4 dozen

In small saucepan over medium-high heat, blend butter and brown sugar. Heat to boiling and boil for 4 minutes. Cover 10x15-inch jelly roll pan with foil and butter lightly. Place single layer of saltines on foil close together. Pour butter mixture over crackers, spreading evenly. Bake at 375 degrees for 5 minutes. Immediately sprinkle chocolate chips on top. Allow to soften and spread evenly over cooked crackers. Sprinkle with nuts. Refrigerate until cool. Break into pieces and store in tin container in refrigerator. *Can be kept in refrigerator for 1-2 weeks.*

Divinely simple. Simply divine.

Wheat Shortbread Cookies

1	cup butter, softened
½	cup packed light brown sugar
1	cup whole wheat flour
1	cup all-purpose flour
	pinch of salt
1	large egg yolk
1	tablespoon water
⅓	cup ground almonds or hazelnuts

3 dozen

In large bowl, cream together butter and sugar. Mix flours and salt together and blend into dough. On lightly floured surface, roll out dough to ¼-inch thickness. Cut dough into rounds or shapes with cookie cutters and place on ungreased cookie sheet. Beat egg yolk with water and brush mixture on dough, leaving rim of cookie plain. Sprinkle nuts on egg yolk mixture. Bake at 350 degrees for 12-15 minutes.

A delicate, nutty flavor! You don't have to be a health food devotee to love these.

Larimer Toffee Squares

24	graham cracker squares, regular or cinnamon crisp
1	cup butter
1	cup packed dark brown sugar
1¼	cups chopped nuts (pecans, walnuts or almonds)

24 squares

Line 11x17-inch jelly roll pan with foil and place whole graham crackers in single layer on foil. In small saucepan, heat butter and brown sugar until sugar dissolves. Spread evenly over crackers. Sprinkle with nuts. Bake at 325 degrees for 10 minutes. Cool for 5 minutes, then transfer to waxed paper to cool completely.

Desserts

Brown Sugar Cookies

½ cup butter, softened
½ cup Crisco
½ cup sugar
½ cup packed light brown sugar
1 teaspoon pure vanilla extract
1 large egg
2 cups all-purpose flour
½ teaspoon baking soda
¼ teaspoon salt

4 dozen

Cream together butter, shortening and sugars until light and fluffy. Add vanilla. Beat in egg until well mixed. Stir together flour, baking soda and salt and gradually add to creamed mixture. Refrigerate dough for 2 hours.

Roll dough into nickel-sized balls and roll in sugar. Place on ungreased cookie sheet 2 inches apart and press down with designed bottom of glass dipped in sugar. Bake at 325 degrees for 10 minutes.

Just like grandma used to make!

Ginger Cookies

1½ cups Crisco
2 cups sugar
2 large eggs
2 teaspoons pure vanilla extract
½ cup light molasses
4 cups all-purpose flour
4 teaspoons baking soda
2 teaspoons ground cinnamon
2 teaspoons ground nutmeg
2 teaspoons ground cloves
2 teaspoons ground ginger
2 teaspoons salt

6-8 dozen

In mixing bowl, cream together Crisco and sugar. Add eggs, vanilla and molasses. Mix well. Add flour, baking soda, cinnamon, nutmeg, cloves, ginger and salt to molasses mixture. Mix well. Roll into 1-inch balls and dip in sugar. Place on ungreased cookie sheet and bake at 375 degrees for 10 minutes. *Cookies stored with a piece of bread will last several weeks. These cookies also freeze well.*

Old-fashioned goodness in every bite. Terrific with fresh fruit desserts.

Strawberry Sauce

1 10-ounce package frozen strawberries in syrup, thawed
2 tablespoons sugar
2 teaspoons fresh lemon juice
2-3 tablespoons Cointreau liqueur

1 cup

In food processor or blender, combine all ingredients and blend until smooth.

*Berry wonderful! A perfect accompaniment to **Chocolate Pâté, Denver Cheesecake, Chocolate Torte** or ice cream.*

Desserts

Pear Sauce

⅔   cup sugar
2½   tablespoons cornstarch
2   cups water
2¼   teaspoons freshly grated
     lemon peel
⅓   cup fresh lemon juice
     pinch of salt
2-3   fresh pears, peeled, cored
     and sliced

4 cups

In medium saucepan, combine sugar and cornstarch. Add water, lemon peel, lemon juice and salt. Cook and stir over moderately high heat until thickened. Gently stir in pears. Remove from heat and cool. Serve at room temperature.

*Fresh pear flavor at its best. Serve with **Denver Cheesecake, Colorado Crème** or fresh fruit.*

Toffee Sauce

1½   cups sugar
1   cup evaporated milk
4   tablespoons butter
¼   cup light corn syrup
     pinch of salt
½   cup crushed toffee candy bars

2½ cups

In medium saucepan, combine sugar, evaporated milk, butter, corn syrup and salt. Heat to boiling. Boil 1 minute stirring constantly. Remove from heat and stir in toffee. Cool.

Transform a scoop of ice cream into an encore presentation.

Caramel Corn

1   cup margarine or butter
2   cups packed dark brown sugar
½   teaspoon salt
¼   cup light corn syrup
¼   cup water
1   teaspoon baking soda
8   quarts popped corn
     (do not air pop)

8 quarts

Melt margarine in 2-quart saucepan. Add brown sugar, salt, corn syrup and water. Heat to boiling. Boil for 5 minutes, watching carefully so sauce does not boil over. Remove from heat and add baking soda; stir well. Pour over popped corn and stir until well coated. Place on 2 cookie sheets and bake at 250 degrees for 40 minutes, stirring occasionally. Bake both batches at the same time using lower and middle racks in oven. Take caramel corn off cookie sheets immediately after removing from oven.

Lip-smacking snacking!

Chocolate

Chocolate

Chocolate Torte with Raspberry Sauce

6	ounces semisweet chocolate chips
1	cup unsalted butter, softened
1	cup sugar
8	large egg yolks
8	large egg whites, room temperature
	sweetened whipped cream

8-10 servings

In top of double boiler over boiling water, melt chocolate. In large bowl, combine melted chocolate, butter and sugar. Cool. Add egg yolks, 2 at a time, beating well after each addition. In separate bowl, beat 8 egg whites until stiff. Gently fold egg whites into chocolate mixture. Pour ⅔ batter into buttered and floured 9-inch springform pan. Bake at 325 degrees for 35-40 minutes or until wooden pick inserted in center comes out clean. Cool to room temperature (center will fall) and spread remaining batter on top. Refrigerate for at least 8 hours or overnight. Use a hot knife to cut into wedges. Serve with sweetened whipped cream and **Raspberry Sauce.**

Raspberry Sauce:

2	10-ounce packages frozen raspberries in syrup, thawed
¼	cup sugar
2-3	tablespoons Grand Marnier liqueur

1½ cups

Drain 1 package raspberries and discard juice. Retain juice from other package. Purée fruit, juice, sugar and liqueur in food processor or blender; strain purée to remove seeds. Chill until ready to use.

Easy, elegant and freezes beautifully.

Richard Grausman's Grand Marnier Chocolate Soufflé

4	ounces semisweet or bittersweet chocolate
4	tablespoons unsalted butter
4	large egg yolks
	freshly grated peel of 1 orange
2	tablespoons Grand Marnier liqueur
4	large egg whites
¼	teaspoon cream of tartar

4 servings

Preheat oven to 475 degrees. Butter and sugar 1-quart soufflé mold. Place chocolate and butter in a saucepan, and allow to melt over low heat. Remove from heat and stir in egg yolks. Pour into a large mixing bowl and flavor with grated orange peel and Grand Marnier.

Beat egg whites until stiff. Fold half of beaten egg whites into chocolate with whisk. Add remaining whites and fold in with rubber spatula. Pour into prepared soufflé mold. Bake in preheated oven 5 minutes. Then turn temperature down to 425 degrees and continue baking for 5-7 minutes. Sprinkle with powdered sugar and serve immediately.

*Baking time given produces a soufflé with a creamy center. Serve on a pool of **Crème Anglaise** for a spectacular dessert.*

Chocolate

Chocolate Pâté

15	ounces Hershey's semisweet chocolate
1	cup heavy cream
4	tablespoons unsalted butter
4	large egg yolks
¾	cup powdered sugar
6	tablespoons dark rum

Garnish:
> *Raspberry Sauce*
> **sweetened whipped cream**

8-10 servings

In top of a double boiler over simmering water, melt chocolate with cream and butter. Beat with wire whisk until mixture is smooth and glossy. Remove from heat and add yolks, one at a time, beating well after each. Add powdered sugar, whisking constantly until smooth. Mix in rum. Butter a small 4-cup loaf pan. Put waxed paper in pan, leaving small overhang, and butter sides and bottom of paper-lined pan. Pour chocolate mixture into pan, cover with plastic wrap, and freeze overnight.

To remove pâté, gently loosen waxed paper from pan. If it sticks, set in hot water for a few seconds. Turn pâté over onto a serving plate and remove waxed paper. Using a hot knife, slice pâté ⅓ to ½-inch thick. Present chocolate pâté slice on a pool of **Raspberry Sauce** and top with a generous dollop of sweetened whipped cream.

*Decorate with candied violets for an exquisite finale. Substitute **Crème Anglaise, Strawberry Sauce** or **Apricot Glaze** for the **Raspberry Sauce,** if desired.*

Chocolate Divine Dessert

½	cup slivered almonds
12	ounces semisweet chocolate chips
3	tablespoons sugar
3	large egg yolks, beaten
3	large egg whites, stiffly beaten
2	cups heavy cream, whipped
1	teaspoon pure vanilla extract
1	8-ounce angel food cake

10-12 servings

Place almonds on ungreased cookie sheet and bake at 350 degrees until light golden brown. Watch carefully so almonds do not burn! Cool and set aside.

In top of double boiler over hot water, melt chocolate chips with sugar. Cool. Mix in beaten egg yolks. Gradually fold in stiffly beaten egg whites. Fold in whipped cream and vanilla. Tear up angel food cake into ½-inch pieces. Put half of cake pieces on bottom of buttered 10-inch springform pan. Cover with half of chocolate mixture. Layer remaining cake and chocolate. Refrigerate at least 24 hours. Remove springform rim. Top with toasted almonds. *May be made up to three days in advance.*

Paradise found!

Chocolate

Chocolate Indulgence

16   ounces semisweet chocolate
¾   cup butter
¾   cup powdered sugar
1   tablespoon all-purpose flour
4   large egg yolks
1½   teaspoons pure vanilla extract
4   large egg whites, room temperature
1   cup sour cream

12-16 servings

In large saucepan, melt chocolate and butter together, then gradually add sugar and flour, stirring constantly with wire whisk. Add egg yolks, one at a time, mixing well after each. Stir in vanilla. Beat egg whites until stiff peaks form and fold into chocolate mixture Pour all but 1 cup of mixture into buttered 8x8-inch pan. Add 1 cup sour cream to reserved 1 cup batter and spread evenly over top of mixture in pan. Bake at 375 degrees for 25 minutes. The center will not look done or set. Cool completely, cover and refrigerate for 4-6 hours. Cut into 1½-inch squares with a hot knife. *Individual pieces can be wrapped and frozen.*

The name says it all — a chocoholic's dream! Garnish with a small dollop of whipped cream.

Chocolate Crêpes

Crêpes:
1   cup all-purpose flour
3   tablespoons sugar
    pinch of salt
2   tablespoons unsweetened cocoa powder
2   large eggs
1   cup whole milk, warmed
2   tablespoons butter, melted

Filling:
1¼   cups heavy cream
1   teaspoon pure vanilla extract
2   tablespoons sugar

Topping:
1½   cups *Hot Fudge Sauce*
4   ounces sliced almonds, toasted

16-20 crêpes

In medium bowl, mix together flour, 3 tablespoons sugar, salt and cocoa. Add eggs, warm milk and melted butter and beat until smooth. Force batter through sieve and let batter stand at room temperature for 2 hours before cooking crêpes.

If using a crêpe maker, follow recommended directions. Otherwise, brush bottom of 6-inch, thick-bottomed skillet with butter. Add 2 tablespoons batter, swirling pan to allow batter to cover entire bottom of pan thinly. Brown lightly on one side and turn with spatula to brown other side. Turn onto paper towel to cool. Repeat with remaining batter. To store, place waxed paper between crêpes and wrap in foil. *Refrigerate up to 4 days or freeze. Allow to warm to room temperature before filling.*

Whip cream with vanilla and 2 tablespoons sugar. Fill each crêpe with whipped cream, roll and place on serving dish. Drizzle with hot fudge and sprinkle with toasted almonds.

A dessert fit for royalty.

Chocolate

Easy Pots de Crème

1	cup whole milk, heated to boiling point
1	cup semisweet chocolate chips
1	large egg
2	tablespoons sugar
2	tablespoons rum or favorite liqueur

Garnish:
fruit
whipped cream
chocolate shavings

6 servings

Combine all ingredients in food processor or blender. Blend on high until chocolate chips are melted and smooth. Pour into 6 pots de crème or demitasse cups. Chill until firm. Garnish with a piece of fruit, dollop of whipped cream, and/or chocolate shavings, if desired.

Easy to make and worth every calorie. Serve with petite, elegant cookies.

Pots de Crème

5	ounces semisweet chocolate
3	tablespoons Kahlúa or Grand Marnier liqueur
3	tablespoons fresh orange juice
3	large egg yolks
⅔	cup sugar
¾	cup heavy cream

Garnish:
whipped cream
chocolate curls
unsweetened cocoa powder

6-8 servings

In saucepan, melt chocolate with Kahlúa and orange juice. Cool. In blender or food processor, mix egg yolks and sugar well. Gradually add chocolate mixture to eggs and blend until well mixed. With machine running, slowly pour in heavy cream. Blend until well mixed. Pour into 6-8 demitasse cups or pots de crème or into 1 large glass bowl. Refrigerate. *Can be made 1 day in advance.* Garnish with whipped cream and sprinkle with chocolate curls or cocoa, if desired.

A rich and luscious way to end a meal.

Down Under Fudge Pudding

½	cup butter
1	ounce unsweetened chocolate
2	large eggs
1	cup sugar
2	tablespoons all-purpose flour
1	teaspoon pure vanilla extract
1	cup chopped pecans
4	scoops vanilla ice cream

4 servings

In saucepan, melt butter and chocolate stirring until blended. In medium bowl, beat eggs. Stir in sugar, flour and vanilla. Add chocolate mixture and mix well. Stir in nuts and pour into 9x5-inch loaf pan. Place loaf pan in pan of hot water and bake at 325 degrees for 45 minutes. Serve warm in dessert bowls topped with a scoop of vanilla ice cream. *Can be made 1 day ahead and reheated in pan of hot water before serving.*

It's gooey, rich and chocolatey.

Chocolate

Chocolate Fluff

3	ounces semisweet chocolate or bittersweet chocolate
4	large egg yolks
½	teaspoon pure vanilla extract
4	large egg whites, room temperature
¼	cup powdered sugar
½	teaspoon pure vanilla extract
4	cups heavy cream
¼	cup powdered sugar
½	teaspoon pure vanilla extract

6-8 servings

In top of double boiler over simmering water, melt chocolate. Cool. Add egg yolks, one at a time, mixing well after each. Continue beating until light; stir in ¼ teaspoon vanilla. Cool.

Beat egg whites until soft peaks form. Gradually add ¼ cup powdered sugar and ½ teaspoon vanilla. Continue beating until stiff peaks form. Fold melted chocolate mixture into egg whites. Volume will decrease. Set aside in a cool place.

Whip cream gradually adding ¼ cup powdered sugar and ½ teaspoon vanilla until stiff peaks form. Fold ½ of whipped cream into chocolate mixture. Spoon a layer of whipped cream into bottom of stemmed glasses, reserving ¼ cup for decoration. Divide chocolate mixture evenly among glasses. Spoon or pipe remaining whipped cream on top. Refrigerate until ready to serve. *Can be made 1 day ahead.*

Heaven on the palate! For extra flair, garnish with chocolate curls.

Grandma's Hot Fudge Pudding

1	cup all-purpose flour
1	teaspoon baking powder
¼	teaspoon salt
⅔	cup sugar
2	tablespoons unsweetened cocoa powder
2	tablespoons butter, melted
1	teaspoon pure vanilla extract
½	cup half and half
1	cup chopped walnuts
1	cup packed light brown sugar
¼	cup unsweetened cocoa powder
1¾	cups boiling water sweetened whipped cream

4-6 servings

Stir together flour, baking powder, salt, sugar and 2 tablespoons cocoa. Mix melted butter, vanilla and half and half. Add to flour mixture, blending lightly; add nuts. Pour into buttered 1½-quart baking dish. Combine brown sugar and ¼ cup cocoa and sprinkle over batter. Carefully pour boiling water over top of batter. Bake at 350 degrees for 30 minutes. Serve immediately with sweetened whipped cream.

An old-fashioned treat.

Chocolate

White Chocolate Mousse

12	ounces Guittard's white chocolate, chopped (do not use coating chocolate)
¾	cup whole milk
1	tablespoon unflavored gelatin
¼	cup whole milk, warmed
2½	teaspoons pure vanilla extract
4	large egg whites, room temperature pinch of salt
2	cups heavy cream, whipped
⅛	teaspoon fresh lemon juice

Garnish:
Raspberry Sauce or
Strawberry Sauce or
Hot Fudge Sauce
Chocolate Leaves

12 servings

Melt white chocolate in ¾ cup milk in top of double boiler over hot, not boiling, water. (White chocolate melts at a low temperature and will become "grainy" if heated too much.) Stir until smooth and remove from heat.

Soften gelatin in ¼ cup milk, stirring until dissolved. Place cup in hot water if necessary. Add gelatin to chocolate, stirring constantly until very smooth. Stir in vanilla. Cool to room temperature.

In small bowl, beat egg whites until foamy. Add salt and continue beating until stiff peaks form. Mix ⅓ of whites into chocolate mixture. Gently fold in remaining whites in two additions. Fold whipped cream into chocolate mixture in three additions. Fold in lemon juice and pour into glass serving bowl. Chill at least 3 hours before serving. Spoon onto individual plates on pool of **Raspberry Sauce, Strawberry Sauce** or **Hot Fudge Sauce.** Decorate with **Chocolate Leaves.**

A delicious variation of the classic favorite.

White Chocolate Fondue

½	cup whole filberts, hazelnuts or almonds
15	ounces white chocolate, chopped
¾	cup heavy cream
1	tablespoon hazelnut or almond flavored liqueur
1	teaspoon pure vanilla extract
2	cups strawberries, washed and hulled
2	large oranges, peeled, divided into segments, membrane removed
2	cups fresh pineapple chunks
2	cups sliced apples
	Wheat Shortbread Cookies

2½ cups

Place whole nuts on cookie sheet and bake at 350 degrees for 10-15 minutes or until skins are golden, shaking pan occasionally. Wrap nuts in towel and rub together to loosen skins. Pick out toasted nuts and discard skins. Cool and chop finely.

Place white chocolate in large bowl and set bowl in pan of hot water to melt chocolate slowly. In small saucepan, bring heavy cream to boil; pour over white chocolate, stirring until smooth. Stir in chopped nuts, liqueur and vanilla. Pour into 3-cup container, cool, cover and refrigerate up to six weeks.

To serve, bring fondue to room temperature or heat in microwave oven until soft enough to spoon into small individual cups. Place each cup on a dessert plate and surround with fruit and cookies. Dip fruits and cookies into fondue or spread fondue on them with butter knife.

*A whimsical twist for the chocolate addict in all of us. Milk chocolate can be substituted for white chocolate. Additional fruits in season, **Chocolate Pound Cake** or nut breads can supplement the suggested fruits and cookies.*

Chocolate

Almond Mocha Pie

Crust:
- ½ cup butter, softened
- 2 tablespoons sugar
- 1 cup all-purpose flour

Filling:
- ⅓ cup chopped almonds
- 6 ounces semisweet chocolate chips
- ¼ cup light corn syrup
- ¼ cup water
- ½ cup sugar
- ¼ cup water
- 1 large egg white, room temperature
- 1 teaspoon instant coffee granules
- 1 teaspoon pure vanilla extract
- 1 teaspoon fresh lemon juice
- 2 cups heavy cream, whipped
- 3 tablespoons *Hot Fudge Sauce,* warmed (optional)

6-8 servings

In small bowl, mix butter and sugar by hand or with mixer on lowest speed. Add flour, stirring until mixture resembles coarse meal. Press all but ⅓ cup onto bottom and sides of buttered 9-inch pie plate. Bake at 375 degrees for 12-15 minutes or until light golden brown; cool. Spread reserved crumbs on cookie sheet and bake at 375 degrees for 10-12 minutes or until golden brown; cool.

Place chopped almonds on cookie sheet and toast at 375 degrees for 5-7 minutes, watching carefully. Cool. In small saucepan, stir chocolate chips, corn syrup and ¼ cup water over low heat until chips melt; cool. In large bowl, beat sugar, ¼ cup water, egg white, coffee granules, vanilla and lemon juice until soft peaks form, about 3-5 minutes. Fold chocolate mixture, whipped cream and almonds into egg white mixture. Spoon into baked crust. Decorate top with warmed **Hot Fudge Sauce** by drizzling chocolate in 3 concentric circles; pull knife tip from center to edge in several places to create web design. Sprinkle top with reserved toasted crumbs. Freeze until firm, about 4-6 hours. *Cover if stored longer.* Let sit at room temperature for 30 minutes before serving.

Guaranteed not to last!

Chocolate Pecan Pie

- 1 unbaked 9-inch *Best Ever Pastry Shell*
- 4 tablespoons butter
- 3 ounces semisweet chocolate
- 1 cup light corn syrup
- ½ cup sugar
- 1¼ teaspoons pure vanilla extract
- ¼ teaspoon salt
- 3 large eggs
- 1½ cups pecan halves
  whipped cream

6-8 servings

Prepare pastry shell and set aside.

In medium saucepan, melt butter with chocolate, stirring until smooth. Remove from heat and beat in corn syrup, sugar, vanilla, salt and eggs. Mix well. Place pecans on bottom of pastry shell. Pour chocolate mixture over pecans. Bake at 350 degrees for 1 hour or until knife inserted 1 inch from edge comes out clean. Serve with whipped cream.

Your taste buds will be forever grateful.

Chocolate

Chocolate Leaves

10-15	fresh leaves with stems
4	ounces white, semisweet or milk chocolate, coarsely chopped

10-15 leaves

Wash leaves and dry well with paper towel. Place waxed paper on cookie sheet. In microwave oven or in top of double boiler, melt chocolate. Hold leaf by stem and use pastry brush to apply chocolate to underside of leaf. Be careful not to get chocolate on top of leaf. Set leaf on cookie sheet. Repeat for all leaves. Place cookie sheet in freezer for 5 minutes. Brush leaves with more chocolate and refreeze. Holding stem, carefully peel leaf from chocolate. **Chocolate Leaves** can be stored in refrigerator or freezer until ready to use.

The ultimate garnish for your desserts! Use rose, lemon, grape or nasturtium leaves.

Chocolate Moussecake

Crust:

1	8½-ounce box thin chocolate wafers, crushed
¼	cup unsalted butter, melted

Filling:

2	large eggs
16	ounces semisweet chocolate, melted and cooled
4	large egg yolks
4	large egg whites, room temperature
2	cups heavy cream
6	tablespoons powdered sugar

16-20 servings

Mix crumbs with butter and press onto bottom and part way up sides of buttered 10-inch springform pan. Refrigerate 30 minutes.

In large mixing bowl, beat whole eggs into melted chocolate. Add 4 egg yolks and beat 4-5 minutes. In small mixing bowl, beat 4 egg whites until stiff. In another small mixing bowl, whip heavy cream with powdered sugar until stiff peaks form. Stir ¼ of egg whites and ¼ of whipped cream into chocolate mixture. Fold in remaining whites and whipped cream, blending thoroughly. Pour into crust. Refrigerate at least 6 hours or overnight. *Can be made 3 days ahead. Freezes beautifully.*

*The pure and wonderful taste of chocolate. Garnish with whipped cream and **Chocolate Leaves** for a spectacular dessert. For a quick and easy **Chocolate Mousse**, prepare half of the moussecake filling and add 1 tablespoon Grand Marnier liqueur.*

Chocolate

Crème de Chocolate Cheesecake

Crust:
- ¼ cup butter, melted
- ¼ teaspoon ground cinnamon
- 1 8½-ounce box thin chocolate wafers, crushed

Filling:
- 32 ounces cream cheese, softened
- 2 cups sugar
- 4 large eggs
- 12 ounces semisweet chocolate chips, melted
- 1 tablespoon unsweetened cocoa powder
- 1 teaspoon pure almond extract
- 1 teaspoon pure vanilla extract
- 2 cups sour cream
  sweetened whipped cream

Garnish:
- toasted almonds
- chocolate shavings

12-16 servings

Mix melted butter and cinnamon with crushed wafers. Press onto bottom of buttered 10-inch springform pan. Chill.

In large mixing bowl, beat cream cheese until light and fluffy. Gradually add sugar and eggs, one at a time, and beat well. Be sure batter is smooth. Add melted chocolate, cocoa, almond and vanilla extracts. Blend in sour cream. Pour cream cheese mixture into crust. Bake at 350 degrees for 1 hour and 10 minutes or until all but a 2-inch diameter in center is set. Cool at room temperature before placing in refrigerator. *May be made 1 day in advance.* Serve with sweetened whipped cream, garnished with toasted almonds and chocolate shavings.

Sinfully rich, a **Crème** *favorite.*

Chocolate Zucchini Sheetcake

- 1½ cups packed light brown sugar
- ½ cup sugar
- ½ cup butter, softened
- ½ cup vegetable oil
- 3 large eggs
- 1 teaspoon pure vanilla extract
- ½ cup buttermilk
- 2½ cups all-purpose flour
- ½ teaspoon ground allspice
- ½ teaspoon ground cinnamon
- ½ teaspoon salt
- 2 teaspoons baking soda
- 5 tablespoons unsweetened cocoa powder
- 4 cups firmly packed grated unpeeled zucchini
- 1 cup semisweet chocolate chips
  powdered sugar

36 servings

In large mixing bowl, cream together sugars, butter, oil, eggs, vanilla and buttermilk. Mix flour, allspice, cinnamon, salt, baking soda and cocoa. Add to creamed mixture. Stir in zucchini. Pour into greased and floured 11x17-inch jelly roll pan. Sprinkle chocolate chips over top. Bake at 325 degrees for 40-45 minutes or until a wooden pick inserted near center comes out clean. Dust with powdered sugar. Let cool before cutting.

No one will ever guess the ingredients of this rich, moist, chocolatey delight. For a beautiful lacy finish, place a paper doily on top of the cake and dust with powdered sugar. Remove doily to reveal your work of art.

Chocolate

Chocolate Trifle

Cream Filling:

7 ounces semisweet chocolate
8 ounces cream cheese, softened
¼ cup sugar
1 large egg yolk, beaten
1 teaspoon pure vanilla extract
2 large egg whites, room temperature
¼ cup sugar
1 cup heavy cream, whipped

Cake:

1⅓ cups all-purpose flour
1 cup sugar
3 tablespoons unsweetened cocoa
powder
½ teaspoon baking soda
½ teaspoon salt
1 large egg
⅓ cup vegetable oil
¾ · cup water
¾ teaspoon pure vanilla extract

¾ cup raspberry or apricot preserves
¼ cup sherry or brandy
1 cup heavy cream
1 tablespoon sugar
½ teaspoon pure vanilla extract
2 ounces sliced almonds, toasted
½ cup fresh raspberries or chopped
dried apricots

12-16 servings

Cream filling must be prepared 1 day before trifle is assembled.

In top of double boiler, melt chocolate over simmering water. In small bowl, beat together cream cheese, ¼ cup sugar and egg yolk until smooth. Add to chocolate, stirring until well mixed. Stir in vanilla and remove from heat; cool. In large bowl, beat egg whites until soft peaks form. Gradually add ¼ cup sugar, beating until stiff peaks form. Fold in cooled chocolate mixture. Fold in whipped cream. Chill in covered bowl overnight.

Sift together flour, 1 cup sugar, cocoa, baking soda and salt. Add egg, oil, water and vanilla. Beat until well blended, about 2 minutes. Pour into greased and floured 8-inch square pan. Bake at 350 degrees for 35 minutes or until wooden pick inserted in center comes out clean. Cool in pan for 10 minutes. Turn out onto rack and let cool completely, as long as overnight.

Split cake in half horizontally and spread preserves on bottom. Replace top of cake and pierce cake all over with fork. Drizzle sherry or brandy evenly over cake. Cut into 1-inch squares and set aside. Grease a 3-quart bowl and line the inside with plastic wrap, smoothing out wrinkles. Put ½ cup cream filling in bottom of bowl. Top with ⅓ of cake cubes. Repeat with 2 more layers of cream filling and cake. Cover with plastic wrap and press down to smooth surface. Chill at least 3 hours, or up to 3 days.

Invert trifle onto serving plate, removing plastic wrap. Whip 1 cup heavy cream with sugar and vanilla. Put into pastry decorating tube and pipe onto cake in spoke design from center and pipe a ring of cream around base. Decorate with toasted almonds and fresh raspberries or chopped apricots.

This spectacular dessert merits applause!

Chocolate

Tivoli Torte

½ cup butter, softened
½ cup sugar
1 teaspoon pure vanilla extract
7 large egg yolks
3 tablespoons cornstarch
⅔ cup all-purpose flour
⅓ cup semisweet chocolate chips
7 large egg whites, room temperature
¼ cup sugar

Topping:
⅔ cup sour cream
3½ tablespoons sugar
½ teaspoon fresh lemon juice

Frosting:
⅓ cup semisweet chocolate chips
1½ tablespoons butter, softened
3 tablespoons sour cream
½ teaspoon pure vanilla extract
1-1½ cups powdered sugar

Garnish:
fresh strawberries, washed, hulled and halved

12-16 servings

Beat butter, sugar and vanilla until fluffy. Add egg yolks, one at a time, beating well after each. Stir cornstarch into flour and stir into butter mixture. Divide the batter in half. Melt chocolate chips in top of double boiler; cool. Mix melted chocolate into one portion of batter; set aside.

Beat egg whites until soft peaks form. Gradually add sugar, beating until stiff peaks form. Divide beaten whites in half. Fold half into the vanilla batter, the other half into the chocolate batter. (Batter may appear curdled.)

Preheat broiler. Spread ½ cup chocolate batter in bottom of greased 9-inch springform pan. Place pan under broiler 5 inches from heat and broil for 1-2 minutes or until baked. Spread ½ cup vanilla batter over baked chocolate layer and broil for 1-2 minutes. Repeat, alternating layers for a total of 10 layers.

Combine topping ingredients and spread over top layer of broiled cake. Broil 1 minute. Cool cake for 15 minutes, then carefully remove sides of springform pan and cool completely.

To make frosting, melt ⅓ cup chocolate chips in top of double boiler, stirring until smooth. Cool. Stir in butter, sour cream and vanilla extract. Gradually beat in powdered sugar until frosting is smooth and of spreading consistency. Use ⅔ of frosting to frost sides of cake; reserve other ⅓ to pipe on top.

Arrange strawberries around top outside edge of cake and in center. Use reserved frosting to pipe between strawberries in a spoke pattern. Chill at least 2 hours or overnight. *Cake does not freeze well.*

A chocolate lover's dream! This torte requires 2 hours preparation time, but its elegant presentation is well worth the effort. Offering more than 10 layers, it will measure approximately 2 inches in height.

Chocolate

Chocolate Pound Cake

1½	cups unsalted butter, softened
3	cups sugar
2	teaspoons pure vanilla extract
5	large eggs
1	cup unsweetened cocoa powder
2	cups all-purpose flour
½	teaspoon baking powder
½	teaspoon salt
1	cup buttermilk
¼	cup water

12-16 servings

In large mixing bowl, cream together butter and sugar. Beat at high speed for 5 minutes, then add vanilla. Add eggs, one at a time, beating well after each. In separate bowl, mix together cocoa, flour, baking powder and salt. Add dry ingredients alternately with buttermilk and water, ending with dry ingredients. Mix until well blended. Pour into greased and floured 10-inch tube pan and bake at 325 degrees for 60-75 minutes or until a wooden pick inserted in center comes out clean. Let cake rest in pan for 20 minutes, then turn onto cake rack. Cool completely before serving.

*Decorate this unbelievably moist cake with chocolate-dipped almonds, sweetened whipped cream or sprinkle with powdered sugar. Serve with ice cream or dip squares in **White Chocolate Fondue.***

Moist Chocolate Cake

½	cup unsweetened cocoa powder
1	teaspoon baking powder
2½	cups all-purpose flour
½	teaspoon salt
1	teaspoon white vinegar
2	teaspoons baking soda
1	cup whole milk
1	cup margarine, softened
2	cups sugar
2	large eggs
1	teaspoon pure vanilla extract
¾	cup boiling water + 1 tablespoon

White Frosting:

3	tablespoons all-purpose flour
1	cup whole milk
1	cup sugar
½	cup Crisco
½	cup margarine, softened
1	teaspoon pure vanilla extract

16-20 servings

In small bowl, stir together cocoa, baking powder, flour and salt; set aside. In measuring cup, add vinegar and baking soda to milk; set aside. Cream margarine and sugar until fluffy. Add eggs and mix well. Add dry ingredients alternately with milk mixture, beating well after each addition. Beat in vanilla until mixture is smooth and creamy. Stir in ¾ cup boiling water, blending gently just until water disappears from top of mixture. Pour into greased and floured 10½x14½x2-inch pan. Bake at 350 degrees for 30-35 minutes or until a wooden pick inserted in center comes out clean. Frost when cool.

In small saucepan, cook flour and milk over medium heat, stirring constantly until mixture thickens and begins to boil. Remove from heat and cool. In small bowl, cream together sugar, Crisco and margarine. Add milk mixture and beat until sugar crystals disappear, about 5 minutes. Add vanilla, beating until well mixed.

You'll want a second slice when nobody's looking!

Chocolate

Mocha Cream Chocolate Roll

6   large egg whites, room temperature
½   cup powdered sugar
1   tablespoon all-purpose flour
6   large egg yolks
1   tablespoon pure vanilla extract
½   cup powdered sugar
6   ounces semisweet chocolate chips
3   tablespoons water

Filling:
1½   cups heavy cream
½   cup powdered sugar
¼   cup unsweetened cocoa powder
1½   teaspoons instant coffee granules
1   teaspoon pure vanilla extract

Garnish:
powdered sugar
whipped cream

12 servings

Grease a 10x15-inch jelly roll pan. Fit waxed paper into pan. Grease again and dust with flour. In a small bowl, beat egg whites until soft peaks form. Gradually beat in ½ cup powdered sugar and flour until stiff peaks form. Cover and set aside.

In large mixing bowl, beat egg yolks with vanilla and ½ cup powdered sugar until thick, about 10 minutes. In small saucepan, melt chocolate chips with water and cool slightly. Stir into yolk mixture. Fold in egg whites. Spread into prepared pan and bake at 350 degrees for 15-20 minutes. Cool for 15 minutes.

Beat together all filling ingredients until cream is whipped. Turn cooled cake onto damp tea towel. Carefully remove waxed paper and let cake sit for 1 minute. Spread mocha cream filling over cake. Roll up as for a jelly roll, lifting the towel to roll the cake. Dust with powdered sugar. Wrap tightly and refrigerate. Before serving, sprinkle with powdered sugar again and decorate around edge with piped whipped cream rosettes.

A dessert fit for a king.

Frosted Chocolate Chip Brownies

1   cup butter
4   ounces unsweetened chocolate
2   cups sugar
4   large eggs, beaten
2   teaspoons pure vanilla extract
1½   cups all-purpose flour
⅛   teaspoon salt
2   cups chopped pecans
6   ounces semisweet chocolate chips
    Cream Cheese Frosting

24 brownies

Melt butter and chocolate in top of double boiler over simmering water. Cool to room temperature. In large mixing bowl, cream sugar, eggs and vanilla; blend in chocolate mixture. Add flour and salt; mix well. Stir in pecans and chocolate chips. Spread batter into greased and floured 9x13-inch pan. Bake at 350 degrees for 25-30 minutes. Cool. Frost with *Cream Cheese Frosting*.

The all-American brownie plus cream cheese frosting!

Chocolate

Brownie Alaska
Brownie Banana Split

Brownie Base:
1	4-ounce bar German sweet chocolate, coarsely chopped
½	cup butter
1	cup sugar
½	cup all-purpose flour
3	large eggs
½	teaspoon pure vanilla extract
⅔	cup chopped pecans or walnuts (use only for Brownie Alaska)

12 servings

In medium saucepan, melt chocolate with butter; cool. Add remaining ingredients and mix thoroughly. Pour into buttered 9-inch springform pan. Bake at 350 degrees for 30-35 minutes or until a wooden pick inserted in center comes out clean. Cool. Cover and freeze until firm. Follow directions for chosen filling.

Brownie Alaska Filling:
¾	quart coffee, strawberry or other favorite ice cream, slightly softened
¾	cup *Hot Fudge Sauce,* warmed to spreading consistency
4	large egg whites, room temperature
⅔	cup sugar
¼	cup ground pecans or walnuts (optional)

Spread ice cream on frozen brownie base, leaving ½ inch of uncovered border around edge. Drizzle **Hot Fudge Sauce** over ice cream. Cover with foil and freeze until ready to use (up to 1 month). Let stand at room temperature for 20-30 minutes before adding meringue.

Beat egg whites in small bowl until soft peaks form. Gradually add sugar, beating until stiff and glossy peaks form. Remove springform pan rim. Spread egg whites over top of ice cream, sealing well around edge of brownie base. Sprinkle with nuts. Bake at 450 degrees until meringue is lightly browned. Watch carefully. Using a hot, sharp knife, cut into wedges and serve immediately.

Brownie Banana Split Filling:
3	scoops vanilla ice cream
4	scoops chocolate ice cream
4	scoops strawberry ice cream
¾	cup *Hot Fudge Sauce,* warmed
¾	cup *Strawberry Sauce*
6	ounces toffee candy bar, crushed
2	bananas, sliced
1	cup sliced fresh strawberries (optional)

Place 3 scoops vanilla ice cream on middle of frozen brownie base. Alternate scoops of chocolate and strawberry ice cream around edge of brownie base. Drizzle hot fudge topping and strawberry topping over ice cream. Sprinkle crushed toffee candy bar on top. Cover with foil and freeze until ready to use (up to 1 month). Before serving, let stand at room temperature for 30-40 minutes. Top with bananas and/or strawberries. Remove springform pan rim and cut into wedges. Serve immediately.

Both versions will earn rave reviews. Any combination of ice cream flavors can be substituted.

Chocolate

Denver Brownies

2	ounces unsweetened chocolate
½	cup butter, softened
1	cup sugar
2	large eggs
1	teaspoon pure vanilla extract
½	cup all-purpose flour
¾	cup finely chopped walnuts or pecans
½	recipe *Chocolate Frosting*

12-16 brownies

In top of double boiler, melt chocolate over hot water; cool. In large mixing bowl, cream together butter and sugar. Add eggs and beat well. Gradually blend in melted chocolate, vanilla and flour. Stir in nuts. Pour into buttered and floured 8-inch square pan. Bake at 325 degrees for 30-35 minutes. Cool. Frost with **Chocolate Frosting.**

Brownies with more chocolate on top — a double treat.

Breckenridge Bars

½	cup butter, softened
1¼	cups sugar
3	large eggs, lightly beaten
3	tablespoons plus 1 teaspoon unsweetened cocoa powder
1	cup all-purpose flour
½	cup chopped pecans or walnuts (optional)
14	ounces sweetened condensed milk
2	cups sweetened flaked coconut

Chocolate Frosting:

1	ounce unsweetened chocolate
1	tablespoon butter
2	cups powdered sugar
2	tablespoons whole milk
1	teaspoon pure vanilla extract

24-30 bars

In large bowl, cream butter and sugar. Beat in eggs. Stir in cocoa, flour and nuts. Mix well. Spread batter evenly into greased and floured 9x13-inch metal pan. Bake at 350 degrees for 20 minutes. In small bowl, mix condensed milk and coconut. Spread on top of crust and bake an additional 18-20 minutes. Frost immediately. When cool, cut into squares.

In top of double boiler over simmering water, melt chocolate and butter, stirring until smooth. Add powdered sugar, milk and vanilla. Beat until ingredients are well mixed.

Chocolate and coconut team up in this wonderful bar.

Chocolate Nugget Bars

First Layer:

11½	ounces milk chocolate chips
½	cup butterscotch chips
½	cup creamy peanut butter

Second Layer:

1	cup sugar
¼	cup whole milk
4	tablespoons margarine
¼	cup marshmallow creme
1	teaspoon pure vanilla extract
2	cups dry roasted peanuts

24 bars

Melt all ingredients. Stir well and spread half of mixture into a buttered 9x13-inch pan. Cool. Reserve other half of mixture for 4th layer.

Boil sugar, milk and margarine for 5 minutes. Add marshmallow creme and vanilla. Pour over bottom layer and sprinkle with roasted nuts.

Third Layer:
- 1 **pound or 14-ounce bag caramels**
- 2 **tablespoons hot water**

Fourth Layer:

Add hot water to caramels and melt in saucepan. Drizzle over peanuts.

Spread reserved half of chocolate mixture on top. Cool completely and cut into squares.

Extra rich and chewy, with a taste like your favorite candy bar.

Rocky Mountain Bars

Crust:
- ½ **cup butter**
- 1 **ounce unsweetened chocolate**
- 1 **cup all-purpose flour**
- 1 **teaspoon baking powder**
- 2 **large eggs**
- 1 **cup sugar**
- 1 **teaspoon pure vanilla extract**
- ½ **cup chopped nuts**

24 bars

Melt butter and chocolate; cool. Sift together flour and baking powder. In medium bowl, beat eggs, sugar and vanilla. Add chocolate mixture to eggs, beating well. Add flour mixture and nuts. Spread in buttered 9x13-inch pan; set aside.

Filling:
- 6 **ounces cream cheese, softened**
- 4 **tablespoons butter, softened**
- ½ **cup sugar**
- 1 **large egg**
- ½ **teaspoon pure vanilla extract**
- 2 **tablespoons all-purpose flour**
- ¼ **cup chopped nuts**
- 6 **ounces semisweet chocolate chips**
- 2 **cups miniature marshmallows**

Beat together cream cheese, butter and sugar until fluffy. Add egg, vanilla and flour. Beat well. Stir in nuts and spread batter over unbaked crust. Sprinkle with chocolate chips. Bake at 350 degrees for 30-35 minutes. Remove from oven and sprinkle with marshmallows. Return to oven for 2 minutes.

Frosting:
- 4 **tablespoons butter**
- 1 **ounce unsweetened chocolate**
- 2 **ounces cream cheese**
- ¼ **cup whole milk**
- 1 **teaspoon pure vanilla extract**
- 3 **cups powdered sugar**

Melt together butter and chocolate; cool. Add cream cheese, milk, vanilla and powdered sugar and beat until smooth. Spread over marshmallow layer. Cool and cut into bars.

Brownie-like texture with rocky road candy flavor. These are delicious!

Chocolate

Chewy Chocolate Cookies

1¼   **cups margarine, softened**
2   **cups sugar**
2   **large eggs**
2   **teaspoons pure vanilla extract**
2   **cups all-purpose flour**
¾   **cup unsweetened cocoa powder**
1   **teaspoon baking soda**
    powdered sugar

5 dozen

In large bowl, cream margarine and sugar; add eggs and vanilla. Beat well. In medium bowl, combine flour with cocoa and baking soda; gradually blend into creamed mixture. Drop by teaspoon onto ungreased cookie sheet. Bake at 350 degrees for 9-11 minutes. (Cookies will still be puffy when taken from oven, then collapse as they cool on cookie sheet.) Transfer cookies onto waxed paper and sprinkle with powdered sugar when they are completely cooled. Store in airtight container with slice of bread to retain chewiness.

Quick and delicious, these can be made in a flash using a food processor.

Seven Minute Chocolate Cookies

4   **tablespoons butter**
12   **ounces semisweet chocolate chips**
14   **ounces sweetened condensed milk**
1   **cup all-purpose flour**
1   **cup chopped pecans**
1   **teaspoon pure vanilla extract**

3-4 dozen

In top of double boiler over simmering water, melt butter and chocolate chips with condensed milk. Remove from heat and add flour, nuts and vanilla. Drop by teaspoon onto greased cookie sheet and bake at 350 degrees for 7 minutes. Cool slightly and remove from pan. Store in an airtight container.

Very chocolatey, very easy, and very delicious. Will keep for several days — if there are any left!

Chocolate Cups

8   **ounces semisweet or white chocolate, coarsely chopped**
2   **tablespoons butter**

8 cups

In top of double boiler over simmering water, melt chocolate and butter, stirring constantly. Using teaspoon, spread chocolate mixture over inside of foil laminated bake cups, until bottom and sides are well covered. Be sure to spread enough on sides so cups will not fall apart. Refrigerate until firm. Just before serving, put in freezer for 15 minutes. Remove foil liner carefully. Fill with favorite filling.

*Easy to make and no end to the desserts you can create. Keep these on hand in your freezer. Try filling with **White Chocolate Mousse, Colorado Crème,** ice cream or fresh berries. Top with sweetened whipped cream.*

Chocolate

Hot Chocolate Sauce

1 cup heavy cream
6 tablespoons unsalted butter
¾ cup sugar
⅔ cup packed dark brown sugar
  pinch of salt
1 cup Droste Dutch-process cocoa
  powder

2 cups

In medium saucepan, combine cream and butter. Stir over medium heat until butter is melted and mixture comes to a slow boil. Add sugars, stirring until dissolved. Reduce heat and add salt and cocoa, stirring until smooth. Remove from heat and serve. *May be kept for weeks in refrigerator.* Sauce should be thick.

Rich, dark chocolate flavor, guaranteed to satisfy your chocolate passion.

Hot Fudge Sauce

6 ounces unsweetened chocolate
4 tablespoons butter
2 cups sugar
1 cup half and half
14 ounces sweetened condensed milk
3 tablespoons brandy, bourbon, rum
  or favorite liqueur (optional)

2½-3 cups

In medium saucepan, melt chocolate and butter over low heat, stirring constantly. Add sugar and half and half, and continue cooking until thick. Gradually add condensed milk. Cook 20 minutes, stirring occasionally. Stir in liquor. Serve warm. *Keeps indefinitely in the refrigerator; reheat before serving.*

Worth cheating on your diet! Wonderful semisweet flavor great over ice cream, or as a fondue with fresh or dried fruit, pound cake and cookies.

Chocolate Crispy Peanut Butter Balls

3¾ cups powdered sugar
½ cup margarine, softened
2 cups crunchy peanut butter
2 cups Rice Krispies cereal

Chocolate Coating:
6 ounces German sweet chocolate
6 ounces semisweet chocolate chips
2 ounces parafin wax

5 dozen

Combine all ingredients in large bowl and mix well. Roll dough into 1-inch balls. Chill.

In top of double boiler over boiling water, melt German and semisweet chocolates with parafin wax, stirring constantly until smooth. Using a wooden pick inserted in ball, dip balls into chocolate mixture, one at a time. Set on waxed paper to harden. Store in airtight container in refrigerator.

A devilishly good combination.

Chocolate

Brandy Truffles

12	ounces milk chocolate
4	tablespoons unsalted butter
¾	cup heavy cream, scalded
1½	tablespoons brandy or cognac
	powdered sugar
6-8	ounces semisweet chocolate

30 truffles

In top of double boiler over simmering water, melt milk chocolate with butter. Slowly beat hot cream into chocolate mixture until all cream is absorbed. Add brandy or cognac. Cover and refrigerate until mixture is firm, about 2-3 hours.

Line cookie sheet with waxed paper. Spoon 1-inch mounds of chilled chocolate mixture onto waxed paper. Refrigerate until firm, approximately 30 minutes. Rinse hands with very cold water; dry. Rub palms of hands with powdered sugar. Working quickly, roll each chocolate mound between the palms to make a ball. Freeze for 30 minutes.

In top of double boiler, melt semisweet chocolate. Line another cookie sheet with waxed paper. Remove ½ the truffles from freezer. Working gently, dip truffles into chocolate and place on waxed paper. Repeat until all truffles are coated. Refrigerate until serving

Drizzle white or milk chocolate over truffles for additional decoration and serve in decorative paper candy cups.

Frontier Fudge

½	cup butter
12	ounces evaporated milk
4	cups sugar
10	ounces large marshmallows
2	ounces unsweetened chocolate, chopped
12	ounces semisweet chocolate chips
12	ounces milk chocolate, chopped
1	tablespoon pure vanilla extract
2	cups chopped walnuts or pecans

5 pounds

In 4-6 quart heavy metal pan, cook butter, evaporated milk and sugar over medium-high heat until sugar is dissolved. Heat to boiling. Turn heat to low, cover and continue boiling for 5 minutes without stirring. Turn heat to warm and stir in marshmallows until dissolved. Add each kind of chocolate in turn, stirring until melted. Stir in vanilla and nuts. Pour into lightly buttered 9x13-inch pan. Let stand until firm, about 8-10 hours, before cutting.

A festive, delicious addition to your holiday cookie tray.

Chocolate

Amaretto Truffles

8	ounces semisweet chocolate, melted
¼	cup Amaretto liqueur
2	tablespoons strong coffee
½	cup unsalted butter, softened
1	tablespoon pure vanilla extract
¾	cup vanilla wafer crumbs
½	cup powdered sugar
½	cup unsweetened cocoa powder

2-3 dozen truffles

In small bowl, mix melted chocolate, Amaretto and coffee until smooth. Add butter, vanilla and cookie crumbs. Mix well. Set bowl in ice water and beat until firm. Form into balls and chill. Mix powdered sugar and cocoa. Roll truffles in sugar mixture and store in airtight container. Refrigerate until serving.

If you prefer, chilled truffles can be dipped in melted chocolate.

Chocolate Dipped Fruit Balls

⅓	cup dried apricots
1	cup pitted prunes
¼	cup raisins
¼	cup walnuts
⅓	cup sugar
2	tablespoons cognac or Grand Marnier liqueur
12	ounces semisweet chocolate chips, melted

3-4 dozen

In food processor, chop apricots, prunes, raisins and walnuts with sugar. Do not over process. Add cognac and mix. Form into ½-inch balls and chill. Dip in melted chocolate. Set on cookie sheet lined with waxed paper. Chill until firm.

Slathered in chocolate, these are sure to please and would make ideal hostess gifts at holiday time.

Rich and Creamy Fudge

½	cup margarine
12	ounces semisweet chocolate chips
2	large eggs
4	cups powdered sugar
1½	teaspoons pure vanilla extract
1	cup chopped pecans or walnuts

2 pounds

In small saucepan, melt margarine and chocolate chips, stirring until smooth. In large bowl, beat eggs until light in color. Add powdered sugar and mix well. Add chocolate mixture. Stir in vanilla and chopped nuts. Pour into buttered 9-inch square pan and refrigerate until firm.

Easy, creamy and oh, so good! May be doubled and put into 9x13-inch pan.

Mexican

Mexican

Chile Peppers

Anaheim

Anaheim peppers (also called green chiles) are the most common large chile in American markets. Medium green in color, these peppers are 4-6 inches long and 1½ inches wide, narrow and slightly twisted. Ranging from mild to hot, depending on growing conditions, Anaheims are available fresh, canned whole or diced.

Poblano

Poblano peppers are dark green, bell-shaped, and range in length from 3½-5 inches. Their flavor varies from mild to medium-hot. In its dried state, the poblano changes into the dark reddish-brown **Ancho,** which forms the basis for many red chili sauces. If ancho peppers are not available, you can substitute 1 tablespoon of chili powder for each pepper.

Pasilla

Pasilla peppers (also called chile negro) are dried, long, slender, medium-size peppers with wrinkled, blackish-brown skin. They are usually very hot and are often used in combination with ancho peppers.

Jalapeño

Jalapeño peppers are small, 2½-3 inches long and ¾-1 inch wide, and dark green. Jalapeños, very hot and flavorful, are available fresh, canned whole or sliced, and pickled. **Chipotle** peppers are smoked and dried jalapeño peppers, with a dull brown, wrinkled skin.

Serrano

Serrano peppers are very small, usually dark green but sometimes allowed to ripen to red, and extremely hot.

Cayenne

Cayenne peppers are small, narrow and red; they virtually breathe fire. Used almost exclusively in dried form, whole or ground, cayenne adds heat to a number of dishes.

The seeds and veins are the hottest parts of any chile. When working with chiles, it is best to wear rubber gloves. Otherwise your fingertips will sting. Be sure not to touch your eyes; the juice will cause a burning sensation. If you accidentally touch your eyes, flush them immediately with water.

Preparation of Fresh Green Chiles

Rinse and drain chiles. Make a steam vent in each chile by pricking with a wooden pick. Place chiles on foil-covered cookie sheet. Put in oven 4-6 inches below broiler unit. Roast chiles, turning frequently, for 6-8 minutes or until uniformly blistered. Remove chiles from oven and place in sealed plastic bag, or small bowl with lid that seals, for 10 minutes. Start at stem of chile and peel outer skin downward. Remove stem and seeds, if desired. (If preparing chiles for rellenos, stem end should be left intact.) Chiles are now ready to use in any recipe. Chiles may be frozen after skins are blistered and before peeling; skins slip off quite easily after chiles are thawed.

Mexican

Margarita

1   6-ounce can frozen limeade
      concentrate
6   ounces bottled sweet and sour
      mixer
6   ounces tequila
12 ice cubes
1   lime, cut into wedges
      lemon-flavored margarita salt

6 6-ounce servings

Thaw limeade and pour into blender. Use empty limeade can to measure sweet and sour mixer and tequila. Add to blender. Fill blender with ice cubes to within 1 inch of top. Blend ingredients until smooth. Rub outside rim of glass with lime wedge and dip into margarita salt. Pour margaritas into salted glasses and serve.

A refreshing drink that sends you south of the border!

Sangria
(Red Wine Cooler)

1   bottle Burgundy wine or other dry
      red wine, chilled (3 cups)
½   cup fresh lemon juice
½   cup fresh orange juice
½   cup sugar
¼   cup brandy
1   small lemon, sliced
1   small orange, sliced
½   cup strawberries, hulled and
      cut in half
1   10-ounce bottle club soda, chilled
16 ice cubes

8 6-ounce servings

Stir wine, juices, sugar and brandy in large pitcher until sugar is dissolved. Stir in lemon and orange slices and refrigerate. Just before serving, add strawberries, club soda and ice; stir and pour into glasses.

Make wine coolers early in the day or as little as 15 minutes before serving. Serve from a glass pitcher or bowl to highlight the brilliant colors of the fruit slices.

Chocolate con Leche
(Mexican Hot Chocolate)

¼   cup unsweetened cocoa powder
¼   cup sugar
¾   teaspoon ground cinnamon
4   cups milk, divided
¼   cup light cream
¾   teaspoon pure vanilla extract
      heavy cream, whipped
      chocolate shavings

4 servings

In small bowl, mix cocoa, sugar and cinnamon. In medium saucepan, heat 1 cup of milk until bubbly. Stir in cocoa mixture and whisk until smooth. Reduce heat to low and heat to boiling, stirring constantly. Gradually stir in remaining 3 cups of milk and return to a boil. Blend in cream and vanilla. Remove hot chocolate from heat and whisk until frothy. Pour into cups and top with whipped cream and chocolate shavings.

Soothes the soul — a beautiful hot chocolate for après ski.

Mexican

Pico de Gallo
(Rooster's Beak)

4 ripe avocados, peeled, pitted and
   chopped
2 medium tomatoes, peeled and
   chopped
1 medium white onion, minced
2 cloves garlic, minced
2 tablespoons minced fresh cilantro
1-2 serrano chiles, seeded and finely
   chopped
3 tablespoons fresh lemon juice
1 tablespoon olive oil
   salt and freshly ground
    black pepper to taste

2½ cups

Mix all ingredients together well. Cover and refrigerate 1-2 hours.

*Filled with chunks of avocado and tomato, this is excellent tucked inside **Chicken Fajitas, Beef Fajitas** or **Pita Fajitas.***

Guacamole

4-5 fresh or canned tomatillos
3 fresh or canned Anaheim chiles,
   seeded
3 medium avocados, peeled and
   pitted
1 tablespoon minced onion
   salt and freshly ground
    black pepper to taste
¼ cup minced fresh cilantro
1 teaspoon fresh lime juice

2½ cups

If using fresh tomatillos, husk and wash. In medium saucepan, cook tomatillos in boiling water just until tender, about 5 minutes. Drain.

Combine tomatillos and chiles in blender or food processor and blend until smooth. In small bowl, mash avocados with fork. Stir in tomatillo mixture and onion. Add salt and pepper to taste. Stir in cilantro and lime juice.

The lemony flavor of tomatillos creates a distinctive guacamole.

Mexican

Salsa Cruda
(Fresh Salsa)

2	large tomatoes, peeled and chopped
4	tomatillos, husked and chopped
2	fresh Anaheim chiles, seeded and chopped
5	green onions, chopped
2	fresh jalapeño peppers, seeded and chopped
1	teaspoon ground cumin
1	teaspoon fresh lime juice
1	teaspoon sugar
1	teaspoon minced fresh cilantro
½	teaspoon freshly ground black pepper
¼	teaspoon salt

2 cups

In lidded jar, combine all ingredients and marinate for at least 1 hour. *May be stored for 2-3 weeks in refrigerator.*

Salsas are the salt and pepper of Mexico. This fresh salsa is a great accompaniment to most Mexican dishes and is a tasty dip for tortilla chips.

Avocado with Gazpacho

1½	tablespoons finely chopped onion
¼	cup finely chopped tomato
3	tablespoons peeled, finely chopped cucumber
3	tablespoons finely chopped green bell pepper
1	teaspoon minced pickled jalapeño pepper
2	teaspoons fresh lemon juice
1	avocado, peeled, halved and pitted fresh lemon juice lettuce tortilla chips

2 servings

In small bowl combine onion, tomato, cucumber, bell pepper, jalapeño pepper and lemon juice. Brush avocado halves with additional lemon juice to keep them from turning brown. Place avocados on bed of lettuce and fill each half with gazpacho mixture. Serve with tortilla chips.

Spicy flavor, brilliant colors and crunchy texture blend with smooth avocados for a special appetizer.

Mexican

Torta de Avocado
(Avocado Torte)

2	10-ounce cans tomatoes with green chiles
½	small onion
1	clove garlic
2	sprigs of fresh cilantro, minced, or ½ teaspoon ground coriander
1	teaspoon sugar
¼	teaspoon salt
2	tablespoons oil
2	8-ounce packages cream cheese, chilled and very firm
	Bibb lettuce
2	large ripe avocados, halved lengthwise, peeled, pitted and sliced
	tortilla chips

12 servings

In blender or food processor, blend tomatoes, onion, garlic, cilantro, sugar and salt until well blended. In medium skillet, heat oil. Add tomato mixture and bring to a boil. Reduce heat and simmer for 5 minutes. Remove tomato sauce from heat and cool. *Sauce may be prepared 2 days ahead and refrigerated.*

On cutting board with long, thin-bladed, sharp knife, cut each brick of cream cheese lengthwise into 4 slices. Arrange bed of lettuce on an oblong platter. Place 2 cream cheese slices together at their narrowest ends. Top cream cheese with avocado slices and thin layer of tomato sauce. Repeat layering three times. Make a second stack alongside first and pour remaining sauce over top. Bring to room temperature before serving. Surround with tortilla chips. Serve with knife to slice through layers and spread on chips.

Creamy, delicious and beautiful.

Camarones en Escabeche
(Marinated Shrimp)

1½	pounds medium shrimp, cooked, peeled and deveined
⅓	cup fresh lime juice
2	medium tomatoes, chopped
1	large avocado, peeled, pitted and chopped
1	small onion, finely chopped
1	tablespoon minced serrano chiles
2	teaspoons minced fresh cilantro
3	tablespoons olive oil
	salt and freshly ground black pepper to taste

6 servings

In large bowl, combine all ingredients. Refrigerate. Serve cold.

This spicy shrimp cocktail is simply sensational. Serve on individual plates with Bibb lettuce and red onion rings. Garnish with lime wedges.

Mexican

Crazy Corn Nachos

1	tablespoon vegetable oil
½	cup diced red bell pepper
½	cup finely chopped onion
¾	cup whole kernel corn
4	ounces diced green chiles
1	cup sour cream
8	ounces cream cheese, softened
1-2	teaspoons chili powder
1-2	teaspoons ground cumin
	cayenne pepper to taste
	salt and freshly ground black pepper to taste
	tortilla chips
4	slices bacon, fried crisp, drained and crumbled
2	cups shredded Monterey Jack cheese (8 ounces)
	chili powder and cayenne pepper (optional)
	thinly sliced jalapeño peppers (optional)

12 servings

In large skillet heat oil and sauté red pepper, onion and corn until soft. Stir in green chiles. In medium bowl, blend together sour cream, cream cheese, chili powder, cumin, cayenne, salt and pepper. Fold mixture into sautéed vegetables. Place chips on 2 10-inch, ovenproof platters. Cover chips with vegetable mixture. Sprinkle crumbled bacon and cheese on top. Add additional chili powder and cayenne pepper, if desired. Arrange jalapeño peppers on top. Broil for 2-3 minutes or until cheese melts.

This fabulous finger food is a definite crowd pleaser!

Chicken Nachos

2	cups shredded Cheddar cheese (8 ounces)
½	cup sour cream
1½	cups cooked and shredded chicken
1	4-ounce can diced green chiles, drained
	tortilla chips
1½	cups shredded lettuce
½	cup chopped tomato
	additional sour cream
	Guacamole
	Salsa Cruda

4-6 servings

In medium saucepan, combine cheese and ½ cup sour cream. Stir constantly over low heat until cheese melts. Add cooked chicken and chiles to cheese mixture, stirring until heated through. Heat tortilla chips on cookie sheet at 400 degrees for 10 minutes. Arrange half the tortilla chips on a serving platter and top with half the chicken mixture. Repeat layering with remaining chips and chicken mixture. Sprinkle lettuce and tomato on top. Garnish nachos with sour cream, guacamole and salsa. Serve on a warming tray.

Whether served as an appetizer or a main dish, this turns any meal into a fiesta!

Mexican

Quesadillas
(Cheese Turnovers)

½   cup unsalted butter, softened
8   7-inch flour tortillas
4   cups shredded Monterey Jack cheese (1 pound)
8   green onions, minced
½   cup chopped pimientos
4   pickled jalapeño peppers, minced
2   tablespoons minced fresh cilantro leaves optional
1   teaspoon ground cumin

48 pieces

Spread butter on 1 side of tortillas and place on ungreased baking sheet, buttered side up. Toast tortillas at 400 degrees for 3 minutes or until lightly browned. *Tortillas may be toasted 2 hours ahead.*

In medium bowl, mix cheese, green onions, pimiento, jalapeño peppers, cilantro and cumin. Sprinkle mixture on tortillas and bake at 400 degrees for 5-8 minutes or until cheese is bubbly. Place quesadillas on cutting board and cut into wedges.

Garnish with sliced black olives, sour cream or avocado slices — muy bueno!

Mexican Layered Dip

2   15-ounce cans refried beans with green chiles
½   cup mayonnaise
½   cup sour cream
2   avocados, peeled, pitted and chopped
2   tablespoons fresh lemon juice
½   cup picante sauce, medium or hot, to taste
1   cup shredded Cheddar cheese (4 ounces)
1   cup shredded Monterey Jack cheese (4 ounces)
4   green onions, chopped
1   4-ounce can sliced black olives
    tortilla chips

8-10 servings

Spread beans in 9x13-inch baking dish. Combine mayonnaise and sour cream and spread over bean dip. Sprinkle chopped avocados with lemon juice; layer over mayonnaise mixture. Cover with picante sauce. Sprinkle with Cheddar and Monterey Jack cheeses, then onions. Top with black olives. Bake uncovered at 350 degrees for 30 minutes. Serve with tortilla chips.

This is also delicious served cold, without baking.

Mexican Pizza

Crust:
- ½ cup all-purpose flour
- ¼ teaspoon sugar
- 1¼ teaspoons quick-rise yeast
- ½ cup hot water
- 1 cup all-purpose flour
- ¼ teaspoon salt
- 1 tablespoon olive oil
- 1 tablespoon yellow cornmeal
    additional yellow cornmeal for
        sprinkling on pan

Topping:
- ½ pound tomatoes, thinly sliced and
        seeded
- 1 clove garlic, minced
    salt and freshly ground black
        pepper to taste
- 5 ounces Monterey Jack cheese,
        thinly sliced
- 1 small onion, thinly sliced and
        separated into rings
- 1 red bell pepper, thinly sliced into
        rings
- 1 pickled jalapeño pepper, chopped
- 2 tablespoons minced fresh cilantro
- 2 tablespoons freshly grated
        Parmesan cheese
- 1 tablespoon olive oil

2-3 servings

In food processor, mix ½ cup flour, sugar and yeast. With processor running, add ½ cup hot water. Turn processor off and add 1 cup of flour, salt, oil and 1 tablespoon cornmeal. Blend mixture until it forms a ball. Pat dough out on 11-inch pizza pan, sprinkled lightly with additional cornmeal, making the crust slightly thicker around the edge. (For a thinner crust, use a 14-inch pizza pan.)

Place tomato slices on dough and sprinkle with garlic, salt and pepper. Cover pizza with an even layer of Monterey Jack cheese. Place onion, bell pepper and jalapeño pepper on pizza. Sprinkle with cilantro and Parmesan, and drizzle with oil. Bake pizza in lower third of preheated oven at 500 degrees for 15-20 minutes, or until crust is golden brown and top is bubbling.

A perfect summer lunch with gazpacho, or cut into smaller pieces for a tempting appetizer.

Cheesy Jalapeño Quiche

- 1 10-inch *Best Ever Pastry Shell*
- 6 ounces cooked ham, chopped
- 4 slices bacon, fried crisp, drained
        and crumbled
- 1 cup shredded Swiss cheese
- 1 cup shredded sharp Cheddar
        cheese
- ¼ cup chopped onion
- 1 medium tomato, peeled and
        chopped
- 2 canned jalapeño peppers, seeded
        and chopped
- 3 tablespoons minced fresh parsley
- 4 eggs, beaten
- 1 teaspoon dry mustard
- ½ cup sour cream

8 servings

In unbaked pastry shell, layer ham, bacon, Swiss cheese, Cheddar cheese, onion, tomato, jalapeño peppers and parsley. In small bowl, combine beaten eggs, mustard and sour cream and mix well. Pour egg mixture into pastry shell. Bake quiche at 450 degrees for 30 minutes or until filling is set. Cover edge of pastry with foil to prevent excessive browning.

A great way to wake up your taste buds.

Mexican

Green Chile

3	tablespoons vegetable oil
2	pounds lean pork, cubed
1	medium onion, cut into large chunks
1-2	cloves garlic, minced
	salt and freshly ground black pepper to taste
1	28-ounce can whole peeled tomatoes
8-10	Anaheim chiles, roasted, peeled, seeded and chopped
2	cups water
1½	tablespoons all-purpose flour
⅓	cup water
6-8	flour tortillas, warmed

6-8 servings

Heat oil in large stockpot. Add pork, onion, garlic, salt and pepper. Sauté until pork is browned. Drain juice from tomatoes into stockpot. Chop tomatoes and add to pork with chiles and 2 cups water. Stir well and simmer covered for 45 minutes. Whisk together flour and ⅓ cup water until smooth. Add to chile mixture and stir constantly until well blended and slightly thickened. Cover and simmer for 15 minutes. Serve with warm tortillas.

*Make double the recipe and freeze in smaller portions so you'll have some on hand. **Green Chile** makes an excellent sauce for enchiladas, burritos and chile rellenos.*

Sopa de Tortilla
(Tortilla Soup)

1	medium onion, chopped
2	cloves garlic, minced
2	tablespoons olive oil
4	cups beef broth
4	cups chicken broth
½	cup tomato juice
1	teaspoon ground cumin
1	teaspoon chili powder
1	fresh jalapeño pepper, seeded and chopped
1	teaspoon salt
¾	teaspoon Worcestershire sauce
4	corn tortillas
	vegetable oil for frying
2	cups shredded cooked chicken
1	large tomato, peeled and diced
1	large avocado, peeled, pitted and sliced
1	cup shredded Monterey Jack cheese

8-10 servings

In 4-quart saucepan, sauté onion and garlic in oil. Add beef and chicken broth, tomato juice, cumin, chili powder, jalapeño pepper, salt and Worcestershire sauce. Heat to boiling, reduce heat and simmer covered for 1 hour. Cut corn tortillas into narrow strips. Heat oil in skillet and fry tortillas until crisp; drain on paper towels. Add chicken and tomato to soup and cook 5 minutes. Place 2-3 tortilla strips in each soup bowl. Pour soup into bowls and garnish with avocado slices and 1 tablespoon of cheese.

One of the most popular soups in Mexico, and sure to become one of your favorites.

Mexican

Black Bean Soup

12	ounces black turtle beans
6-8	cups chicken broth
2	tablespoons butter
1	cup chopped onion
1	cup chopped celery
1	cup shredded carrots
1	cup shredded potatoes
1	bay leaf
2	cloves garlic, minced
1	teaspoon dried oregano
½	teaspoon freshly ground black pepper
3	tablespoons fresh lemon juice lemon slices

8-10 servings

In large stockpot, cover beans with water and soak for 20 hours. Drain beans and return to stockpot. Add chicken broth and heat to boiling. Reduce heat and simmer covered for 3-4 hours.

In large skillet, melt butter and sauté onion, celery and carrots for 3-5 minutes or until crisp-tender. Add to beans along with potatoes, bay leaf, garlic, oregano and pepper. Stir well and simmer covered for an additional 45 minutes or until vegetables are tender. Stir lemon juice into soup just before serving. Pour soup into individual bowls and garnish with lemon slices.

The addition of fresh lemon juice imparts a refreshing tartness to this nutritious soup.

Caldo Colorado (Chicken Soup)

1½	pounds chicken breasts
3	quarts chicken broth
½	cup chopped onion
1	clove garlic, minced
2	tablespoons lard or vegetable oil
1	medium tomato, peeled, seeded and finely chopped
1-2	canned chipotle chiles in adobe sauce, drained and rinsed
12	radishes, thinly sliced
3	green onions, including tops, thinly sliced
1	cup garbanzo beans
2	medium avocados, peeled, pitted and thinly sliced
8	ounces Monterey Jack cheese, cut into ¼-inch cubes
3	limes, quartered

12 servings

Cook chicken breasts in broth until tender, about 20 minutes. Remove breasts and set broth aside. Bone and skin breasts. Cut meat into ¼-inch strips; set aside. Sauté onion and garlic in lard until onion is transparent. Add tomato and cook uncovered, stirring frequently, until mixture is somewhat dry, about 5 minutes. Remove mixture from heat.

In food processor, purée chipotle chiles with ½ cup reserved chicken broth. Stir chipotles and tomato mixture into remaining broth. Simmer for 15 minutes. Divide chicken strips, radishes, green onions, garbanzo beans, avocados and cheese among 12 warmed soup bowls. Ladle chicken stock into bowls. Serve immediately with lime wedges on the side.

Mexican

Black Bean, Corn and Bell Pepper Salad

½ pound black beans, soaked overnight
1 10-ounce package frozen corn, thawed
1 green bell pepper, chopped
1 red bell pepper, chopped
1 jalapeño pepper, seeded and chopped
3 green onions, thinly sliced
2 tablespoons minced fresh parsley
⅛ teaspoon salt
2 tablespoons olive oil
3 tablespoons fresh lime juice
 freshly ground black pepper to taste
 lettuce leaves (optional)

6 servings

Drain beans and cover with fresh water; cook for 1 hour or until tender. Cool beans and drain. Combine beans, corn, green and red bell peppers, jalapeño pepper, green onions, parsley and salt. Add olive oil and lime juice. Grind black pepper generously over salad. Mix well. Serve on lettuce leaves, if desired.

A brilliant palette of colors. Serve in hollowed-out tomatoes topped with a sprig of cilantro.

Creamy Jícama Salad

1½ pounds jícama, peeled and shredded (3 cups)
1 small head red cabbage, shredded (2 cups)
1 large red onion, finely chopped
4 carrots, finely chopped
1 medium green bell pepper, finely chopped

Dressing:
¾ cup sour cream
¾ cup mayonnaise
¼ cup Dijon mustard
2 teaspoons fresh lemon juice
2 teaspoons dried tarragon
2 tablespoons vegetable oil
1 teaspoon celery seeds
¼ teaspoon freshly ground black pepper

8 servings

In large bowl, combine all vegetables. Whisk together all dressing ingredients until well blended. Pour over vegetables and toss well. Cover and refrigerate overnight.

Toss again before serving.

Jícama, a crisp vegetable sometimes called the "Mexican potato", is usually eaten raw. It's a favorite appetizer when sliced and soaked in lime juice.

Mexican

Ensalada de Pollo
(Chicken Salad)

2½   **cups diced, cooked chicken**
½   **teaspoon lemon pepper**
1   **medium head iceberg lettuce**
1½   **cups chopped tomatoes**
½   **cup shredded longhorn Cheddar cheese**
½   **cup shredded Monterey Jack cheese**
1   **4-ounce can diced green chiles**
½   **cup toasted pine nuts**

Dressing:
¼   **cup tarragon vinegar**
¼   **cup vegetable oil**
2½   **teaspoons lemon pepper**

6 servings

In medium bowl, toss cooked chicken with ½ teaspoon lemon pepper. Line large serving bowl with 4 to 5 lettuce leaves. Tear remaining lettuce into pieces and place in serving bowl. Add chicken, tomatoes, longhorn cheese, Monterey Jack cheese, green chiles and pine nuts, tossing lightly. Combine all dressing ingredients, mix well and pour over salad. Toss again. Refrigerate for 30 minutes before serving.

This spicy salad will delight your palate!

Shrimp and Jícama Salad with Chile Vinegar

Chile Vinegar:
⅔   **cup white wine vinegar**
¼   **cup sugar**
2-3   **tablespoons seeded, minced fresh jalapeños**
2-4   **tablespoons minced fresh cilantro**

2   **cups shredded, peeled jícama**
1   **pound tiny shrimp**
4   **large, ripe tomatoes, sliced**
4   **large tomatillos, husked and sliced salt to taste**
   sprigs of fresh cilantro (optional)

4 servings

Combine all **Chile Vinegar** ingredients and stir well.

Mix shredded jícama with ⅓ cup **Chile Vinegar** and set aside. Mix shrimp with ⅓ cup **Chile Vinegar** and set aside.

Arrange tomatoes and tomatillos in an overlapping pattern on 4 dinner plates. Mound jícama on top of or beside tomato and tomatillo slices. Arrange shrimp over jícama. Spoon remaining **Chile Vinegar** over all. Sprinkle with salt to taste. Garnish with sprigs of fresh cilantro.

*Crunchy jícama and shrimp combine with **Chile Vinegar** for a Mexican taste sensation.*

Mexican

Corn Muffins with Jalapeño Jelly

1 cup all-purpose flour
1 cup yellow cornmeal
¼ cup sugar
1 tablespoon baking powder
1 teaspoon crushed red pepper flakes
1 egg
½ cup plus 1 tablespoon milk
¼ cup corn oil
1 17-ounce can creamed corn
¼ cup jalapeño pepper jelly

12 muffins

In large bowl mix together flour, cornmeal, sugar, baking powder and pepper flakes. Whisk together egg, milk, oil and corn. Pour liquid mixture over dry ingredients and stir lightly, using no more than 15-20 strokes to mix. Generously butter 12 2½-inch muffin cups. Fill each muffin cup ½ full with batter. Reserve ⅓ of batter. With back of teaspoon, make small depression in center of each muffin and drop in 1 teaspoon of jalapeño jelly. Divide reserved batter over muffins to cover jelly. Bake in preheated oven at 375 degrees for 25 minutes or until light golden brown. Let muffins rest in pan for 2 minutes. Using blunt knife, ease muffins out onto wire rack and let cool for 20 minutes.

Spread with butter for melt-in-your-mouth flavor.

Squash Corn Bread

1 cup yellow cornmeal
1 cup plus 1 tablespoon all-purpose flour
2 tablespoons packed light brown sugar
5 teaspoons baking powder
1 teaspoon salt
½ teaspoon ground cumin
½ teaspoon dried salad herbs
2 tablespoons minced fresh parsley
 dash of cayenne pepper
1 cup spaghetti squash or acorn yellow squash, cooked and mashed
2 eggs
1 cup milk
¼ cup olive oil
½ cup diced Monterey Jack cheese
1 2-ounce jar pimientos
1 4-ounce can diced green chiles
¼ cup sliced black olives (optional)

10-12 servings

In large bowl, mix together cornmeal, flour, brown sugar, baking powder, salt, cumin, herbs, parsley and cayenne pepper. In separate bowl, blend squash, eggs, milk, oil, cheese, pimiento and green chiles. Pour dry ingredients into squash mixture and blend. Pour squash-corn bread mixture into greased 9x13-inch pan. Arrange black olives on top and bake at 425 degrees for 25-30 minutes or until a wooden pick inserted near center comes out clean.

*The unique flavor of this special corn bread goes well with **Ensalada de Pollo (Chicken Salad).** Use in place of flour tortillas at your next Mexican meal.*

Mexican

Breakfast Burritos

¼ pound bulk chorizo sausage
2 tablespoons finely chopped onion
2 tablespoons finely chopped green
   bell pepper
2 eggs
2 tablespoons milk
   freshly ground black pepper
      to taste
1 tablespoon butter
4 6-inch flour tortillas
1 tomato, peeled, seeded and
   chopped
½ cup shredded Cheddar cheese
   Burrito Sauce or mild salsa,
   warmed

Burrito Sauce:

1 cup chopped onion
2 tablespoons vegetable oil
3½ cups finely chopped tomatoes
½ cup chopped green chiles
½ teaspoon sugar
½ teaspoon salt
¼ teaspoon garlic salt
   freshly ground black pepper
      to taste
2 tablespoons minced fresh parsley
2 tablespoons minced fresh cilantro

2-4 servings

In medium skillet, cook sausage, onion and green pepper until done. Drain off grease; set aside.

In small bowl, beat eggs, milk and pepper. Melt butter in 8-inch skillet over medium heat. Add egg mixture. Cook without stirring until eggs begin to set on bottom and around edges. Using a spatula, lift and fold partially cooked eggs so uncooked egg flows underneath. Continue cooking until cooked through. Remove from heat.

Divide sausage mixture among 4 tortillas. Top sausage mixture with ¼ of eggs, tomato and cheese. Fold in sides, fold bottom up and top down to enclose filling. Secure with wooden pick. Arrange on baking sheet. Bake at 350 degrees for 15 minutes or until heated through. Serve with warmed *Burrito Sauce.*

3 cups

Sauté onion in oil for 5 minutes. Add tomatoes, chiles, sugar, salt, garlic salt and pepper. Simmer for 15 minutes or until slightly thickened, stirring occasionally. Stir in parsley and cilantro.

*Whether you're in a hurry or not, this quick and easy meal is a great family-pleaser. The wonderful mild sauce is perfect with burritos or **Huevos Rancheros (Country Eggs).***

Huevos Rancheros (Country Eggs)

   unsalted butter
4 eggs
   unsalted butter
2 8-inch flour tortillas
1½ cups shredded Cheddar cheese
4 tablespoons mild salsa, *Green
   Chile* or *Burrito Sauce*
3 tablespoons sour cream
   salsa

2 servings

In crêpe pan over medium heat, melt butter and fry eggs to desired doneness. Remove eggs to warm plate. Melt enough butter to cover bottom of pan. Place 1 tortilla in pan to soften for 30-45 seconds; flip. Place 2 eggs, ¾ cup cheese and 2 tablespoons salsa to one side on tortilla and fold over. Cover pan to melt cheese. Cook 1 minute. Uncover and flip tortilla. Cover and cook 1 minute longer or until cheese is melted. Repeat with second tortilla. Serve topped with sour cream and additional salsa.

Mexican

Pescado Veracruz
(Fish Veracruz)

1   small onion, thinly sliced
2   tablespoons water
1   pound red snapper or orange
      roughy fillets
1   cup mild salsa
1   medium tomato, chopped
½   cup sliced pitted ripe olives
½   cup shredded Cheddar cheese

4 servings

Place onion on bottom of ungreased 7x12-inch microwave baking dish. Add water and cover with vented clear plastic wrap. Microwave on highest power for 3-5 minutes or until onion is crisp-tender. Place fish fillets on top of onion slices and cook covered for 4-5 minutes or until fish flakes easily when tested with a fork. Give dish a half turn after 3 minutes. Drain well. Spoon salsa, tomato and olives over fish. Cook uncovered for 2 minutes or until heated through. Top with cheese and cook for 1 minute or until cheese melts.

Chicken Enchiladas
with Tomatillo Sauce

⅓   cup half and half
6   ounces cream cheese, softened
2   cups shredded cooked chicken
¾   cup finely chopped onion
½   teaspoon salt
      Tomatillo Sauce
12   8-inch corn tortillas
      vegetable oil
¾   cup shredded Cheddar cheese
¾   cup shredded Monterey Jack
      cheese

Condiments:
      shredded lettuce
      chopped tomatoes
      ripe olives
      sour cream

Tomatillo Sauce:
2   dozen tomatillos, husked
4-6   serrano peppers, stemmed, seeded
      and minced (to taste)
3   cups chicken broth
2   tablespoons cornstarch
1   teaspoon salt
2   tablespoons chopped fresh cilantro

6-8 servings

Beat together half and half and cream cheese until smooth and fluffy. Add chicken, onion and salt to cheese mixture and blend well. Soften tortillas in hot oil or heat for a few seconds in buttered dish in microwave oven. Spoon thin layer of *Tomatillo Sauce* in 9x13-inch baking dish. Spread each tortilla with thin layer of *Tomatillo Sauce.* Place approximately ¼ cup of chicken mixture down center of each tortilla. Roll tortillas and place seam side down in baking dish. Spoon *Tomatillo Sauce* to taste over tortillas. Cover with foil and bake in preheated oven at 350 degrees for 20 minutes or until hot. Remove foil and sprinkle enchiladas with Cheddar and Monterey Jack cheeses. Bake chicken for 5 minutes longer or until cheese melts. Serve with shredded lettuce, chopped tomatoes, ripe olives, sour cream and remaining *Tomatillo Sauce.*

2 cups

Boil tomatillos and peppers in chicken broth for 7-10 minutes. Dissolve cornstarch in small amount of cold water and add to boiling mixture along with salt and cilantro. Boil sauce for 5 minutes. Remove sauce from heat, cool slightly and purée until smooth.

The flavor shouts "Ole!". Tomatillos are small green fruit covered with brown, thin, papery husks that you remove before using. **Tomatillo Sauce** *is excellent with tacos or tostadas, or as a dip for fried tortilla chips.*

Mexican

Seafood Enchiladas

2	medium white onions, coarsely chopped
1	7-ounce can diced green chiles
1½	tablespoons butter
1	pound crabmeat
1	pound tiny shrimp
1	cup walnut halves, toasted
1	12-ounce can medium pitted ripe olives, drained and halved
1	pound Monterey Jack cheese, shredded
1	pound Cheddar cheese, shredded vegetable oil
16	corn tortillas
2	cups half and half
1	cup sour cream
½	cup butter, melted
1½	teaspoons dried oregano
1	teaspoon garlic salt

Garnish:
shredded Cheddar cheese
sliced pimientos
avocado slices
sliced black olives

8 servings

In large skillet, sauté onions and chiles in butter until onions are transparent. Remove from heat and add crab, shrimp, walnuts and olives. Combine cheeses. Set aside 1½ cups of cheese for top of casserole. Stir remaining cheese into seafood mixture.

In skillet just large enough to hold tortillas, heat ¼ inch oil. Fry tortillas, one at a time, just long enough to soften, about 30 seconds. Drain on paper towels. Fill each tortilla with seafood filling, roll up and place seam side down in large, greased baking dish. *Can be prepared in advance and refrigerated or frozen. Defrost before proceeding.*

In medium saucepan, combine half and half, sour cream, butter, oregano and garlic salt. Stir frequently over medium heat until lukewarm and well blended. Pour over enchiladas. Sprinkle enchiladas with reserved cheese. Bake at 350 degrees for 30 minutes or until bubbly. Garnish with additional shredded cheese, pimiento, avocados and olives.

Simply sensational! Cooked and shredded chicken can be substituted for seafood.

Southwestern Orange Roughy

2	pounds orange roughy fillets
¾	cup sour cream
½	cup cream cheese, softened
1	cup shredded white Cheddar cheese
1	tablespoon minced onion
1	tablespoon fresh lemon juice
½	teaspoon garlic salt cayenne pepper to taste
1	4-ounce can diced green chiles minced fresh cilantro paprika

4-6 servings

Cut fish into serving pieces and place in single layer in greased baking dish. Blend sour cream and cream cheese until smooth. Add Cheddar cheese, onion, lemon juice, garlic salt, cayenne and chiles and mix well. Spread over fish. Bake at 375 degrees for 10-15 minutes or until fish flakes easily. Garnish with cilantro and paprika.

Red snapper, flounder or other white fish can be substituted for orange roughy.

Mexican

Chicken Tostadas

Avocado Dressing:
    3   tablespoons vegetable oil
    2   tablespoons cider vinegar
    2   teaspoons minced pickled jalapeño
        peppers
    ½   teaspoon sugar
    ½   teaspoon salt
    1   avocado, peeled, pitted and
        chopped
    1   tomato, chopped

    2   tablespoons vegetable oil
    1   clove garlic, minced
    2½ pounds chicken breasts, cooked,
        boned, skinned and shredded
    1   4-ounce can diced green chiles,
        drained
    ½   cup sour cream
        vegetable oil
    4-6 6-inch flour tortillas
    ½   small head iceberg lettuce, thinly
        sliced
    1   cup shredded Cheddar cheese
    1-2 tomatoes, chopped

4-6 servings

In small bowl, combine all dressing ingredients; mix well. Cover and refrigerate.

In 3-quart saucepan, heat 2 tablespoons oil over medium heat. Add garlic and cook until tender. Add shredded chicken, green chiles and sour cream; stir well. Cook over medium heat until hot; keep warm.

In 10-inch skillet, heat ¼ inch vegetable oil over medium heat. Fry flour tortillas in hot oil, one at a time, for about 30 seconds on each side or until lightly browned and blistered. Remove with tongs and drain on paper towels.

Arrange lettuce on each tortilla. Top with chicken mixture. Sprinkle with cheese and tomato. Spoon **Avocado Dressing** on top and serve immediately.

Enjoy this outstanding version of a traditional favorite. Mound a crisp flour tortilla high with vegetables, chicken and cheese to create the ultimate open-faced sandwich.

Chicken Fajitas

    8   large chicken breast halves, boned
        and skinned
    ½   cup fresh lime juice
    ½-1 teaspoon freshly ground black
        pepper
    ¾   teaspoon garlic salt
    1   large onion, sliced into rings
    1   tablespoon butter
    1   large green bell pepper, sliced into
        strips
    6-8 flour tortillas

Condiments:
    Guacamole
    Pico de Gallo or *Salsa Cruda*
    shredded Cheddar cheese
    sour cream

4-6 servings

Sprinkle both sides of chicken breasts with lime juice, pepper and garlic salt. Cover and refrigerate overnight.

In large skillet, sauté onion in butter for 2 minutes. Add green pepper and cook 2 more minutes or until vegetables are crisp-tender. Remove from heat and set aside.

Grill chicken breasts over hot coals for 2 minutes per side. Slice diagonally into strips. Add to vegetables in skillet and cook until heated through. Fill warmed flour tortillas with chicken mixture. Add **Guacamole, Pico de Gallo,** cheese and sour cream to taste. Roll and serve immediately.

*Close your eyes and you're in Acapulco. Serve sizzling hot with **Frijoles Refritos (Refried Beans).***

Mexican

Pastel de Montezuma (Montezuma Pie)

2	cups sour cream
⅓	cup milk
2	13-ounce cans tomatillos, drained
2	cloves garlic, minced
1	tablespoon minced fresh cilantro
2	tablespoons vegetable oil
1	cup chopped onions
2	4-ounce cans diced green chiles
12	6-inch corn tortillas, cut into quarters
2½	cups shredded, cooked chicken
2	cups shredded Monterey Jack cheese

6 servings

Mix together sour cream and milk and set aside. In blender or food processor, blend tomatillos, garlic and cilantro. In skillet, heat oil and cook onions and chiles until onion is transparent. Mix onion and chili mixture with tomatillo mixture and set aside.

In microwave oven, warm tortillas for 30 seconds. Spread ⅓ of tortillas over bottom of greased 3-quart casserole. Layer ½ of chicken, ⅓ of sauce, ⅓ of sour cream and ⅓ of cheese. Repeat layers. Top with layers of remaining tortillas, sauce, sour cream and cheese. Bake at 350 degrees for 40 minutes.

A delicious casserole layered with tortillas, chicken, chiles, cheese and sour cream. This dish is best if assembled ahead of time and heated before serving.

Stuffed Chicken Breasts with Enchilada Sauce

4	whole chicken breasts, boned and skinned
4-5	Anaheim chiles, roasted, peeled, seeded and chopped
¼	pound bulk chorizo sausage, cooked
½	pound Monterey Jack cheese, cut into 4 slices
½	cup fine dry bread crumbs
1	tablespoon chili powder
½	teaspoon ground cumin
	salt and freshly ground black pepper to taste
6	tablespoons butter, melted
	chopped green onion tops
	minced fresh cilantro (optional)

4 servings

Pound chicken breasts between sheets of waxed paper until thin. Spread each piece with equal amounts of chiles and chorizo. Top with cheese slice and roll up. Combine bread crumbs, chili powder, cumin, salt and pepper. Dip each chicken breast in melted butter and roll in crumb mixture. Place breasts seam side down in baking dish. Chill for at least 1 hour.

Bake chicken at 400 degrees for 30 minutes. Pour **Enchilada Sauce** over baked chicken. Garnish with green onion and cilantro.

Enchilada Sauce:

1	8-ounce can tomato sauce
1	teaspoon ground cumin
1	teaspoon chili powder
½	teaspoon ground coriander
¼	teaspoon freshly ground black pepper
	salt and freshly ground black pepper to taste

Combine all sauce ingredients and heat to boiling.

Mexican

Beef Fajitas

1	1½-pound beef skirt or round steak
½	cup fresh lime juice
¼	cup tequila
3-4	cloves garlic, finely minced
1	teaspoon salt
½	teaspoon freshly ground black pepper
1	small onion, thinly sliced into rings
1	tablespoon vegetable oil
1	green bell pepper, sliced into strips
12	flour tortillas, warmed

Condiments:
Guacamole
Pico de Gallo or *Salsa Cruda*
shredded Cheddar cheese
sour cream

6 servings

Cut beef into 4 pieces. Put in plastic bag with lime juice, tequila, garlic, salt and pepper. Close bag securely and marinate in refrigerator for 2-3 hours or overnight.

In heavy, cast-iron skillet, sauté onion in oil for 2 minutes. Add green pepper strips and cook for 2 more minutes or until vegetables are crisp-tender.

Drain marinade and discard. Broil steak over coals (mesquite to be authentic) or fry in a heavy, cast-iron skillet over medium-high heat. Cook for 3-4 minutes per side. Carve into thin slices across grain. Quickly stir beef and vegetables together in skillet and cook for 1-2 minutes or until heated through.

Fill warmed tortillas with beef and vegetables. Add **Guacamole, Pico de Gallo,** shredded cheese and sour cream as desired. Roll and serve immediately.

*For a taste of Mexico, serve this regional specialty sizzling hot, with **Frijoles Refritos (Refried Beans)** on the side.*

Spinach Enchilada Casserole

1½	pounds lean ground beef
1	clove garlic, minced
½	cup chopped onion
	salt and freshly ground black pepper to taste
2	tomatoes, chopped
8	ounces tomato sauce
2	4-ounce cans diced green chiles
	juice of ½ lime
1	tablespoon sugar
1	10-ounce package frozen chopped spinach, thawed and squeezed dry
10	6-inch corn tortillas
½	cup butter, melted
3	cups shredded Monterey Jack cheese
1	cup sour cream

8 servings

In large skillet, cook ground beef with garlic, onion, salt and pepper until beef is crumbled and no longer pink. Add tomatoes, tomato sauce, green chiles, lime juice, sugar and spinach. Mix well. Cover and simmer for 10 minutes.

Cut tortillas into quarters and dip into melted butter. Cover bottom of greased, 9x13-inch baking dish with half the tortilla quarters, overlapping slightly. Spoon half of beef mixture over tortillas. Sprinkle with half of cheese. Arrange rest of tortilla quarters over cheese, overlapping slightly. Spread with sour cream. Spoon remaining beef mixture over sour cream. Sprinkle with remaining cheese. Bake at 350 degrees for 30 minutes.

A winning combination of tastes and textures.

Mexican

Mexican Fillet

4	small fillet steaks, 1½-inches thick
	Worcestershire sauce
	garlic salt
	freshly ground black pepper
1½	ancho chiles
2	pasilla chiles
	water
½	clove garlic
	salt
4	slices Monterey Jack cheese, ¼-inch thick

4 servings

Cover both sides of each fillet with Worcestershire. Sprinkle with garlic salt and pepper. Marinate at room temperature for 2 hours.

Open chiles and remove seeds and stems. Soak in very hot water for 30-45 minutes or until softened. Place chiles in blender with garlic, salt to taste and 4-5 tablespoons of water in which chiles soaked. Blend until puréed.

Grill steaks over medium-hot coals for 5-7 minutes per side for medium-rare. Two minutes before end of cooking time, cover each fillet with a slice of cheese. Cook until cheese melts. Spoon chile purée over cheese and serve immediately.

Juicy fillets for those who like it hot.

Tenderloin Stuffed with Chiles and Cheese

1	tenderloin of beef (3-4 pounds)
4	poblano or Anaheim chiles, roasted, peeled, seeded and chopped
3	medium onions, chopped
6	cloves garlic, minced
¼	cup vegetable shortening or lard
1½	teaspoons salt
1	teaspoon freshly ground black pepper
6	ounces white Cheddar cheese, shredded (1½ cups)

Garnish:
Salsa Cruda
chopped green onion tops

6 servings

Place tenderloin on edge and cut lengthwise to within 1 inch of opposite edge. Spread open and flatten to an even ¾-inch thickness with meat pounder. Cover meat and let sit at room temperature while cooking filling.

In large skillet over medium heat, sauté chiles, onions and garlic in shortening until onions are transparent. Remove from heat and cool to room temperature.

Season butterflied tenderloin with salt and pepper. Spread chile and onion mixture on bottom half of tenderloin. Sprinkle with cheese. Fold over to enclose filling. Secure with skewers. Grill over hot coals, turning once, for about 14 minutes total for rare or until desired doneness. Slice across grain. Serve with salsa and garnish with chopped green onions.

For festive flavor, fire up the grill for these fabulous fillets.

Mexican

Pita Fajitas

4½ pounds bone-in beef chuck roast
1 7-ounce can diced green chiles
3 tablespoons chili powder
1 teaspoon dried oregano leaves
2 cloves garlic, minced
1 8-ounce can stewed tomatoes
 salt to taste
 cayenne pepper to taste
8 whole pita breads

Condiments:
 Guacamole
 sour cream
 Salsa Cruda

8 servings

Place roast on sheet of aluminum foil 12x25 inches. Mix together green chiles, chili powder, oregano and garlic. Spread mixture on top of roast. Wrap aluminum foil around roast and seal. Place roast in pan and bake at 300 degrees for 4-4½ hours or until meat is so tender it falls apart. Unwrap roast and discard fat and bones. Shred meat and put meat and drippings in large pan. Stir in tomatoes and heat until hot. Stir in salt and cayenne pepper to taste. Cut pita breads in half to form pockets. Fill with shredded beef mixture. Serve with **Guacamole,** sour cream and **Salsa Cruda.**

This **Pita Fajita,** *with south-of-the-border flavor, is perfect for moveable feasts. Use the tasty filling for* **Mexican Tortilla Baskets,** *burritos, tacos and enchiladas as well.*

Mexican Tortilla Baskets

Spicy Meat Filling:
1 pound boneless pork butt or
  shoulder, cut into 1½-inch pieces
2 cups water
2 tablespoons cider vinegar
3 tablespoons diced green chiles
1 clove garlic, minced
¼ teaspoon dried oregano
¼ teaspoon ground cumin
½ cup salsa

 vegetable oil
8 6-inch corn tortillas
1 avocado, peeled, pitted and halved
½ small head iceberg lettuce, thinly
  sliced
2 medium tomatoes, diced
1½ cups shredded Monterey Jack
  cheese
½ cup pitted ripe olives, sliced

8 servings

Put pork into 3-quart saucepan. Cover and cook over medium heat for about 10 minutes. Uncover pork and cook on high heat until liquid evaporates and meat browns well, stirring frequently. Add water to meat. Cover and simmer until meat is tender, 1-1¼ hours. Uncover meat and boil over high heat until liquid is gone. Add vinegar, green chiles, garlic, oregano and cumin to meat. Remove from heat and cool. Shred meat and stir in salsa.

Heat 1 inch vegetable oil in 10-inch skillet over medium heat. Place a tortilla in a 7 or 8-inch strainer and press the tortilla inside the strainer to form a basket. Place strainer in hot oil while holding tortilla in place with the back of a slotted spoon. Fry for about 1 minute or until crisp. Tilt strainer to fry tortilla edges. Remove tortilla basket and place on paper towels to drain. Repeat until eight tortilla baskets have been made.

Cut avocado halves crosswise into slices. Place some lettuce in each tortilla basket. Top with pork filling, diced tomatoes, shredded cheese, avocado slices and olives.

For ease of preparation, use a bird's nest fryer to make the baskets. Baskets can be filled with **Pita Fajitas'** *shredded beef if you prefer.*

Mexican

Chiles en Nogada
(Chiles in Walnut Sauce)

12	Anaheim chiles
1	onion, chopped
2	cloves garlic, minced
2	tablespoons butter
1	pound ground pork or shredded cooked pork roast
1	cup tomato purée
½	teaspoon ground cinnamon
⅜	cup raisins
⅜	cup blanched almonds
½	teaspoon sugar
	salt and freshly ground black pepper to taste
2	peaches, diced
2	pears, diced
4	egg whites
4	egg yolks
	all-purpose flour
1	cup vegetable oil

Walnut Sauce:

50	walnuts, shelled
⅜	cup blanched almonds
4	ounces goat's cheese
2	cups milk
	sugar to taste

12 servings

Roast chiles under broiler, turning with tongs until skin is blistered. Seal in plastic bag for ½ hour. Skin chiles. Slit them lengthwise to remove veins and seeds. Set aside.

Sauté onion and garlic in butter. Add ground pork and cook until no longer pink. Add tomato purée, cinnamon, raisins, almonds, sugar, salt and pepper. Stir in peaches and pears and simmer until thick. Stuff prepared chiles with filling and chill for 1 hour.

Beat egg whites until stiff. Beat yolks and fold into whites. Dip stuffed chiles in flour and then in beaten eggs. Fry in vegetable oil. Serve hot covered with cold **Walnut Sauce.**

In food processor, grind together walnuts and almonds; mix with cheese. Add enough milk to make a thick sauce; add sugar to taste. Cover and chill until ready to use.

One of the most famous dishes in Mexico, served to celebrate Mexico's independence from Spain. Decorate with pomegranate seeds and parsley and you'll have all the colors of the Mexican flag.

Frijoles Refritos
(Refried Beans)

2	cups dried pinto beans
1	onion, sliced
1	clove garlic, sliced
½	pound salt pork, cut into strips
2	tablespoons chili powder
2	tablespoons bacon grease
2	cups shredded longhorn cheese (8 ounces)
½	cup chopped green onions

4-6 servings

Cover pinto beans with water and soak overnight.

Drain beans, rinse and place in 4-quart saucepan. Add water to 1 inch above beans. Add onion, garlic, salt pork and chili powder. Simmer for several hours until beans are tender. Add more water as necessary. Remove salt pork pieces.

In large skillet, melt bacon grease and add beans a spoonful at a time, mashing well. Cook over low heat for at least 1 hour, stirring occasionally and adding more water as needed. Serve mounded in a large bowl, covered with cheese and sprinkled with green onions.

Spanish Squash

1 clove garlic, minced
2 cups summer squash, sliced
2 cups zucchini, sliced
½ cup dry bread crumbs
½ cup freshly grated Parmesan
    cheese
½ cup milk
1 tablespoon minced fresh parsley
½ teaspoon salt
⅛ teaspoon freshly ground
    black pepper
½ teaspoon dried oregano, crushed
2 4-ounce cans diced green chiles
½ cup shredded Cheddar cheese
2 eggs, beaten
½ cup soft bread crumbs
¼ cup butter, melted
½ cup shredded Cheddar cheese

6 servings

In large covered saucepan, cook garlic, squash and zucchini in small amount of water until tender; drain. Stir dry bread crumbs, Parmesan cheese, milk, parsley, salt, pepper, oregano, green chiles and ½ cup Cheddar cheese into vegetables. Fold in beaten eggs. Pour mixture into 6x10-inch baking dish. Toss soft bread crumbs with melted butter. Sprinkle casserole with buttered bread crumbs and ½ cup Cheddar cheese. Bake at 325 degrees for 25-30 minutes.

A velvety blend of flavors in every bite.

Chile Chicken Rellenos

16 Anaheim chiles, roasted and peeled
2 whole chicken breasts, cooked,
    boned, skinned and shredded
1 cup grated longhorn Cheddar
    cheese
½ cup sour cream
    salt and freshly ground
    black pepper to taste
5 egg yolks
2 tablespoons all-purpose flour
¼ teaspoon salt
¼ teaspoon baking powder
5 egg whites
¾ cup vegetable oil

8 servings

Slit chiles lengthwise and remove seeds and veins; set aside.

In large bowl, combine shredded chicken, cheese, sour cream and salt and pepper. Mix well; mixture should be sticky and hold together. If mixture is too dry, gradually add more sour cream. Roll one tablespoon of chicken mixture between palms to form into a cigar shape. Insert into slit chile. Continue until all chiles are filled. Place in single layer on cookie sheet and chill for 1 hour.

To make batter, mix together egg yolks, flour, salt and baking powder. Set aside. Beat egg whites until stiff peaks form. Just before ready to use, fold egg yolk mixture into egg whites.

Heat oil in large skillet. Dip each cold chile into batter. Fry, turning only once, until golden brown on both sides. Drain on paper towels and serve immediately.

*Oozing with flavor! Top with **Green Chile** or **Salsa Cruda** and serve with **Frijoles Refritos (Refried Beans)**.*

Mexican

Mexican Zucchini

2	tablespoons olive oil
4	cups thinly sliced zucchini
¾	cup chopped celery
½	large onion, chopped
½	cup sliced red or green bell pepper
1½	teaspoon dried basil, crumbled
½	cup picante sauce, hot or mild (to taste)
1	teaspoon salt
	freshly ground black pepper to taste
1	cup shredded Monterey Jack cheese

4-6 servings

In large skillet on high heat, heat olive oil. Sauté all vegetables at once for approximately 3 minutes in hot oil, stirring constantly. Add basil, picante sauce, salt and pepper; stir well. Cover vegetables and cook for 3-5 minutes. Add Monterey Jack cheese to vegetables and mix well. When cheese is barely melted, serve immediately.

A festive Mexican side dish.

Flan
(Caramel Custard)

2	cups whole milk, scalded
3	eggs, lightly beaten
½	cup sugar
1	teaspoon pure vanilla extract
¾	cup sugar
¼	cup water

4-6 servings

In medium bowl, beat scalded milk, eggs, sugar and vanilla extract until smooth. Set custard aside.

In small saucepan, melt sugar with water over medium heat, stirring constantly until sugar crystallizes into hard lumps. Continue cooking and stirring until sugar remelts into a golden brown liquid or caramel. Quickly spoon caramel into 4-6 custard cups to coat bottom. Pour custard over cooled caramel. Place custard cups in pan of shallow water and bake at 300 degrees for 1 hour or until knife inserted in custard comes out clean. To serve, run knife around edge of custard cup and quickly invert cup onto dessert dish. Serve warm or at room temperature.

*Probably the most popular of all Mexican desserts, **Flan (Caramel Custard)** is an inheritance from Spain, where it enjoys equal popularity. We proudly present this version.*

Mexican

Kahlúa Mousse

1 cup heavy cream
½ teaspoon instant coffee powder
¼ cup Kahlúa liqueur
2 tablespoons sugar
1 egg white
2 teaspoons sugar
  chocolate curls

4 servings

Chill medium bowl and beaters. Combine cream and coffee powder in chilled bowl and beat until soft peaks form. Add Kahlúa and 2 tablespoons sugar and beat until stiff peaks form. In small bowl, beat egg white until soft peaks form. Gradually add 2 teaspoons sugar, beating until stiff peaks form. Fold egg white into whipped cream mixture. Transfer to dessert bowls, cover and chill several hours or overnight. Decorate with chocolate curls.

Elegance was never so easy! Chill in a 1½-quart soufflé dish if you prefer.

Natillas

3 egg whites
1 tablespoon sugar
3 tablespoons cornstarch
¾ cup sugar
1 cup milk
3 egg yolks
1¼ cups milk
  ground cinnamon
  raisins

8 servings

Beat egg whites until stiff, gradually adding 1 tablespoon sugar. Set aside. In saucepan over low heat, dissolve cornstarch and ¾ cup sugar in 1 cup milk. Remove pan from heat. In small bowl, beat egg yolks thoroughly. Stir yolks into sugar and cornstarch mixture until it resembles a paste. Gradually stir 1¼ cups milk into paste mixture and cook over low heat, stirring constantly, for 10-12 minutes or until mixture thickens. Fold egg whites into hot custard mixture. Pour into 8 custard dishes and chill until ready to serve. Sprinkle with cinnamon and top with raisins.

A traditional Mexican dessert, the perfect ending to a spicy meal.

Mexican Wedding Cookies

1 cup butter, softened
½ cup powdered sugar
1 teaspoon pure vanilla extract
1 teaspoon pure almond extract
2 cups all-purpose flour
¼ teaspoon salt
1 cup finely chopped pecans
  powdered sugar

4 dozen

Cream butter, sugar, vanilla and almond extracts together. Blend flour, salt, and pecans into butter and sugar mixture. Mix dough until it holds together. Form into 1-inch balls. Place balls on ungreased baking sheet about 1 inch apart. Bake at 400 degrees for 10-12 minutes or until lightly browned. Cool cookies for a few minutes and roll in powdered sugar several times until well coated.

Mexican

Baked Pineapple with Vanilla Sauce

1   **large pineapple**
4   **tablespoons dark rum**
¼   **cup packed light brown sugar**
    butter
    toasted coconut (optional)

Vanilla Sauce:

2   **cups half and half**
¼   **cup sugar**
1   **whole egg**
2   **egg yolks**
1   **teaspoon cornstarch**
1   **teaspoon pure vanilla extract**

6 servings

Cut a slice from side of pineapple, avoiding green top, to form a boat. Reserve slice. Scoop out insides of pineapple, being careful not to puncture sides. Discard core and cut fruit into cubes. Mix cubes of pineapple with rum and sugar. Return them to pineapple boat. Dot pineapple cubes and boat with butter. Cover pineapple and its green top with aluminum foil. Bake at 350 degrees for 20 minutes or until warm. Top with reserved slice and immediately bring to the table to serve. Drizzle **Vanilla Sauce** over pineapple cubes and sprinkle with toasted coconut.

In top of double boiler, scald cream; cool slightly. In mixing bowl, beat sugar and whole egg. Add egg yolks, cornstarch and vanilla. Beat well. Add egg mixture to scalded cream and cook in double boiler over hot water, stirring constantly, until smooth and thickened. Chill sauce before serving.

*The creamy **Vanilla Sauce** brings a new taste sensation to pineapple.*

Strawberry Margarita Ice

1   **cup sugar**
2   **cups hot water**
2   **pints fresh strawberries or frozen strawberries, thawed**
6-8 **tablespoons lime juice**
6   **tablespoons tequila**
¼   **cup Triple Sec liqueur**
      pomegranate seeds
      tequila (optional)

8 servings

Dissolve sugar in hot water and cool. In food processor, purée strawberries. Add lime juice, tequila and Triple Sec. Stir in sugar syrup . Add additional lime juice if desired. Freeze in metal pan at least 6 hours, stirring occasionally to break up. Serve in sherbet bowls sprinkled with pomegranate seeds. Pour additional tequila over the ice for more pronounced flavor.

Surround with sliced fruits such as papaya, mango, pineapple, kiwi or strawberries and garnish with mint.

Mexican

Mexican Chocolate Ice Cream

8   ounces milk chocolate (preferably imported), chopped
3   cups half and half
1   cup heavy cream
4   egg yolks
¾   cup sugar
½   teaspoon ground cinnamon
1½ tablespoons pure vanilla extract
¼   teaspoon pure almond extract

1½-2 quarts

In double boiler over gently simmering water, melt chocolate. Stir chocolate until smooth. Remove top pan and set aside off heat.

In large, heavy saucepan, mix half and half and heavy cream. Heat to boiling and remove from heat. In large bowl, whisk egg yolks until foamy. Combine sugar and cinnamon and slowly beat into egg yolks. Whisk until mixture is thick and lemon colored. Whisk cream mixture into sugar and egg yolks. Pour mixture into saucepan and cook over low heat, stirring constantly, for 7 minutes or until thickened. Remove custard from heat. Whisk in melted chocolate and both extracts. Cover custard and chill for at least 3 hours, stirring occasionally. Put custard in ice cream freezer and freeze according to manufacturer's instructions. Freeze in covered container for several hours. Let ice cream soften slightly in refrigerator before serving.

*Wonderful cinnamon flavor makes this chocolate ice cream extraordinary. Serve with **Churros** or **Cinnamon-Sugar Tortillas.***

Mexican Fried Ice Cream

½   gallon French vanilla ice cream
4   teaspoons ground cinnamon
3   cups cornflakes, coarsely crushed
    vegetable oil
    honey
    sweetened whipped cream

8 servings

Shape ice cream into 8 balls. Sprinkle each ice cream ball with cinnamon and roll in crushed corn flakes. Place on cookie sheet and freeze until very hard. Chill serving bowls. Heat enough oil in deep fat fryer to cover ice cream balls. Heat to 375 degrees and fry each ball, one at a time, for 3-5 seconds. Serve immediately after frying topped with honey, whipped cream and a sprinkle of ground cinnamon. Serve with **Cinnamon-Sugar Tortillas.**

Cinnamon-Sugar Tortillas:

½   teaspoon ground cinnamon
¼   cup sugar
4   8-inch flour tortillas, cut into quarters
    vegetable oil

In small bowl, combine cinnamon and sugar and mix well. In large skillet, heat ½ inch of oil over medium heat until haze forms. Fry tortilla quarters, a few at a time, for 1 minute or until golden. Drain on paper towels and sprinkle with the cinnamon-sugar mixture.

Mexican

Churros
(Mexican Doughnut Strips)

1½ cups water
½ cup unsalted butter
2 teaspoons freshly grated lemon peel
2 teaspoons sugar
¼ teaspoon ground cardamom
¼ teaspoon salt
1½ cups unbleached all-purpose flour
3 eggs, room temperature
vegetable oil for frying
½ lime
1 slice day-old bread
sugar

2 dozen

In medium saucepan, combine water, butter, lemon peel, 2 teaspoons sugar, cardamom and salt. Heat to boiling. Add flour and immediately remove from heat. Beat with electric mixer until batter is fluffy. Cool slightly. Add eggs, one at a time, beating well after each. Spoon warm batter into pastry bag fitted with ½-inch star tip.

In large, heavy saucepan, heat 2 inches of oil to 370 degrees. Squeeze juice from lime and reserve for another use. Add lime shell and bread to oil and fry until bread is dark brown. Remove bread and lime with slotted spoon. Pipe batter onto oil in 2-inch lengths. Fry several at a time, but do not crowd. Cook 1½-2 minutes or until golden brown, turning occasionally. Drain on paper towels. *Can be made 6 hours ahead. Reheat at 250 degrees for 5 minutes.* Roll churros in sugar and serve warm.

Street vendors sell these light and crispy pastries at festivals and markets in Mexico. Try them with a mug of steaming **Chocolate con Leche (Mexican Hot Chocolate).**

Dulce con Nueces
(Brown Sugar Pralines)

1 cup buttermilk
2 cups sugar
1 cup packed dark brown sugar
1 teaspoon baking soda
⅛ teaspoon salt
⅔ cup light corn syrup
2 teaspoons pure vanilla extract
2 tablespoons butter, melted
1½ cups pecan halves
1 teaspoon hot water

14-16 pralines

In 4-quart saucepan cook buttermilk, sugar, brown sugar, baking soda, salt and corn syrup over medium-low heat, stirring occasionally. (Slow cooking gives the pralines the dark and rich color.) Insert candy thermometer into mixture and heat to 230 degrees or soft ball stage. Remove from heat. Mix vanilla and butter together and add to sugar mixture. Blend until thick. Add pecans and beat until creamy and thick. Stir hot water into mixture and drop by tablespoon onto waxed paper. Cool for 1½ to 2 hours before wrapping individually in clear plastic wrap. *Pralines will keep for several weeks when stored in an airtight container.*

A delightfully different dessert to conclude your Mexican dinner.

HealthMark
Recipe Modifications

HealthMark Recipe Modifications

Susan Stevens, M.A., R.D., *is the nutritionist for HealthMark Centers, Inc., preventive medicine clinics located in Denver. She has written* Cooking For A Healthier Everafter, *a cookbook featuring recipes which have been reduced in fat, cholesterol, sodium, sugar and calories. The focus at HealthMark is teaching dietary and lifestyle changes which will reduce risk for heart disease, stroke, cancer, diabetes and obesity.*

Light, lean, natural, fresh, nouvelle cuisine, nutritious, heart-healthy — all are terms which characterize the way we eat today. But at the same time terms such as elegant, gourmet, luscious, decadent and sinfully rich also reflect contemporary cooking and eating. Which is the true state of the art?

The truth is we want the best — la crème — always. We want wonderful, delicious, beautifully presented food that will both delight the palate and be kind to the waistline as well as the arteries. Unfortunately, there is often a conflict between our desire for health and the ingredient list of a recipe.

Current dietary recommendations encourage consuming less fat (especially saturated fat), cholesterol, salt and sugar and increasing fiber intake in order to reduce risk of disease. The health-conscious cook reads recipes with an eye toward reducing or eliminating some of the ingredients that play havoc with our health. With a bit of modification most recipes can be "lightened" without sacrificing taste or visual appeal.

Making substitutions and modifications soon becomes second nature, and meals will be as appealing and tasty as ever — but much healthier. Once the sources of unnecessary fat, cholesterol and sodium are known, they become easier to eliminate.

Cholesterol — A type of fat found only in animal products.
• Red meats
• Chicken and poultry
• Fish and seafood
• Dairy products
• Egg yolks
• Organ meats such as liver, kidneys, sweetbreads and brains

Saturated Fat — Usually (but not always) solid at room temperature. Undesirable because it elevates blood cholesterol levels.
• Animal fats such as butter, meat fat and lard
• Dairy products: whole milk, yogurt and cottage cheese made from whole milk, ice cream, cheese and butter. (Lower fat dairy products will have less saturated fat and cholesterol.)
• Shortening
• Solid (stick) margarine (Liquid and tub margarines have less saturated fat.)
• Coconut and palm oil
• Hydrogenated vegetable oils

Sodium — Naturally present in many foods, much is added to processed foods.
• Canned, processed and convenience foods
• Seasoning salts, bouillon, MSG, meat tenderizers, soy sauce, Worcestershire sauce, steak sauce and other condiments
• Pickles, olives, sauerkraut, capers and anchovies
• Lunchmeats, ham, bacon and sausage

Cultivate the art of recipe modification and the resulting delicious, healthy food will become a family tradition. The best — the Crème de Colorado — can be just as wonderful as before with a few changes. This new cuisine will enrich both your health and your palate.

Here's how to do it:

Reducing Fat and Cholesterol

1. Buy lean cuts of meat and trim all visible fat. Serve smaller portions of meat, 3-4 ounces per person.

2. Avoid organ meats, which are very high in cholesterol.

3. Broil, bake, roast, poach or stir fry meat, poultry and fish instead of pan frying or deep-fat frying.

4. Sauté in non-stick cookware using a minimum of oil, 1-2 teaspoons, or sauté with broth, wine or water. (Chefs call this "sweating".)

5. Serve poultry, fish, whole grains, dried beans, peas and lentils more often.

HealthMark Recipe Modifications

6. Cook poultry without the skin; reduce cooking time by ⅓-½ to prevent overcooking.

7. Make stock, soups and stews ahead of time, chill and remove all hardened fat. If there is no time to do this, skim off as much fat as possible, then add several ice cubes. Fat will congeal and cling to the ice cubes, which can then be discarded.

8. Reduce the amount of fat in baked goods by ⅓-½. Use vegetable oil (safflower oil is the least saturated) or soft margarine whenever possible. Quick breads, muffins, pancakes and waffles turn out perfectly well made with oil rather than a more saturated fat such as butter, shortening or stick margarine. Soft margarine can be substituted for butter or stick margarine in many recipes.

9. Use non-fat or 1% dairy products (milk, yogurt or cottage cheese). Use evaporated non-fat milk in soups, sauces and baking.

10. Substitute non-fat yogurt or puréed cottage cheese for sour cream. To make a reduced fat "sour cream", purée 1 cup non-fat or 1% cottage cheese with 1-2 tablespoons lemon juice or ¼ cup buttermilk. If buttermilk is not available, add ¼ cup non-fat milk and 1-2 tablespoons powdered buttermilk.

11. Substitute 3 tablespoons unsweetened cocoa powder and 1 tablespoon oil for 1 ounce baking chocolate.

12. Eliminate nuts from a recipe or use only ¼-⅓ cup.

13. In baking, substitute 1-2 egg whites for each whole egg.

Reducing Salt

1. Eliminate or reduce salt in all recipes except yeast breads where salt is necessary to control growth of the yeast.

2. Use onion and garlic powders instead of salts.

3. Use salt-free canned vegetables and soups.

4. Use light (reduced sodium) soy sauce — sparingly.

5. Use salt-free beef and chicken broth. For a more concentrated flavor, boil to reduce by half. Be sure to defat canned broth by chilling until fat hardens, then skimming.

6. Rinse canned tuna, salmon, shrimp, crab or clams to reduce salt content.

Reducing Sugar

1. Reduce sugar by ⅓-½. In cookies, bars and cakes, replace the eliminated sugar with non-fat dry milk.

2. When sugar is reduced, enhance flavor with spices (cinnamon, nutmeg or cloves) and extracts (vanilla, almond, orange or lemon).

3. Substitute brown sugar or honey for white sugar; use less because the flavor is sweeter.

4. When reducing sugar in quick breads, cakes and cookies, use fruits which add sweetness naturally such as raisins, dried apricots, dates or bananas.

Adding Fiber

1. Use whole wheat flour whenever possible. As it is heavier than white flour, use less: ⅞ cup whole wheat flour to 1 cup white flour.

2. Add wheat bran or oat bran to baked goods, cereals, casseroles, soups and pancakes.

3. Use potatoes unpeeled ("country style") whenever possible in soups, stews or oven-fries.

4. Use more vegetables, whole grains (bulgur, corn, barley and oatmeal), dried beans, split peas and lentils.

HealthMark Recipe Modifications

Toasted Pecan Fruit Spread (Original)

3   tablespoons honey
1   tablespoon apple-flavored brandy
2   tablespoons milk
8   ounces cream cheese, softened
½   cup dried apple chunks, chopped
¼   cup chopped pecans, toasted

1¾ cups

In medium bowl, gradually add honey, brandy and milk to cream cheese, mixing until well blended. Stir in apples and pecans. Cover and chill.

For a variation, use ½ cup dried fruit medley (apricots, apples, peaches, pears and raisins) in place of the apples. Delicious spread on crackers or as a dip for fruits.

Toasted Pecan Fruit Spread (Modified)

3   tablespoons honey
1   tablespoon apple-flavored brandy
1   cup low-fat (1%) cottage cheese
2   tablespoons non-fat milk or apple
     juice (as needed)
½   cup dried apple chunks, chopped
¼   cup chopped pecans, toasted

1¾ cups

Combine honey, brandy and cottage cheese in food processor or blender. Blend, adding milk or apple juice as needed, until puréed. Stir in apples and pecans. Cover and chill.

HealthMark Recipe Modifications

Very Lemon Bread
(Original)

⅓ cup butter, melted
1 cup sugar
3 tablespoons lemon extract
2 eggs, lightly beaten
1½ cups sifted all-purpose flour
1 teaspoon baking powder
1 teaspoon salt
½ cup milk
2 tablespoons freshly grated
 lemon peel
½ cup chopped pecans

Lemon Glaze:
¼ cup fresh lemon juice
½ cup sugar

1 loaf

In large bowl, mix butter with sugar, lemon extract and eggs. In separate bowl, sift flour with baking powder and salt. To butter mixture, add flour mixture alternately with milk, stirring just enough to blend. Fold in lemon peel and pecans. Pour batter into greased and floured 9x5-inch loaf pan and bake at 350 degrees for 1 hour or until a wooden pick inserted in center comes out clean. Remove bread from pan and with a wooden pick poke holes at 1-inch intervals on all sides. While loaf is still warm, drizzle lemon glaze mixture over top and sides. Wrap in foil and store for 1 day before slicing to serve.

Very Lemon Bread
(Modified)

⅓ cup safflower oil
¾ cup sugar
3 tablespoons lemon extract
4 egg whites
1½ cups sifted unbleached flour
1 teaspoon baking powder
½ cup non-fat milk
2 tablespoons freshly grated
 lemon peel
¼ cup chopped pecans

Lemon Glaze:
½ cup lemon juice
½ cup sugar

1 loaf

In large bowl, mix oil with sugar, lemon extract and egg whites. In separate bowl, sift flour with baking powder. Add flour mixture to oil mixture alternately with milk, stirring just enough to blend. Fold in lemon peel and nuts. Pour batter into lightly oiled and floured loaf pan and bake at 350 degrees for 1 hour or until a wooden pick inserted in center comes out clean. Remove bread from pan and with a wooden pick poke holes at 1-inch intervals on all sides. While loaf is still warm, drizzle glaze over top and sides. Wrap in foil and store for 1 day before slicing to serve.

HealthMark Recipe Modifications

Lodestone Lasagne
(Original)

Sauce:

1	cup chopped onion
2	cloves garlic, crushed
1	28-ounce can crushed tomatoes
1	16-ounce can crushed tomatoes
1	6-ounce can tomato paste
¼	cup minced fresh parsley
1	tablespoon packed light brown sugar
1	teaspoon salt
1½	teaspoons dried oregano
¼	teaspoon dried thyme
1	bay leaf
1	whole stalk celery, leaves removed
2	cups water

1½-2	pounds Italian sausage in casings
1	cup water
8	ounces lasagne noodles, cooked al dente and drained
16	ounces ricotta cheese
1½	pounds mozzarella cheese, sliced

10-12 servings

In large saucepan, combine all sauce ingredients and simmer for 3 hours, stirring occasionally. Remove bay leaf and celery stalk.

In large skillet, cook sausage in water over moderate heat. Cook until water evaporates. Reduce heat to low and brown sausage for 5 minutes. Cut into ½-inch pieces. Add sausage to sauce. In a 9x13-inch pan, layer half of the noodles, sauce, ricotta and mozzarella. Repeat layers a second time. Cover with greased foil. Bake at 350 degrees for 1 hour.

Lodestone Lasagne
(Modified)

Sauce:

1	cup chopped onion
2	cloves garlic, crushed
1	28-ounce can salt-free crushed tomatoes
1	16-ounce can salt-free crushed tomatoes
1	6-ounce can salt-free tomato paste
¼	cup minced fresh parsley
1	tablespoon packed light brown sugar
1½	teaspoons dried oregano
¼	teaspoon dried thyme
1	bay leaf
1	whole stalk celery, leaves removed
2	cups water
1	pound lean ground round or ground turkey
1	teaspoon fennel seeds
½	teaspoon crushed red pepper flakes
8	ounces lasagne noodles (eggless), cooked al dente and drained
16	ounces low-fat (1%) cottage cheese
1	pound part-skim mozzarella cheese, sliced

10-12 servings

In large saucepan, combine all sauce ingredients and simmer for 3 hours, stirring occasionally. Remove bay leaf and celery stalk.

Brown ground round or turkey in large skillet; drain fat. Add meat to sauce along with fennel seeds and red pepper. In a lightly oiled 9x13-inch pan, layer half of the noodles, sauce, cottage cheese and mozzarella. Repeat layers a second time. Cover with lightly oiled foil. Bake at 350 degrees for 45-50 minutes.

Acknowledgements

Testing Committee

The Junior League of Denver dedicates Crème de Colorado to those whose commitment to excellence have made this book possible: the members of the Testing Committee who have given so generously of their time and talents to assure the quality of the recipes.

Sue Vandergriff Akers
Karen Keck Albin
Barb Anstett Barnard
Julie Clark Baxter
Liz Beard
Lindsay Bacon Bell
Gail Classon Berliner
Sheila Schweiger Bernardi
Sherman Todhunter Blosser
Martha McKown Brock
Sandra Hertz Brown
Jo Garverick Byyny
Debbie Krebbs Carr
Mary DuBois Carrothers
Bar Chadwick
Bonnie Lecker Clements
Sue Clinton
Diane Cecil Cousins
Diane Wolach Curd
Sally Hewitt Daniel
Jane McLaughlin Davis
Glenna Callahan Day
Barbara Trupp DeGroot
Lee Yanus Doyle
Sally Campbell Drennen
Cheryl Davis Dutton
Karlene Alt Elder
Caroline Kelley Ely
Sally Sharrer Engle
Sally Boekelman Erdmann
Candy McAdam Ergen
Linda Arndt Fengler
Diann Wittman Ferriell
Katie Eldridge Fitchett
Judith Sewald Fitzgerald
Lucy Bauer Footlik
Carolyn Drescher Gamba
Deborah Hughes Garrity
Lee Binley Golub
Kathy Humphreys Gravely

Anne Kuzell Hackstock
Linda Green Hanson
Nancy Gean Harding
Lynn Harris
Barbara Young Hart
Sharon Hartman
Marianne Hayes
Pamela Dervey Heckenkamp
Debbie Fagan Heikens
Lorayne Paoletti Henderson
Kaye Maxaxis Isaacs
Connie McConnelee Jacoway
Maggi Poncher Johnson
Patti Talbot Johnson
Fleta Cooke Johnson
Donna Bielski Kabrud
Virginia Hall Kelly
Heidi Dake Keogh
Alanna O'Meara Kimmel
Mona Pratico Kinnevy
Sally Bolln Kneser
Roger D. Knight
Barbara Eckhardt Knight
Janet Allman Kritzer
Susan Roberts Lake
Nan Hawks Lee
Merrilyn Maurer Leuthold
Linda Redden Lillie
Larry Lohmeier
Sherry Sieck Lohmeier
Barbara Temple Lorenz
Randall H. Lortscher
Marsha Murphy Lortscher
Anne Grant Lowdermilk
Billee Leonard Madsen
Janet Benson Manning
Kathy Litton McConahey
Nancy Anderson McKeever
Donna Evans Miedema
Melissa Pickering Miller
Michele Morris
Mimi Wilkinson Nelson
Maryann Austin Nelson
Jane Watson Netzorg
Gretchen Miller Nygaard
Jane Askew O'Connor
Dee Baluh Pallasch
Sue Walsh Palmer
Nancy Ervin Panasci
Virginia Lawhon Park
Merlaine Meyers Peede
Sue Browne Pfeiffer
Marilyn Mock Pickering
Sandy Gramms Pjesky
Judy Pardue Polidori
Mary Poor
Sherry Drab Richardson
Donald Ringsby
Karen Ringsby
Sharon Meisler Ripps
Gerry Crow Roeder
Hindi Bergmann Roseman
Mary Noteman Rosenberger
Jeanne Heller Ruggles
Loretta Lohmeyer Rule

Katharine Carah Schlosberg
Kathy Edwards Schmidt
Scott C. Schroeder
Kimberly Watkins Schroeder
Sukie Klie Schroeder
Cindy Crowell Schulz
Sandy Lemcke Scott
Sharon Early Severance
Linda Stevenson Sheehan
Lynn Sheridan
Susan White Siegesmund
Wendy Johnston Sinton
Jean Mason Smith
Loyce Helgerson Sorrell
Nancy Thornburg Stamper
Margaret Lutz Stavros
Liz Boone Steinbrueck
Luann Stratton
Carol Landler Strickland
Lorinda Stewart Swenson
Sonnie Mutz Talley
Nancy Tawse Tankersley
Nancy Jewett Tillman
Wendy Hall Trigg
Kay Bliss Truitt
Ruth Ann Campbell Tucker
Julia Harlow Valeski
Jane Vondache
Mary Anne Shirley Watters
Janet Tracy Wenzel
Sharon Kullgren Wilkinson
Pamela Porter Wolper
Marcia Langton Wood
Elaine Sack Woodworth
Francine Frank Yeddis
Sherrie Tobin Zeppelin

The 1987 Marketing Committee

The Junior League of Denver wishes to extend a very special thank you to the members of the Marketing Committee for their dedication, time, and expertise in making the tremendous success of this book possible.

Rickie Anderson Jones
  Chairman, C & C Publications
Sally Hewitt Daniel
  Marketing Chairman
Hindi Bergmann Roseman
  Marketing Co-Chairman

Barbara Anstett Barnard
Ellen Beller
Lucy Bauer Footlik
Anne Kuzell Hackstock
Kathryn Bixby-Haddad
Linda Green Hanson
Barbara Young Hart
Heidi Dake Keogh
Cydney Murray Marsico
Ann Hatfield Merritt
Deanna Hergert Person
Judy Pardue Polidori
Suzanne Jardine Robinson
Mary L. Wenke
Francine Frank Yeddis

Acknowledgements

Recipe Contributors

The Junior League of Denver thanks its members, families, and friends who have contributed recipes. It is our sincere hope that no one has been inadvertently overlooked.

Andree Abouzeid
Edithann Peters Acsell
Lorraine Ruskin Adams
Sue Vandergriff Akers
Karen Keck Albin
Linda Allen
Ann Reeves Allison
Margo Dreudahl Anastassatos
Jeaneene Fischer Anderson
Cindy Hamilton Anderson
Barbara Anderson
Beth Wier Anderson
Ann Kelly Anderson
Bobbie Helgerson Anderson
Carol Antonoff
Alice Townsend Applebaum
Tamara Arendt
Elaine Feintech Asarch
Be Merritt Aspinwall
Barbara Lien Bader
Sue Dawson Baker
Linda Lewis Bandy
Allyn Bader Barclay
Margaret McDonald Bathgate
Cynthia Gore Bauman
Julie Clark Baxter
Mary Bayers
Suzanne Luomala Becker
Lindsay Bacon Bell
Ellen Beller
Cherry Blume Belstock
Elaine Blomgren Bennion
Marsha Pirie Berger
Gail Classon Berliner
Sheila Schweiger Bernardi
Barbara Kennedy Bess
Deborah Wright Bevans
Glenda Bielski
Linda Blair Black
Ann Neisley Black
Leslie Burch Blauman
Patricia Knesel Blizzard
Sherman Todhunter Blosser
Kay Newlin Blue
Judith Peterson Boat
Charissa Boedecker
Dorothy M. Bonham
Shirley Sidles Bowman
Ruth Boxer
Alice Schwab Boyer
Christy Stambaugh Boyle
Lisle Loosli Bradley
Judith Brase
Brenda Breadon
Susan McWethy Brewer

Martha McKown Brock
Sandra Hertz Brown
Marguerite Coon Brown
Jane Holsteen Brown
Jane Crouse Brown
Susan Truitt Brown
Geil Mitchell Browning
Marlene Rosenberg Brubaker
Suzanne Groteluschen Bryson
Susan Gurney Buchanan
Marilyn Bulkey
Jane Bullock
Nancy Ehrenberg Burchfield
Joyce Ann Walsh Burgett
Jackie Andrews Burghardt
Sue Henderson Burleigh
Glory Isham Burns
Rosemary Major Burris
Janis Sparks Burrow
Sherry Hester Caldwell
Lecy Gumowitz Callender
Kathleen Koch Callender
Sydney Cambias
Wendy Weiner Cameron
Sparkie Cannon
Hildegarde Carlson
Lin Adams Carlson
Jan Davidson Carpenter
Judy Carpenter
Debra Krebs Carr
Mary DuBois Carrothers
Catherine Caton
Kathleen Cavalier
Barbara Cecchet
Sugar Schmidt Chalus
Sharon Hagar Charlton
Nancy Hall Chase
Susan Wilcox Chenier
Jeannie Pinkerton Clancy
Bonnie Lecker Clements
Sue Yale Clinton
Celia Colbitt
Christine Colunza
Wendy Pierce Connor
Melinda Cook
Susan Coombe
Carol Cortez
Janice Gillespie Cortez
Layne Price Corzine
Frances Hoffman Cosby
Elizabeth Cottingham
Diane Cecil Cousins
Nanette Cox
Sarah Jane Sloan Crabtree
Mrs. C. W. Cross
Diane Wolach Curd
Gay Curtiss-Lusher
Sally Hewitt Daniel
Dr. Warren A. Daniel
Catherine Bell Darnell
Sally Hendricks Davidson
Jane Tamplin Davis
Barbara Wagner Davis
Glenna Callahan Day
Wendy Metzger Debell
Judith Steele Debord
Mildred Gaston Deese
Barbara Trupp DeGroot
Kerry Maley Delva
Jean Dent
Flo DePalo
Florence Bellumori DePolo
Debra Deverell
Adda Dickerson
Louise Dilatush

Laura McClure Dirks
Ann Durant Disborough
Lena Dolce
Corry Mack Doty
Bonnie Page Downing
Elizabeth Seeley Downs
Lee Yanus Doyle
Ivy Majlinger Doyle
Fay Pearson Dreher
Susan Knierer Dreisbach
Nancy Wikler Dubelman
Cheryl Davis Dutton
Jeanne Duval
Patricia Poisson Eberle
Mary Eckels
Patricia Lorraine Edwards
Nancy L. Ego
J. B. Elberson
David Elder
Karlene Alt Elder
Susan Flanagan Elliott
Caroline Kelley Ely
Sally Sharrer Engle
Ellen McEwen Enoch
Mary Erickson
Doris Rogers Erickson
Elizabeth Evans
Margaret Hazlett Fagin
Constance Wean Farmer
Allie Low Broderick Farwell
Ann Brooks Fawcett
M. Kay Willson Feinberg
Ricki Hetts Feist
Linda Arndt Fengler
Diann Wittman Ferriell
Louise Fettinger
Sharon Sorensen Fightmaster
Mary Frances Finch
Lucile Finch
Janie Fisher
Ellen Kingman Fisher
Judy Sewald Fitzgerald
Billie Jean Andrews Fitzgerald
Sue Fitzsimmons
Susan Coyne Flanagan
Linda Newman Flynn
Lucy Bauer Footlik
Dixie Forrester
Julia Frick Foster
Carolyn Beise Fournier
Barbara Chain Fowles
Barbara Newton Framsted
Wendy Francke
Nancy Solma Franks
Vicki Vickland Franks
Dan Frantz
Sharon Frayer
Sally Huestis Frerichs
Katherine Upton Fulford
Diane Galbraith
Carolyn Drescher Gamba
Mitten Howell Gates
Sharon Gatline
Nancy W. Gegen
Cheri Gerou
Norma Evans Gerwin
Carole O'Brien Ghella
Lisa Emerson Gibson
Nancy Cole Gobel
Joanne Goldcamp
Suzanne Seeley Golden

Lee Golub
Marilyn Taylor Gordon
Linda Widdersheim Gordon
Constance Fox Graham
Richard Grausman
Kathy Humphreys Graveley
Ellagwen Shaw Green
Janice Cruzen Griffith
Marilyn Groff
Norma Jean Carpenter Grow
Susan Grupe
Delores Guerreno
Karen Rolf Gulley
Laura Brown Hackstaff
Anne Kuzell Hackstock
Cindy Hagan
Cynthia Griffin Halaby
Karen Rohde Haley
Susan Greterman Hall
Marilyn Hall
Lindee Hallin
Denise Hamel
Susan Nye Handwerk
Elizabeth Hanson
Linda Green Hanson
Brewster Hanson
Nancy Gean Harding
Dorothy Ellen Hargrove
JoAnn Harman
Patricia Schweiger Harmon
Jane Allison Harper
Lyn Gebhard Harris
Melissa Harris
Lo Harrison
Betty Hart
Barbara Young Hart
Sharon Hartman
Patricia Anderson Harwood
Penny Oliver Hawkins
Vicki Hayden
Marianne Hayes
Dorothy Warren Hayward
Colleen Miller Healey
Pamela Dervey Heckenkamp
Debbie Fagan Heikens
Peggy Byrne Heinz
Peggy Greer Helgerson
Carol Peterson Heller
Marsha Helling de Farro
Lorayne Paoletti Henderson
Billye Moser Heoft
Susan Lee Herstedt
Frances Rogers Hewitt
Susan Wessels Hiatt
Pat Hill
Dottie Hills
B. C. Hills
George Hills
Susan Anderson Hills
Casey Hine
Arlene Friedman Hirschfeld
Sarah Hoper Hite
Nancy Walker Hohfeler
Sydney Cambias Hollinger
Cathy Carlos Hollis
Elizabeth Alexander Holtze
Dianne McWhorter Honig

Acknowledgements

Merrilee Carlson Hooker
Nita Watson Horner
Karel Wright Horney
Jane Snodgrass Houston
Margaret Houtchens
Linda Adams Hovland
Reba Clarkson Hudgins
Sheilagh MacKinnon Hudon
Ellen Guglielmo Hufft
Charles Hull
Donna de la Ossa Hultin
Heidi Hummel
Carol Robinson Hutchins
Gwen Mooney Hutchinson
Janie Shover Hutchison
Judy Ingersol
Francine Ingraham
Faye B. Irelan
Kaye Mataxis Isaacs
Liz Jackson
Connie McConnelee Jacoway
Sue Ann Brownlee James
Ann Cozad Jansson
Patricia Talbot Johnson
Maggi Poncher Johnson
Lucia Moore Johnson
Kay Durey Johnson
Gayle Bergman Johnson
Margorie Wallace Johnson
Sally M. Jones
Mrs. R. Carter W. Jones
Terri Wolfe Jones
Rickie Anderson Jones
Sharon Joseph
Kathye Post Julander
Judi Kahn
Cornelia Wyma Keatinge
Debra Abbott Kelin
Mary Wallis Masengill Keller
Debbie Keller
Suzanne Woodward Kelly
Sarah Graef Kennedy
Heidi Dake Keogh
Barbara Kieswetter
Alanna O'Meara Kimmel
Cyndi Potestio Kingdom
Melly McGreev Kinnard
Mona Pratico Kinnevy
Elaine Kizzie
Mary Lou Knapp
Sally Bolln Kneser
Sue Kopine
Nancy Kopp
Barbara Knauf Kowalsky
Valarie Kozak
Judy Winter Krass
Jane Smith Krichbaum
Susan Roberts Lake
Sharon Rogers Lamberton
Ruth Mary Bangs Lancaster
Kathy Langton
Michele Larson
Linda Laskey
Lisa Citron Laudeman
Susan Gathers Law
Debby Lawrence
Nan Hawks Lee
Diana Hess Leher

Margaret Griffith Leiser
Merrilyn Leuthold
Lori Lynne Roebuck Lewis
Hannelore Gatzka Lichtenfels
Leslie Erb Liedtke
Raymond Liegl
Linda Redden Lillie
Susan Stellor Linkow
Karen Littlefield
Ann Garney Livingston
Lori Livingston
Mary Funk Logan
Sherry Sieck Lohmeier
Pat Jackson Long
Marcia Murphy Lortscher
Randall H. Lortscher
Cynthia Losasso
Vicki Breznikar Luengo
Diane Muckerman Luppens
Carol Krieger Macfee
Debbie MacGowan
Sue MacKenzie
Della Mack
Billee Leonard Madsen
Pamela Kirk Magill
Cinny Mahoney
Sherry Parker Maloney
Jennifer Lamme Mandelson
Janet Benson Manning
Donna Marsh
Vera Martin
Elizabeth Hosanna Mascitelli
Sean Brewer Massad
Renie Shields Max
Carrie Welch McClellan
Peggy Gralino McClintock
Theresa McClure
Kathy Litten McConahey
Patricia Hughes McConaty
Helen Gilmour McConaty
Cherie McCracken
Virginia S. McDonald
Virginia McDonall
Sandra Dietl McGuire
Carolyn Plylar McKenzie
Anne McKinnon
Anne Love McKown
Jane McMahon
Shirley Sue Jackson McMillan
Bonnie McMillen
Suzanne McNitt
Lynn McWilliams
Ann Hatfield Merritt
Debbie Hillmer Mersfelder
Bitsy G. Meyers
Frank W. Meyers
Carol Suoboda Michuda
Donna Evans Miedema
Melanie Milam
Melissa Pickering Miller
Mary Lee Filgo Miller
Ann Miller
Ann Durstine Miller
Mary Miller
Trish Millia
Dorothy Mock
Kathy McGrath Mohn
Louise Watkins Molthop
Penny Montgomery
Susan Hill Moore
Louise Gaither Moore

Pasey Morah
Michele Fugere Morris
Mary Sinclaire Morris
Bea Moss
Alice Hruschka Mouton
Helen Ruth Fogel Mozer
Monica Ziegler Munroe
Sue Murray
Claudia Boles Myers
Cynthia Fels Nagel
Barbara Wyckoff Neal
Barbara Lynn Neil
Beverly Benn Neilson
Mimi Wilkinson Nelson
Mary Ann Austin Nelson
Karen Wennerstrom Nelson
Jan Berne Netting
Jane Watson Netzorg
Alvina Helgerson Neuner
Diane Marcuson Newcom
Muriel Staniford Newell
Jane Vonderahe Nicola
Belinda Gammon Nields
Suzanne Nielson
Marge Nielson
Ed Nielson
E. J. Nielson
Susan Nixon
Amy Noonan
Loretta Booth Norgren
Barbara Alexander Norwood
Gretchen Miller Nygaard
Cynthia Bailey Oakes
Kathleen O'Connell
Barbara Sumner O'Connell
Deborah Doyle O'Connor
Patrice Rahel O'Donnell
Nancy Wilson O'Donnell
Ann Barlow O'Donnell
Ann Batchelder Ogg
Nancy Newsham Orcutt
Susan Rowan Paddock
Dee Baluh Pallasch
Sue Walsh Palmer
Nancy Ervin Panasci
Tunu Panda
Lynn Mueller Parham
Virginia Lawhon Park
Susan Mihevic Pasek
Diana Elzey Pearson
Jill Pedicord
Didge Pedicord
Marlene Peede
Merlaine Meyers Peede
Sandra Stephens Peltier
Edie Brown Pepper
Hilary Perlov
Barbara Perrin
Karen Perry
Barb Perry
Deanna Hergert Person
Susan Peterson
Elizabeth Cowles Peyton
Pat Henning Pezzella
Susan Browne Pfiffer
Barbara Buck Phillips

Kathleen Kaup Pickering
Marilyn Mock Pickering
Melaine Pierce
Carol Ransom Pierce
Jolynne Pierce
Ann Dunlap Pierson
Mrs. Arthur Pinkerton
Jean Ann Pisceatta
Jane Pjesky
Judy P. Polidori
Mary Van Steen Poor
Inge T. Popke
Margaret Evans Porter
Kathryn Sager Potts
Janet Poyser
Alice Sawaya Prendergast
Linny Pretekin
Fonza Bell Price
Lynne Trego Quoy
Karen Hayes Ragsdale
Mary Ward Rankin
Allison Rath
Dru Dugas Ray
Judith Recht
Melanie Reed
Betty Rees
Toni Reimers
Sharon Drab Richardson
Brenda Dunn Rickert
Nancy Blue Riley
Sharon Meisler Ripps
Michael Ritz
Kathyleen Rourke Roberts
Julie Robertson
Suzanne Jardine Robinson
Joan Roe
Gerry Crow Roeder
Willie Mae Youngblood Rogers
Hindi Bergmann Roseman
Mary Noteman Rosenberger
Marcia Muller Rothenberg
Jane Rothlisberger
Romaine Rouse
Joyce Rubin
Dr. John Ruge
Jeanne Heller Ruggles
Loretta Lohmeyer Rule
Catherine Walz Rundle
Jayne Belvedere Russell
Betty Lou Wagoner Russell
Kathryn Records Ryan
Vivian Porter Sabel
Muriel May Sack
Mary Ann Yanus Samborski
Dianne Pfeiffenberger Saul
Mary Presley Sawyer
Carolyn Sack Schaefer
Marcia Schafer
Norma Schambow
Katharine Carah Schlosberg
Persis Wolf Schlosser
Kathy Edwards Schmidt
Sukie Schroeder
Kimberly Watkins Schroeder
Scott C. Schroeder
Cindy Crowell Schulz
Linda Schwartz
Sandy Lemcke Scott
Gail Schaeuble Scott

Acknowledgements

Adelia Sebald
Margaret Wagner Seep
Martha Carey Segelke
Carole Semple
Lorraine Sewald
Karen E. Johnson Shander
Katrina Shanks
Thais Duel Shapiro
Pierce Shaw
Linda Sheehan
Litamae Sher
Sally Sheridan
Marilyn Matteson Sheridan
Caryl Silversmith Shipley
Pat Shockley
Jeanne Siebert
Violet Cressio Sieck
Susan White Siegesmund
Sara Thomsen Siegesmund
Michelle Sims
Nathalie Osgood Simsak
Wendy Johnston Sinton
Marjie Endsley Skalet
Patti Ryden Skirving
Elizabeth Walker Slifer
Jan Smedley
Ronda Barlow Smith
Melanie Arrington Smith
Jean Mason Smith
June Smith
Patricia Anselin Snider
Sharon Trautman Sorenson
Loyce Helgerson Sorrell
Ann Taylor Speidel
Mrs. James B. Spice
Diane M. Stanbro
Barbara Schilling Stanton
Margaret Lutz Stavros
Constance Mattson Steeples
Elizabeth Boone Steinbrueck
Betsy Sabin Stettner
Mimi Haentjens Stone
Fran Hewitt Strange
Luann Stratton
Janet Greer Streich
Barbara Stubbs
Martha Sullivan
Lorinda Stewart Swenson
Pamela Fay Swenson
Sondra Mutz Talley
Jennifer Robinson Tallmadge
Nancy Tawse Tankersley
Katherine Heinemann Taucher
Katherine Palmer Tautz
Nancy Taylor
Sally Paige Tejan
Phyllis Falenzer Thompson
Deborah Rice Thurlow
Debbie Tidler
Carol Kenna Tierney
Deborah Leo Tilton
Susan Deese Tracy

Kay Bliss Truitt
Linda Segebrecht Truitt
Ruth Campbell Tucker
Ann Hinds Tull
Marie Ungeman
Patricia Searles Vairin
Addie Donnan Valentine
Kimberly Valentine
Julia Harlow Valeski
S. H. Van Steen
Kathryn Barrington Vanneman
Ann Vazquez
Ann Verbrugge
Jane Curtin Vertuca
Elisabeth Emery Vinton
Mary Elizabeth Vitale
Joan Vought
Linda Jensen Wade
Lee Wadsworth
Jodi McFarland Waggoner
Ellen Kelly Waterman
Michelle Korry Waters
Fay Walker Watkins
Connie Brennan Watts
Barbara Webb
Jacquelin Blanch Weber
Nancy Fisher Weidenhamer
Sonia Lazere Weiss
Martha Richter Welborn
Pamela Nagle Welch
Sharon Wendelson
Janet Tracy Wenzel
Christine Davis West
Nancy Alleman Wester
Cynthia Crowell Westergaard
Maureen McDermott Westerland
Kathy Weydert
Marilyn Wheat
Carol Wheeler
Janet White
Miriam Ellis Whitney
Nikki Widdersheim
Penny Wertz Wiedeke
Sue Wild
Jeanne Wilkins Wilde
Sharon Kullgren Wilkinson
Madeline William
Nancy Seiwert Williams
Mary Burrus Williams
Cynthia Williams
Mary Schwertz Willis
Jodi Wilson
Glenda Carter Winker
Martine Ernst Wollenweber
Marcia Langton Wood
Elaine Sack Woodworth
Doris J. Woodworth
Bob Woodworth
Tricia Delano Worcester
Sally Ann Cadman Wormley
Nancy Seacrest Wright
David C. P. Wyman
Jane Ponting Yale
Mary Ann Kripaitis Yanus
Fran Yeddis
Liz Young
Betty Zacker
Sandra Shollenberger Zayle
Sherrie Zeppelin
Nancy Wheless Zimmerman
James V. Belvedere
Maureen Lienart
Diana Charlton Lyford
Kathleen Ryan Kaufman
Sharon Thayer

The Junior League of Denver wishes to express its appreciation and gratefully acknowledges those who have supported this project by providing valuable assistance and professional expertise.

A. Barry Hirschfeld
A. B. Hirschfeld Press, Inc.
Adolf Coors Company
Jeff Anderson
Nancy Barger
Bay Wolf
Jaydee Boat
Michael Bush
Charles Court at the Broadmoor
William E. Daniel
Joanne Davidson
Helen Dolloghan
John Fielder
The Fish Market Restaurant and Oyster Bar
Gallery Louisianne
Gregory Gorfkle
C. Andrew Graham
Richard Graussman
HealthMark
International Villa
Charlotte Isoline
Randall H. Lortscher
Mae Norcross Linens
Matrix International
Marty Meitus
Dr. Harlan Meyers
Marilyn Mishkin
Mocha Cafe
David R. Murphy
Reed Photo Art
Michael Ritz
Ellen Rolfes
Robert J. Roseman
Martha Mayne Smith
Susan Stevens
Martha Stewart
Strings Restaurant
Tandoor Kitchen
The Tended Thicket
Mrs. James Vanderveck
Mr. James Vanderveck
Mary L. Wenke
Westcliffe Publishers
Duane D. Wiens

Index

Index

Index

Index

Index

Index

Index

Index

Index

Index

Index

Index

Index

Index

C & C
Publications, Inc.
Colorado Cache ● Creme de Colorado

The Junior League of Denver, Inc.
6300 East Yale Avenue
Denver, Colorado 80222
(303) 782-9244

Name _____

Address _____

City/State/Zip _____

Telephone _____

TO: _____
_____
_____
_____
_____

Please send me the best-selling classic cookbooks indicated below:

Mailing Label – Please Print

Title	Quantity	Price	Tax (Colorado residents only)	TOTAL
COLORADO CACHE	_____	$14.95	$ .62 per book	$.
CRÈME DE COLORADO	_____	$16.95	.70 per book	$.
Total number of books ordered	_____	plus $2.00 each for shipping and handling (Canadian orders: $3.00 additional for each book ordered.)		$.
		TOTAL ENCLOSED		$.

Please charge to my   VISA _____ or MasterCard _____

Card number _____

Expiration date _____

Cardholder's
signature _____

Please make checks payable to:
JUNIOR LEAGUE OF DENVER, INC.
Please do not send cash. Sorry, no C.O.D.'s.

Send to: C and C Publications
The Junior League of Denver, Inc.
6300 East Yale Avenue, Suite 110
Denver, Colorado 80222
(303) 782-9244

Profits from the sale of these cookbooks are used to support the purpose and programs of the Junior League of Denver, Inc.

C & C
Publications, Inc.
Colorado Cache ● Creme de Colorado

The Junior League of Denver, Inc.
6300 East Yale Avenue
Denver, Colorado 80222
(303) 782-9244

Name _____

Address _____

City/State/Zip _____

Telephone _____

TO: _____
_____
_____
_____

Please send me the best-selling classic cookbooks indicated below:

Mailing Label – Please Print

Title	Quantity	Price	Tax (Colorado residents only)	TOTAL
COLORADO CACHE	_____	$14.95	$ .62 per book	$.
CRÈME DE COLORADO	_____	$16.95	.70 per book	$.
Total number of books ordered	_____	plus $2.00 each for shipping and handling (Canadian orders: $3.00 additional for each book ordered.)		$.
		TOTAL ENCLOSED		$.

Please charge to my   VISA _____ or MasterCard _____

Card number _____

Expiration date _____

Cardholder's
signature _____

Please make checks payable to:
JUNIOR LEAGUE OF DENVER, INC.
Please do not send cash. Sorry, no C.O.D.'s.

Send to: C and C Publications
The Junior League of Denver, Inc.
6300 East Yale Avenue, Suite 110
Denver, Colorado 80222
(303) 782-9244

Profits from the sale of these cookbooks are used to support the purpose and programs of the Junior League of Denver, Inc.